The Politics of Passion

BETWEEN MEN ~ BETWEEN WOMEN

The Politics of Passion

Women's Sexual Culture
in the Afro-Surinamese Diaspora

Gloria Wekker

Columbia University Press
New York

Columbia University Press

Publishers Since 1893

New York   Chichester, West Sussex

Copyright © 2006 Columbia University Press

The publication of this book was made possible by a grant from the
Netherlands Organization for Scientific Research (NWO).

Library of Congress Cataloging-in-Publication Data
Wekker, Gloria.
The politics of passion : women's sexual culture in the Afro-Surinamese diaspora
/ Gloria Wekker.
p.   cm. — (Between men—between women)
Revision of the author's thesis published in 1994 under title: Ik ben een gouden munt,
ik ga door vele handen, maar ik verlies mijn waarde niet.
Includes bibliographical references and index.
ISBN 0-231-13162-3 (cloth : alk. paper) — ISBN 0-231-13163-1 (pbk. : alk. paper)
1. Women—Suriname—Paramaribo—Sexual behavior. 2. Women—Suriname—
Paramaribo—Identity. 3. Sex customs—Suriname—Paramaribo. 4. Lesbianism—Suriname—
Paramaribo. 5. Creoles—Suriname—Paramaribo. I. Wekker, Gloria. Ik ben een gouden munt,
ik ga door vele handen, maar ik verlies mijn waarde niet. II. Title. III. Series.
HQ29.W476 2006
306.76'5089960883—dc22

2005054320

Printed in the United States of America

c 10 9 8 7 6 5 4 3 2 1

p 10 9 8 7 6 5 4 3 2 1

BETWEEN MEN ~ BETWEEN WOMEN
Lesbian, Gay, and Bisexual Studies

Terry Castle and Larry Gross, Editors

Advisory Board of Editors
Claudia Card
John D'Emilio
Esther Newton
Anne Peplau
Eugene Rice
Kendall Thomas
Jeffrey Weeks

BETWEEN MEN ~ BETWEEN WOMEN is a forum for current lesbian and gay scholarship in the humanities and social sciences. The series includes both books that rest within specific traditional disciplines and are substantially about gay men, bisexuals, or lesbians and books that are interdisciplinary in ways that reveal new insights into gay, bisexual, or lesbian experience, transform traditional disciplinary methods in consequence of the perspectives that experience provides, or begin to establish lesbian and gay studies as a freestanding inquiry. Established to contribute to an increased understanding of lesbians, bisexuals, and gay men, the series also aims to provide through that understanding a wider comprehension of culture in general.

For three Caribbean women

Esseline Fredison, 1922–1982
Juliette Cummings, 1907–1998
Audre Lorde, 1934–1992

Contents

Mi go—m'e kon
sootwatra bradi
tak wan mofo,
ala mi mati,
tak wan mofo.
m'go m'e kon . . .

[I went away—I am coming back
the ocean is wide
conjure up the ancestors
all my friends,
conjure up the ancestors
I went away
I am coming back . . .]

TREFOSSA, 1957

Preface and Acknowledgments

This book is one incarnation of an interest that first presented itself to me about twenty-five years ago. While working on my master's thesis in cultural anthropology at the University of Amsterdam (1981), I came across the book *Suriname Folk-lore* (1936) by Melville and Frances Herskovits. It was a treasure trove to me, child of a first generation of post–WWII middle-class Surinamese migrants to the Netherlands whose main ambitions were for their children to forget the past and step unquestioningly into the Dutch "promised land." My parents' ambitions for us included becoming model Dutch citizens, which meant first and foremost studying hard. Being versatile in Creole culture or the Surinamese creole they sometimes spoke with each other, Sranan Tongo, was not high on their lists of priorities. Sitting in the library of the Royal Tropical Institute in Amsterdam, I relished the Herskovitses' lively accounts of Creole working-class women's culture. I was intrigued by their accounts of the *mati* life and the institutions supporting it like the birthday party and *lobi singi*. The Herskovitses opened up a new world to me and at the same time, like a lightning bolt, made me see connections with phenomena I perceived around me in Amsterdam, where a new, more heterogeneous group, in terms of ethnicity and class, of Surinamese migrants had settled after independence (1975). Too late to change my M.A. thesis, whose focus was matrifocality, I made myself a promise to return to that world of working-class Surinamese women at a later date. The dream I dared to entertain was to make a contribution to the contemporary ethnography of Afro-Surinamese women's lives.

This dream has since blossomed and transformed into the book you now hold in your hands. It first took root in the work in sociocultural anthropology that I pursued as part of my doctoral research at UCLA. It has involved living, working with, and interviewing twenty-five working-class women. In the past decade and a half I have made more than six trips to Suriname, keeping in contact with many of these women. My initial dream has transformed into a longitudinal, transcontinental study, realized in the pages of this book. Its manifestation is threaded with webs of friendships and indebtedness that span three continents, North America, South America, and Europe, where I am located.

In March 1990, having just arrived in Paramaribo, I went to a traditional Afro-Surinamese afternoon birthday party, given in honor of the sixtieth birthday of a prominent male union leader. I went with an older woman whom I'd met through the YWCA where I had started to volunteer. The majority of guests were older Creole[1] women in full regalia, smoking fat cigars. The verb used in Surinamese Dutch for going to a party without an official invitation is *boren,* literally "drilling"; in small-town Paramaribo society, where partying is such an important and pleasurable part of life, boren carries benevolent connotations. I "drilled" the party and came away full of powerful impressions, dizzy with the certainty and relief that I *had* found mati culture—that sixty years after the Herskovitses did research for *Suriname Folk-lore,* women were still involved in upholding their institutions. Brimming with excitement, that same evening I wrote a poem, "Creoolse Vrouwen"/"Creole Women,"[2] as a tribute to the women who were to become central to my studies and to my life in the years that followed.

Creole Women

Like stately ships they are
bobbing and streamered
fully adorned
whispering chintz skirts
lined gold braided

digressing
from board to water line
anyisa, anyisa
motyo tie

let them talk
sailors tie[3]
like stately ships they are
swaying cleaving climbing
to the beat of their own drummer

A redskirted robust flagship
leads the squadron
enlarging
grace of gracefulness
she glides to the side
cigar in hand
prepares the others
on their way to the harbor
a triumphal arch, a beacon
chivalrous and eager
like a young naval officer
and always always
dancing flowing floating
to the beat of her own drummer.

First and foremost, I want to thank Misi Juliette Cummings and the many other women in Suriname who opened their hearts so that I could understand their lives. In the same way in which the armadillo hides underneath its carapace, these women will remain pseudonymous here, carrying their mostly self-chosen names. Without them, I could not have written the texts that I have authored in the past decade and a half. More than that, their influence on my life has been immeasurable. I can never hope to repay this debt, but I trust I have succeeded in accomplishing what several women have explicitly asked me to do: "mek' mi tyar' den tori go moro fara"/may I carry their stories further.

I want to thank the Anton de Kom University of Suriname, staff and personnel of the division of Culture Studies of the Ministry of Education and Culture and of the Surinamese Museum for their collegiality and support of my research. U.S.I.S. and the European Economic Community in Paramaribo were helpful in supplying me with data and access to telecommunications during the first research period.

My travel companions and coauthors Judy Reichart, Laddy van Putten, and the late Ben Scholtens and Stanley Dieko gave more depth to my stay in Suriname. I traveled with them to Asindoopo, the seat of government of the Saramaka Maroons, on the Upper Suriname River, where we witnessed two unique historical events, limba uwii, the end of the period of mourning for Aboikoni, the paramount chief of the Saramaka Maroons (November 1990) and buta Gaama, the installation of Songo, his successor (December 1990)[4].

I want to express gratitude to Tieneke Sumter, Loes Monsels, Twie Tjoa, Henna Malmberg, Carla Bakboord, my late uncle Just Wekker, and Reinout Simons for their willingness to brainstorm and their help in gathering data. For their friendship I thank Hillary de Bruin, Christine van Russel, Annette Djamin, Eudya Vos, and Ineke de Miranda. I also want to thank the representatives of the various women's organizations in Paramaribo, among others Siegmien Staphorst and Juanita Altenberg, who gave freely of their time and insights to help me accomplish this study. Joanne Werners made my stay more productive by keeping me informed of Dutch publications on Suriname in an environment that has suffered depression very acutely in the realm of information.

Several remarkable women have helped me to give birth to this project. I wish to acknowledge the centrality of Audre Lorde. We first met in Amsterdam in the summer of 1984 when she came on a short visit at the invitation of Sister Outsider, a group of black lesbians who organized literary salons. I was a founding member of this group, and she empowered me to pursue my dream. A staunch supporter throughout the process, she urged me to tell the stories she needed to hear. We stayed in touch during our itineraries of the following years. It is a small consolation that she was still able to read and discuss the dissertation with me, in October 1992 in Berlin, just one month before her death on St. Croix, U.S. Virgin Islands, in November of that same year.

I owe special thanks to the chair of my dissertation committee, Claudia Mitchell-Kernan, professor in linguistic anthropology and director of the Center of African American Studies at UCLA when I enrolled. I became Claudia's research assistant at CAAS. Even before I came to UCLA, she welcomed and encouraged me. Her support of my endeavors, her incisive comments, and her African American sense of style have made an indelible impression on me. She was my first black female teacher, which cannot easily be overestimated. Her ability to be "girlfriend" as well as mentor to her students has shaped my own teaching praxis. I also want to thank Karen Brodkin, then director of the budding Program of Feminist Studies, for her rigorous contribution to my work and for posing the "hamburger" question. Over hamburgers in her backyard in Venice, we came up with the central organizing question of my research: what is it that makes Afro-Surinamese working-class women survive amidst the manifold crises they confront? Each of the other members of my committee, Robert Edgerton, Gail Wyatt, and Jacqueline DjeDje made my work more insightful and precise. I always

enjoyed my interactions with Jim Turner, who gave freely of his encyclopedic cross-cultural knowledge of self and "the winds." Edward Dew's timely
presence in Los Angeles in the last stages of the final draft of my dissertation
was much appreciated.

My initial research in Suriname was made possible by generous fellow-
ships from the Inter American Foundation (Washington, DC) and the Institute of American Cultures at UCLA. I also received support from the Dutch
Fullbright Committee, which facilitated my first year in Los Angeles greatly.
I am indebted to the staff of the Center of Afro-American Studies for being
my home away from home during the first two years at UCLA. Ann Walters,
graduate adviser in the Department of Anthropology, was an invaluable
source of information and support in all those years. I want to thank my
friends in Los Angeles, Renee Cowhig, Natalie Beausoleil, Rachel Chapman
and James Pfeiffer, Sheila Arthur and Lynne Harper, Toke Hoppenbrouw-
ers and Jane Peckham, Kashmira Sabir and Michael Woodard, who lived
through the ups and downs of these years with me. Chinosole's friendship
and our common appreciation of Audre's work helped me through some
gloomy days. Many of my friends were gracious enough to accompany me,
at one time or another, to my favorite night "hangout," Dolores on Santa
Monica Boulevard, to eat pancakes and drink their awful coffee. I found
much truth and consolation in Audre's words:

> . . . for the embattled
> there is no place
> that cannot be
> home
> nor is.

AUDRE LORDE, "SCHOOL NOTE" (1978)

My friends in the Netherlands have kept my place in our circle. I want
to thank Diny Zanders, Andrée Douglas, Marjan Sax, Zus de Graaf, Thea
Doelwijt, Marijke van Geest, Rachelle Tjin-A-Djie, and Anita van den Berg
for being there or for coming to visit me in L.A. or in Paramaribo. I want to
thank my father and his partner, my siblings, their partners, and my nieces
for their continuing loyalty and support. My absences from the family circle,
punctuated only by stopovers in the Netherlands, made me more aware of
how fortunate I am to be a member of this family. Whether it was my oldest
brother's insistence on coming to get me in Suriname where I was sick with
malaria or their relay telephone system to keep up with my whereabouts
during this whole period, I was always deeply comforted by their care. I
acknowledge the spirit of my mother, Esseline Fredison, who links me to the

Creole working class. Her courage sustained me throughout this project. My research has been a journey into the culture of her ancestors.

After the North American and Surinamese years, I have been fortunate in finding a fruitful academic environment in the Netherlands at the University of Utrecht. The Department of Women's Studies in the Humanities has brought me colleagues like Rosi Braidotti, Maaike Meijer, Berteke Waaldijk, Rosemarie Buikema, and Kathy Davis. I have greatly benefited from the comments of Kathy Davis, Helma Lutz, and Halleh Ghorashi on the first draft of the chapter on sexual globalization. I want to thank my coworkers at GEM, the Expertise Center on Gender, Ethnicity and Multiculturality in higher education at Utrecht University, of which I am the director, who supported me in numerous ways in completing the manuscript. Mari Hermans, Maayke Botman, Nancy Jouwe, Marjolein Verboom, Lulu Helder, Ada Ruis, Marlise Mensink, Nanda van der Laan, Liesbeth Minnaard, and Elsje Dicke never allowed me to forget this book. Manu Bühring and Adam Garcia Flight were particularly indispensable in the completion of the manuscript.

From October 2000 through April 2001 I spent a six-month sabbatical at the Oral History Project at Columbia University in New York City, and I want to thank its director Mary Marshall Clark for making that possible.

Inevitably, during such a long period, some of the friends and family members who were present at the outset of the project have not lived to see the branches of the tree flower. Among them I especially want to mention my mother, mischievous Mis' Juliette, the indomitable Ms. Audre, three Caribbean women to whom I dedicate the book. In addition, I call upon my oldest brother and colleague Herman, the talented historian Ben Scholtens, my uncle Just, with his encyclopedic knowledge about Suriname, and my Amsterdam comrades Tania Leon and Mea Venster. Many thanks to the anonymous reviewers of the manuscript for their intellectual companionship.

Last but not least, I want to thank M. Jacqui Alexander, sister in arms and cotraveler in the black Diaspora. Maggy Carrot has shared my dream in most of its incarnations. Both, in their very own ways, have accompanied me on this journey. They taught me many things about the world and about myself, but, most important, how easy it is to love and, its most difficult part, to be a generous witness to their growth.

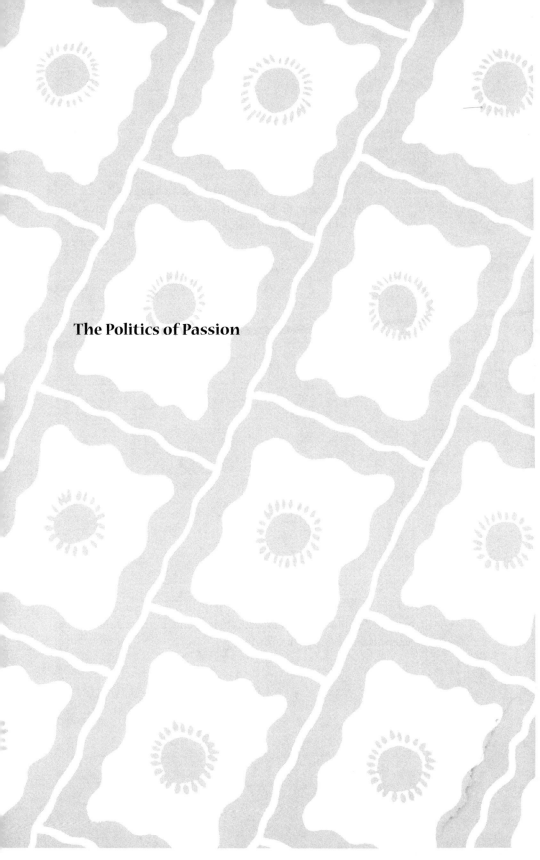

The Politics of Passion

It was an acknowledgement that ethnographic research, whatever else it is, is a form of human relationship. When the lines long drawn in anthropology between participant-observer and informant break down, then the only truth is the one in between; and anthropology becomes something closer to a social art form, open to both aesthetic and moral judgment. The situation is riskier, but it does bring intellectual labor and life into closer relation.

MCCARTHY BROWN 1991

1

No Tide, No Tamara / Not Today, Not Tomorrow: Misi Juliette Cummings's Life History

This chapter centers on the life history of an eighty-four-year-old Afro-Surinamese working-class woman, Misi Juliette Cummings. She had five male partners in the course of her life, bore twelve living children and her *wan ai karu*, literally "corn with one eye," the apples of her eye, were women. She had a relationship with a woman that lasted for forty years and numerous sexual liaisons with other women. I recorded her life history over the course of a nineteen-month period, in 1990 and 1991, when I lived in her backyard in the capital of Suriname, Paramaribo. Juliette's life history is the cornerstone of this book; her life is worth telling because it addresses, in a highly condensed form, all of its major themes.

First, the narrative of her life foregrounds the sexual subjectivity of a black diasporic woman, an Afro-Surinamese or Creole woman, whose construction of self challenges many received anthropological notions about gender, sexuality, marriage, kinship, and family. Juliette's sexuality was based on a sense of agency and self-worth that made sexual fulfillment and not the sex of the object of her desire the most important factor. She displayed tremendous joy in sexuality with other women, coupled with considerable sexual prowess, skills, and narrative capabilities in the domain of sex. She inhabited a space where the *mati work* is prominent. The mati work is an old institution, first mentioned in Dutch colonial literature in 1912, in which women have sexual relations with men and with women, either simultaneously or consecutively. The prevalence of this institution in Afro-Suriname points to a more broadly based cultural repertoire. In one of my central understandings, the mati work is expressive of the West African–based cultural archive of sexual subjectivity as slaves belabored it under specific demographic and colonial-political circumstances in the former Dutch colony, Suriname. As such it has significance for the construction of sexual subjectivity in other parts of the black Diaspora. Juliette' s narrative also charts her relationships with men and the way she managed to reconcile her primary interests in women with her male partner(s). There are few, if any, testimonies in the anthropological literature in which a black woman talks so openly about sex, displays the agency to order her life in that domain, and informatively reports on what gave her pleasure.

Second, there are still few Caribbean women's life histories of any class background. A woman's life, lived with resourcefulness and savvy, reported with considerable insight and spanning almost the entire twentieth century, is rare enough in itself. While her narrative is a uniquely individual story, it is as much a collective story, a story of women of her generation, her ethnic and class background, enacting the same versatile sexual behavior. She saw herself as *poti sma*/a poor woman, a member of the subordinate *volksklasse*/"popular class." The narrative of her life opens windows onto the ways working-class Afro-Surinamese women survived in the twentieth century, how they ordered their universe and what values they lived by. Juliette was firmly embedded within women's working-class culture and honored its sensibilities by being a *dyadya uma*/a real woman, a sturdy woman, who knew how to take care of the business of managing life, her own and those lives entrusted to her, economically, religiously, culturally, politically, and sexually.

Third, Juliette's life history and specifically her lexicon in the domain of subjectivity offer a reading of a multiplicitous self; a self that is multilayered, complex, integrating various instantiations of "I." There are numerous ways in which Juliette made pronouncements about her self in her first language, the local creole, Sranan Tongo: in singular and in plural terms, in feminine and in masculine terms, and in terms of third-person constructions. This conceptualization of self is underwritten by the worldview embedded in the Winti religion, which is firmly present in the working class. Juliette conceived of her sexual activities as behavior, not in terms of a deep-seated core identity. This complex "I" is not the fragmented self postulated under postmodernity and should not be equated with it. Amidst all the multiplicity of the self, there is simultaneously, in Juliette's life history, a search for unity of the self. In the narrativization of her life, certain enduring themes emerge, which give unity to her life: her love for economic and social independence, refusing to be "under a man," wanting children, living well with her mati, taking care of spiritual balance in her own life and in that of those around her.

The representation of Juliette's life in this chapter is highly condensed, but in the following chapters several themes and institutions, constituting her life like concentric circles or like the famous layers of an onion (Geertz 1973; Ross and Rapp 1997), will be taken up again and laid out in more detail. It is important to note at the outset that my rendering of Juliette's life, as well as the entire book, underwrites the importance, in the study of sexuality, of a brand of social constructionism that is simultaneously deeply aware of political economy. By political economy I mean

> the attempt to constantly place culture in time, to see a constant interplay between experience and meaning in a context in which both experience and meaning are shaped by inequality and domination (and the) attempt to understand the emergence of particular peoples at the conjunction of local and global histories, to place local populations in the larger currents of world history
>
> (ROSENBERRY, QUOTED IN LANCASTER AND DI LEONARDO 1997B:4).

The combination of social constructionism and political economy means that I will as consistently as possible bring together a critical analysis of sexual experiences and meanings and a careful consideration of material practices. Sexual lives cannot be understood apart from the changing political economies in which those lives are embedded, and those economies include

> dominant and contesting constructions of gender, race, sexual "perversions" and nationality—constructions that themselves carry traces of long and complicated histories of conquest, resistances, exploitation, ... and neocolonial structures. They also include ... "sexualized" states—states' ubiquitous uses of gender, sexual, and racial ideologies in order to enact their own legitimacy and control over citizens.
>
> (LANCASTER AND DI LEONARDO 1997B:4, 5)

How do I tell the story of Misi Juliette Cummings's life, a life that spanned almost the entire twentieth century, 1907 through 1998? It is clear that the narrative that unfolds in these pages is a story that we, in a very real sense, crafted together, and thus I am as present in these pages as she is. In seeking the truth in between the participant-observer and the informant, I do not play the "God trick." I cannot hide myself behind the role of an invisible and omniscient third-person narrator (Haraway 1991). Having finally tapped into Juliette's seemingly endless source of stories about women she had sexually connected with, I teasingly remarked one day: "Luku, Juliette, a gers' ef' ala sani den umasma ben du, in' a ten dati, a ben de fu didon makandra"/Look, Juliette, it looks like the only thing women in the olden days did was to lie down together. She was indignant: that was not true at all. I was the only one who wanted to know everything about her life and hear her stories. On the most obvious level, then, Juliette and I crafted this narrative together. No one had ever asked her in such a sustained way about her life, her friends, how she made a living, what she expected from and enjoyed in male and female sexual partners, or about her children. Inspired by my ceaseless questions, events that had become shrouded in the mists of time came to light again for her.

On yet another level, this narrative is a coproduction, a segment of the lives of each of us that was crossed. In that sense I want to acknowledge the ways in which our, both mine and Juliette's, erotic subjectivity were crucial in its forging. My positionality as an Afro-Surinamese anthropologist who loves women was vital in helping me gather thick information about her and other Afro-Surinamese women's sexuality. In the past decade the debate has been opened on the powerful vantage point that acknowledgment of the erotic subjectivity of the ethnographer affords. Instead of the ideal agent of value-free, objective knowledge, which "requires a notion of the self as a fortress that must be defended against polluting influences from its social surroundings" (Harding 1991:158), fieldwork by an ethnographer who starts from the premise of equality and who acknowledges difference yields less biased, more valuable and sensitive data.

If in participant observation it is the person of the researcher, which serves as the most central and sensitive instrument of research, it behooves us to be transparent, accountable and reflexive about the different modalities in which the self engages with others. Acknowledgment of sexual subjectivity should not be misread as a license for an unbridled, honorless exploitation of the Other on a more intimate level than has thus far generally been acknowledged. I am suggesting that methodology provides information about the various ways in which one locates oneself—psychologically, socially, linguistically, geographically, epistemologically, and sexually—to be exposed to experience in a culture (Wekker 1998a). This position entails a fundamentally different relationship between the researcher and the people with whom she works than traditionally has been envisioned. I work from an inverted model, which starts with a simple but rather fundamental acknowledgment: but for the grace, patience, and interests of the people involved, there would be little research. Both researcher and the people involved are subjects, active agents with their own emotions and agendas. Moreover, all knowledge is gained at the intersections of race, gender, class, and sexual locations; thus, "all scientific knowledge is always, in every respect, socially situated . . . neither knowers nor the knowledge they produce are or could be impartial, disinterested, value-free, Archimedean" (Harding 1991:11). There is not *one*, optimal position from which to do research; the positions are as varied as we are. At the very least we must own and acknowledge our locations, and there is no good reason to exclude sexual locations from our work, either as an a priori or a posteriori excision.

So, by way of preliminary answer to the question I posed at the beginning of this chapter: I will tell Juliette's story as faithfully as she told it to me, and the process of her telling me her stories, embedded as it was in an atmosphere of being mutually attracted to each other, is a part of this narrative as well, with all the joys and difficulties our positions entailed.

I want to ask this question in a second sense: how do I tell Miss Juliette's life history, and the sexual stories of other Creole working-class women, in light of a dominant Euro-American history of representing black women's sexuality as excessive, insatiable, the epitome of animal lust, and always already pathological? How do I avoid staging a latter day Sarah Baartman show, with Juliettte as the traveling spectacle this time? In this second sense, as well, I feel implicated. The question has preoccupied me in the many years since I first embarked on this project. Ultimately, the only pertinent answer is that I expressly call attention to the history of dominant representations of black female sexuality in order that this deeply racialized, lethal imagery can be deconstructed. By now it has become commonplace to say that sexuality is gendered and classed—and I will discuss these interconnections elaborately in the course of this text—but the imbrication and foundational inscription of sexuality with "race" is still something that can be overlooked, in many studies, without too many serious consequences. Thus not only black sexualities suffer from these inscriptions, white and other ethnicized and racialized sexualities are also constructed by various inscriptions, resulting in differential positions regarding appropriate and "normal" sexuality and corporeality. In lending my pen to Creole working-class women who speak in their own words about their sexualities, I hope to contribute to that deconstruction.

On Oral History

> To tell a story is to take arms against the threat of time, to resist time, or to harness time. The telling of a story preserves the teller from oblivion; the story builds the identity of the teller and the legacy which she leaves for the future.
>
> (PORTELLI 2001:59)

Juliette was a gifted storyteller, who obviously enjoyed being my center of attention over an extended period of nineteen months and incidentally also after the first period of my fieldwork when I returned to Suriname or when she came to visit her children, including me, in the Netherlands. The point in her life cycle at which she told me her stories, in 1990–1991, was significant. She had a lot of time, because she did not have any children that she was responsible for and she did not have to work anymore. She accommodated her life, more or less, to mine. In addition, she still was very sharp and remembered minute details of events that had happened seventy years earlier. When I last was with her, in 1997, she could not tell me those stories any more, although she vividly remembered our time together. The length of the period in which I interviewed her resulted in my hearing several stories repeatedly as well as different versions of one story, e.g., she told me two versions of the first time she had sex. As rapport grew and she trusted me more, she gave me more details and her stories started to include quite intimate details.

Juliette did not tell me her life history chronologically; one day she preferred to tell me *odo*/proverbs and sing songs; another day something propelled her to recount an event in her life or to give me an interpretation of the characters of her children. Yet I have chosen to reconstruct her life mainly, but not exclusively, chronologically because that has seemed the most accessible form to me. Oral historian Alessandro Portelli notes that when the narrator herself does not perceive one particular event or epoch as a key event or pivot in her life, that is to say, when she sees her entire life as meaningful, then that makes it easier to take chronology as the organizing factor (2001:66).

Sometimes the story wanted to be told differently, however, jumped ahead of itself. As I reconstructed her life, I have encountered problems dating events. Often I have had to estimate her age in the context of public events or the length of intimate relationships. Like her, I used the ages of her children or grandchildren, or other significant events like World War II, as signposts.

In interviewing Juliette about her life, I have worked on the assumption that I was dealing with verbal artifacts (stories) shaped by Juliette's self-perception, by the encounter with me as the interviewer, and by my perception and interpretation of Juliette and her words (Portelli 2001). It should thus be clear that oral history as an ethnographic practice cannot lay claim to the impossible dream of attaining the absolute "truth" of a life or of history. Since Juliette's telling of her life is part of her life, what we have is something that may not be the truth, but it is something otherwise invaluable: her interpretations of her experiences. These are colored in the light of what she perceived me to be interested in. I have no doubt that with a different interviewer, interested in other themes, she would have come up with other stories. The question to be contemplated is not "what is the relation *between*

life and story," but, far more interesting, rather, "what is the place of the story
within the life" (Portelli 2001)? How does she construct the story in order to
project a particular persona? What are the characteristics of that persona?
What is important for her to bring across?

In order to answer those questions, it is necessary to introduce another
way of analyzing Juliette's story. In addition to the chronological or horizontal mode, which narrators may or may not pay attention to in their narration, they often use three different vertical levels to organize the narrative
of their life: a personal, a collective, and a national and global level. Portelli
describes these levels as follows:

> *Personal*: private and family life; the life cycle of births, marriages, jobs, chil-
> dren, and deaths; and personal involvement in the two other levels. Space refer-
> ent: the home.
>
> *Collective*: the life of the community, the neighborhood, and the workplace;
> strikes, natural catastrophes, and rituals; and collective participation in "institu-
> tional" episodes. Space referent: the town, the neighborhood, and the workplace.
>
> *Institutional*: the sphere of politics, government, parties, unions and elec-
> tions; the national and international historical context; and ideology. Space
> referent: the nation and the world
>
> (PORTELLI 2001:70)

These, admittedly, are analytical levels, and in Juliette's life history these
levels are not watertight; they interplay and impinge upon one another. In
my rendering of her life I will indicate when a particular sequence or event
can be read as inhabiting a particular level. The major emphases in Juliette's
story were on the personal and collective levels, since these two were the
grounds overwhelmingly upon which she organized her life.

Meeting Mis' Juliette

> *There are always two subjects to a field situation, and . . . the roles of "observed"
> and "observer" are more fluid than it might appear at first glance.*
>
> (PORTELLI 2001:30)

Having arrived in Suriname to do research at the end of January 1990, I
asked friends and acquaintances to help me find housing in a working-class
Creole neighborhood. Annabel, a friend I had known in the Netherlands in
the eighties, had migrated back to Suriname, and she introduced me to Mis'
Juliette, whom she called Ouma Juliette/Grandma Juliette. Juliette lived in a
neighborhood close to the center of town, Land van Dijk, consisting mostly

of Creole and Maroon inhabitants, which is reputed to be *dyango*/unruly and tough. Many streets in the neighborhood are unpaved, except for the main thoroughfares that surround it. At the end of Juliette's street is the dr. Willem Campanjestraat, which harbors a large day market where fruit, vegetables, meat, and bread are sold. Even though it has been around for decades, it is still called the temporary market, and it is a center of neighborhood activity and gathering. In her backyard Juliette had an empty, wooden house without running water but with electricity, and she agreed that I could live there. My sturdy little wooden house consisted of three tiny rooms: a living room, a bedroom where I hung my hammock, and a kitchen area. I paid rent to Anton, one of her sons, who had built and owned the house, and moved into it in March, after I had whitewashed the walls, hung posters and pictures of family and friends, and collected kitchenware and the barest of furnishings through my Surinamese network. I was ready to start.

At eighty-four years old, Juliette was a beautiful and attractive woman. When we got to know each other better, she often reminisced about how attractive she had been when she was young, with her *krin kleur*/light skin color, her round face, and her long, "good hair." Good hair refers to hair that is long and straight or wavy, not unruly, short, frizzy, or natural, which is still often called or considered "bad" hair. Short, quicksilvery, with her gray hair in two braids, which are tucked under her colorful *angisa*/headdress, she still went to the market every day to do her shopping and to chat with her *stamans*/male and female friends. It soon became clear that she had had her own booth at the market until she was in her seventies. Her angisa always matched the color of her dress, and she carried an orange plastic bucket to the market in which she put her fish or meat, onions, and tomatoes. Juliette never, never had problems coming by the products that were regularly scarce for ordinary human beings: bread, milk, sugar, rice, Maggie cubes (who would seriously consider cooking a meal without them?). Juliette knew everything about what was going on in the neighborhood, was loved and respected, and was often consulted in ritual—cultural matters. In her yard, she grew plants and herbs, like *kuswe*/Bixa orellana (Bixaceae), *stoypiwi-wiri*/Ruta graveolens (Rutaceae) against seizures, and *strun*/lemongrass, that are necessary to make home remedies against all kinds of ailments (Sordam and Eersel 1989). After a while I was present when Juliette would tell people exactly how to make those remedies, and she was often asked to preside over *fanowdu*/matters in the spiritual domain.

Juliette's first and main language was Sranan Tongo,[1] or *Nengre*/Negro language, as she called it. The linguistic situation in Suriname is complicated and needs some clarification. A former possession of the Netherlands, Dutch is still the official language in Suriname, written and spoken in schools, in government settings, in newspapers, and on TV. Dutch is still accorded higher status than Sranan Tongo, but both serve as linguae francae among the many different ethnic groups that make up its population of 440,000 people. Sranan Tongo (ST) or Sranan is an English-based creole that originated in the first years of the plantation colony, around 1650. Surinamese Dutch (SD) is the local variety of Dutch spoken by many people in Suriname (and in the Netherlands). SD has many "flavors"; some varieties are almost indistinguishable from Standard Dutch, others are literal translations from Sranan into Dutch (Wekker and Wekker 1991).[2] Most of the working-class women I worked with spoke both Dutch and Sranan. Typically, Sranan would become the vehicle when they were inspired, excited, or just well at ease. Especially older women, like Mis' Juliette, spoke mainly Sranan. But sometimes she would surprise me with a quaint and archaic Dutch expression. If she could not make sense of someone's behavior, she would say, for example: "Andermans boek is duister om te lezen, baya"/Someone else's book is hard to read, you hear. Or, when she thought that I was pulling her leg: "Verneuk de gek; dat is toch geen zonde"/There is no sin in making a fool of a crazy person. I have translated the direct utterances of women, whether the source language was Surinamese Dutch or Sranan Tongo, into English. The target variety of English I have chosen is intended to be closer to Black English Vernacular than to Standard American English.

It took us several months to get used to each other and to figure each other out. I was not very fluent in Sranan Tongo when I arrived, so our early conversations were somewhat halting. I tried to explain to her as best as I could what my study was about, phrasing it in terms of my curiosity about how Creole working-class women were keeping their heads above water, under the ever deteriorating economic circumstances, and what gave them joy, psychologically. Although Juliette would nod emphatically, especially when I talked about the economic hardship afflicting women, I had the distinct feeling that I was not making a very deep impression on her. She would grant me:

"Ay, dyakasa, mi bret' so te dat' mi ben nyan prisiri[3] te mi ben de yongu, a 'er' kondre, a libi kon pori now"/(exclamation) I am so glad that I had fun when I was young, because this country, our entire life has become spoiled now. "Ala sani kon moro diri ala dey"/Everything is becoming more expensive every day and "un ben de poti sma, ooktu, ma un no ben pina lek' den sma e pina now"/women of my generation were poor, too, but we did not suffer like people are suffering now.

Our initial conversations were mainly about how she had survived, how she had raised her many children, and the grief she had known about the deaths of some of the children. It should be emphasized, however, in my initial explanations to her of my work, that I did not mention that I was especially interested in meeting and spending time with *mati*/female friends, lovers, women who are sexually involved with women. Lacking the cultural competence to decide whether and when I could openly talk about mati, I was reluctant to mention the word *mati* at all.

While I thus initially posed as a disembodied, objective researcher, only allowing a limited view into my objectives, the answers I reaped from her were equally limited, staying on safe ground, not volunteering much information that I did not already know from the literature. I gradually realized that I was not the only one trying to read her; she was also trying to read me. Her signposts were different than mine; while I was interested in hearing about working-class women's lives, sexuality, and the mati work from her—without indicating that clearly—she was giving me a political reading. Later on, she told me that, in the beginning, she had not trusted me politically. She did not know where to place me: was I in the Desi Bouterse camp?[4] Juliette, being a lifelong member of NPS,[5] the largely Creole National Surinamese Party, would not think of sharing her stories with someone who might be NDP, the National Democratic Party, a multiethnic political party founded by members of the military regime that had seized power in February 1980. After she had come to trust me and saw that I had few good words to say about any of the male-dominated political parties,[6] unfortunately including her own NPS, she started to open up to me.

Daily Living

"Pikin aksi e fala bigi bon"/The little ax fells the big tree.

JULIETTE

In the first month after I had moved into the house in her backyard, Juliette began offering me platters of food when she had cooked. At first she asked one of her unemployed grandsons, Charly, who was always hanging out in our backyard, to bring me the food, but later on she came over herself and sat chatting with me, while I ate, smoking a fat cigar[7] and rubbing her teeth with its ashes. When she invited me to take showers in her house, instead of washing with buckets in the shed in the backyard, I knew that I had made some progress. Gradually, I also acquired access to the telephone in her house. Still later we developed a routine where she would shop and cook for us every day. I thought the appropriate course of action was to give her money, but that was hardly her objective and my suggestion, in fact, insulted her. This was a too direct, a too calculated gesture, which she did not appreciate. Instead, I began to pay the electricity bills for both our houses and I paid the laundry woman who came once a week to wash our clothes. I knew this pleased her when she said: "Let' anu e was' krukt' anu"/ The left hand washes the right, pointing to a deeply felt wisdom in working-class women's circles that cooperation is absolutely necessary if one wants to accomplish anything (Wekker 1997). I was just beginning to see the contours of that worldview.

To me her cooking was no mean thing, because, beside the fact that she cooked really well, before I had had to spend precious time finding and standing in line for milk, bread, and other food items. Gradually I recognized that when things were well between us she would put the food on my plate and serve me, sit with me, and entertain me with stories, things that had happened that morning in the neighborhood, or give me her comment on what the politicians had cooked up now, whereas when she was angry at me I had to serve myself and sit alone at the table. Equally expert at showering me with attention and giving me the cold shoulder, food took a privileged place in expressing those different modalities.

Food (*nyan* in Sranan) is a language rich in symbolic content. Food may serve as a medium for multiple complicated social transactions, as individuals and social groups use food to control others, establish and maintain sexual relations, avoid or initiate conflict, or express some aspect of cultural identity (Scheper-Hughes 1992:131). Both in same-sexed and in opposite-sexed Creole relational spheres, there is a strong connection between food and eroticism. Being served by the loved one, in opposite-sexed spheres usually the woman and in same-sexed spheres the one who is performing the "feminine" role,[8] is experienced as a testimony to the well-being of the relationship.

Our days together were always full: after I came home from my morning round, having spent time with one of my twenty-five informants sweeping streets, selling produce in the market, or cleaning a government building, Juliette would be waiting impatiently for me in her house, having cooked one of my favorite meals. After our meal we would go to my house, where she would tell me stories and odo or sing songs she had thought of that morning. While I tried to work out my notes of that morning on my laptop, she taught me *fos' ten singi*/songs of the olden days, e.g.:

> Mi trow kaba
> Mi trow kaba
> Eliza na fu mi (2x)

Basi Kupu[9]
Kon prey a poku
Eliza na fu mi (2x)

[I am married already
I am married already
Eliza is mine (2x)

Boss Kupu
Come play the music
Eliza is mine (2x)]

Another old song is:

Fefi yuru mamanten
Granmisi mek' wan manpikin (2x)

Fa' a nen? (2x)
Buriki kakumbe (2x)

[At five in the morning
The older woman gave birth to a son (2x)

What's his name? (2x)
Donkey chin (2x)]

In the beginning of June 1990 I had to go back to Los Angeles for a conference. I had intended to be away for a week and a half, but I was unexpectedly delayed much longer. Later she told me that she had thought I would not come back, even though I had called her a couple of times to keep her informed of my whereabouts. Our growing attachment was evident from the fact that we missed each other terribly during the time I was away; our daily living together and talks had become an anchor in both our lives.

One morning in July, at breakfast, she told me that she had been to a *lobi singi* the night before. I reacted as if stung by a bee, because I knew lobi singi from the literature (Comvalius 1935, 1939; Herskovits and Herskovits 1936) as gatherings where mati sing self-composed love songs for each other and was not sure at that moment whether they were still performed. I expressed my disappointment that she had not taken me with her, because this was just what I was interested in. I finally explained to her that I was especially interested in *mati,* and the dams broke. The mati work lit up like a lighthouse in the landscape of her life's experiences. From then on, one story after another about the women she had been with in her younger days came tumbling out. Still,

I wanted to make sure that I understood her right. It was almost too good to be true: I had come to Paramaribo wanting to study whether mati life was still around and here I found myself living with one; one, as I teased her, who had invented it. One evening I asked her directly: "Juliette na wan matisma, no?" literally, "Juliette is a mati, no?" i.e., are you a mati? Impatient at such stupidity, she answered me: "Ma di m' e srib' nanga umasma, dan m' e mati"/But since I am sleeping with women, then I mati. In using the verb *na*/to be and the noun *mati,* asking her whether she belongs to the category of mati, I was inscribing an identity for Juliette, whereas she was answering me in terms of verbs, that is, describing her behavior and actions. Here I just want to note that our different phrasings, signaling identity versus activity, are significant, because they bespeak two different models, a dominant Euro-American and a working-class Afro-Surinamese model, of how sexual subjectivity is envisioned. I will elaborate on this crucial issue in the chapters that follow.

We now joined the endless round of secular and spiritual events that were taking place in Paramaribo, in spite of the dire economic situation. The Surinamese guilder was on a dazzling inflationary course and, especially for people who did not have access to foreign currencies, either Dutch guilders or U.S. dollars, the possibilities of making ends meet were grim. Being able to give a party almost certainly meant access to foreign currency. We became regulars at these parties, she twice my age and half my height, taking me out in her colorful *koto,* traditional, multilayered skirts, and matching angisa. Her cronies at the market and at parties teased her about me. At first I did not understand, but later, as my language skills improved, it was quite clear what they were saying, in the typical cutoff and elliptical way that odo are deployed: "Aiiiiiii, owru kaw . . ." Literally, they said, "Yes, old cow . . ." alluding to the odo "Owru kaw e nyan yong' grasi"/Old cow eats young grass. This odo is used especially, when there is a large age differential between partners. Juliette would beam, when they said it, neither denying nor affirming it, making good-natured *tyuri*[10] and dismissive hand gestures. She herself used another expression for us that was far more humbling: "pikin aksi e fala bigi bon"/the little ax fells the big tree.

Gradually I felt free to confide in her about the rather unhappy affair I was involved in since I had come to Paramaribo. I was seeing a middle-class woman who was in a longstanding relationship with another woman. Juliette was empathetic, but she also felt that I was pretty stupid to have opened my heart to Carmelita. She made it no secret that she had managed things differently and more smartly, when she was young, so she took considerable pleasure in counseling me on what to do:

"Meisje, m' o ferter' i wan sani"/Girl, I will give you some advice. When you are doing it with somebody, who already has someone else, do not give all

your love to that person. Just do it with her, but keep your love with your own sma/person, woman. This is the way I have always done it.

Juliette was outraged at my openness about my relationship with Carmelita, at the fact that her lover was my friend, too, and that I visited them at their home:

"Mi patu no ben bor' a nyan disi, yere! Yu na f' fur' man, y' e f' fur' en uma. A kompe wroko na wan lawlaw sani. Noit' mi ben du sani lek' y' e du now, mi ben sa du en kibri fasi; a visiti fu mi vriendin no ben sa sabi. Yu no mus' go drape; mek' Carmelita kon' dya"/My pot did not cook this food, you hear? You are a thief, you are stealing her woman. The mati work truly is a crazy thing. I would never have done what you are doing now, I would have done it much more discreetly; my lover's mati would never have known. You should not go there. Have Carmelita come here.

Despite the vicissitudes of my affair with Carmelita, those were happy days for Juliette and me and we were both aware of how we were filling each other's needs. I had come to Paramaribo with an academic purpose, but also with the personal aim to learn about my deceased working-class mother's cultural background, looking for answers to questions I had not been able to ask her. Exchanging stories with Juliette, having a best friend and a confidante, laughing at each other's idiosyncrasies, going places together, being taken care of by her, gave me a sense of belonging and safety. I felt thoroughly at home in Paramaribo, no mean feat since I was one and a –half years old when my family had migrated to the Netherlands. Juliette introduced me as her daughter to neighbors or friends who asked who I was, making me feel in place and that I was welcomed. She was the "informant" I could not have dreamed up in my wildest dreams: intelligent, lively, a storehouse of knowledge, and as curious as I was about how people lived and the reasons they attributed to the things they did. Had Juliette had the opportunity to study after elementary school, she would have liked to be a teacher, and it was clear that I could not have found a more adept one.

I had come to her in the winter of her life and telling her about my affair with Carmelita enabled her to comment on my unspeakable behavior. That was the best incentive for her to provide relief with stories about her own life. The stories we weaved together about the women in our lives made her come alive again. She clearly enjoyed giving all her *tori*/stories to someone who was so obviously interested and hanging on to her every word. I learned thickly about her and my own construction of sexuality. As she lived alone, it was gratifying for her to have someone nearby who looked after her on the few days that she was not feeling too well. I accompanied her to the doctor, because her *krammenade,* her spleen, was impaired, and I became her hero when I protested vociferously when she had to take off her clothes in a room where painters were at work. She often became mute in middle-class environments, loosing the self-confidence and flourish she had in her own surroundings. Through my adoring eyes she experienced herself as the attractive and irresistible woman she had been. She saw me as her daughter, her *pikin s' sa*/little sister, her *pikin fowru*/little chicken and her *wan ai karu*/ her "corn with only one eye."

Power and the "Erotic Equation in Fieldwork"

> *My informants are not just interesting cases. Over the years many have become friends of mine. … I fully recognize this common affinity and use it to understand my informants better, to engage in discourses with them, and, through these dialogues, to develop my own insights into their culture and personality.… I am one with them, yet not one of them.*
>
> (OBEYESEKERE 1981:11)[11]

> *The field researcher, therefore, has an objective stake in equality, as a condition for a less distorted communication and a less biased collection of data.*
>
> (PORTELLI 2001:31)

Not nearly enough has been written about the psychological underpinnings of "the erotic equation in fieldwork" (Newton 2000), either from the point of view of the anthropologist, much less from that of the "informant." I will assume that the days and the gendered dangers of being labeled a "field groupie," committing professional suicide, are long gone. Or, worse, that my relationship with Juliette would be considered as taking advantage of a poor, lonely, older woman. I believe it is important that we continue a frank conversation about the erotic subjectivity of the ethnographer who is doing fieldwork. I was confronting a psychologically extremely potent mixture of loneliness, being without the context of family and friends, of dependency, my "normal" persona of a professional erased or simply not relevant (Kondo 1992), at times being very different from the women around me, feeling reduced to somewhat childlike status, and at others being like one of them, gratitude for being seen by another person, even if Juliette's gaze only included particular aspects of my self. Admittedly, these were aspects of self that I had not been interpellated by before, such as Juliette reading me as being carried by Amerindian spirits, meaning that she saw me as warmhearted and friendly; yet she also saw me as extremely argumentative, always taking things too seriously, thinking too much, "full of tricks," not having proper mati manners, not showing respect at the right moments and in the required ways. At times I was aware that I eroticized Juliette's knowledge. Interestingly, the relationship between Juliette and me reminded me in some ways of a relationship between a client, me, and a very special and wise therapist. When new knowledge is part of the stuff that eroticism is made of, then Juliette provided me with plenty. My appreciation for and excitement about the knowledge I was acquiring of the way the world functioned, my development of cultural, linguistic, and religious insights and skills, knowledge of her and myself, was considerable. The setting, very accepting and very loving, in which it was possible to say, ask, and share everything and in which I had the feeling she saw me in—by and large—favorable ways, worked toward that perception too. Knowing Juliette renewed me, it shed new light on me in ways that I had not known before. My research was an adventure that taught me not only about a sexual culture but also about myself. Our encounter was a mutual benevolent sighting; we liked each other and each of us came to see the other as a gift, a very unexpected one. All these ingredients resulted in fertile conditions for me to connect erotically with her.

Not nearly enough has been written yet either about the differential power aspect in a same-sexed erotic relationship between an "informant" and an anthropologist (but see Whitehead and Conaway 1986; Kulick and Willson 1995; Lewin and Leap 1996; Newton 2000). At the time it was important to me not to be the initiator of the relationship. For mostly ageist reasons I never imagined Juliette as a possible sexual partner or that she had erotic interests in me. Had I been the initiator, it would have been hard to sort out my motivations, whether I was doing it to get better data—which would have been unacceptable to me—or because I was "simply" and genuinely attracted to Juliette. Ironically, although the end result ostensibly is the same, I note the different positioning of Ralph Bolton (1996), who made an intentional decision to use male same-sex sexual encounters as a form of data collection in the field of sexual practices in the time of the HIV/AIDS plague. I am less concerned with ethical aspects of his methodology, although he generally does not seem to address power dynamics and imbalances sufficiently and he unproblematically assumes that a sexual encounter will carry the same weight and meaning for his sex partners. More interesting in these configurations are the gendered positions a gay male and a lesbian anthropologist occupy in the field of sexuality, which underscore that gayness and lesbianism, within Euro-American contexts, are not symmetrical positions, that we need to be far more atttentive to such differences, and that one of the ways to uncover them is precisely through being transparent about our sexual positionings.

During my research I was not consistently aware that, while I was ostentatiously learning about the construction of her sexuality, I was also and simultaneously learning about my own. Many insights came afterward as I was reading through my extensive field notes. There is a rich field of oppositions in the ways in which she and I constructed desire and acted on it; whereas for her an age difference of more than forty years did not play a role, for me this difference was—initially and also in the long run—largely prohibitive. In my diary at the end of July 1990 I noted:

> *This morning, when I came out of the shower, I passed Juliette in the kitchen and, laughing loudly, pleased with herself, she cupped my breasts with both hands. To her grandson Raymond, visiting from the Netherlands with his wife and sitting in the living room, she exclaimed: "Mi fas' en bobi, yere!"/ I touched her breasts, you hear! I was somewhat taken aback and said: Ee-eeh!?! She said: "M' e kon grani kaba, mi pikin s' sa, na granisma kan du den san' disi"/I have grown old already, little sister, it's older women's prerogative to do this.*

I took her gesture for what she said it was and thought it rather charming. In hindsight I have come to interpret it as Juliette already expressing her sexual interest in me. This gesture could have gone unnoticed to Raymond and his white Dutch wife Rita, who was appreciably older than him, since they were in the living room and Juliette and I were in the kitchen. But Juliette expressly called their attention to it. Coupled with her clear pleasure in her own audacity, she was not only playing and flirting with me, but she was also showing herself as a sexual persona to her grandson. There was a naughty and ingenious touch to this gesture: in the first place, she seemed to be signifying a well known odo to him: "M' e owru, ma mi n' e kowru"/ I may be old, but I am not cold. Raymond, who was about my age, responded by chuckling, which I read as his applauding his grandmother. Thus, in this reading, she was showing off to him: look, I am much older than you, but I am still capable of flirting with a woman of your age, while you have a much older woman. The second reading I offer of the gesture is that it is ingenious because it remains ambiguous whether a sexual overture is being made or not. It *is* true that older women may teasingly touch younger girls' budding breasts, but I could not possibly be counted in that age category. I felt her gesture as a sexual overture, and she implicitly conceded that it might be sexual, but that did not matter anyway. Since she was old already, it was her prerogative to do so, implicitly pointing me to the privileged position of older women in Creole culture. I later regarded this as a key signifier in how she conceived of our relationship.

In my diary of August 1990 I jotted down the following thoughts, struck by the directness of Juliette's sexual overtures, which contrasted with my own, until then largely implicit, standards in this matter.

How is it possible that in a culture that has been called so "roundabout," e.g., by Herskovits in his diary at the Schomburg (1928), I am being propositioned so directly? Her way of courting me is so incredibly direct, according to my standards. No double entendres here—maybe they are lost on me?—but I do not think so; the objective is sex. No vanilla sex is intended, no cuddling and stuff; she wants sex, genital sex.

On the one hand, it is sort of embarrassing that our flirting and teasing got so out of hand. On the other, incredibly funny, rich, true to life. I have to admit that I do like the thought that she finds me attractive and that I get the old mati treatment. But am I really drawn to her?

What am I to do? I don't think having sex is a very good idea, I want to remain her daughter rather than become her mati. How would we continue to live together, if things do not work out? I am not prepared to move out, look for another place to live, and lose her, the worst scenario.

With Juliette as the initiator, I, having ended the relationship with Carmelita by then, but socialized into the notion that being sexually intimate with "an informant" was certainly not the thing to do, kept on hesitating for a while, going back and forth, trying in my diary to come to clarity about the nature of my feelings for her, struggling with my ageism. I sometimes hoped that her desire would dissipate, that it would vanish as silently as it had come, and that things would return to being warm and unproblematically mother-daughterish. Sometimes I enjoyed her ardency, making the knot of contradictory emotions even more inextricable. I have no doubt that I sent contradictory messages. I thought she was attractive and I liked flirting with her, but I did not want to pay the price that was apparently attached to a relationship. I was living on her premises and I had her and my house to lose if things did not work out. Moreover, I had reasons to believe that my freedom to go and come as I pleased would be seriously jeopardized—specifically, that she would object to my sleeping with someone else. Having had multiple simultaneous relationships in the past, this was not an academic issue. I had socialized, during the seventies and eighties, in mainly white lesbian circles in Amsterdam that put premiums on individuality and on inventing and living models of relating in which monogamy and possessiveness were avoided (Wekker 1993, 1998a). Jealousy was just not cool, and one would not want to be caught at it. I was quite competent at performing in these modes. At a later stage the Eurocentric model of lesbian relating had become tiresome to me: "equality" along several dimensions, age, education, income, and status, was deemed important, with ethnicity playing a more problematical part, and one's lesbian "identity" inescapably meant sexual incarceration with only women. But I knew experientially no other models. From the the late eighties on, I mainly had relationships with black women, but that did not necessarily guarantee different models of relating, largely correlating with how long a partner had lived in the Netherlands and whether she had mainly dwelt in white or black circles. Nor was I really prepared to change my ways when someone wanted another, monogamic, way of relating to each other.

My ways of handling the situation with Juliette, stalling, explaining why I did not think it was a good idea, interrogating her about what would change if I did sleep with her, negotiating with her, did not make much impression on her. She had made up her mind that she wanted me and was not about to take no for an answer. As I came to understand her perspective in due course, the fact that she, as the older woman, was propositioning me made it something I could almost not refuse. There was no ambiguity in Juliette's answer when I queried about the sustainability of my love of freedom: "I mus' denk' m' e law"/You must think that I am crazy.

Oral historian Alessandro Portelli reminds us of the importance of thinking through the roles of equality and difference in field research. The two concepts, equality and difference, are related:

> Only equality prepares us to accept difference in terms other than hierarchy and subordination; on the other hand, without difference there is no equality—only sameness, which is a much less worthwhile ideal. Only equality makes the interview credible, but only difference makes it relevant. Fieldwork is meaningful as the encounter of two subjects who recognize each other as subjects, and therefore separate, and seek to build their equality upon their difference in order to work together.
>
> (PORTELLI 2001:43)

How can these notions of equality and difference be unpacked in the encounter of Juliette and me? And, more specifically, did our landscapes of equality and difference, as we would have described them to ourselves or to a sympathetic outsider, look the same? Putting the matter in the latter terms already points to a fundamental point of difference in the domain of the formation of our subjectivities. While I would have welcomed the occasion to piece myself together by laying out my understanding of the relationship to a trusted outsider, who came along later in the person of Delani, Juliette would never have directly or fully described the relationship to someone else. She might have dropped hints about it to her peers, as she did with Raymond and Rita and other family members, on occasion, and she might have listened to others jokingly allude to it, but she would never have openly discussed the ins and outs of the relationship. Writing about our relationship now means that I am engaging in a practice that is foreign and not necessarily congenial to her. Even though we agreed that her life was worth telling, and she was very supportive of my writing a book about mati, it was understood that I would only write about our relationship after her death (Wekker 1998a). In seeking the truth of the relationship from her point of view, it might seem as if I am ventriloquizing her. I base myself upon my descriptions of her behavior and utterances, as they are recorded in my field diaries. The extent to which I manage to describe the relationship as it appeared to her, and describe it with integrity, is also the extent to which I have come to understand the world from her point of view. The encounter between Juliette and me, in this land in-between, is open to aesthetic and moral judgment (McCarthy Brown 1991).

It might be easy to assume that I had more power than Juliette in the relationship. In many respects and contrary to what the few descriptions of sexual relationships between (white) male anthropologists and informants of color have told us, Juliette on balance had more power than I. As Creole women, although I was a "prodigal daughter," we were on a level playing field in our negotiations with respect to the intersection of gender and ethnicity. My unpracticed eye put us within the same range of light skin colors, but her insiders' eye did not fail to notice several shades of color between us. This signified differently in her universe than it did in mine: since I had not grown up in Suriname, I did not automatically make connections between lighter skin color and class status. On several occasions it became clear to me that part of her pride in showing me off had to do with the combination of my age and my lighter skin color. Our class situation as measured by income was not radically different, neither she needing me financially nor the other way around. We both had income in foreign currency, the most desired financial modality; she received her most important means of living from her children in the Netherlands, while I had two consecutive U.S. scholarships. Certain elements of my middle-class status, e.g., being a Ph.D. candidate—which to me was very meaningful—were virtually erased in her universe; my professional accomplishments simply were not visible and thus did not mean much to her. She did like the poem "Creole Women," which I wrote in March 1990,[12] and she was proud when, shortly after, it was published in one the national dailies, *De Ware Tijd*.

Other possibilities that my class position, in conjunction with my nationality, might and did entail in my interactions with others, e.g., entry into the Netherlands by acting as someone's guarantor or even the possibility of Dutch citizenship by being in a relationship with her/him, simply were not relevant in my relationship with Juliette. She had her children to ease her entry into the Netherlands whenever she wanted to visit and, at her age, had no need whatsoever for the Dutch nationality. The intersection between class and nation did not carry significance in our case.

Besides being meaningful as regards skin color, class, in its lived reality, was accentuated for us both at different moments. I already mentioned the occasions when I accompanied her to the doctor and protested against the treatment that was deemed appropriate for someone of her class. She became strangely mute in middle-class environments, where working-class people are often treated with disrespect. However much I liked my house and the neighborhood where we lived, I did occasionally experience the need to be away from the noise—with different kinds of music coming from four corners—the crowding and the basic living conditions. Sometimes, when the chance presented itself, I stayed in the homes of middle-class friends, who were traveling, and twice Juliette and I spent a weekend in a luxurious hotel. In the environments where I was most at ease she was least at ease, and the other way around was true too; where she blended in, e.g., in our neighborhood, at Winti Prey, and at parties, I was initially uncertain as to the proper behavior. At the hotel we would sit on the terrace by the swimming pool, on a Sunday afternoon, drinking high tea. I enjoyed our outing immensely, while she was mostly silent. I realized that she enjoyed being with me, but not necessarily the location where I took her. People of her class background, which was evident by her traditional working-class Creole attire, had never been welcomed at the hotel before. When we got home she would not fail to tell our next-door neighbor, however, where we had been that weekend.

In the end, it was culture and age that played out most in her favor in the balance of equality and difference between us. She was the expert in a culture, a politics of passion, that I wanted to understand. Moreover, she was older and thus within a Creole context where respect is due to older people, especially women, she was "always right." By the end of October I accepted her standing invitation to "lie down with her." I was enamored of the deeply cultural explanation she had given me of her feelings for me, how her *yeye*/her "soul" had taken to mine and had clearly recognized the *Inyi Winti*/the Amerindian spirits that were carrying me. These were the same Winti carrying her. Interestingly, at other times, she used a biological discourse to explain her feelings. She supposed that the blood-building injections and pills the doctor had been giving her for her spleen had given her blood more strength and had made her feel alive again: after all, she was not made out of wood.

In *Death Without Weeping: The Violence of Everyday Life in Brazil* Nancy Scheper-Hughes writes about the strong connection poor Brazilians make in their autoethnography between poverty and sex. Sexual vitality is the only thing that reminds them that they are not dead. She movingly describes an old woman, a bag of bones, her infected foot doused in iodine, dancing sexily and suggestively with a young boy (1992:164–165). Poverty and hunger have not been as endemic and systemic in Suriname as in Brazil's Nordeste, and thus the Surinamese configuration, although in some respects reminiscent of the Brazilian, is not the same. I have understood Juliette's zest for life and sex within the context of a culture that grasps sexuality as an extraordinary joyful and healthy aspect of life, possibly a feature of the West African "grammatical behavioral principles" (Mintz and Price 1992 [1976]) in the domain of sexual subjectivity, the expression of which does not need to end in an advanced stage in life. This is in stark opposition to the representation of asexuality that predominantly characterizes older Euro-Americans, with all its limitations and loss of pleasure. The latter representation works toward limiting sex to that venerated stage of life, youth, and is in need of as much explanation as the Afro-Surinamese modality.

Juliette was extraordinarily frank with me in discussing her feelings and behavior and to the extent that I have come to understand the mati work and Creole working-class culture, I owe it largely to her. Our relationship was complex, multilayered, by no means easy, or to be taken for granted. I felt a mixture of love, gratitude, and sometimes transferred anger toward her as a dominant, demanding mother and a jealous lover. She was my most important informant, collaborator, commiserator, supporter, friend, mother substitute. She saw me as a child with Surinamese roots, her little sister, who did not know the first thing about the culture and who badly needed educating in terms of the language and culturally appropriate manners. Juliette's openness toward me was a mirror of my attitude toward her and it certainly helped that in my life, too, mostly women have been the "apples of my eye." We often exchanged information and I would tell her as much from my side of the world as she would tell me about hers. I discussed different theories about the mati work with her, e.g., that some people who had studied the phenomenon thought that women engaged in it because of the absence of men. She responded with a tyuri, sucking her teeth. I told her about developments with regard to homosexuality on the African continent; that the leaders of some African nations held whites responsible for spreading homosexuality. Her concise comment: "No wan bakra ben leri mi, mi pikin s'sa"/no white person has taught me, my little sister. We shared our stories about the women who had been important in our lives and laughed till we cried about ourselves and the women who had broken our hearts: cathartic sessions for us both. Juliette would repeatedly sigh: "a mati wroko na wan law sani"/the mati work can drive you crazy. And after an exchange about different techniques of having sex, she summed it up: "baya, ala sortu nay de"/my word, there is all kinds of screwing. I told her my coming out story and how my father, at first, had not liked my being a lesbian at all. I explained to her that, where I came from, to be a woman who loves women had long been disparaged and brought feelings of shame and hiding. Such feelings were unthinkable in Mis' Juliette's universe; she had never heard of anything of that kind. "Sortu, syen? Meisje, un kon mit' a wroko dya. A no un' mek' en"/What do you mean, shame? Girl, we found the mati work when we got here. It was not us who invented it. It was one of the early markers of her radically different value structure and the formation of her sexual subjectivity.

Life as a Young Girl

"A ka kor' patu f' i n' e interesseer mi lek' a doosje fu Ma Joosje"/That damn coal pot of yours does not interest me as much as Ma Joosje's pussy.

Juliette had two younger brothers and one sister and we sometimes went to visit the one brother and the sister who were still alive. She was not particularly close to them, because, when growing up, Juliette lived with her aunt Anna, her mother's sister, who did not have children of her own and who *kwek' en*, raised her. One of the West African features of the Creole kinship system, which has survived to this day, is that children are easily exchanged between households. Especially when a woman is without children of her own, she is "given" children of her siblings, of other relatives, or of her mati to raise. There is continuity in this practice. Thirty years later, Juliette's oldest daughter, Mama Matsi, who was in her middle twenties and could not have children of her own, raised Juliette's youngest daughter, Floortje, from the day she was born. When Juliette was in her middle thirties and pregnant with her ninth child, she had temporarily taken in her mati, at that time, Wanda. Wanda was very poor, she neither had children nor a place of her own, so Juliette helped her out until she found her own house. Wanda helped her when the baby was born and *fu kwek' en*/helped to raise her. The baby was named after her. Until that time, big Wanda had been crazy about Juliette's youngest child, a boy called Humphrey. Wanda now only had eyes for little Wanda, she took the care of the baby upon her and did not pay attention to Humphrey any more. Juliette says: "Mi no mu' ley g' en, di a ten dat' Wanda geboren, mi no ab' fu was' wan pis' duku f' a pikin dati."/I should not tell lies about her, since the time that Wanda was born, I did not have to wash one diaper for that child.

This is a very typical way for Juliette to open an exegesis on a person or a matter that she wants to do justice to: "Mi no mu' ley g' en"/I should not tell lies about her/him, or, alternatively: "San mi sa taki sondro fu ley?"/ What shall I say without telling lies? It is a formulaic opening that attests to the truth she is about to tell; she also creates time to think about what she will say and how she will present it. It is a way of speaking that other older women also engaged in, making it more than an idiosyncracy.

When Wanda moved out, she took the baby with her and raised her. Juliette says she never would have taken the baby away from Wanda; that would have been a heartless and unforgivable thing to do and is part of working-class women's etiquette. The practice of giving birth to a child, while doing the mati work, is referred to as "kisi pikin na sma anu"/getting a child in your woman's hands. Very literallly, Juliette gave birth to a child in her mati's hands, even when she was living in concubinage with Dorus, the man with whom she had the longest relationship. The sequel to this tale of the sharing of children is instructive, too, and sheds a more nuanced light on the role of biology in the families people make and on the heterosexist assumptions underlying studies of kinship (Weston 1992; Blackwood 2005; Lewin 2002). Years later little Wanda suddenly died at the age of forty, pregnant with her fourth child. Suffering from an infection, she had to go see a doctor but kept postponing it. Juliette remembers that the day Wanda died a black butterfly was in her house, the whole day. At six in the evening it flew away. The next morning she heard that Wanda had died the day before. Juliette went to sit with big Wanda for days, as one of the obligations, implied in the expression *mati work*, that (ex-)mati have toward each other. In effect, big Wanda had become the mother of little Wanda and the grandmother of the three young children—the oldest was six—that she continued to raise. These grandchildren, now in their late twenties, sometimes came to visit Juliette, but Wanda is their "real" (grand-)mother. Family connections are not only made in opposite-sexed spheres but also between mati. These family ties remain intact, even when the women involved have separated or have died.

In Aunt Anna' s home Juliette was raised in the EBG religion,[13] the Protestant Evangelical Brethren Gemeinschaft, also known as the Hernnhutters, and she went to an EBG school. When Juliette was twelve she started spending time with older women who were crazy about her. "Mi no ben ab' leti verstand ete, y' e yongu, y' e sport. Mi ben lob' fu ab' prisiri"/I did not have a brain yet; you are young, you go out. I loved to have fun. The *bigisma*/older women, took her to Winti Prey, to dances, to excursions, to *boiti*, literally, "outside," rural districts outside of Paramaribo. She started to work at the age of thirteen as a domestic servant in a private home. She reminisces:

I worked for this nice lady in the Zwartenhovenbrugstraat; "a ben ab' krin kleur en a ben ab' bun ati"/she was light skinned and goodhearted. The work was not hard and I was young and strong. I always had the time to run errands and go see my friends on the way. She would always ask me, very friendly: can you sweep and mop the floor? Do the dishes? There was someone else to do the laundry. If I only had had to deal with her, I would still be working for her. Her husband owned a pharmacy. When the lady was not at home, a ben fufer' mi/he pestered me. He promised me money if I would lay down with him. But, "mansma no ben interesseer mi nooit"/ men never interested me.

She found another private home to work, but again the man of the house harassed her. Juliette became sick and tired of men making sexual overtures toward her. The pattern described here, in which men consider it their pre-rogative to have sexual access to women, especially working-class women, dates from 1920. It is noteworthy that sexual harassment has been operative for so long, but it has only received public attention in Suriname, under the influence of the globalization of the women's movement, in the nineties (see chapter 6).

On the personal level, here is an important theme that keeps coming back in Juliette's utterances about the way she constructed her subjecthood. There were myriad ways in which she expressed that men were not impor-tant to her sense of self: "mansma no ben interesseer mi nooit"/men never interested me; "mi no ben de frammejaar so nanga mansma"/I was not so familiar, at ease with men; "mi ik no ben lob' mansma"/"I" did not love men; "mi no ben dipidipi so nanga mansma"/I was not so intimate with men. Her sense of self is deeply embedded in the discourse circulating within the Afro-Surinamese Winti religion where people are carried by various spirits. One of Juliette's main spirits was a male Apuku who did not tolerate real-life men in her life.

As I go back over my notes I notice that Juliette has told me two compet-ing stories about the first time she slept with a woman. In my diary of August 8, 1990, I find the following notes:

Juliette told me today about the first woman she slept with; she was fourteen and it was a girl of her own age. "Un ben du fisti sani makandra, ma a ben sab' griti ooktu. Dan, mi no sab' fa, wan sma ben mus' fu konkru nanga fer-ter' en ma, so dan en ma ben suku mi tu. Mi srib' nang' en, dan later mi sribi nanga en bigi s'sa umapikin. Dan wan dey, wan bigi sma ben kar' mi en a' e taki: 'Juliette, yu ben nay dri Kasnika uma now. A sari.'"/We did nasty things together, but she also knew how to rub. Then, I do not know how, somebody must have been gossiping with her mom and telling her, so the next thing I know is that her mother is after me, too. I slept with her, too. Then later I slept with the daughter of her older sister. One day, an older woman called me and told me: Juliette, you have been having sex with three Kasnika[14] women now. That's enough.

Thus, although Juliette had her eye on a fourth woman from the same large family group, she refrained from that. The term *griti*/rubbing, is, as we will see developed in chapter 5, the most colloquial term used by mati to indicate tribadism, according to many accounts a favorite sexual position.

The other story about Juliette's first sexual encounter that I recorded is about an older woman, Yaya, who was about thirty-five years at the time; this is a pattern that still occurs in mati circles today. Yaya already had a *visiti*/girlfriend of her own, Martha. Yaya was thus engaged in what mati call *f furu*/stealing or *uru*/whoring around. In this version, too, Juliette was fourteen years old. She sums it up succinctly: "A mek' mi kon sribi nanga en"/She made me come sleep with her. It was the older woman who took the initiative in expressing interest in the young girl. It is a matter of respect that a younger person, especially when there is a large age gap, should not take the initiative. In general, the initiator stakes a claim to the dominant position in the relationship. Asked what it was like to be with this woman, Juliette recalls:

"We, san mè sa taki, dan?"/Well, what shall I tell you? Here I was, fourteen years old, with my beautiful round face, my light skin color, my full braids, and all the neighborhood women were going crazy over little Juliette. "A mus' de tak' mi yeye, mi kra ben de nanga umasma"/It must have been that my "soul," "I," was with women. Yaya, my first krin visiti/real mati, taught me everything there was to know, she spoiled me, bought me dresses and jewelry, she always gave me little tidbits or money, she helped me set up my room. People in the olden days knew things, you hear? They were really careful with me, too. We did everything; "un ben freri, un ben bosi, un ben griti, ma den no ben broko mi"/we made love, we kissed, we "rubbed," but they did not break me, i.e., deflower me.

The bigisma that she slept with had taken care not to break her *t'te*, literally, "rope," hymen, because that was deemed appropriate for the first man to do. In Juliette's case that happened when she was about eighteen years old. The man is supposed to give the "self" of the young girl a present of gold, because it is considered a great honor. Terborg (2002:67–70) states that there is no strict virginity ideal among Creoles, in the sense that loss of virginity would be a sin or a shame. She relates the importance of virginity both to Christian ideals and to African cultural traditions. Virginity is not so much connected to male honor but to female pride. It is also an instrument in the negotiations with men. The fact that that honor is reserved for men may be interpreted as the privileging of men, in this respect, but it may also indicate the notion that it is from connections with men that children result and that the first time with a man thus carries a rite-of-passage character, which should be marked with a present. In other words, I am suggesting that there may be less significance to the fact that the honor is reserved for a man than to the fact that the woman is indicating her readiness to have babies. Juliette remembers that Yaya told her "a no mus' go suku masra"/she should not look for a man. Since Juliette wanted children, she did anyway, after a while.

Yaya was to have her birthday, Juliette wanted to give her a nice present, and she had to go looking for a *kopro beki,* a copper basin, to put the present in. Working-class women, in their many-layered skirts, carry the decorative copper basin on their heads on festive occasions. The basin is filled with flowers and shrubs, red and yellow *fayalobi* (Rubiaciae) and amaranths. After seventy years, Juliette still recalls what the present was that she bought for Yaya: a beautiful pink bowl with little purple roses on it. It was a bowl to simply have around for decorative purposes or to eat *tom-tom* soup from, the thick soup made from ripe green bananas. When Juliette had to run an errand, strong almond essence, for her aunt Anna, she passed by Aunt Hilda and wanted to borrow a kopro beki from her. Aunt Hilda went to Anna and, probably alarmed by Juliette's precociousness, told her that Juliette, all of fourteen years old, was looking for a copper basin to give a present to Yaya. Her aunt had told Juliette that she did not appreciate the mati work and that she should stay away from it. When she confronted Juliette, there was no choice but to lie. She said that another friend of Yaya's, Noldi, had sent her to go look for the beki, because Noldi wanted to give Yaya a present. Aunt Anna went straight to Noldi, and the latter had her wits together enough to confirm this story and help Juliette out. She could not go to the birthday proper, because Yaya's mati Martha and all her *speri*/age-mates, friends, were there, but she managed to get the present over there. When the older women saw the present, they all started talking about how Juliette's present was more beautiful than Martha's, and the latter got so flustered that she smacked Yaya across the mouth. Somehow word got to Aunt Anna that Juliette had sent a present after all. But still Juliette did not confess. This scenario is familiar from the description given by the Herskovitses of the mati birthday party in *Suriname Folk-lore* (1936) and I will come back to it in chapter 5. Already schooled in the rules of the mati work, Juliette posed an institutionalized challenge to the exclusive claims of the steady partner, Martha, on Yaya, the woman who is celebrating her birthday. Juliette was quite precocious.

Juliette's and Yaya's courting occurred in 1921. Hearing these stories, of which Juliette seems to have had an endless supply, I felt excited and blissful. But the stories also evoked a bittersweet melancholy. They speak of working-class women who had been able to build a culture in which they enjoyed and celebrated each other openly, in which they helped each other cope with daily living, sharing hardships and pleasure, and in which there was a lot of sleeping around and teasing. Most of the protagonists in the stories are dead now. The only way in which they can be called to live again, in which we will get to know them and their politics of passion, is by entrusting Juliette's stories to paper.

After Yaya, Juliette, still in her late teens, had another lover, Shanna, who was one year her junior. She says that she loved Shanna most of all the women in her life. She was lovers with her *wan bun tujari*/a good many years. But since they were both very young, there was also a lot of sleeping around and jealousy between them. Once Juliette went to a dance and got very drunk. She did have her eye on a woman there, but was too drunk to be very effective about it. She had put her shoes somewhere in the house and was barefoot. Shanna was told of Juliette being at this party and unexpect-

FIGURE 1.1 Suriname *kottomissies,* women in traditional Afro-Surinamese dress, ca. 1920. *KITLV, Leiden, the Netherlands, no. 8828*

edly showed up and made her leave. She made Juliette look for her shoes and, when they had found them, at first Shanna carried them, but then she said: "I did not make you take them off, so you carry them yourself." When they got home, Shanna told the drunk Juliette that Juliette could not go to sleep before she had made love to her. Juliette was not up to it.

From my diary of September 19, 1990:

There is an element in the kompe wroko/mati work that reminds me of S&M. This is one example. Another one was when Juliette told me that Shanna at some point did not want to sleep with her anymore. According to Juliette this was because Shanna had another visiti/girlfriend. Juliette said: "Dan en ede at' en; dan a bere at' en, dan en futu at' en. Mi ben nak' a sma baldadig fosi, dan mi ben mek' en sor' mi, fa a ben du nanga en visiti. Dan kan de mi ben nak' en agen. Mi pur' en futuwiri. Ai baya"/Then her head was hurting her; then her belly, then her "foot," i.e., her vagina, was hurting her. First, I hit the shit out of her, then I made her show me how she had done it with her girl-friend. Then maybe I hit her again. I would pull her pubic hair [a deep sigh]. But you know how things like that go; I do not have to tell you anything. She will tell you that it was no big thing. That she did not come and the other one made herself come. "En futu b'o saka, mi pikin s'sa. En futu b'o saka"/I would make her lust go away, my little sister, I would make it go away.

After the relationship with Shanna ended, because of jealousy and their two pairs of roving eyes, Juliette says that she did not want to get in the *mati wroko* again. She felt hurt and did not like the jealousy and madness of mati life.

She continued to work as a domestic, renting a room of her own in a backyard house. When she was eighteen years old, she met Rinaldo, who was in his late twenties, and when I asked her about the nature of this relationship and how being with a man combined with having female lovers, she explained:

"Sensi mi ben de yongu, mi ben aks' Gado fu gi mi pikin. Vooral mi ben wani umapikin. Mi las' pikin. Ma noit' mi ben pur' bere. San Gado ben wan' gi mi, mi ben teki. Yu abi man fanodu, fu gi yu pikin sensi, fu yep' yu pai a yuru, fu bai yu wan japon. Mansma srefi mi no ben lobi, ma di a ben yep' mi, mi ben mus' gi en wan pikinso"/Since I was young, I asked God to give me children. I wanted daughters especially. I lost children, but I never had an abortion. What God wanted to give me, I took. You need a man, to give you some money, to help you pay the rent, to buy you a dress. I did not really like men, but since he was helping me out, i.e., giving me money, I had to give him some.

But, I countered, all those things a woman could have given you too, some money, a nice dress. Exasperated, she replied:

"Dan fa mi b'o kis' den pikin? A tru tak' a kan gi mi sensi tu, a kan gi mi yapon, a kan lob' mi. Ma mi ben wani den pikin, den sorgu yu in' yu owru yari. Mansma e go lib' yu, kompe e go lib' yu, ma yu pikin d' o tan ala yu libi"/Then how would I have gotten the children? It is true that she can give me money too, she can give me a dress, she can love me. But I wanted the children, they take care of you in your older years. Men are going to leave you, mati are going to leave you, but your children will stay all your life.

Rinaldo became her steady partner, visiting her regularly, and he fathered her oldest daughter. Having a baby did not mean that Juliette was prepared to give up on going out. One evening she got into a fight with Rinaldo, because he wanted her to stay at home in order to control her movements. In her research on heterosexual relationships in the Creole population Terborg (2002) notes that, at the end of the 1990s, the most serious bone of contention is the man wanting to control the woman's sexuality by proscribing her movements. Many women with steady male partners are not at liberty to come and go as they please, and there is remarkable continuity in the pattern. Juliette could not be bothered with Rinaldo, "a ben wani fu sidon na mi tapu"/he wanted to sit on me. This was also the main reason for her refusal to marry. Disdainfully, she exclaims, her nostrils flaring: "Trow? Suma? Mi? Noit' mi no ben wani trow. Mi na wan sma di altijd lob' mi onafhankelijkheid"/Marry? Who? Me? I never wanted to marry. I am someone who always loved my independence. She did not want to have to put up with a man in her house, who might permit himself all kinds of liberties, like telling her: "No durf fu trap' wan poot na dorosey, dineti"/Don't you dare to put a foot outside this house tonight. In the olden days when a man had told his woman to stay at home and she defied him, choosing instead to go out to a dance, for instance, her friends would warn her, when he turned up at the dance: *Luku, Blaka de*/Watch out, Blackie has come. The woman then would leave by the backdoor and be at home by the time he got back there. Juliette stressed the element of shame for the woman in such an arrangement. Her female friends would make fun of her. She always wanted to come and go as she pleased, and the man she had later in her life never gave her trouble on that score. She is convinced: *Uma koni moro man triki*/Women's smartness outweighs men's antics.

Rinaldo wanted her to stay home and lay down with him, but Juliette refused because "a ben mek' afspraak nanga Ma Joosje"/she had a date with

Ma Joosje, a *bonuman,* a healer in the Winti religion, with whom she was involved at the time. Rinaldo then hit her. As Juliette says: for the first and the last time. He bought her presents to win her back, among others a new coal pot. But she told him, relishing the story as she tells it to me:

> *"Mi ben de wan sani tu, yere, mi ben de wan brede. Mi ferter' en: a ka kor' patu f' 'i n' e interesseer mi lek' a doosje fu Ma Joosje. So dan a nak' mi agen, ma mi ben breti mi ben fen' reden. Mi ben wan' mi fri"*/I was something else, you hear, I was nobody's fool. I told him: that damn coal pot of yours does not interest me as much as Ma Joosje's pussy. So then he hit me again, but I was glad to have found a reason. I wanted my freedom.

The same night she moved out and went to live with Ma Joosje.

When she was young, Juliette's relationship with her own mother was not close. While living with Aunt Anna, her mother sometimes came to visit and brought her a new dress or shoes. Juliette does not tell many stories about her mother, but one story strikes me as significant for reasons that have to do with the debate on dating the emergence of the mati work. Once, Juliette, who was then in her early twenties, went to visit her mother with Ma Joosje, who was in her fifties. Her mother was very unpleasant to Ma Joosje and Juliette on that occasion and more or less told them to leave; she did not want to receive them. I initially made the assumption that her mother was against the mati work and was not in the life herself. This assumption turned out to be incorrect. In a later conversation Juliette told me she realized when she was older that her mother and another woman who was always around her, Aunt Pauwtje, must have been mati too. Aunt Pauwtje was with Juliette's mother from as far back as Juliette can remember. Her mother only objected to Ma Joosje because she had the name to be an *obia* woman, someone who entertains the evil forces of Winti. An important element of this story is that it helps us to date the emergence of the mati work before 1900, which is the period most commonly held to mark its emergence. Around 1900 many working-class men left Paramaribo to do migrant labor in the gold and wild rubber industries in the rain forest, leaving women to fend for themselves in the city. Men had unprecedented amounts of money to spend when they returned to the city and prostitution flourished. Working-class women reacted to the commodification of heterosexual relations by upgrading their sense of worth, which was evident in all aspects of Creole culture, proverbs and songs (van Wetering 1998:132). According to this argument, women then started to have sexual relationships with each other. Juliette's mother probably was born in the 1870s or 1880s, and I assume that she would have become sexually active before 1900.

When she was about a year and a half, Juliette's first baby, whom Juliette invariably calls *sargi*[15] Zus, "blessed Zus," died of liver illness. All the other relatives who have died are preceded by sargi. There is sargi Wanda, her daughter who died at forty years of age. There is also sargi Humphrey, the son who, at seventeen, drowned, and finally sargi Dorus, her concubine for almost two decades. Juliette was nineteen when the baby fell so seriously ill, and by the time she went to see a doctor for Zus it was already too late.

I ask her whether Ma Joosje stood by her when Zus died. Juliette explains that Joosje could have been her grandmother and that with older women you did not talk that much, that was what you did with your *speri*/age-mates. Ma Joosje was good to her in that she helped Juliette organize her life and helped her financially. Younger women like herself would dance their money away. Juliette was not Ma Joosje's only girlfriend; Ma Joosje had her own mati and several young lovers, in addition, and from Juliette's stories she appears to have been in a position in which she thoroughly enjoyed having sex with multiple partners without being possessive or jealous.

Talking about Ma Joosje sent Juliette on a trail of reflections about her preference for older women when she was young:

> *I always got along well with older women. Mi skin ben de yongu/"My body,"*
> *"I" was young, was alive. My face did not have wrinkles yet, I had a very*
> *round face. They loved me. I did not have sex every day. If I had to count*
> *all the older women that I had sex with … I also could make a pass at her,*
> *it wasn't only she who would be after me. When we went to bed, it did not*
> *make any difference anymore. She played with me, I played with her. We*
> *were equal. But what I do not like, when you are with an older person, you*
> *should not be sassy with her. Because you really are not equal. You have to*
> *give her respect.*

Here, at the end of the quote, besides giving information about the importance of respect in relationships, Juliette was also signifying. By then, December 1990, our conflicting visions of etiquette in a relationship had begun to appear. She thought that I was *vrijpostig*/sassy and she could not believe that I really did not know any better, that I did not know how to behave myself properly as the younger partner in the relationship. She believed that I was willfully not showing her any respect.

I remember the day that this first became apparent to me, a stifling hot day near Christmas when I was ill with malaria.[16] I was so weak that the only way I could continue my work was to interview women at home. Juliette was exceedingly jealous of this trickle of women dropping by and suspected me, with "my roving eye" to be having it on with some of them. The irony was that at this point I was merely doing my work. It made me furious to be suspected of something I was not doing. Meeting women outside, as my work entailed, was one thing, but having them come to the house was an outright insult in her eyes. By this time she also refused to introduce me to some of her acquaintances whom I wanted to interview because she did not trust me with them. Her fits of jealousy, ranting, raving, and hitting me were hard to bear. We exchanged bitter words, because I felt bad about being ill and loosing time in the first place. In addition to this, she was making my work only harder. When I finally convinced her that her jealousy was unfounded, she made light of the whole episode: "Mi s'sa, ef' yarusu no de bij, dan a no tru lobi"/Sister, if I am not jealous, then it is not true love. She felt that I was always too serious, thinking too much, too argumentative, when she accused me of being unfaithful. To her, it was all part of staging the relationship. I should not answer her back, since that was a sure sign of disrespect. Rather, I should *kor' kor' en*/humor, appease, sweet-talk her. I was no good at that skill.

It became apparent that no woman was exempt from her suspicions, but she strongly applauded it when men came to visit me. In particular, one colleague, a tall, lean, very white Dutch man, was her favorite, and she even advised me to start a relationship with him: You are young and if you want to have a man "kon waka na yu baka, dan mi n' a' trobi. A man kan gi yu wan fef' sensi" /walk after you, then I do not have problems with it. The man can give you some money. I was taken aback: "Aren't you jealous of a man then?" "No," she replied, "with women it is another story, but you can have something with a man." Obviously the Dutchman's color worked in his favor, he had a car and white Dutch men were, in Juliette's worldview—and given the selection mechanisms during a long period of Dutch colonial history she was to a large extent factually correct in this—by definition in a favorable economical position. In short, in her eyes, I should decide to have children with him before it was too late. I was forty; it was still possible. Who would take care of me in my old age, when I did not have children? Our different worlds could not have been juxtaposed more sharply. Retrospectively, I am moved by the fact that she was worried about my future. But at the time I was irritated by her admonitions, which did not resonate at all with my construction of being a woman who loves women. She obviously did not have a conception of me as being able to take care of myself financially. She was giving me the best advice that she had to offer, based on the deeply ingrained notions that women ought to have children and need men for money.

Partners and Children

No tide, no tamara/not today, not tomorrow.

JULIETTE

After blessed Zus died, Juliette was pregnant with twins, but she miscarried. At twenty, finally, she had the daughter, whom I know as mama Matsi. Mama Matsi is indicated as *dosu*, the term used for the child coming after twins. Three different men fathered Zus, the twins, and Matsi, but Juliette lived with none of them. "Mi ben wani pikin, ma ala ten dat' mi ben sribi nanga mansma, mi ben kis' bere gelijk"/I wanted children, but every time I slept with a man, I was pregnant immediately. Those men were too young and troublesome to live with. She wanted them to help her *nanga wan kwartjie*/with a quarter, but she always wanted her freedom, most of all. If they had other women, she did not care. *We, den ben sa abi*/well, they undoubtedly did have (other women), she comments offhandedly. It was important to her to know the fathers of her children, she did not want to do *stukwerk*/sleep with men on a commercial basis, but they should not get any ideas. Since she knew that she was into the kompe wroko, she wanted *wan owru p'pa*[17]/an older man, who would not bother her too much, who would let her do whatever she wanted to do. And who would not beat her or be jealous, as a young man would likely be. It took her six years to find a man like that. This pattern, too—a younger woman with an appreciably older man—shows historical continuity.

Dorus was a balata bleeder in the rain forest, away from home very often. He was living with Mis' Magda and in a visiting relationship with Mis' Corry when Juliette came into his life. He had children with both Magda and Corry. According to Juliette, he was crazy about her. I ask Juliette what gave her the edge over his other women. She was younger, lighter skinned and more beautiful than they and in the end she had more children with him. Dorus was in his late forties, and she was twenty-five when she started living with him. Dorus and Juliette were together for eighteen years, until he died. They had eight children together.

They had a boy first, Stephan, and when the next child was born, Nancy, he moved in with Juliette. Mis' Magda almost died, she sent one of her daughters, Adriana, to Juliette's house to beg Dorus to come see her. She was miserable. I asked Juliette how she felt about that. Did she empathize with Magda?

> *Nono. It was Dorus's decision, I did not ask him to come live with me. I was young, "mi no ben prakser' a zaak kwet' kweti"/I did not think about it at all. Whenever I saw Dorus go into some woman's house, I never called him or asked him what he was doing there. I was in the kompe wroko, so I did*

*not want him to ask me anything either. I myself told him to go see his other
women when I was busy doing my own thing.*

While in many respects, e.g., her wish for economic independence, for
freedom, for not wanting to be "under a man," Juliette has a feminist consciousness, avant la lettre, in her relationships with her *meti*/her "cowives,"
that is, Dorus's other women, it seems, on first sight, strangely lacking. However, there was no animosity among the women. Juliette would sometimes
take care of Corry's and Magda's children. One of these children, Cecilia,
Corry's daughter, still comes to visit Juliette and brings her fresh bread, every
other day, since she works at the bread factory. Magda, Corry, and Dorus
have all died a long time ago, but Cecilia considers Juliette kin and vice
versa. Thus we see that another bond of kinship was formed, not through
heterosexual ties, but through "cowives" who considered each other and
each other's children kin. When Dorus would return to town, after having
been away in the forest, Juliette wholeheartedly agreed that he had to give
some money to her meti too. Juliette, having found a reliable, older man who
was able to support her and who did not pester her because of her activities
with women, was not about to let go of him. Dorus knew that Juliette was in
the mati work because other people had told him. It was not a topic of much
conversation between Dorus and Juliette; it was simply understood.

I am curious whether Dorus ever said anything to Juliette about her female
lovers. "Wins' a tak' wan sani, mek' en gwe. Mek' en komopo na mi tapu"/
Even if he would have said anything, he should get lost. He should leave me
alone. She would not take nonsense from him. One time Dorus came back
from the forest, unexpectedly, and Juliette had already made plans to go on an
excursion with her friends. She did not want to change her plans for him, so
she said, and she later told her girlfriends: "Tide mi no man, tamara m' o weri
tumsi, na tra tamara"/Today I cannot, tomorrow I will be too tired, so the day
after tomorrow (I will have time for you). Everybody broke up. That became
her nickname, *no tide, no tamara*/not today, not tomorrow. Some people, like
Coba's brother, would say that to her whenever he saw her, telling her that if
she would have said that to him, he would not have stood for it, after being
away, *in a kowru, tu wiki*/in the cold, i.e., alone, two weeks. Dorus, according to Juliette, was not mad. Indulging her, he said: "Ga voor je, me schat, go
nanga yu mati, i de yongu"/Go, my sugar, go with your mati, you are young.

Sex with Dorus was something she wasn't too excited about, in the
first place.

*"Mi nanga en no ben de frammejaar so, so dipi-dipi so. Y' e nay, dan y' e opo.
Nanga mansma mi no ben de so ge' echt. Ef a aks' mi dineti, dan a no mus'*

kon baka di mus' dey. Nanga vriendin, dat ben de trafasi"/Me and him were
not so close, so familiar, so deep-deep. You screw, then you get up. I was not
so connected to men. If he asked me tonight (to have sex), then he should not
come back again in the morning. With a female lover, that was different.

She didn't like oral sex with him, never did it. "Libi mi nanga a morserij
dati"/Don't start that dirty stuff with me, is what she says when I query her.
If he wanted to do it with her, that was OK. "Mi ben de syat' futu nanga ef'
mi nanga Dorus ben speel klaar tegelijkertijd, dan mi ben kis' bere"/I used to
come pretty quickly and if Dorus and I came at the same time, then I would
be pregnant. The reason that she knew that she was pregnant was that right
the next day, her pipe was not tasteful to her any more. She became *duister/*
nauseous, and had to extinguish the pipe. She would always try again and if
the same thing happened once more, then she knew for sure. She couldn't
smoke for about four months, then she would resume.

The transactional nature of sex, which is called *kamra prikti*/sexual obligations, by working-class women, even during pregnancy, is evident here.
In exchange for money from men, women give sex. In the first three or four
months of her pregnancies she did not feel like having sex with Dorus. "Sex
ben de lek' wan dresi in' a ten dati"/Sex was like medicine at that time. In
general, she could abstain from having sex with him for a month or two, but
since he gave her money that was about the limit and then she had to do it,
whether she wanted to or not.

Juliette has her own theory about the widely differing skin colors of
her children, who had the same father. Nancy is very light skinned, while
Wanda, for instance, was dark. When you conceive just after you have had
your menstruation, your belly is very clean and then the child turns out
light. But when you are about to have your menstruation and you become
pregnant, then the child will be black. She has seen this work in her own
experience, and the older women told her that was the way it worked and
they were usually right.

Not only did Juliette continue to have relationships with women, she
was intimate with her own sexual prowess as well as that of other women.
One of Juliette's stories—she must have been in her thirties then—is that
one evening she went to see two women who lived in the same backyard.
She stayed with one, until midnight, "when the ground was getting wet,"
and then crept away toward the other and stayed there *te broko dey*/until
the day broke. Sometimes at a party, when she was dancing with a woman,
they would get so raunchy that they would go home, either to her place
or the other woman's, have sex, then wash up and come back to the party
again. I asked whether some women did it outside. She said she heard that

some did it *na baka fu plee o was' oso*/in the back of the lavatory or the washing shed, they spread *wan seri*/tarpaulin, "ma fa mi ben wani fu miti a uma" (rubs her hands diagonally together) "mi no ben wani fu du en na dorosey"/but since I wanted to "meet" the woman, I did not want to do it outside. She assumes that the way other women did it was standing up and fingering each other, but "a sani dat' b' o mek' mi moro razend"/that would have made me more crazy.

Juliette's descriptions of her encounters with women are full of joy, naughty. She makes it no secret that she liked women much better than men, that it is *swit' a ben switi*/exceedingly sweet to have sex with a woman. When I ask her to elaborate on her preference and to explain to me why it is that some women like sex with women better and others prefer men, she says:

> *Some women are easy. They do not like to tire themselves and want to be on their backs only and to come when a man puts his tollie/penis, inside of them. When you are with a woman, both of you are expected to be on top sometimes and to do some work. Some women are like that. It is your "soul," your "I," that makes you so. "Mi yeye no ben wan' de ondro man"/My "soul," "I" did not want to be under a man, it wanted to be with a woman, it is more equal. "Ma mi skin mus' lob' a trawan, a mus' tek' en, no so mi no kan du en"/but my "skin," my "I" has to love the other, has to take her, otherwise I cannot do it.*

In this last utterance Juliette is firmly placing herself within the context of the Winti religion. The multiplicitous self is given center stage. It is the "I" that makes some women prefer women and others go for men.

Juliette's understanding of her own sexuality differs radically from the more normative anthropological approaches to the position of women within matrifocality. Whereas the literature depicts women as the losers in this family system or otherwise attributes the origins of mati work to the psychological and physical unavailability of men and their penchant for *buitenvrouwen*/outside women, Juliette gives another impression. She was the piper who called the tune. She consciously chose an older male partner who was very fond of her. He indulged her and thought that she was very beautiful. She wanted to have children and he could give them to her. She was the one who wanted to have female lovers; she set her own schedule to which Dorus had to accommodate. This interpretation that Juliette took all the room she needed to maneuver is borne out by an observation that Dorus made, late in his life. Dorus would sometimes sit at night, on the stoop in front of their house, and look at their big sons, Stephan, Anton, and Simon, getting ready to go out. He would muse: "Luku den bigi boi now, ma noit' te mi ben wani, yu ben gi mi"/Look at those big boys now, but you never gave me any (sex) when I wanted it. The subtext was, "Look, I gave you those boys"—meaning you will be secure in the future—"but you never gave me sex willingly." Juliette is compassionate with Dorus, but would not have led her life differently. She only regrets that he did not live to see his children into adulthood and did not profit from their taking care of him. They were too young when he died. He never traveled to the Netherlands with her.

When Juliette was in her seventies, she went to the Netherlands for the first time. Her daughter Nancy took her to a Surinamese hairdresser. To Juliette's expert eyes, the hairdresser clearly was in the mati work and she would have sought her out, had she been younger and had the hairdresser's mati not been present. When Juliette met one of her old cronies at the market in Rotterdam a little while later, they compared notes on Holland. Juliette said: "You know, Helene, they are doing our thing over here, too." "What thing do you mean"? Juliette just rubbed her hand palms diagonally. The two women burst out laughing.

The War Years

Being with a balata bleeder or a fisherman, there was not much money to go around. Dorus did not leave any money behind when he left. It was even more difficult to make ends meet during periods of economic crisis, like the Great Depression in the thirties and during World War II, when Suriname, as a colony of the Netherlands, was at war with Germany too. At the beginning of the war, due to Suriname's weak military defense, two thousand American soldiers were stationed in Suriname to safeguard the production of bauxite. Suriname supplied 60 percent of the bauxite needed for the U.S. war industry (Scholtens 1985). Under the influence of the American troops, who had many dollars to spend, the increased importance of bauxite production, the building of defense works, roads, and Zanderij Airport, a short and lopsided economic boom resulted. Favorable for traders, producers, and artisans, the boom was disastrous for people with a fixed income, like civil servants. One third of the population in the city became undernourished. The Committee of Christian Churches in Suriname depicted a period of moral decline during the war years: "a craving for entertainment, licentiousness, alcohol abuse, deterioration of family life, increase of prostitution and STD's" (Scholtens 1985:37).

The war years were not so bad for Juliette and her family, however. Enterprising as she was, she was able, together with one of her neighbors, to secure work as a laundress for the American soldiers at the base at Zanderij. She was paid in dollars and her weekly earnings easily quadrupled her monthly salary as a domestic. She recalls that an American soldier on a big motorcycle, a Harley Davidson Liberator, once gave her a ride home. After the U.S. soldiers left it was hard going back to domestic service again, with a monthly wage of sf 10. Juliette joined the Surinaamse Sociaal-Democratische Vrouwenbond (Surinamese Social-Democratic Women's Union), which had been founded in 1937 under the leadership of E. J. Temmes (Scholtens 1985:38).

For those women who found work with the American soldiers, either doing laundry, cooking, cleaning, or engaged in sex work, mati life went on as usual, and even more luxuriously in the presents they could give each other, jewelry, dresses, parties.

Community Life

"Wan finga n'e dring' okro brafu"/One finger does not drink okra soup.

In this section, I will pay attention to the community level of Juliette's life: women's organizations, the street, her membership in *banya* and *susa*— choirs and in her political party. My thesis is that, over the years, Juliette organized her life in such a way that women were centrally present in it, both at an organizational and at a personal level. Her multiple connections with women were enabled by her organizational activities, which were largely patterned by gender.

There are the myriad women's associations of which she was a member and for which Paramaribo is famous. The proliferation and strength of women's voluntary organizations, following the end of slavery, has often been commented upon in the literature (Pierce 1971; Coleridge 1958; Brana-Shute 1976, 1993). Women's organizations with a religious, social, recreational, economic, educational, or political character, or a combination of these elements, have long been part of the Surinamese landscape. The degree and denseness of organization bespeaks the well-known odo "Wan finga n'e dring' okro brafu"/One finger does not drink okra soup,[18] reflecting the collective insight that one finger is not capable of accomplishing anything; one needs a whole hand[19] (Wekker 1997).

The cluster of ideas behind the organizations—the deeply felt responsibility to support and take care of one another; to be there in matters of love, life, and death; to nurture and to make positive contributions to each other's lives—has continued to this day. Often working-class women were members of three or four organizations at the same time, thus creating an overlapping patchwork of women's networks all over town. The members of the organization often had the same traditional dress that was worn on special public occasions, such as when the organization celebrated its founding day.[20]

Organizations had a formal structure. Interestingly, many of these associations had a man as their leader, while the membership was exclusively female. He was the ceremonial leader of the club, but he was not allowed to vote and generally did not have real influence. I tell Juliette that it is hard for me to understand why such *dyadya uma*/sturdy women would take a man as the chair of their organization. She does not see this as a problem; it was just the way things were done. Possibly it was a way of being taken seriously by the outside world, which, in view of the dominant public gender regime, could be done by installing a man as leader; possibly, too, it pointed to an implicit principle of harmony, needing the presence of a male in these all-female endeavors.

The clubs were led by elected officers, called "mothers," who had specific duties, and members, "sisters," were expected to contribute fees regularly. "Mothers" delegated tasks to the other women. There was a *siki moeder* who went to visit the sick members. In addition, a *ronde commissie*/committee that makes the rounds, functioned, and people were asked to volunteer for the positions. Juliette said she could not have done that work, having a lover like Mis' Coba. The women in the committee and the siki moeder went to visit the members at home, also to collect their dues, and often, I understood, helping the sick did not stop at pouring tea. It was the activities within the organizations that made me exclaim that it was as if all women did in that time was to lie down together.

Juliette belonged to several groups, e.g., Blaka Watra/Black Water,[21] a dancing association, Ons Doel/Our Goal, Ons Hoekje/Our Little Corner. With the members saving weekly in the organization, some of the fees were used for recreational purposes: going on excursions together to Blaka Watra, Creola, or Carolina, with lots of good food and *sopi*, alcohol. Frequently, after having walked for four or five hours to their destination, with gear on their head, the women enjoyed themselves with *nyanfaro* or *geflons*/flirting, singing, dancing and *kot' odo*. They often had to stay overnight, which was one of the main attractions. Other activities of the women's organizations included dancing formal dances (Setdansi), praying, singing Christian hymns or secular songs, saving in *kasmoni*/rotating credit association. Not all members of these working-class organizations were mati, but mati and nonmati alike shared, to a significant extent, in the same working-class culture.

Juliette's reminiscences about her clubs reminded her of the love triangles that took place, both between women and between men and women. Some of these affairs took a quite violent turn. The male chair of one organization had affairs with two women in the group and had his eye on a third one. Trouble had to come. The *masra*,[22] "husband," of one of the women had told the chair not to show his face at his woman's house anymore, but the chair did not heed his warning. When he went to visit the woman again and was washing up, the "husband" threw a firebomb into the washing quarters and the man burned alive. Juliette was very sorry for the chair to have found such a cruel death.

Her circle of friends also included women in the neighborhood, like Hanna, whom she knew for close to sixty years. Hanna lived a couple of houses down the street and she had a very pretty little face, reminding me of Alice Walker. She was a heavy drinker when she was young. Juliette was very fond of Hanna, in spite of her preference for men. Whenever there was a dance Hanna loved to come and get Juliette to dance with her, because they both loved the way the other danced: *dan un ben bloko. Bloko,* literally, *broko,* is breaking, and I suspect that the etymology of the term may have something to do with *bloko a t'te,* deflowering. It is dirty dancing and Juliette, after dancing with Hanna, had to bear her mati's anger. Hanna had an affair with another male chair of an association. Her *meti*/cowife, competitor, was Irma, who *kis' bere f' en*/got pregnant by the chair. There was trouble between Hanna and Irma. Sometimes associations fell apart because of these trials and tribulations of sexual intrigue. According to Juliette's stories, our section of the street was, when she moved there in her early forties, a busy beehive of women, raising children, working as domestics, cleaning and market women, having (itinerant and irregular) male partners, while they also busily engaged in connections with each other. According to Juliette, a good friend with whom you do not sleep is called *kompe,* but the ambiguity of the term was evident from the fact that she often used it when she was speaking of a sexual friendship; she in fact used *mati wroko, kompe wroko,* and *uma wroko*/women's work interchangeably. One by one I was told the histories of our neighbors and "suma ben mati nanga suma ben didon zo maar"/who had been in a steady mati relationship with whom and who had just had incidental sexual connections with women, without the obligations of the mati work. One of her good kompe in the street was Elsa. They always stood by each other in difficult times and helped each other:

"*Elsa ben wan' didon nanga mi, ma mi no ben wani. Mi ben meki lek' mi no ben ferstan san a ben wani. Sensi mi de, mi ik, mi skin mus' lob' yu, mus' wani fu du en nanga yu*"/Elsa wanted to lie down with me, but I did not want to. I pretended that I did not understand what she wanted. Always, my "I," my body, must love you, must want to do it with you.

With other women in the street she would never have started anything sexual, because they dressed and behaved too much like men. In our section of the street, containing about twenty houses, about half the women had had some kind of sexual history with other women, according to Juliette's reports. It does not seem too far-fetched to conclude that there was a lot of same-sex sexual activity, in the different modalities that mati discern, going on in the street when she was in her middle years, in her thirties and forties. When I lived there in the beginning of the nineties, all these women were in their seventies and eighties; some were in frail health, and there was a lot of mutual visiting and taking care of each other going on. When I once visited an elderly neighbor, Hilda, bringing her some rum and a cigar, Juliette, conscious of her reputation and her past exploits, forbade me to go see *a beest dati*/that "animal" (but meant in good humor, a naughty person) again. Hilda had tried to seduce Juliette; when Juliette had knocked on her door, Hilda was sitting at the top of the stairs, her legs spread, without drawers.

Winti Prey, susa and *banya*—traditional men's and women's dances for the ancestors with all-female choirs accompanying them—often took place outside of Paramaribo and provided another context for Juliette's organizational attachments. Through her relationship with Ma Joosje she learned about the culture. Juliette was an indefatigable singer, always invited to come to cultural events and loved for her stamina, since these events would last the entire night. She knew the lyrics of many songs to call the Winti of the different pantheons to come down and manifest in people: the songs for Mama Aisa, her husband Loko, Sofiabada, a Koromanti of the sky, a heavy Winti, which makes you bleed.

A final source of women in her life was her political party, Nationale Partij Suriname (National Surinamese Party), NPS, which she joined in the fifties, after she had been able to build her house with a loan that the first dark skinned leader of the party, Johan Pengel, made available to his constituency.[23] Women were the main propagandists for the party, canvassing neighborhoods and convincing people to vote for male politicians. The women were often called upon, on short notice, to cook large meals for parties of hundreds of men, to perform all kinds of auxiliary activities from a subordinate position (Brana-Shute 1976, 1993). During my research period, preceeding the elections of May 1991, I accompanied Juliette several times to pep rallies at *grun dyari*, literally, "green yard," the NPS party headquarters, and I was struck by the gendered scenarios played out in public: the men were on the podium, pontificating, showing off their verbal skills, joking, grandstanding, and the women in the audience, working, serving, clamoring, applauding them. A telling incident occurred after one of those rallies; a group of about twenty-five women, including Mis' Juliette and me, had been picked up by a party bus in our neighborhood, but after the rally we found out that the bus was now needed for male party brass and that it was up to us, near midnight, to see how we would get home. None of the neighborhood women, who otherwise were never at a loss for words, protested against this treatment. When Juliette and I got home that night, having walked for about an hour and a half, and discussed the event, she forcefully defended the party, understanding that the bus was needed for more important people than us and that it must have been an emergency. It again marked a moment when gendered and classed differences were operative. Neither in the past, nor in the present has the large female presence in the party translated into commensurate public, female political power or attention to women's articulated concerns (Wekker 1997, 2001).

Mis' Coba and the Later Years

> "Ef' yarusu no de bij, dan a no trutru lobi"/If jealousy does not play a part, then it is not true love.

> JULIETTE

While Dorus was still alive the family moved to the street where Juliette has been living for forty-five years. Through her endless activities, planning carefully, saving in kasmoni, and with the help of her male children when they got older, she was able to buy a plot of land and eventually build her own house. The house is a one-story wooden structure consisting of two bedrooms, a large living room, a kitchen and a washing area. On birthdays and ritual events Juliette is able to receive large numbers of people in the areas to the side and the back of the house, which are paved with concrete. Located in a working-class Creole neighborhood, one of the traditional strongholds of the Nationale Partij Suriname, Juliette's living room is presided over by a large portrait of Johan Adolf Pengel, affectionately called Jopie, erstwhile leader of the NPS. On the portrait, his large palms outstretched, Jopie, a heavy, dark-skinned Creole, urges his followers: "Wacht even, weest gerust, alles komt terecht"/Wait a little bit, be assured, everything will be all right. This is a message that has become increasingly inappropriate over the past decades, but in his political apogee (1958—1969) Pengel and his party made it possible for Juliette and her neighbors to buy plots of land by extending loans to them. Pengel and the political leader who followed him, Henck Arron, are the closest Juliette comes to worshipping men. Under Pengel clientelism became a prominent feature of the political system and, as the spoils extended to loyal party members, Juliette became a cleaning woman in government service. She not only had medical insurance for herself and her children but also built up a pension, which in 1990 amounted to sf 75 a month. In addition to that, she received the sf 110 governmental allowance to which all elderly people, above sixty-five years, were entitled. There was no way that people could survive on this income, however, so Juliette was fortunate and successful in the fact that she had children in the Netherlands who supported her.

Across the street from Juliette lived Mis' Coba, with her daughter and numerous grandchildren. Coba had had her eye on Juliette for a long time and, even though friends warned her not to start with Coba, because she had *takru maniri*/ugly ways, Coba insistently courted her and Juliette gave in. This relationship started when they were both forty years old and ended when they were eighty.

When they meet in the streets or on the market, they just nod at each other and say hi: "Dag Juliette," "Dag Coba." It is only after several months that Juliette points Coba out to me as her former mati. When I ask what was the reason that they broke up after forty years, I get different answers. One reason she mentions is that Coba gave herself all kinds of liberties, like having other women, while Juliette could not do anything of the sort. Coba also liked picking fights in public with Juliette. Moreover, she liked to put herself above Juliette. Even Coba's brother could understand it when Juliette broke the relationship off after forty years, saying that Juliette had put up with enough.

Juliette does not like talking about Mis' Coba. The only remarks she volunteers are that Coba's spirits *no mu' kon lul mi*/must not come and harass me after Coba dies. She explains that that will never happen, anyway, since Coba and she never made *sjweri ef verbontu*/an oath or "association," i.e., taking an oath that you will never sleep with another person again till death do you part. She has heard stories about matisma who did this; it brings disaster because it also entails that after one partner dies the other cannot take another lover, since the yeye of your dead lover will come haunt and trouble you.

In the course of different conversations more pieces of the puzzle of her relationship with Coba accumulate, and it is interesting that Juliette's explanations about the reasons for the breakup fit into two different discourses: there is a Winti discourse and a Christian discourse. She is, at times, remorseful about the relationship; she should have ended it much sooner. But being together for so long, *y' e tron famiri*/you become family. In the same way that, when starting a relationship, her yeye /her "soul," had to "take," like, be in harmony with the other person, so her yeye got fed up with Coba. Juliette's yeye, in their plural form, that is the male and female parts, had been humiliated so many times they did not want Coba anymore. At other times the remorse is clothed in terms of a Christian discourse: God does not approve of mati relationships, but when you are young you do not have any business with that: your blood is boiling, you are not made out of wood, so you just go ahead and do it with women. Before Juliette and I embarked on our relationship, she had told me:

> "*Di mi ben yongu, mi ben lob' fu ab' prisiri. Yu de yongu, y' e sport. Ma now mi kon grani, m' e kon verander. Fu a uma wroko di mi ben du, ala neti m' e begi Gado pardon. Gado no poti umasma nanga umasma makandra. Gado poti umasma nanga mansma makandra. Gado poti Adam nanga Eva makandra, dan sneki kon verlei Eva, a ben nyan apra. Mi ben sie na in' na Buku*"/When I was young, I loved having fun. You are young, you are "*sporting,*" painting the town red. But now that I have grown old I have changed. For the mati work that I have done, every night I am praying God to forgive me. God did not put woman together with woman. God put woman and man together. God put Adam and Eve together, then the snake came and seduced Eve, she ate the apple. I saw it in the Book, the Bible.*

Here we see two discourses, which at first sight seem to converge in rejecting same-sex sexual behavior, but there is an important difference; while the Afro-Surinamese Winti discourse captures the ending of the relationship in terms of Juliette's yeye not "taking," not tolerating Coba's yeye anymore, it does not reject same-sex behavior tout court. It was this particular person, Coba, that Juliette's yeye did not want to live with anymore. The superseding Christian discourse is far more punishing, demanding, and oppressive: it brings her to ask God every night for forgiveness for her sexual behavior with women. The behavior, that, as we have seen, she so enjoyed, that gave her immense pleasure in her life, and that, in a very real sense, made her survive, is deemed unacceptable. Even though there are varieties of Christianity in Suriname, some stricter than others, some more inclined toward syncretism than others, in general, the dismissal of homosexuality would seem a firm article of faith for all currents. The Christian discourse is a (re-)colonizing discourse that dismisses same-sex behavior out of hand, while it goes without saying that Christianity rejects Winti and its *afkodrey*/idolatry, in the same movement. Both discourses held validity for Juliette: with the prospect of appearing before His throne, she deemed it wiser to end the relationship with Coba. These same discourses still circulate among younger mati, as we will see in chapter 6. When I appeared in her life, however, and she felt attracted to me, she was confronted with a dilemma she had not believed would occur anymore: she thought that she had finished with the mati work. She had her own internal struggles, which she did not fully share with me but the contours of which I could sometimes discern. In her own way she was negotiating her desire. In the end, luckily, the Winti discourse won, enabling her to enjoy her last mati relationship with me. As I will elaborate more fully in chapter 3, Winti is an enabling discourse, opening up possibilities for people, while Christianity is forbidding, limiting, exclusionary, dismissing same-sex behavior and offering people who like to engage in it a negative self-image.

As the *work* in mati work suggests, Juliette and Coba had mutual obligations. They helped each other raise their dependent (grand-)children, they shared resources, helping each other financially. They shared a market booth, selling fish and fruit, until they were in their seventies. When one bought fabric for a new dress, she made sure to get enough so that her mati could get a dress too. Juliette felt that Coba did not live up to her side of the deal, she was often miserly and did not like to spend money on Juliette; Juliette felt that she took better care of Coba than the other way around. Coba also did not come up to Juliette's expectations in days of grief; when her daughter Wanda died Coba should have supported Juliette, should have sat with her and helped with expenses. Instead, neighbor Elsa, Juliette's kompe, did all those things. Coba and Juliette also had sexual obligations, the kamra prikti, that feature in both same-sex and opposite-sex spheres, where one's partner has to oblige the other's sexual desires. Absent that, one is entitled to seek gratification elsewhere.[24]

Although Juliette continued to enjoy her life in the four decades that she remained with Coba, jealousy is a constant theme in her accounts of those years. Juliette says because Coba was "stealing" all the time, she herself did not want to stay behind. There is no knowing whether this is the correct story; much as I wanted to, I could not interview Coba, given my relationship with Juliette and the distress this would have caused her. One characteristic story unfolded, when they were both in their fifties. Coba was seeing someone else and Juliette also took another *visiti*/girlfriend:

"*A dame ben rij wan fiets. Wan dey, mi no sab' suma ben ferter' Coba, a dame ben kon fu si mi, en fiets ben de na nengredoro, dan plotseling Coba ben kon ooktu. A kon storm na ini, a sidon nanga begin fu kos' a dame nanga beledig en. A taki 'Juliette, we, mi moi moro yu mati, yere.' Mi no ben tak' noti. Mi ben sab' ef' mi pik' en, feti o de. Mi ben prakseri: yu no sabi ef' yu moi moro en, yu n' e tek' en na yu bedi. A dame ben de moro yongu, ooktu. A dame tenapu, di a' e gwe, a' e taki: We, Juliette, later, no? Coba ati ben bron so te*"/The lady had a bicycle. One day, I do not know who told Coba, the lady had come to visit me, her bicycle was at the gate,[25] then suddenly Coba came in, too. She came storming in, she sat down and began to curse and insult the lady. She said: "Well, Juliette, I am prettier than your mati." I did not say anything. I knew that if I answered her we would have a fight. I thought: you do not know whether you are prettier than she, you don't take her to bed. The *lady was younger [than us], too. The lady got up, as she was leaving, she said: Well, Juliette, [I'll see you] later, no? Coba was furious.*

A couple of days later, Juliette's friend attended a *Winti Prey*/a Winti gathering in which the spirits are called up, which could only be reached by boat. The boat sunk and she could not swim, so she and a boy drowned. That day a neighbor came by Juliette's house and asked: "Did you hear that so-and-so drowned?" Juliette was sitting on her doorstep with Coba and she saw Coba looking at her, at how she would react, so she did not show any of her emotions, though she was terribly shaken. She had seen the woman shortly before she left on the boat and knew she was going to the Winti Prey. "Doro-doro Coba ben tanteer' mi fu a uma"/Continuously Coba was nagging me because of the woman. Juliette wore mourning clothes, a blue dress and a white anyisa, for her friend, but Coba did not want her to wear blue, because then everybody would know that she and the woman had been close. Shortly afterward there was to be a *Prey* and Juliette did not feel like going at all. But Coba put a lot of pressure on her and also wanted her to wear a red dress, since the Prey was for the Amerindian spirits, who wear red trousers or dresses themselves and love for their children to wear the same color. She quarreled with Juliette the entire day. Meanwhile, Juliette says, Coba had a girlfriend at the very same time. She had heard that Coba was meeting her friend on the corner of Willem Campanjestraat, *fu beslis*/to make a date. "Well, when I saw Coba on that corner, I had taken a can with me, an empty butter can, and I hit her on her head with it. Blood flowed." Juliette is still bitter about it after thirty years:

"Na Coba zaak, kis' en moi. A ben kon na mi oso, ma mi no ben dres' en ede. A no ben kan go n' en oso, bika en masra ben de d' ape"/That was Coba's business, served her right. She came to my house, but I did not help her to bandage her head. She could not go to her own house, because her man was there.

Juliette has many other narratives like this one, fraught with jealousy and violence, describing the longest relationship she had in her life. It shows, first, that Coba's man was not as accommodating and indulging toward her as Dorus was toward Juliette. Coba knew better than to go home with a bleeding head. Second, the culturally sanctioned form and direction that jealousy takes and the violence that comes into play with it become transparant. When Juliette talks about jealousy, she opens windows onto different worlds, depending on whether it was her man or her woman who had been unfaithful. She did not mind when Dorus went to see other women. Frankly, she thought: Well, it is better that he harasses her than me.

She also did not mind when her mati lay down with a man. If she could find some money with him, why not? But neither she nor Coba would stand for it when the other slept with another woman. Yet, this occurred on a fairly regular basis. Having interviewed numerous mati of different generations, I concluded that having multiple sexual partners is still part and parcel of the mati work. Sometimes it is considered the prerogative of the dominant partner, and some women argue that when she does it it is less serious, because it is more "natural." When the "feminine" partner sleeps with someone else or is suspected of it, it is a serious blow to the self-esteem of the "male" partner. Coba and Juliette did not have a relationship in which the roles were clearly demarcated as male and female; in practice both partners had sex with others. Jealousy is often taken as a sign of true love: if you are not jealous, when your partner sleeps with someone else (of the pertinent sex), then what kind of love is this? Jealousy and violence are as much part of the intimate landscape of the mati work as are love, obligations, friendship, and companionship. Jealousy and violence are operative in both same-sex and in opposite-sex spheres.

Part of Juliette's politics of passion became transparent when she was having sex with someone else: *di a ben mati*/when she was in a steady relationship, and she felt she wanted to sleep with somebody else, she would *bedank mi visiti*/thank my lover, i.e., end the relationship. This was only a temporary measure, however, and when she had satisfied her curiosity—and whatever else—she would return to her mati. The point of honor to her was never to give the woman she was having an affair with *ede na tap' mi visiti*/a place above my mati, humiliate my mati in favor of the incidental contact.

In the course of their forty years together, Juliette's children and Coba's grandchildren became family who still now visit each other, both in Suriname and in the Netherlands. I have interviewed one of Coba's grandchildren, herself in the mati work, about the relationship between Juliette and Coba. Jet was thirty-nine when I met her in 1990, and she is named after Juliette. She looks back with pleasure on the years of her youth:

> Since I have grown older and am in the mati work myself, I have realized that my grandmother and Aunt Juliette were "friends of the heart." I did not see it like that as a child. They had an ideal to support each other and to stay together for life. Grandmother was very strict, but all of us children loved Aunt Juliette, because she had a soft heart. We could get things done by talking to her first and then she would persuade grandma that it was all right. Both of them were our mothers.

Reading Juliette Within the Context of Working-Class Culture

What is the place of the story within Juliette's life?

I want to come back to the questions I formulated earlier: what is the place of the story *within* Juliette's life? in other words, how does she use her narrative to construct and project a particular persona? And what are the characteristics of that persona? It is useful to come back to the three levels by which she ordered the narration of her life: the personal, the collective and, finally, the national and global level. Most of her narrative centered on the first and second levels. On the personal level she projected a story of an attractive, precocious girl child who loved the company of older women and who grew into an adult who preferred to be surrounded by women. She was proud of the numbers of women with whom she had connected sexually, as proud as she was of her large *bere*/the children and grandchildren she had produced. There is continuity in those stories and their corollaries are the utterances concerning her not feeling connected to men, her rejection of marriage, her seeking and finding an older male partner who was able to support her financially, give her children, and not beat her or cramp her life with women. Juliette projected the persona of a responsible adult woman, embodying cultural ideals, in the ways in which she dealt with her meti, Magda and Corry, and their children, who became kin. So did her former mati and their (grand-)children. Central values that guided her life were to live well with others, both with her mati, with nonsexual friends, with family and neighbors, but also, equally important, with the Gods and spirits that carried her. She worked for spiritual balance for herself, her (grand-)children, and people who asked her advice. From an early age she worked hard to support her family economically, and this continued until she could enjoy the support of her adult children. In her home Juliette organized her life so that women could be central to it.

Straddling the personal and the collective level is her sexual self. She self-presented to me as someone who is sexually savvy, had considerable prowess, experience, and skills; someone who was attractive and sought after, first by older women and then by her peers; someone who was fun to be with, naughty, could tell good, tall tales. But also someone who was respectful and who had good mati manners. If she had fifteen cents, she would share it with her mati; if she bought fabric for a dress, her mati would get one too. She would not think of withholding a child that she had given birth to from her mati who wanted to raise the child. None of her ex-mati had any reason to bear grudges against her after they split up. This was important to her, to prevent the situation that the spirits of a deceased, disgruntled mati might come trouble her.

On the collective level her narrative invoked a person who was loved and appreciated, both because of her personality and because of her cultural capital. She had valued cultural knowledge and healing powers and she gave others advice in matters of love, life, sickness, and death. She sang and danced indefatigably at Winti Prey, susa and banya. Her membership in women's organizations, also spoke significantly to working-class cultural ideals of cooperation, mutual help, and the accomplishment of common goals. Her membership, again, enabled her to be surrounded by women.

Juliette's narrative spoke less to the national and global levels, although there surely were elements present, such as her membership in the NPS political party and the union of domestics, but also her encounter with American soldiers during World War II and her travels to the Netherlands. She could have foregrounded those elements, had she so chosen.

It is no coincidence that she did not stress the national and global levels in her narrative; Juliette used her narrative to project a persona who embodied, to a significant extent, the idealtypical working-class dyadya uma, the sturdy, real, woman who knows how to manage her own life and that of those around her, politically, economically, emotionally, culturally, religiously, and sexually. The sites in which the dyadya uma operated, for women of Juliette's generation, were overwhelmingly the home and the community. As we will see in chapter 6 on the globalization of the mati work, younger mati use the global as their field of operation much more intensely. Since the independence of Suriname (1975), the mati work has moved to the Netherlands and forms part of the transatlantic exchanges constituting Suriname and the Netherlands. Thus the three levels are not in themselves gendered, but there is a difference in the degree of involvement at each level for different generations. The characteristics of a dyadya uma will be laid out in more detail in chapter 3. It is worth noting that, within working-class culture, Juliette did not need to make amends for her sexual activities but could fully embody cultural ideals.

Epilogue

> *I was no good at the rules of her game and she did not see any honor in mine.*
>
> GLORIA

The multifaceted relationship I developed with Misi Juliette has been pivotal in my understanding of the mati work. In my diary of March 1991 I wrote:

I stayed home today to get all kinds of things done, but can't say I was very productive. Have mainly been chatting with Juliette. We talked about how it will be when I move back to L.A. again in July. It made me very sad and she noticed it and said that I should not cry. She is so beautiful and wise. I do feel utterly safe with her and when, as last night, she is sitting with me and chatting a mile a minute, while I am working on my paper, my whole heart melts for her and I find myself wishing and expressing to her that she was forty-five years old again. She said that if we would have been the same age, we would have stayed together all of our lives. I told her that I love her as my mother, and that that is really not a bad thing, because it will last forever. We have become family. She said that she knew that, but that she loves me more than I love her, since I am her last mati. After me she will take no other lover and she knows that I will.

But times were not always so edenic. In fact, in hindsight I learned most intensely on occasions of conflict and misunderstanding, moments when my ideas and values as a Europe-centered lesbian sharply clashed with her mati world. Inadvertently I caused wounds and a cultural crisis by my, in her eyes, unspeakable behavior. Shortly before I wrote the above entry, I met Delani McDonald, a thirty-eight-year-old schoolteacher, and I thought that it would be possible to openly have a relationship with her, because I had now defined my relationship with Juliette as family. Although I suspected that it would be no simple matter, I still believed that as long as I was clear about my feelings, and if I took care to keep on spending considerable time with Juliette, it would have been possible. My attitude baffled and scandalized Juliette, and this she made clear in no uncertain terms.

In Juliette's view I was still her last mati, her little "chicken," whom she spoiled mercilessly, but in return for which she demanded absolute fidelity. And if she could not have absolute fidelity, she wanted me to hide artfully my other liaison from her. Delani was not to come to my house or to parties and events that Juliette and I attended. Delani's attempts to be on good terms with Juliette, by sending over a bouquet of flowers and fruit on her birthday, were met with flat refusal: the flowers were immediately thrown in the trashcan. Unfortunately, there were some *lemki*/little limes,[26] in the basket, which Juliette read as a sure sign of Delani's bad faith: her wish for the relationship between Juliette and me to go sour.

My job, the prescribed way of placating Juliette, was to make her feel that my eyes were on her only, whatever it took. I could not do that. Her jealousy drove me crazy, my "roving eye" made her furious, wanting to beat me up, although she was so tiny and fragile. I was no good at the rules of her game and she did not see any honor in mine. She always thought that I really knew better, that I was willfully violating mati codes. For my part, I was desperately groping to make her see my view of the situation. She exposed me, on several occasions, for behaving callously and selfishly toward her, of behaving like a man—the ultimate putdown—when I thought I was merely being my own autonomous self, putting a lot of store in a situated and, under the circumstances, myopic version of being "transparent and honest." I often thought of Adrienne Rich's words in her noteworthy essay "Women and Honor: Some Notes on Lying":

> An honorable human relationship—that is, one in which two people have the right to use the word "love"—is a process, delicate, violent, often terrifying to both persons involved, a process of refining the truths they can tell each other.... And so we must take seriously the question of truthfulness between women, truthfulness among women...so that lying (described as *discretion*) becomes an easy way to avoid conflict or complication? Can it become a strategy so ingrained that it is used even with close friends and lovers?
>
> (1979:188–190)

These insights were of little help, indeed counterproductive, in my situation. Juliette and I shared some important aspects and values of a same-sexed universe, but others we decidedly did not.

I became sharply aware that we both inhabited a *specific* same-sexed sexual space. Not only did I thus learn about her world, I also came to see characteristic aspects of my own construction of sexuality. Knowledge about the proper ways to embark upon and to end a relationship, which I so took for granted, is deeply culturally inflected. There can be no doubt that "same-sexual activities in distant cultural settings are *not* transparently comparable to such relationships at home" (Lewin 2002:114). It was in the domain of how to end a relationship that I fell most seriously short of Juliette's norms because, according to her, I gave *Delani ede na tap' en*/placed Delani above her. I had humiliated Juliette. Juliette reproached me with never having formally ended the relationship with her, after which I could have had sex with Delani and then returned to Juliette. She preferred to see Delani as an incidental sexual interest and continued to treat me as her mati, because I had not followed the culturally prescribed way to end the relationship: *mi no ben bedank en*/I had not "thanked" her, temporarily ended the relationship. She felt very strongly about the fact that she had been there first, before Delani; since I had not ended the relationship with her, it was still going on, as far as she was concerned.

I preferred to blur the fact that my sexual relationship with Juliette had ended. I did not want to have sex with her anymore, but, apart from that, I did not want to end or change my relationship with her at all. I wanted two

simultaneous relationships, with her and with Delani. In a typically bound-
ary-blurring mode, however, I did not want to openly state that. It was too
painful to tell her that the sexual part of our relationship had ended.

Further intercultural puzzles were presented by the cultural markers
that indicate one is in a relationship with another woman, by the different
modalities in which one can relate to another woman, the proper ways to
deal with one's mati—which, to me, seemed oppressive, violent, and insin-
cere at times—or about the best techniques to have sex with a woman; all
this I learned and all this was different from the knowledge I possessed. My
relationship with Juliette confronted me with my ageism, my preconcep-
tion that an octogenarian would not be interested in sex, would not be jealous, would willingly and wholeheartedly give me the space I wanted. I also
came to see that my preferred configuration of autonomy, transparency, and
sexual freedom was, from the perspective of the mati work, highly situated,
individualistic, self-centered, and really untenable.

In the end, Juliette, Delani, and I were, not without struggle, able to come
to terms and to live with ourselves and each other. I learned a bit of *kor'kori/
sweet-talking*, humoring her; she, being always right, stated that she did not
have to learn or change anything. When I behaved in a decent and respectful mati way, that is, kept Delani out of her sight as much as possible, she
was quite pleased. But gradually she indulged me by consenting to Delani's
more frequent presence. Again, food played a symbolical role in the process
of rapprochement between Juliette and Delani. While for months Juliette
refused to feed Delani when she came to visit me, she eventually would give
her food, too, although naturally she would not serve her. Juliette made
sure that there was enough food on my plate so that I could share it with
Delani. Sleeping arrangements were another issue when the three of us were
together, either in Paramaribo or later in Amsterdam. Invariably I slept in
Juliette's bed, giving her *ede na tap' Delani*/honoring her above Delani. In
the end I became her daughter again. We have continued to share important
moments, joy and grief, in each other's lives, by telephone, letters, and by
mutual visits. Juliette was present in Amsterdam when my Dutch book *Ik
ben een gouden Munt* was launched in September 1994. So were her sons and
daughters and several of her grandchildren, living in the Netherlands, who
have become my family. She always reminded me in telephone conversations that I had left Suriname just in time and that it was because of her that
I did not end up dead, by getting myself in deep trouble with *den wenke*/the
girls, through my lousy mati manners. I never quite measured up, in that
respect, to her standards.

I last saw Juliette in December 1997 in Paramaribo, when she was already
ill and weakened, small as a twelve year old in her pink housecoat. Her face

resembled a Benin death mask. I sat and lay in bed with her, feeding her okra soup, chatting, laughing, and reminiscing about the days we had lived together. When Mama Matsi called me two months later to say that Juliette had passed, just days before her ninety-first birthday, I arranged ads on the Surinamese Kankantri radio station in Amsterdam, listing myself as her daughter, and I observed mourning rites, as she had taught me to do them properly.

Back in the United States or in the Netherlands, when people have asked me: "What did you actually do during your research period?" I have been able to truthfully and simply say: I lived. I lived with gusto, with passion, with curiosity, meaningfully connected with illuminated parts of my self and with significant others. I could not wait to begin every new day, never having been as productive before: coauthoring a book and writing several articles besides doing the research. I sometimes wondered whether this was real: one of the happiest periods in my life and being funded to live it. Comparing this fieldwork experience with a previous one in France, I know that the intensity of my feelings in Suriname was and is deeply connected to my bringing my whole self into the situation: my Creole, woman-loving self met its karma. In the encounter of my selves with various other significant selves, I have received some lasting gifts. The (self-)knowledge I gained through my connection to Juliette has become part of the universe I inhabit. One of the legacies Juliette has left me is that she has given me a glimpse of how *mati* of her generation spoke with each other; moreover, by becoming fluent in Sranan Tongo under her guidance, she has bequeathed their speech to me. She has enlarged my *bere*/my matrikin by giving her family to me. Simultaneously, she has given me to her family: we attend each other's *bigi yari*/crown birthdays; I dance at their Winti Prey for the *kabra*/the ancestor spirits of the family, thus for Juliette. As my family, they come to my book launches and they attended my oration, when I accepted the IIAV chair[27] at the University of Utrecht. Juliette gave me the most exquisite and intimate gift: understanding the lived reality and the beauty of the mati work, its sociocentricity, its passion, its longevity, and its survival wisdom.

"Optimism," said Cacambo, "what is that"? "It is the madness of asserting that everything is good, when it is evil." Candide looked again at the negro, and burst into tears; thus weeping, he entered Surinam.

VOLTAIRE 1993 [1759]

2

Suriname, Sweet Suriname: A Political Economy of Gendered and Racialized Inequality

Globalizing forces have always been at the heart of Suriname, this former plantation colony that quite literally was a Dutch creation in the service of "King Sugar" in the seventeenth century. Great Britain and Holland fought for possession of the colony and the Dutch were able to establish hegemony in 1667 (Wolbers 1861; van Lier 1977 [1949]). Later, in the eighteenth and nineteenth centuries, the princes of tobacco, coffee, and cotton were served. In the twentieth century bauxite, rice, fish, oil, wood, and gold became the main export products.

In Voltaire's *Candide or Optimism,* Candide and his traveling companion Cacambo visit Suriname in their search for the "best of all worlds." On entering Suriname they find a negro lying on the ground. He is only wearing a pair of blue linen breeches and his left leg and right hand have been cut off. When interrogated about his condition, he says: "When we labour in the sugar-works, and the mill catches a finger, they cut off a hand. When we try to run away, they cut off a leg. I have suffered both these misfortunes. This is the price at which you eat sugar in Europe" (1993 [1759]:55).

Beside illustrating the representation of Suriname as one of the cruelest slave regimes,[1] there is another significant aspect to the black man 's words: they bring the interconnectedness between Suriname and Europe, which has existed from the beginning of European expansion, into focus. By pointing out the sweet material presence of Suriname in Europe, Voltaire invokes the significance of globalization processes. In fact, globalization has been at the heart of Suriname's genesis and in that sense Suriname, like the rest of the Caribbean, has always been modern.[2] Suriname, to paraphrase Mintz's words, has not been on the margin of the world system but, historically, squarely in the system's foundation.

Mis' Juliette's life history forms part of a larger and longitudinal research project, which, in its broadest formulation, seeks to understand the sexual configuration that she inhabits in both an African diasporic and a global context. In this chapter I want to begin to lay the groundwork for this undertaking by addressing three themes. First, I want to introduce Suriname as a political economy of gendered and racialized inequality in which women are consistently postioned in less favorable, more marginal locations than men of their class and ethnic background. Human sexual lives cannot be considered apart from the political economies in which those lives are embedded (Lancaster and di Leonardo 1997b). I focus on the last decade of the twentieth century. Second, I want to situate *The Politics of Passion* in current theoretical work in gay, lesbian, bisexual, transgender, and queer (glbtq) studies on the construction of sexualities. In addition, I will outline the contents of the book, the themes that are central to it and make its intellectual investments explicit. Third, I will provide a brief genealogy of the project and provide some methodological information.

Suriname is a relatively little known part of the black Diaspora. Located on the northeast coast of South America, Suriname, formerly Dutch Guyana, is the middle part of the Guyana Shield, and it is neighbored by Guyana and French Guiana. Suriname is home to about 440,000 people, who mainly live in the northern strip. Suriname celebrated its independence from the Netherlands in 1975, but independence did not bring the expected prosperity. Independence provoked massive outmigration. In its most recent past the country has known a brutal military dictatorship under the leadership of D. D. Bouterse (1980–1987, 1990–1991) and a civil war between the military and Maroons (1986–1992). Even though Suriname has returned to civilian government, the consequences of the dictatorship are still palpable and visible.

Following patterns that were established during the colonial era, the nexus that the Dutch Caribbean—Suriname and the Dutch Antilles—is embedded in still privileges connections with the former European metropole, the Netherlands, more so than ties with the Caribbean region. Few studies on Suriname are written in or translated into English, which means that comparative work, involving the Dutch Caribbean, is rare (Trouillot 1992).[3] Additionally, the bulk of research on the Caribbean has tended to focus on the English-speaking region. The complexity of Suriname's genesis and its cultural and linguistic richness, based on the presence of a large variety of ethnic groups, has failed to attract the attention it deserves. Based on its cultural and linguistic diversity, Suriname, together with Trinidad, Belize, and Guyana, has been classified as the most complex type of society found in the Caribbean.

An Inegalitarian Political Economy

The gendered and racialized inequality of Suriname's political economy, especially the ways in which women are positioned as marginal both within the economy and within the political apparatus of the state, is the general backdrop against which women organize their lives. My central understanding is that even though Afro-Surinamese women have a long tradition of economic independence and authority within the household, they, like all other women in Suriname, are still maneuvred into secondary status within society at large. Like women elsewhere in the Caribbean, they are made to defer widely to male authority in the public domain and are confronted with several problems arising from gender discrimination in the labor force and violence from men (Brydon and Chant 1989). The secondary status of women in the public sphere is the backdrop against which Afro-Surinamese women have assumed primary responsibilities in the domestic sphere, and have managed to give continuity to their constructions of sexual subjectivity.

Scholarship on Caribbean societies has, in most traditions, naturalized masculinity. It is only in the past decades that feminist scholarship has started to understand gender, class, and race oppression as parts of a unitary system (Shepherd, Brereton, and Bailey 1995; Beckles 1999; Yelvington 1995; Barrow 1996). The pertinent statistical data are not always available to make these intersectional analyses. I understand gender inequality, moreover, to be integrally related to broader processes of uneven development, articulated both in national and in international spheres (Harrison 1988; Sassen 1998). The world capitalist system embodies a structure of labor market segmentation wherein workers of peripheral countries receive no more than one sixth of the wages received by their counterparts in the advanced industrial center (Amin 1980). Since female workers receive considerably less than their male counterparts, Third World women represent a *cheaper than cheap* segment of the international work force (Harrison 1988). The brunt of these exploitative relations is borne by Third World women.

Since the last census of 1980 in Suriname, a policy decision was made no longer to register people by ethnic status because of its potentially disruptive consequences for the precarious racialized balance of power. Suriname consists, in order of size, of seven main population groups: Hindustani, Creoles, Javanese, Maroons, Chinese, Amerindians, and Europeans. Data from Household Survey Statistics by the General Bureau of Statistics for the period 1995–1997 estimate the following percentages:

TABLE 2.1 Surinamese Population by Ethnic Group

Hindustani	33.5 percent
Creoles	31.8 percent
Javanese	16.0 percent
Maroons	5.4 percent
Indigenous people	5.4 percent
Chinese	2.0 percent
Europeans	0.4 percent
Other	1.0 percent
Mixed	5.9 percent

Algemeen Bureau voor de Statistiek, 1993–1997, *Huishoudens in Suriname.*
Note that the total exceeds 100 percent.

The total population of Suriname was estimated at 433,517 persons at the end of 1999, of which 65 percent live in Paramaribo.[4] Creoles, or Afro-Surinamese, are the second largest ethnic group, comprising about 32 percent of the population. Afro-Surinamese working-class women of different ages and with different sexual styles take center stage in this book. Creoles are an urban population, the descendants of slaves, and they distinguish themselves—ethnically, culturally, linguistically, and psychologically—and are distinguished by others from Maroons. The Maroons[5] nowadays consist of six nations, with their own territories and languages. They are the descendants of slaves who fled from the plantations starting in the seventeenth century to form autonomous communities in the interior of the rain forest. Creoles and Maroons continue to be sharply distinguished groups, both in Suriname and in the Netherlands.

After the abolition of slavery (1863), indentured laborers from India, Java, and China were imported to work on the plantations. The ex-enslaved went to the capital in large numbers, working as artisans, laborers, in domestic service, and as washerwomen, while the Hindustani[6] and Javanese,[7] after their periods of indentureship, initially stayed on the plantations in small agricultural enterprises. The Chinese set up neighborhood grocery stores, after their indentureship. The Lebanese,[8] who have always just been a frac-

tion of the total population, came to Suriname from the end of the nineteenth century on as traders and merchants.

At the beginning of the twentieth century Surinamese society could be
divided into an upper class consisting of white Europeans, mainly senior
officials and their families who only stayed in Suriname for a short period
and who—unlike their predecessors—did not mix with other groups; the
middle class was made up of Jews and light-skinned Creoles; finally, a large
working class consisted of blacks, Hindustani, and Javanese (van Lier 1977).
While, three decades ago, it was still possible roughly to identify specific ethnic groups with specific positions in the class structure in Suriname (Brana-
Shute 1976; Kruijer 1973; van Lier 1977), today the picture is less clear-cut.
Several factors have played a role here: there has been considerable ethnic
mobility, both in a horizontal sense, since Amerindians and Maroons have
moved into Paramaribo in significant numbers, and in a vertical sense, since
Hindustani and Javanese have moved into positions in the bureaucracy, which
used to be a Creole stronghold.[9] In addition, foreign labor[10]—in the eighties
Guyanese, Koreans, and Haitians and in the late nineties an estimated forty
thousand Brazilians and an unknown number of Hong Kong and mainland
Chinese—has filled positions in agriculture, fishing, construction, domestic
service, and in gold digging, retail trade, and supermarkets. Most important,
a group consisting of Creoles and Hindustani has, since the eighties, moved
into the center of power. The state has not been capable—and some would
say not willing—of controling this group of "new rich," but rather is challenged and infiltrated by them. President Venetiaan (1992–1996, 2000–2004,
2005–) coined the term *tarantulas* for this group. Dividing spoils from various
illegal activities, the group is made up of connected and overlapping circles of
those formerly in the military, which staged a coup in 1980 and again in 1990,
politicians, international traders, cocaine and weapons dealers.

In the most general terms, global inequities between First and Third World
inhabitants have persisted and intensified in the past decades, making the rich
richer and the poor poorer. In Suriname the influence of accelerating globalizing processes since the end of the cold war has been visible and palpable in
a variety of indicators. The selling out by the government of the timber and
gold industries to foreign multinational interests and the large-scale insertion
of Suriname in a transnational drugs economy now form part of the Surinamese landscape. The government has aggressively sought investment in the
gold sector to exploit the substantial gold and diamond deposits thought to
underlie much of the interior, which, incidentally in the view of the government, is home to Maroons and Amerindians (Kambel and MacKay 1999).
With the gold mining industry, damaging extraction technologies, releasing
substantial amounts of mercury into the environment, have been introduced

and many waterways have become unfit for human consumption. Moreover, multinationals from Indonesia and Malaysia have obtained favorable government contracts to cut timber in the rain forests, upsetting ecological balance, ruining infrastructure, and, under soft obligations to replant, leaving large gaping areas in the interior. The consequences of these globalizing developments, the debt crisis in which Suriname finds itself, its chronic lack of foreign currency, and the neoliberal measures taken by the government, such as the Structural Adjustment Program (1993–1996), made themselves felt in the everyday lives of working-class women.[11] This is not only the case for the inhabitants of the interior, Amerindians and Maroons. Until the 1950s Indigenous peoples, that is, Amerindians, and Maroons were not considered to be part of Surinamese society (Kambel 2002). They were constructed as having no rights to the territories they inhabit and had, as Kambel convincingly argues, come to "fulfill the role of the undeveloped, pre-modern 'Other' whose claims to natural resources cannot be justified," primarily because they are construed as obstacles to national development (2002:15, 126). City dwellers, too, have increasingly felt the deteriorating spirals of an economy in recess.

This study focuses on the sexual subjectivity of women in the underclass and in the lower strata of the working class, in Suriname called the volksklasse. At the beginning of the nineties, after a decade of economic decline, the middle class comprised 27 percent and the elite 6 percent of the Paramaribo population, according to a survey study (Schalkwijk and de Bruijne 1999). Almost 70 percent of Creoles in Paramaribo belonged to the underclass (15 percent) and to the working class, or volksklasse, the popular class (51 percent). These segments of the lowest strata in themselves are very heterogeneous. The differences between the working class and the underclass are located in highest educational levels; in the working class one typically finds lower levels of secondary education, and in the underclass it is primary education. The underclass typically lives in wooden houses without running water and has the largest number of persons in the household (4.9 persons versus 4.7 for the popular class). Other differentiating factors are the number of wage earners and the number of appliances, e.g., refrigerator, TV, washing machine, car, and air-conditioning in the house (Schalkwijk and de Bruijne 1999:59). Among Creoles in the popular and underclass, families with women as single heads of households are three times as frequent as in the middle class (Schalkwijk and de Bruijne 1999). Ultimately I have found that the quality of the national and, more important, international, networks that people can access is decisive in determining class status. Poverty in Suriname is correlated with one's educational level, but, most important, with not having effective networks of relationships, locally but, far more consequentially, globally. The breakdown in percentages for the different class strata—elite, middle class, volksklasse, and underclass, must by the end of the nineties most certainly have taken more polarized forms, but there are no data to support this. In general, accurate statistical data are notoriously hard to come by in Suriname. Moreover, most statistics pay attention to ethnicity, not to gender or to both gender and ethnicity. At the end of the nineties important Surinamese government agencies like the General Bureau of Statistics (Algemeen Bureau voor de Statistiek: ABS) were forbidden to publish poverty rates and poverty lines.[12] In the summer of 2004 the bureau burned down, the fire destroying all its records.

Despite the differences between the underclass and the working class, in this study I will generically use the term *working class.* My informants came from both segments of the class structure and in the section on methodological decisions I will come back to the issue of class in Surinamese society.

Surviving the vicissitudes of urban life for Creole working-class women, who are often single heads of households, is an intricate task for which one must muster appreciable savvy. Social capital in the form of networks of (grand)mother, sisters, neighbors, and friends, either near or far, is indispensable. Often unable to count on the financial contributions of the father(s) of their children and with negligible quarterly amounts of governmental child support coming in, it is up to women to keep their households afloat.

In 1990 women were estimated to form about 40 percent of the labor force (Tjoa 1990a), and this percentage has, with some fluctuations, remained the same. But it is generally acknowledged that this percentage is not accurate, since women suffer more intensely from unregistered unemployment and underemployment. In addition, labor market trends indicate loss of real income and an increasing movement toward informal employment among women.

The government has remained the largest employer over the past decade and while the exact number of civil servants is unknown, it was estimated in 1997 at 60 percent of the total labor force, or thirty-seven thousand people. Women comprised one third of that number and were overwhelmingly located in the lowest salary brackets (Ketwaru-Nurmohamed 2000). Women, especially women who are single heads of households, cannot possibly survive on their government salaries and need to find additional income in the informal sector. When talking about single heads of households, it is overwhelmingly Afro-Surinamese women who come into view, since in the other large urban ethnic groups, Hindustani and Javanese, marriage is more common, as we will see in chapter 4. Women are found in the least profitable sectors of the informal market, which comprise an extension of women's "housewifely" duties: baking, catering, hairdressing, washing, ironing and sewing clothes, cleaning houses, selling produce in the market, and peddling lottery tickets. Men, on the other hand, are located in the better paying sectors of the informal sector: driving a taxi, auto repair, furniture manufacturing, shoe repair, buying and selling foreign currencies, drug trafficking, and gold mining.

In 1990 ten of the twenty-five working-class women in my study worked in government service, as office and school cleaners, street sweepers, and low-level office personnel. They fell in the lowest salary scales, but a government position was still attractive because it supplied health insurance for the entire family and a pension. The actual salaries in the formal, bureaucratic sector are low, with the government as the largest employer serving as a safety net. The vast majority of civil servants earned a monthly income on or under the poverty line, which in 1990 was sf 1,300 for a family of four. This amount, which at the time translated to about U.S. $65, underlined the necessity to seek additional income. In actual terms it meant that women worked, yet remained in poverty.

In 2001, when I last spent an extended research period in Suriname, there were visibly wider discrepancies between rich and poor and there was a conspicuous cash flow, evident in luxurious new mansions, complete with swimming pools, and luxury cars. Under the Wijdenbosch government (1996–2000) there had been a striking increase in commodities for sale in the stores—food, computers, bikes. These were only accessible for the middle and upper classes who had the capacity to spend. Moreover, nine casinos had opened their doors.

The conspicuous wealth, which was evident in 2001, was largely attributable to illegal funds from trading and drug trafficking that were plowed back into the economy. The Surinamese guilder had been on a inflationary course since the eighties.[13] Suriname is heavily dependent on its main exports of bauxite and aluminum, constituting about 77 percent of all exports, while domestic production and consumption strongly rely on imports as well as development aid (Kromhout 2000). Access to foreign currency had become vital to one's position in the class structure in Suriname. Due to falling world market prices for bauxite, the periodic suspension of Dutch development aid, consumptive overspending of successive governments made possible by monetary financing, and generally poor governance, the economy had suffered greatly and per capita real income fell from U.S. $2,028 in 1984 to U.S. $880 in 1997 (Schalkwijk and de Bruijne 1999:24). During a short period, at the instigation of the IMF, a Structural Adjustment Program (1993–1996) was implemented, which further undermined the financial position of the low income groups in particular as well as their access to health care and other government services. Poor governance is manifest in the endless growth of the bureaucracy, which in an ethnically organized spoils system[14] expands with each new government that comes into power; the eroding of once succesful industries (sugar, rice, glass, brick); the focus on grand top-down development schemes, which were doomed to failure; the unwillingness to decentralize and to effectively involve the population in decisions (Ketwaru-Nurmohamed 2000). The Inter American Development Bank calculated in 1996 that only three countries were poorer than Suriname in the Western Hemisphere.

While traditionally the working class has always comprised the largest number of people, at the beginning of the twenty-first century their numbers had swelled even more, because one could safely say that people who did not have access to foreign currencies had fallen below the poverty line. This included middle-class women, e.g., nurses and teachers, who did not have such access and who were solely dependent on their own incomes. In 2000 70 percent of households in Suriname were classified as poor (ABS 2001).[15]

Of the twenty-five women I had worked with in 1990, three had died in 2001, seven had migrated, six to the Netherlands and one to the U.S., and fourteen had survived in Suriname. The majority of these had had financial help of a mother, an aunt, or a sister in the Netherlands, but almost all had had to intensify their activities in the informal sector. The most decisive factor in survival in 1990, but even more so in 2001, had become access to foreign currency, either in U.S. dollars or Dutch guilders. Foreign currency may come from one of five sources:

First, from family members in the Netherlands. Several researchers agree that Creoles and Hindustani received more support than other groups (Kromhout 2000). Suriname is a transatlantic community that includes all the various ethnic groups. This community is bound through ties of kinship, friendship, political and economic interests and, importantly, financial support by the Dutch Surinamese in the form of packages—containing in the beginning of the nineties everything from food, clothes, popular magazines to toilet paper and toothpaste—and transmittances. The total financial impact of Dutch Surinamese on the Surinamese economy, in terms of tourist spending, transmittances, and parcel post, is estimated at U.S. $110.7 million, that is, 23.4 percent of the annual average national income, during the period 1992–1997 (Gowricharn and Schuster 2001:168). Although precise data regarding the development of this financial support over the past two decades are lacking, it is argued that the amount of the support has risen. The economic situation in Suriname has deteriorated explosively, while that in the Netherlands has improved, including for migrants from Suriname, which is expressed in more generous support to family members in Suriname (de Bruijne, Runs, and Verrest 2001).

Second, access to foreign currency takes shape through services rendered to Surinamese from the Netherlands who spend money in the city. Of all migrant groups in the Netherlands the Surinamese display the strongest wish to remigrate (Pieper 2000), fueled by a nostalgia for "Suriname, sweet Suriname," which is one of the strong but power-evasive images representing Suriname among both those who lived in Suriname and those who migrated (Wekker 2004b). The traveling back and forth of Dutch Surinamers to Suriname makes the trajectory Amsterdam-Paramaribo one of the most profitable for the Dutch and Surinamese national carriers. The transfer of foreign currencies is related to personal services like sewing and washing clothes for tourists; hairdressing, cooking, catering for parties, and rendering spiritual services in the domain of the Winti religion. Entire Creole families go to Suriname to fulfill their spiritual obligations to the ancestors. Musicians in Paramaribo, too, benefit from the intense traffic. Fully catered tourist trips to the interior form another source of foreign income. Another important source is sex services. A number of 35 registered brothels and 152 locations where sex business is conducted in Suriname is striking for such a small population (Stichting Maxi Linder 2000:4, 16). Sex work benefits both women and men; young men are popular sex workers.[16]

Third, foreign currency may be accessed from a pension, (part of) a salary, a fee, or social security benefits in U.S. dollars or Dutch guilders. This modality is applicable, for instance, to the workers and the retired from Suralco, the U.S.-based bauxite company, and to retired military personnel, who served in the TRIS, the Dutch colonial army. A parastatal company like Staatsolie paid its higher employees partly in dollars. These groups consisted predominantly of the elite working corps, i.e., males. Increasingly, professionals such as doctors and lawyers demanded payment in foreign currencies.[17] Social security benefits from the Netherlands can legally be taken to Suriname when one is sixty-five years old, but it is common knowledge that younger people, both men and women, manage to do so.[18] Dutch social security for a single person was about nf 1,450 or E. 650 a month in 2000. Someone who had this income—well over sf 1,200,000—is definitely not working class but rich in a Surinamese context. At that time, a teacher at a teacher's training college made approximately sf 300,000 a month; a director of a ministery sf 500,000. A new development over the past decade, from which some middle-class men and women benefit, is the local establishment or expansion of international agencies like IDB, WHO, UNDP, FAO, UNESCO, and UNIFEM that hire local consultants to draft policy papers.[19] A number of men and women left positions in government service to start their own consultancies.[20]

The fourth source of foreign currencies is legal trade activities. An important characteristic of former plantation economies is the dominance of the import sector; the biggest segment of national income is traditionally spent on import products. While 55 percent of goods and services used in Suriname are imported, comparable import quotas for the U.S.A. are 7 to 8 percent. In general, it has been very difficult for governments to impose import restrictions, not only because of the well-developed "First World" taste of many Surinamese consumers, but also because the state is successfully pressured by national trade interest groups (comprador bourgeoisie) not to support import-substituting industries. Since even for local industries import of parts and ingredients is necessary, trading is a most profitable endeavor. In the import trade of cars and other means of transport, food and beverages, building materials and technological equipment, again men dominate.

Fifth and finally, there is a variety of illegal activities, including gold digging, cocaine trade, and trafficking,[21] in which foreign currency is obtained. Both men and women smuggle cocaine, but it is predominantly men who organize the trade and thus profit disproportionately from it.

Access to appreciable amounts of foreign currency is thus not gender-blind. It follows clear gender-based patterns and working-class women have most probable access to it through remittances from their family members, male or female lovers in the Netherlands and from tourists. While classes have become more multiethnic since the eighties, women have not kept equal pace with men of the same ethnic group in gaining access to the higher classes. As far as I have been able to ascertain, there was only one woman in 2001 who was part of the highest income brackets, through her activities in building and gold digging. Women have typically gained access to the highest echelon in the class structure as spouses or as *buitenvrouwen/ outside women*. In chapter 4 we will follow twenty-three-year-old Andrea Zorgzaam, who, unable to make ends meet on her own income, was on the lookout for a man who preferably had access to foreign currency.

Thus, the overall picture of a dually segmented labor market has continued and exacerbated during the decade (1990—2001) under review. In the "heavier" and more profitable sectors of the formal and informal economy we consistently find men, working under better conditions and earning higher salaries. Women, on the other hand, work in the "softer" sectors of the economy, for the government where wages are notoriously low and in the informal sector. Moreover, as Ketwaru-Nurmohamed states: "decreased economic growth was clearly visible in private sectors that employ the majority of women, for example agriculture, fishery, manufacturing, restaurants and hotels. In sectors where mostly men were involved, such as mining, quarrying, transport and technical sectors, there was a relative growth" (2000:16). The implications are that clearly over the past decade all women in the lowest income groups have suffered, in ways which sometimes are similar and different in other respects.

The inegalitarian income situation is facilitated by the false, patriarchal premise, upheld in a powerful discursive formation that includes the state, business, and much commonsense thought, that women have a male head of household at home and thus need only worry about additional income. This premiss damages all women. Clearly Maroon and Amerindian women who migrated to Paramaribo, as a result of the civil war (1986–1992), came unfamiliar with city life, with little formal eduation and without formal sector job skills. Their ideological positioning as being "outside of the nation" made it possible for the government to deny any support to them, except the social support to which everyone is entitled (Ketwaru-Nurmohamed 2000:16). Hindustani and Javanese women, while they often are not single heads of households, have suffered progressive declines in their standard of living, because the proceeds from fishing and agriculture, have fallen dramatically. Since they are, moreover, conceptualized as "housewives," their labor is virtually invisible. They, too, number among the poorest in society. Afro-Surinamese women are located at a juncture where the contradictions between a traditionally heterosexist political economy and their own constructions of subjectivity are acutely felt. It is among this group that we find more single, female heads of households than in other ethnic groups.[22] Since we know that there is an inverse relation between poverty and the number of income earners per household and that among all ethnic groups Creole households have a disproportionately high number of female heads, it follows that the number of Creole female headed households under the poverty line will be significant. Poverty in Suriname is feminized and also has ethnically divergent patterns.

A final, brief word about political empowerment. Politically, women have made some progress in the past decade. Of the highest political and bureaucratic offices, president, vice president, fifteen ministers and secretaries of state, numerous government and policy adviserships and the Auditor General's Office, none was occupied by a woman in 1990–91. None of the fourteen judges were women. In the National Assembly, the highest representative body, three of the fifty-one members were women. In 1991, a first in history, three female directors of ministeries were appointed, of which two were appointed ad interim. Of the managerial layer within the government, the largest employer, 83 percent were men and 17 percent were women in 1992. Numerical relations between men and women in other important sectors, like higher education, the medical professions, banking and business, consistently showed the same patterns (Malmberg-Guicherit 1993).

Malmberg-Guicherit (1999, 2000) notes that women's participation in the National Assembly had risen to 16 percent in 1996, and in the judiciary from 27 percent in 1994 to 39 percent in 1998. There are still no women ambassadors, against 10 men in that position. After a failed attempt to found a women's political party, PVVU (Politieke Volks Vrouwen Unie) in 1991 (Wekker 1997), in 1999 two new political parties were initiated, Naya Kadam and Doe, who had women, Marijke Djwalapersad and Monique Essed-Fernandes respectively, as chairperson. Malmberg concludes that the growing number of highly educated women, who are outperforming men, is not mirrored in a sufficient number of women in leading decision-making and executive positions.

In summary, a political economy of gendered and racialized inequality is forcefully present in Surinamese society. As elsewhere, male dominance is secured by the ideological move of presenting the sexual division of labor as "natural," i.e., that women's place is in the home, even when economic conditions do not allow women the luxury of being without paid work. Racialized, sexualized and classed images construct women as inherently different not only from men, but also from each other. The intersectional work of ethnicity, class, sexuality and gender that goes into these constructions is ignored, so that they pass for eternal, cultural "truth." But these images in their turn play a part in allocating women to particular economic positions; positions in the informal sector, in the lowest income scales, in sectors of the economy that are most vulnerable to economic turbulence (Wekker 2004b). Women are in structurally disadvantaged positions in comparison with men. Afro-Surinamese women in the working class are culturally prominent, however. The tensions that arise from contradictions in different important domains of life, play themselves out in sexual spheres.

Theoretical Engagements of *The Politics of Passion*

What's love got to do with it?

TINA TURNER

The Politics of Passion sums up several insights that are central to my understanding of sexuality. The title points to the constructed nature of passion and the sociocultural arrangements that undergird and construct it. Instead of understanding passion and sexuality as "natural" phenomena, as God-given, context-free, and eternal, the title is a reminder that sexuality in a particular setting is something that people shape collectively on the basis of their cultural archives and changing political and economic circumstances. Furthermore, *The Politics of Passion* centrally addresses to issues of power. Instead of indulging in romantic notions about relationships, *Politics* acknowledges that power is negotiated both in cross-sex and same-sex relationships, that there is a politics to passion. In both types of relationships passion is not something that can be engaged blindly and spontaneously. Finally, the title speaks about the agency of women in the sexual domain. Women are not mere pawns in someone else's game; rather they have collectively given shape to an alternative and parallel sexual culture in which they protest the power inequities inherent in the dominant gender regime. *The Politics of Passion* needs to be situated in ongoing debates within anthropology in general and within the blossoming field of gay-lesbian-bisexual-transgender-queer (glbtq) studies and I want to make some of its investments clear. The book is novel in that it deals with an African diasporic sexual culture, which includes women who are sexually active with men and/or women and women who are exclusively involved with men. Women's sexual practices and relationships, no matter who the object of their love or passion is, arise from the same ideas about sexual subjecthood, thus offering a configuration that moves outside of the sexial identity binaries that are so characteristic of Euro-American cultures. I will insist upon alternatively using "indigenous" terminology for the women who are central in this book and terms like same-sex and opposite-sex sexual activity, instead of opting for a universalized use of the situated terms *lesbianism/homosexuality* and *heterosexuality*. I will locate the book within the sexual identity versus sexual activity debate. I will, moreover, note its bridging of the chasm between traditional preoccupations within gay male studies, that is, sexual activities, and within lesbian studies, that is, gender (Wekker 1999; Lewin 2002); I will situate the work within a strong version of social constructionism theory, that moreover takes note of political economy and I will place it within the "transnational turn" in glbtq studies.

This study, in centralizing a concern with a female black diasporic sexuality, engages with the ways in which some received anthropological understandings in the fields of kinship, family and marriage, subjecthood and globalization are modified and enriched, when the naturalized heterosexual contract is interrogated, deconstructed and laid to rest. Ethnographic discussion of glbtq themes is productive, meaningful and rewarding (Lewin and Leap 2002:5). The blossoming of these studies in a variety of adjacent disciplines in the humanities, the social sciences and their intersections— has allowed new, eye-opening insights into the anthropological canon and some of its established concerns.

Although my work evolves within the intellectual tradition of feminist anthropology, I refuse to choose to locate this study, either within lesbian or within queer studies, the two most likely candidates. To the extent that lesbian studies has usually taken a fixed sexual identity, something called "female homosexuality" or "lesbianism" as its starting point, this study does not fit in. Queer studies, on the other hand, defines itself by its difference from hegemonic ideologies of gender and sexuality (Weston 1998:159; Duggan 1992; de Lauretis 1991) and thus there is more affinity here. Queer studies has neither overwhelmingly impressed me so far as being a site where a radical scholarship, grounded in a sexual politic of anti-colonial and antiracist feminism could flourish, nor have extratextual approaches been prominent. I thus remain somewhat awkwardly situated between these different communities of discourse and, as a "scavenger theorist" (Halberstam 1998), this is not the most unproductive site to be located at.

I will avoid the signifiers "lesbian," "female homosexuality" and heterosexuality throughout this study, because of their Euro-American situatedness and their unwanted baggage. In the hands of the Church, medicine, psychology and psychiatry for over a century, sexuality, especially homosexuality, has been molded and recast as "sexual identity" (D'Emilio 1984), the most "authentic" part of self. The concept of "lesbianism," too, has firm connotations of a fixed sexual identity and it is highly problematical to impose the term on practices and relationships that have very different meanings, embeddedness and a genealogy in other cultures. The mati work shows a very different construction and underlying belief system of same-sex sexuality than lesbian identity as it exists in contemporary Western Europe, North America and other "Western" locations. Importing the Euro-American terminology means unwitting acceptance of the legacy of guilt, sin, disease, of notions of male activity and female passivity, of the "natural" superiority of heterosexuality, which can only hamper an understanding of the black diasporic cultural-sexual complex I describe and analyze. Moreover, it means endorsement of the deeply essentialist fallacy that female homosexuality crossculturally carries the same meanings. The terms that I will use, e.g., *female same-sex relations, same-sex* and *opposite-sex sexual activities,* are more neutral and inclusive. In many instances I will simply use the translated local term, *a mati wroko*/the mati work.

Weston has opposed the move to employ indigenous categories "as no more neutral in its effects than the earlier, less reflective application of "homosexuality" to a multitude of occasions" (1998:159). According to this view, using indigenous terms constructs the subject of inquiry as always and already Other and these "foreign terms" "become implicated in a renewed form of Orientalism in which linguistic terms subtly reify differences and buttress ethnographic authority" (1998:159). I read Weston's statement as symptomatic of power relations within the field of lesbian studies, buttressed and reflected in the insufficiently problematized dominance of Euro-American terminology. The tendency to offer up Euro-American terminology as the approximate substitute for the universal and the reluctance even among lesbian theorists to let go of that dominance and to imagine other sexual universes, is deeply troubling and has all the trappings of a neo-imperial gesture.

The Politics of Passion is, as far as I know, the first monograph that centrally deals with black diasporic women's sexualities. In the twenty years that have passed since Hortense Spillers lamented the situation of black women as "the beached whales of the sexual universe, unvoiced, misseen, not doing, awaiting *their* verb" (1984:74), only slight progress has been made towards uncovering "the pleasures and dangers" in the sexual lives of black women (see Rose 2003). It is not without significance, in the context of North American society in which black female sexuality has historically been maligned and vilified, in which black women chose to don "the cloak of dissemblance" after slavery (Clark Hine 1989) to hide their sexual personae, that this field of study has not been as productive as might have been expected. The professionally disastrous course that still attaches to writing about sex in a North American context may have lost some of its sharpest edges in the past decades, but it still holds sway, and a fortiori for black American feminists, making it hard to write about sex.

The majority of feminist studies of same-sex sexuality is still overwhelmingly located in or pertains to white North American communities and only a few of these have paid attention to the intersections of gender, "race" and sexuality (but see Kennedy and Davis 1993). According to the hegemonic logic, which sees gender only as pertaining to women and ethnicity as having pertinence only for people of color and in which gender is fundamentally separated from ethnicity (Wekker and Lutz 2001; Wekker 2004a) male gender and white ethnicity are still seldom thematized in sexuality studies. Many studies have foregrounded and normalized whiteness, without problematizing it and treating whiteness as if it were not a racialized position, while paying scant attention to non-white sexualities. Particular local, "Western" constructions of female same-sex sexuality have thus often unproblematically been universalized as normative. "Third World" women have for a long time typically been portrayed not as sexual agents but as sexual victims in such a framework (Mohanty 1991). While recent work has taken up that challenge, we should remain careful with assuming that the genealogies of sexual subjectivity in a female African diasporic context are the same as those constructed in Western contexts. A recent development that is to be applauded is that female same-sex studies have gone outside the usual geographical orbit , e.g., China (Sang 2003), Japan (Robertson 1998) and Greece (Kirtsoglou 2004) have come into view. This book goes outside of two usual orbits, by centralizing black women and the Caribbean. In addition, *The Politics of Passion* hopes to offer a template for thinking about black diasporic women's sexualities more generally, as building—to varying degrees—on a West African cultural heritage in the domain of sexual subjecthood.

In cross-cultural same-sex studies, intersections of sexuality and "race"/ ethnicity have been implied but not foregrounded and studies of male same-sex sexuality have been dominant (Herdt 1987; Herdt and Stoller 1990; Parker 1991, 1999; Lancaster 1992). Ellen Lewin (2002) has insightfully commented on gay and lesbian studies as an "unhappy marriage" because of their diverging trends. Gay studies are preoccupied with sexual behavior, while lesbian studies mostly engage with gender, without trespassing on each other's main terrains. In my study I break with this binary by paying attention to both sex and gender in describing women's sexual practices. As an "outsider within" (Hill Collins 1986), looking in on lesbian studies, I cannot escape the strong impression that this field of study is first and foremost a North American affair, dispaying the same ethnopsychological attitudes toward sex, that society at large holds. Like dutiful daughters, feminist anthopologists have, by and large, honored their civilization's discomfort with sex, by overwhelmingly not writing about its specifics, thus reinforcing dominant representations of women's sexuality. Gayle Rubin' s words are still well worth quoting in this respect. Writing on what she calls "sex negativity," Rubin notes:

> Western cultures generally consider sex to be a dangerous, destructive, negative force. Most Christian tradition, following Paul, holds that sex is inherently sinful.... . This culture always treats sex with suspicion. It construes and judges almost any sexual practice in terms of its worst possible expression. Sex is presumed guilty until proven innocent. Virtually all erotic behavior is considered bad unless a specific reason to exempt it has been established. The most acceptable excuses are marriage, reproduction and love.... *But the exercise of erotic capacity, intelligence, curiosity, or creativity all require pretexts* that are unnecessary for other pleasures, such as the enjoyment of food, fiction, or astronomy [my emphasis].
>
> RUBIN 1984:278

The abundant erotic enjoyment and "mastery," the capacity to talk about and to tell sex that is evident in many mati relationships, stands in stark constrast to what I still consider to be the most prevalent Euro-American sexual "mood" and mode.

Cross-cultural studies of female same-sex sexuality remain relatively marginal in feminist studies and unjustly quarantined, as if they do not have anything meaningful to contribute to the study of sexuality generally (but see Blackwood 1986a, b; Newton 2000; Blackwood and Wieringa 1999; Manderson and Jolly 1997; Elliston 1995; Lewin and Leap 1996, 2002).

The Politics of Passion is not solely concerned with same-sex sexuality, however. It provides an account that deals both with opposite-sex sexuality and same-sex sexuality. This inclusiveness, a both/and stance (Hill Collins 1990) claimed by many, is in keeping with the way in which Afro-Surinamese working-class women themselves conceptualize their sexuality. The book lays out a black female sexual configuration in which both women who are only involved with men and women who engage in relationships with men and with women partake. Afro-Surinamese women's sexual practices and relationships arise from the same conglomerate of beliefs and ideas about sexual subjecthood, which, as I argue, build on unconscious West African "grammatical" principles (Mintz and Price 1992 [1976]) in the domains of subjecthood and sexuality. With this configuration, Afro-Surinamese women move outside of the identity binaries that have characterized sexual being in Euro-American settings, during the last century. A female same-sex sexual culture has maintained itself, according to most scholars at least during a century but in my understanding appreciably longer, in the framework of a general sexual culture, with which it shares ways of understanding the world, practices, women moving between various sexual locations and, importantly, the idea that the sex of the object of one's passion is less important than sexual fulfillment per se.

One of the central debates in glbtq studies over the past decades has been the question of whether same-sex sexual activity can best be understood as identity or as behavior. It is also a prominent issue in *The Politics of Passion* and I explicitly take a stand on the side of behavior. I have much sympathy for Elliston's thoughtful (1995) critique that dividing up the world between those who have a sexual identity and those who engage in sexual activities, leaves unexamined the core problem of what will constitute "sex" or "the sexual" in either category. This distinction "happens," moreover, to coincide with a First World/modernity–Third World/tradition split. Nonetheless, I arrive at this position by taking Afro-Surinamese women's own accounts seriously, when they talk about their sexuality in terms of activity, when they use a verb, *m'e mati*/i.e., I am doing the mati work, instead of a noun, *mi na wan mati*/I am a mati, which would linguistically and grammatically have been equally possible. Yet, they do not use the latter construction at all, pointing to the importance of their cultural construction of same-sex sexuality. The problem that Elliston quite rightly discerns—what is to count as "sex"?—did not play out in this context: there is no ambiguity whatsoever about what constitutes "sex" or "the sexual." In chapters 4 and 5 I will outline linguistically the Afro-Surinamese landscape in which the politics of passion takes shape. My research on mati work unsettles some "received feminist truths" about the nature of women's sexualities. Mati are part of and form a configuration in which women unabashedly enjoy sex; they talk about it openly, within parameters of mutual trust; they take it seriously, in the sense that sex is important to them; it is seen as healthy and as an extremely joyful and exciting part of life. With mati we typically do not encounter problems prevalent among white North American lesbian middle-class couples, among whom a sharp dropoff in sexual activities frequently occurs after the second year of the relationship, due to the "merging/fusion/enmeshment" of selves (Nichols 1987; Boston Lesbian Psychologies Collective 1987). "Sexual death" in bed was unheard of; according to all accounts, mati are active sexual partners and it is possible in their universe not only to make distinctions between sex with men and women, but also to disentangle sex from love, without the moralistic overtones that so tend to shroud Western feminist discussions of sex. Mati are not the proverbial Prisoners of Love; indeed, more often, it might appropriately be asked, "What's love got to do with it?"

Mati work challenges received notions of female sexuality as passive, muted and non-genital, in that it is the opposite of all these characteristics. It is active, vocal, often genitally oriented and above all, self-driven. Women are conceived as sexual beings who can act on their desires. Mati work presents a configuration where erotic and sexual relations between women are public, acknowledged, validated and often openly celebrated. It offers a radically alternative configuration to the historical genesis of "homosexual identity" under capitalism (D'Emilio 1984; D' Emilio and Freedman 1988; Faderman 1991). Mati work is seen by the actors in terms of behavior; no "true, authentic" homosexual self is claimed. And, finally, it flies in the face of the supposedly simple relationship between gender and sex, with sex either seen as derivative of gender or gender as a product of sex. The Afro-Surinamese gender system in the working class is flexible, a system of possibilities, not constraints, and it is undergirded by a conceptualization of subjectivity which allots "masculine" and "feminine" characteristics to all people. As has been noted for other working-class gender systems in the black Diaspora, differences between biological men and women are not stressed, but a remarkable degree of likeness and social equality between men and women is noted. So, for instance, both black American working-class men and women display emotional expressiveness, mothering behavior, individualism coupled with strong interpersonal connectedness, take independent sexual initiative and they possess a strong sense of selfworth (Lewis 1975; Stack 1986). My own data on Afro-Suriname bear this out. The Afro-Surinamese gender system is buttressed by a linguistic system with genderless aspects, which undermines a strict incarceration in one's biological body. It allows women, without incurring stigma or other social punishment, to "lie down" with other women.

This book is committed to a form of social constructionism that deeply takes political economy into account. I read the mati work as expressive of a strong form of social constructionism (Vance 1989). Instead of a purely textual approach, which often has a tendency towards autism, this study is informed by and combines multiple and inclusive interdisciplinary approaches: starting from ethnographic practice, it builds on insights from history, African American and Caribbean studies, cultural studies, linguistics, religious studies, queer theory and political economy. In that sense, the book may be characterized as employing scavenger theory, as well as a "scavenger methodology" (Halberstam 1998). In attending to material practices in that supposedly most intimate domain of sexuality, which seemingly only involves the personal, the micro level, I also pay attention to changes at the macro level, e.g. changes in the economy, in globalization processes, which effect what everyday life looks like. While I pay close attention to the local context, I also take the broader global contexts into account that these women inhabit, reflect and rework. Recent work in glbtq studies, too, has taken up the call for a "transnational turn" in studies of sexuality and to stop taking the nation-state as the privileged and self-evident site for investigation (Povinelli and Chauncey 1999; Patton and Sánchez-Eppler 2000; Grewal and Kaplan 2001; Cruz-Malavé and Manalansan IV 2002). I fully agree with Sang that this well-meaning injunction is a reminder more useful to queer theorists who are preoccupied with Western sexualities than to scholars who have been studying sexuality in modern Third World nations, who have had to think transnationally all along. She argues that "even when a particular non-Western space for inquiry is ostensibly identified as the nation, it is always already shot through with colonial, imperial, transnational, cosmopolitan, global—whatever we call it—presence and valence" (2003:9). This is singularly true for Suriname and its traveling sexual cultures and in following the women, study of the Netherlands as a postcolonial and postimperial space became inescapable. Often such recent, transnational studies of gay and lesbian men and women have focused on the surfaces and commonalities of such movements, "reading social life off external social forms—flows, circulations of people, capital and culture—without any model of subjective mediation" (Povinelli and Chauncey 1999:445). In-depth ethnographic analysis, allowing precisely for such subjective mediation and agency, has not been one of the strong points of such studies. In chapter 6, I will focus on mati women who have migrated to the Netherlands in the nineties and I will show how they negotiate the new lesbian discourse of identity with their own understandings of the mati work, against the backdrop of largely unexamined, dominant metropolitan representations of black women's sexuality.

The Politics of Passion engages with several communities of discourse that usually do not communicate. Sexuality studies have not often taken the Caribbean as their place of action, while insights from religious studies, linguistics, or globalization studies are not usually wedded to theories of subjectivity. I try to bring insights from these various discursive communities together, in order to do justice to the depth and the complexities of Afro-Surinamese formations of sexual subjectivity.

There are five central themes that the book seeks to address.

Caribbean Women's Life Histories

Few life histories of Caribbean women exist. There are beautiful literary evocations of Caribbean girls and women (e.g., Brand 1994, 1996; Kincaid 1983, 1992, 1996; Cliff 1987, 1995; Danticat 1994, 1996, 1998; Condé 1986) and some collections of interviews with and stories about Caribbean women (Ford-Smith 1986; Elwin 1997), but there are no first-hand social scientific testimonies that foreground the sexual subjectivities of Caribbean women. Here they tell in their own words, filtered, obviously, through my translation and composition, about their lives. Alongside the general circumstances and vicissitudes of their lives, and the ways in which they made a living, I was especially interested in issues of subjectivity and sexuality.

Kinship and Naturalized Heterosexuality

This book challenges the dominant representation that exists in anthropology of working-class Caribbean women, culled from that pervasive and perniciously deployed concept, advanced to explain family relationships in the black Diaspora, matrifocality (Moynihan 1965, Whitten and Szwed 1970; Smith 1996). Women and men are constructed in particular ways within the framework of matrifocality. Anthropologists have implicitly or explicitly contrasted the ways in which men and women perform their partnership and parenthood with the "normal" ways of partners in the Western nuclear family. The Caribbean protagonists in this familial drama have come up seriously short, giving rise to gendered pathologies in the literature. Peripheral to any particular household, men spend their time in various households and form unstable relationships with partner(s), being more attached to their mother and sisters. The imagery about men that is called up in matrifocality is that of the tireless sexual hunter. Women are constructed in contradictory ways. On the one hand, they are the too powerful, castrating figures around which the household orbits, psychologically, emotionally, as well as economically. On the other hand, women come to the fore as sexual victims, waiting patiently for the sexual hunter to bestow his favors on them. They are continuously duped by men whose sweet-talking induces them time and again to have babies in hopes of holding on to them. The lives of several of the women who are central to this book show that this dependent, passive imagery lacks substance in the case of many Afro-Surinamese women.

Another received cluster of wisdom that *The Politics of Passion* wants to critique is the implicit naturalization of heterosexual relationships upon which kinship universally is thought to be based (Blackwood 2005). Instead of the nuclear unit, consisting of a man and a woman, whose offspring cement blood ties with family members on both sides, this study shows that kinship relationships also stem from long-term relationships between two women. Whether it is the children of two mati, who have grown up together and who consider each other kin, or connections formed through two meti/"cowives," as we saw in the case of Mis' Juliette's meti Corry whose daughter Cecilia considered Juliette kin, kinship ties are formed through and between women. In fact, the notion of family, so precious and valued among a population whose forebears in majority did not have relatives when they first set foot on Surinamese soil, became one of the building blocks of "New World" societies (Mintz and Price 1992 [1976]). "Family" is a strong metaphor among mati and nonmati alike, *un tron famiri*/we have become family, indicating the indissoluble bonds that have been established.

Black Female Sexuality

To date, we have no comprehensive full-length historical and sociological understanding of the meanings of sex in the lives of women of African descent, wherever they find themselves. In fact, much of social science research has focused upon the ostensibly negative indicators of an unbridled sexuality: high fertility rates and teenage pregnancies, disproportionately high rates of sexually transmitted disease (STDs) and HIV/AIDS infection, out of wedlock births, rape and "broken" family structures. But the inner sexual lives of black women, how they think about themselves sexually, remain a mystery. What we have learned about black female sexuality has been culled primarily from the work of literary authors, critics, and historians (Spillers 1984; Lorde 1982; Clark Hine 1989; Carby 1986; Davis 1998; Brand 1994, 1996; DeCosta-Willis, Martin, and Bell 1992; Constantine-Simms 2000; Carbado, McBride, and Weise 2002; Rose 2003).

The social scientific study of black female sexuality remains a gaping wound. Both in colonial and postcolonial contexts, black female sexuality has in Euro-American dominant discourses been mainly constructed as immoral, pathological, excessive, animal-like, insatiable, transmitting disease, or otherwise as instrument of destruction. The particular intersections of gender, "race," class, and sexuality in which black women's sexuality gets constructed bears the ineradicable mark of Otherness. Whether in cultural artifacts—paintings, literature, and film (Young 1996)—or in everyday life, this sexuality always already carries the burden of various displacements and projections. Systemic and epistemic violence has been enacted against black female sexual bodies (Gilman 1985; Hammonds 1997).

This anthropological study of the ways women in Suriname, a meaningful part of the black Diaspora, think and talk about their own sexuality may begin to fill this tremendous and painful gap.

Cultural Continuity in the Domain of Sexual Subjectivity

The elaboration of West African heritage in the black Diaspora has been researched with regard to languages, religions, family structures, arts and aesthetic principles, music, motor behaviors, and philosophies, but so far constructions of sexual subjecthood have not been engaged. I imagine the West African grammatical principles governing personhood and sexuality operating like jazz. Improvising upon certain basic themes—a notion of personhood in which the secular and the spiritual are intertwined, the importance of fertility and parenthood for both men and women, the full sexual subjectivity of women, sex as an extraordinarily pleasant part of life that may be engaged in to an advanced stage in life, sexuality as activity rather than exclusive identity—musicians (m/f) in various parts of the black Diaspora have produced riffs that are remarkably similar: working-class women, who typically have children and sexual relations with men and women.

If my line of reasoning holds any validity, we need to ascertain whether phenomena resembling the mati work can be located in Africa and in other parts of the black Diaspora. Data about same-sex sexuality from the African continent and its underlying psychic and spiritual economy are frayed. Yet the scant data that are available about Ashanti (Herskovits 1967 [1938]; Christensen 1950–51) and Zimbabwean women (Epprecht 1998; Aarmo 1999) who have sex with other women point tantalizingly to a construction similar to that which organizes the mati work: women who engage in same-sex are conceptualized as having a "heavy 'soul'"—a "masculine soul" that likes to lie down with women. It is, furthermore, telling that phenomena comparable to Surinamese mati work are found elsewhere in the Caribbean, e.g., *zami, making zami*[23] on Grenada, Cariacou, and Dominica (Lorde 1982; Elwin 1997), on Trinidad (Brand 1994, 1997), and on Barbados; *antiwoman* on St. Kitts; *malnom, antiman* on Dominica (Elwin 1997), *sodomite* and *man royal* on Jamaica (Silvera 1992; Ford Smith 1986); *kapuchera* on the Dutch Antilles (Clemencia 1995); *ma divine* in the French speaking Caribbean,[24] all pointing to a broad-based West African cognitive and behavioral repertoire that found expression and acceptance, under different circumstances in various former slave societies. In the African American context I am reminded of the openness with which the classical blues singers Bessy Smith and Ma Rainey sang about their love for women, e.g., in "Prove It on Me Blues" (Carby 1986; Davis 1998). According to Carby, if we want to hear the voices of working-class women, we need to listen to the blues.

In African American literature that is situated in the fifties and sixties we find descriptions of female same-sex relationships, that are accepted in the working class (e.g., Lorde 1982; hooks 1997). In Lorde's biomythography *Zami* she describes the sexual relationship of the protagonist with her colleague at the factory, Ginger. Sleeping over regularly at Ginger's home and in her bed, Ginger's mother Cora comments offhandedly: "Friends are nice, but marriage is marriage" and on a night when Ginger has gone out: "And when she gets home don't be thumping that bed all night, neither, because it's late already and you girls have work tomorrow" (1982:142).

The mere possibility of cultural continuity in the domain of sexual subjectivity is not welcomed by some vocal constituencies. Apart from Christian fundamentalists globally, homophobic Afrocentrists and black nationalists in Euro-America reinvent black masculinities and femininities to suit their images of "productive" families, which, exclusively conceived, are the only ones who can continue the nation. These groups find themselves consonant with conservative voices from the African continent who maintain that homosexuality is not indigenous to Africa but an aberration taken over from Europeans (Epprecht 1998; Aarmo 1999; Gevisser 2000; Mburu 2000). With this book I want to join those who argue that same-sex sexuality has firm roots in the African heritage. This statement does not imply that I believe sexual configurations are static and bounded. I will in fact show that the mati work is simultaneously changing, both in Suriname and as it establishes itself in the former metropolis, as well as holding on to its organizing principles. I argue that the specificities of local sexual cultures can only be understood as they are caught up within the crosscurrents of global processes of change (Lancaster and di Leonardo 1997b). I thus walk a fine line between being sensitive to continuity and to change in a necessary analytic tension between an emphasis on local meanings and an understanding of global processes (Parker 1999).

Sexual Globalization

The Netherlands occupies a privileged position in the global cartography inhabited by Suriname. Since Suriname reached its constitutional independence from the Netherlands in 1975, when so many Surinamese "voted with their feet" and left for the Netherlands, Suriname can best be imagined as a transnational community that has almost the same numbers of people living on either side of the Atlantic. To every four Surinamese in Suriname, three live in the Netherlands.[25] Ninety-five percent of Suriname's outmigration is to the Netherlands, with the U.S., Aruba, and the Dutch Antilles making up the remaining 5 percent. This points to the centrality of the Netherlands as a social and cultural point of reference in the Surinamese imagination and reality.

The feminist genealogy that best allows me to understand the globalization of Afro-Surinamese working-class women's culture is transnational feminism (Grewal and Kaplan 1994, 2001; Alexander and Mohanty 1997). This brand of feminism pays close attention to the local, the specific geographies women inhabit, as well as to the global: the ways in which global political, economic, and cultural processes reverberate with local realities. Transnational feminism tries to understand women's positionalities through a relational and comparative frame. Moreover, it does not limit itself to an analysis based on the hegemonic category of gender alone, but wants to investigate women's positions from the complex intersections of gender with race, ethnicity, class, sexual preference, and nation. At stake is the insight that women's and men's lives anywhere cannot be fruitfully understood by focusing on gender only and that to persist in this power practice means naturalizing the hegemonic poles of various other relevant binaries: white racial/ethnic positions and heterosexualities. Finally, transnational feminism is deeply interested in the persistent production of inequalities, through the complex intersections of gender with "race," class, sexuality and nation.

I am committed to raising questions about what happens to this black diasporic sexual culture both in Suriname and in the Dutch sexual landscape. As an appreciable number of the women migrated in the past decade, I became increasingly curious about the ways in which migration and transcultural shifts shaped their sexual subjectivity. Instead of following the recurrent trope in discourses of globalization, that of teleological development, i.e., cultural homogenization in the field of sexuality through international travel, TV, the Internet, and other new media, my work focuses on the empirical details of female same-sex connections as they are lived in Suriname and in postcolonial space in the Netherlands. By working with local and global meanings, *The Politics of Passion* provides depth and thick description to a transnational sexual phenomenon and looks in detail at the bricolage that Afro-Surinamese women engage in to make sense of themselves.

My work, finally, also brings a transnational perspective to bear on representations of white Dutch women's sexuality in Dutch postcolonial space since the advent of migrant women of several groups.

A Genealogy of *The Politics of Passion* and Some Methodological Issues

The book explores approximately a decade in the lives of twenty-five women, ranging in age from twenty-three to eighty-four years of age at the start of the research, who are involved in cross-sex and/or in same-sex relationships. *The Politics of Passion*'s original questions were how do working-class Afro-Surinamese women survive amidst the manifold crises that afflict society and how do they organize their sexual subjecthood? The project started with my doctoral field research in 1990–1991 (Wekker 1992a) and has become an ongoing, longitudinal study that follows the women I worked with in their daily living, in their transatlantic crossings and relocations, in their relationships, and in what gave them joy amid the multiplicitous economic, political, and moral crises characterizing Surinamese society. In the past decade I have regularly been back to Paramaribo. In 1992, 1993, 1996, 1997, 2001, and 2002 I visited, for two weeks to two months each time, to look up the women and to update my data, for example, the development of income and cost of living. Moreover, I wanted to know what the impact of ten years of economic roller coaster rides had been on their sexual culture, understandings, and practices.

I initially met the women through volunteer work at the YWCA in Paramaribo and subsequently through different methods, such as the snowball method. When I started doing research with twenty-five women in 1990, I selected them on the basis of a combination of income and occupation. There was no misunderstanding between me and the people whom I asked for help in locating Afro-Surinamese working-class women. The income of the women was to be around or under the poverty line, which was 1,300 Surinamese guilders (= sf), for a family of four in 1990. Often these women would be single heads of household, responsible for taking care of several children and sometimes other dependents, and they would simultaneously have two or three different jobs in the unskilled or informal sector. They lived in working-class neighborhoods all over town, Abrabroki, van Dijk, Schimmelpenninck, Pad van Wanica, Flora A and B, Kasabaholo, and Tammenga Project. Their occupations included street and market vendor, street sweeper, religious specialist, factory worker, domestic servant, lower office personnel, seamstress, washer woman, disk jockey, musician, bartender, waitress, huckster, caterer, baby-sitter, hairdresser, "broker"[26] or intermediary for department stores, and cleaner. Two women were full-time specialists in the Afro-Surinamese Winti religion. Many women had more than one occupation; they often held two jobs a day, and one worked three jobs a day. Many women had one job in the formal sector, mostly working for the government, the largest employer who forms a safety net, in order to be assured of medical insurance, and worked in the informal sector on the side.

During the research process I used a multiplicity of methods, amounting to what Halberstam has called a "scavenger methodology, combining information culled from people with information culled from texts" (1998:12). My methods have included participant observation, semistructured interviews, collection of life histories and family stories, folk seminars, collection and analysis of popular and religious song lyrics and of odo/proverbs, collection of the lexicon of the self, content analysis of stories in popular magazines and newspaper articles, and ethnosemantic analysis.

The number of children the women had varied between none and eleven, with older women having more children. Of the twenty-five women, six had no children (yet). Of four of these, it was certain that they would not have children anymore, either because of their age, their health situation, or because they expressly said they did not want them. The relational situation was less clear-cut, because it changed during the course of my 1990–1991 research. At the beginning of the research period twelve women did not have a relationship with a man, seven had a visiting relationship, six women lived with a man, of whom two were married. In a visiting relationship a man usually comes to visit a woman. At the end of that first research period nine women did not have a relationship, thirteen had a visiting relationship, and three lived with a man, of whom none were married. One man of the two married couples had been killed during a brawl and the other couple had separated. Behind these dry numbers there are real people, with their histories and stories. The situation is even more complicated because both in the category of "concubines" and among the "visitors" there are changes in the composition of the couples. It may be the case that a woman who was living with a man, at the beginning of the research, was still living with one, at the end, but the man was another. Some women had more than one male partner.

I did not approach women on the basis of their supposed varied sexual repertoire. I was not sure, in the beginning, how to go about phrasing sexual behavior as a sampling criterion and assumed that if I had a wide enough range in terms of other criteria, such as age, occupation, domestic situation—with and without male partners—there might be a good chance that I was also indirectly sampling for different sexual activities. This turned out to be the case. Later ten women told me that they had (had) mati relationships. These women are in all three categories of relationships with men: they may not have relationships with men at all, they may live with a man (and be married), and they may have a visiting relationship. It is only rarely that mati live together; women usually have their own home that they rent or possess. They live with their children and they have visiting relationships with each other.

By 2001 three of these twenty-five women had died, including Mis' Juliette. Seven women, the younger ones, the most ambitious and resourceful, had migrated to the Netherlands, and one, who originally was a migrant from Guyana to Suriname, had moved to the U.S. I have kept in touch with several of these women. One of them, Lydia de Vrede, we will encounter centrally in chapter 6, in the context of sexual globalization. The life of Andrea Zorgzaam, a twenty-three-year-old administrative assistant at the beginning of the research, will be foregrounded in chapter 4.

Afro-Surinamese women have been my main interlocutors in this research. As far as men are concerned, my data are mostly limited to my own observations about men and to women's accounts about them. Inevitably, however, over the course of such a long period of involvement, I have come to know some men quite well, e.g., neighbors, sons, and lovers of women I have worked with and whom I have interviewed. I have also come to know several male mati and younger men who call themselves gay.

Content of the Book

The next chapter, 3, deals with the worldview and the discourse encapsulated within the working-class Winti religion, with its galleries of Gods and spirits and its implications for gendered personhood and sexuality. The cosmology of Winti, whether women are active practioners of the religion or not, underlies the organization of this black diasporic sexual culture. The focus on Winti is followed in chapter 4 by one on relationships between women and men, specifically on a complex among Afro-Surinamese women that attests to the undesirability of marriage and the desire to be economically independent and have children. I investigate whether and how they accomplish this and what the attendant ideas and practices about family and kinship are. Chapter 5 foregrounds the institution of the mati work with its characteristic roles, rituals, and regulations. I will present historic data that are pertinent to the phenomenon and offer a black diasporic reading of mati work. In chapters 4 and 5 collectively I explore features of Afro-Surinamese working-class women's sexual culture and which of these should be attributed to the West African heritage. Finally, in chapter 6, I present a reading of the globalization of Afro-Surinamese sexual culture, both in Suriname and in the Netherlands. In addition, I reflect on representations of white women's sexuality in Dutch postcolonial space.

Mimpana mimpana popo o
W'e begi a kara
Mimpana mimpana popo o
W'e begi a misi
Mimpana mimpana popo o
W'e begi a masra
Mimpana mimpana popo o

[We are begging the "soul" (to come)
Mimpana mimpana popo o
We are begging the woman[1]
Mimpana mimpana popo o
We are begging the man][2]

ANONONYMOUS WINTI SONG FOR THE "SOUL"

3

Winti, an Afro-Surinamese Religion, and the Multiplicitous Self

Before I began doing field research in Paramaribo in 1990, I was wary that it would take me into the domain of Winti, the Afro-Surinamese religion mainly practiced among the working class. Until then I fleetingly witnessed signs of Winti in Amsterdam at the few ritual events I had attended and at parties. I was slightly awed by these events and made sure to get myself out of the immediate way.

As a child, Winti was only talked about in my family in a dismissive, disparaging way. When either my siblings or I had a temper tantrum, my mother would scold us to "dance our Winti" elsewhere, not in her house. Moderateness and rational, controled behavior reigned supreme in our home and Winti represented the opposites: being out of control and irratio-nal. No doubt, my initial wariness of Winti was influenced by those not so subtle messages. Many middle-class Afro-Surinamese have internalized the centuries-long colonial dismissal of *negerachtigheid*/negrolike behaviors and manifest a potent mixture of awe, fear, alienation, ignorance, and disdain toward the religion. One of the markers of being middle class has long been to have left Winti behind. I intended to keep away from Winti. Even in the beginning of my stay, I still hoped I might study constructions of selves, gen-der, and sexualities without having to get into Winti. I thought that it would be possible to simply bypass a cosmological system, not fully understanding then the extent to which it pervades so many aspects of working-class life and consciousness. As the evidence began to pile up that the women with whom I was working frequently attended Winti Prey/ritual gatherings and consulted religious specialists in matters of love, sickness, health, and prosperity for themselves and their loved ones, I wrote in my diary about the emerging struggle between what I was witnessing and my own denial:

May 19, 1990
Somebody came by today to consult Juliette because her man is running around and not treating her well. She has just had a baby and when the parents live in disharmony, it affects the baby badly, causing the child to get sick. Juliette explained to me that this is called fyofyo. I am intrigued by the models people have in their heads about what their problem is and what the solutions are, but at the same time I don't feel much affinity. I think that Winti will really complicate my study. Also, it does not really fit into my research design. I never seriously considered that it would become part of the research. Unless it becomes inescapable, I don't think I will get into it.

In a mind filled with class admonitions about Winti, it was very possible to separate life from what I then thought of as the superstructure religion.

In this chapter I will outline the epistemic framework of Winti in order to explore the various ways in which constructions of selfhood and gender ideologies are embedded in it. Understanding this framework is crucial because it is the discursive context in which the multiple meanings of gender and working-class sexual subjectivity take shape. Winti shapes the ways working-class people think and talk about themselves and the ways in which they act out of understandings of what a person is. Even when women are not actively involved in Winti, its discourse extends beyond active practitioners and is a primary locus for the construction of selves for all women (and men) who are embedded within working-class culture.

As to selfhood, I will argue that the Creole self is multiplicitous, dynamic, that its aspects become contextually and strategically salient. Rather than playing out a self-society opposition, particular aspects of self are marshalled to be foregrounded in specific contexts. The elaborate lexicon of the self, the multitudinous ways in which "I" can be expressed in Sranan Tongo, confirms the multiple ways people present themselves and their "identities." It may very well be more appropriate to think in terms of "selves" rather than of a singular self.

The Afro-Surinamese conception of self is in opposition to what, in spite of postmodern insights, is still the dominant liberal, Western way of considering the self, as fixed, bounded, essential, in opposition to society. As postmodernist theorists have asserted in the past decades, subjectivity within Western contexts is also much more fragmented, malleable, and changeable than had been assumed earlier. I will argue, however, that the nature of the fragmentation and malleability postulated for the postmodern self is different from the ways in which personhood is constructed by Afro-Surinamese working-class people. While, on the surface, fragmentation, as a key concept, may appear to signal the same processes in Western and Afro-Surinamese selves, it would be a matter of gross distortion to equate these identity constructions. Equating the two sets of processes would obscure more than that it discloses; in essence, it would obscure the West African "grammatical principles" (Mintz and Price 1992 [1976]) that underpin Afro-Surinamese personhood. Understanding various constructions of self is, as M. Jacqui Alexander and Chandra Mohanty also argue, a complicated and context-sensitive enterprise that cannot be simply invoked by suddenly claiming fluid or fractured identities (1997).

As far as gender is concerned, I discern an essentially egalitarian, non-rigid gender ideology embedded within the folds of Winti. This is evident not only from women's numeric dominance in the religion as practitioners but also in the influential roles they've assumed as *bonuman*/ritual specialists. Female bonu explain that men are ritually unclean because they have sex with too many women. Many women believe that the Winti prefer to descend on women and thus favor women because they are ritually cleaner than men.

A second indication of egalitarianism is that the Gods, ancestors, and spirits are conceptualized as male and female. In fact, the most powerful Winti, Mama Aisa, the upper Goddess of the earth, desired by one and all in the working class, because of the promises she holds out for affluence, beauty, fertility and prosperity, is female. Thus the culturally prominent role of women as mothers is underpinned by and embedded within a religious system that strongly validates women. In chapter 2 I described the structurally disadvantaged positions that women occupy economically compared with men. Marginalization in the secular world holds no sway in the world of the sacred. The tensions generated by these contradictions in different important life domains are enacted in sexual spheres.

In order to understand Afro-Surinamese working-class women's subjecthood, I will pay attention to the textual, that is, local linguistic complexes in the domain of selfhood, while I also seek to identify features in the spiritual context, which reverberate with understandings of subjecthood. The relationships as envisioned between the Gods, who are thoroughly anthropomorphized, and humans are mirrored in the relationships between humans. In Winti religious practices practitioners make offerings to the Gods to placate and please them, to keep them in harmony, so that they will go on protecting their "children." The Gods, in turn, also give things of various kinds to humans—protection, knowledge, dreams, success, and prosperity in life and business. The reciprocity in these relationships should also be a feature of relationships between humans, pertaining as well to women exchanging sex with men for money.

A Koromanti Prey

Let me begin by conveying the atmosphere of the first Winti Prey/Winti Play I attended, a Koromanti Prey, which took place in the afternoon[3] and was intended to placate the Gods of the sky pantheon. The excerpts are taken from journal entries of August 1990, three months after the earlier entry that was overlaid with resistance.

Friday afternoon 08–24–1990
Friday at 12.30, when I went to see Muriel at the school where she works as a cleaner, she invited me to come to a Koromanti Winti Prey with her and her mother that same afternoon. This prey is given for the Winti of the pantheon of the sky. The only thing Muriel knew about the person who was to give the Winti Prey, was that she is a teacher and that it was going to be in town, which is rare, because most Winti Preys take place outside of Paramaribo. Muriel had told me that it was appropriate to wear something blue or gray.

The Winti Prey had started at 2 P.M. There was a large crowd of at least a hundred people, mostly women, only a handful of men. All the women were dressed in tones of white, pale through dark blue and gray, most of them wearing angisa/headdresses in the same colors.

I did not know whether I should go and greet the person who was giving the Winti Prey. Later I asked Muriel and she said that she had greeted her, so that when I passed the woman later, when dancing, I greeted her by nodding. Muriel and I sat near the palisade, made out of large banana leaves. I could see better there and did not feel so exposed in my ignorance.

The Setting

Anna, the woman who gave the Winti Prey, was sitting on a wooden chair to the side of the house. The chair was covered with a cloth, representing Princess Juliana[4] as a young woman, probably made for her accession to the Dutch throne (1948). The colors were red, white, blue, and orange. How paradoxical: such a blatant royalist symbol, the old colonial days played out in an atmosphere that so fiercely attests to the African spirit. On each of Anna's sides were short-legged wooden tables, covered with white lace cloths. On the table to her right were about ten bottles of liquor: small bottles of Heineken beer, Martini, Black Cat rum, orgeade,[5] Malibu, and whiskey. On the table to her left was a candle that was kept burning all night, a calabash filled with a colorless liquid, and the Bible. Next to that table was a white flag on a long pole. At the bottom of the flagpole was a large bottle of beer, whitened with pemba doti.[6]

The entire courtyard was cast in a pale blue light because a blue plastic screen was suspended over it, in the event of rain. From the blue ceiling about thirty beautiful triangled cloths were suspended, very colorful all. Two men were recording the entire event on video camera.

The Activities

Everyone shuffled barefoot in a circle, to the rhythms of the drums, which were played by men. The drumming was accompanied by singing by several members of the band and by women standing behind them, shaking sek' sekis/hollow calabashes filled with seeds. The singing shaped itself according to a call-and-response pattern, where a precantor (troki) was answered by a chorus of voices. I could not understand the words of the songs and Muriel later explained to me that the songs are sung in various languages, e.g., Koromanti, or Saramakan, or archaic Sranan Tongo. The songs are intended for different Winti: Opete/Vulture, Aradi, Sofiabada. The Koromanti are all flying Gods and believed to have come from Africa.

Anna was dressed all in white and her face and arms and feet were whitened by pemba doti. It was an impressive sight; she danced with two whitened wooden sangrafu/herblike plant sticks in her hands, facing the sun. She had braids and on top of her head a white kerchief was standing up, tied like a crown. She was dancing alone in the circle surrounding her. She danced very lightly, high on her feet, like she was ready to take off, though she was a pretty sturdy woman. Soon another white figure emerged from the house, her white dress adorned with silver figures. This was an older woman; she turned out to be the bonu and played the role of "mistress of ceremonies," paying close attention to what was going on, directing the pace of the whole event, e.g., when Anna should go and change her clothes for a new set of Winti to descend and when the drummers could take a rest.

The drummers, on their agida, kwakwa bangi, and apinti drums, worked up a mountain of insistent and forceful sounds. Suddenly, Anna's body became very stiff and immediately thereafter she started to move, shiver, run, jump, and crawl tempestuously, covering the whole length and width

of the courtyard, all the time irresistibly drawn back to the drums. From
everywhere women, including the other woman in white, descended on her
to embrace her. With their fronts turned toward each other, a sequence of
embraces followed with two women bending simultaneously but crosswise
through their knees. With this elegant gesture the women greeted the Winti
who had taken possession of Anna. The embrace itself kissed several women's
Winti alive, because right after they too would go through similar impetu-
ous movements. The bonu made Anna a drink from the calabash, gave her
a big cigar, and put new pemba on her face and arms. After this more Winti
came onto people on the dance floor: it is considered syen/embarassing if the
Winti of visitors come[7] before those of "the host" have made their appearance.
According to the rhythm of the drums, which invites particular Winti to come
and dance, Vulture and other flying creatures made their appearance.

Alakondre Winti Prey

After the Koromanti Winti Prey was over, around 5.30 P.M., there was an
Alakondre Winti Prey, literally, a play for all countries, where Winti of the
other pantheons, earth, forest, and water, came and danced. Anna went and
changed her clothes for every one. When Winti have taken possession of a
person, the asi, literally, "horse," the person who is "possessed" dresses and
behaves according to the personality of the possessing God. They also speak
the God's language, which they normally, when not ridden by the God, do
not know. In fact, asi are believed to temporarily be the God who is using the
body of the asi.

All in all, Anna wore six different outfits, one more elaborate and beautiful
than the next. With all the food and drinks, the musicians, singers, and her
clothes, Muriel estimated that the whole "performance" must have cost well
over sf 20,000.[8]

One does not necessarily have to know the hosts of a Winti Prey in order
to attend. Part of the reason, undoubtedly, is Suriname's small scale and
hospitality, which is normative. But another important reason is that the
religious ideology of Winti itself dictates the hospitality and openness. The
Gods, conceptualized as human beings, who are very experience near, like
prisiri/to make merry, they welcome occasions to sing and dance, they are
gregarious, so that anyone who is prepared to participate, instead of "giving
her chair a fever," i.e., be a wallflower, is welcome.

The openness of Winti Prey merits three other observations. Unless it
strictly concerns family business, which is usually taken care of in seclu-

sion in the days preceeding the festive finale which is the Winti Prey, visitors—tourists, even—can attend the Winti Prey. Many Surinamese like to take their (foreign) guests, who are interested in special, cultural gatherings to Prey. Everyone is urged to dance and I have heard bonu or other family members admonish the visitors for not doing so, since the descent of the Winti who are supposed to alleviate the emergency situation in which the host finds herself can only be accomplished collectively. If one only sits passively and observes, one is not, therefore, participating in the collective work of helping the Winti to come. By their serious and often strident tones, the bonu not only keep the purpose of the event in full view, they also refuse to become the object of somebody else's gaze, explicitly resisting being made into a spectacle. Presence assumes participation: either you are in this with us, they are saying, or you should not be here.

The description in the diary entry above bears remarkable resemblances to Candomble rituals in Belem, Brazil, as described by Fry (1986), in Bahia by Staal (1992), to Voodoo in New York City and Haiti (McCarthy Brown 1991), and to Voodoo and Santería in New York City (Alexander 2005). According to McCarthy Brown, healing is at the heart of the religions that African slaves bequeathed to their descendants, healing not only in health problems but "in the full range of love, work, and family difficulties." Like African diasporic healers elsewhere in the Caribbean and South America, the central figure Mama Lola in her text "combines the skills of a medical doctor, a psychotherapist, a social worker and a priest" (1991:5).

Since the event was recorded on video, my last observation concerns the proliferation, during the nineties, of technological equipment, like videos and (digital) cameras, within this scared space. This technology has made it increasingly possible to record Winti Prey for family members in the Netherlands who cannot be present. But it also works in the other direction these days: Winti Prey in the Netherlands are recorded for family in Suriname. A local TV channel in Amsterdam, Salto TV, regularly broadcasts images of Winti Prey in Suriname and in Amsterdam. This is an illustration of the transnational community that Suriname has become in the past three decades. The spirit of community can be sustained through the use of the new technologies. The juxtaposition between the ancient worldview embedded in Winti, the secrecy with which the rituals used to be surrounded,[9] and the newness and the public nature of the technologies is striking. The videos and digitized images are a symbol that Winti Prey have broken out of their original secluded atmosphere and become situated in the realm of the public and the global.

Cosmology of Winti

In order to get an emic understanding of why people go to such lengths to devote time, energy, and money to please the Gods, it is necessary to have a closer look at what Winti is. Wooding (1988 [1972]), a Surinamese sociologist, who has thus far studied Winti most profoundly shows the West African provenance of the cosmological system. According to his definition: "Winti ... centres around the belief in personified supernatural beings, who take possession of a human being, eliminate his [*sic*] consciousness, after which they unfold the past, the present and the future, and are able to cause and cure disease of a supernatural origin" (1988 [1972]:290–291). I make an important addition to this definition. Wooding's definition is limited, focusing as it does on the religious domain and the moment of possession, and, important as that is, as a worldview Winti contains much more than possession. It pertains to many different aspects of everyday life, to food, relationships, work, health, matters of life and death, to subjectivity and sexuality, as the examples offered below will illustrate. Winti offers templates for how to act in particular situations and explanations of why certain events occur. A synonym for Winti is *kulturu*/culture, and in its broadness that is exactly what it signals: a way of living, a way of being in the world. So that even when working-class women and men are not actively involved in Winti practices—and sometimes, they may speak about Winti with the same disparagement that I was brought up in—its worldview is shared in the way they think and speak about themselves, in the etiology they assign to events, and which course of action is necessary in a particular situation.

Winti as a cosmology is neither a static nor a unitary system. There is a lot of variation in beliefs and practices by region, city, district, or the interior, where Maroon versions of Winti are extant. Since Winti is a purely oral, noncanonical religion and does not have a central authority or written tradition that makes pronouncements about correct interpretations, differences can also be attributed to the personal predilictions and interpretations of practitioners.

Coming from West Africa, from the Fante-Akan, Ewe-Fon, and West Bantu regions, (roughly, Ghana, Dahomey, and Congo-Angola), Surinamese slaves carried with them African beliefs that centered around an upper God, Keduaman Keduampon, who has removed himself far from the Earth; a belief in an immortal soul that reincarnates, and an ancestral cult (Wooding 1988 [1972]). These characteristics have been retained in Winti, which literally means "wind." Like the wind, spirits and ancestors are invisible but can move swiftly and take possession of human beings and natural phenomena like trees and animals.

The word *Winti* is used in three ways. First, it signals the religion itself. Second, it refers to the Gods[10] that constitute it, and, third, it embodies the state of being "possessed" by a God.[11] Let's consider first the beings that constitute Winti by focusing upon the interaction between the upper God, Winti/higher and lower Gods, human beings, and *takru sani*/evil things.

The Upper God

At the top of the hierarchy, there is the upper God who is known as Anana Keduaman Keduampon, a Fante-Akan term, meaning "God The Creator of Heaven and Earth" (Wooding 1988 [1972]:69). After creating all visible and invisible beings and things, Anana went away far from the earth and does not meddle directly in human affairs. Anana is genderless.[12]

The Gods

Anana has left the governing of the world to anthropomorphic higher and lower Gods, who are divided into four pantheons: those of the sky, the earth, the water, and the forest. Chief deity of the sky pantheon is Opete/Vulture; he has a number of brothers: Yaw, Awese, and Aradi Koromanti. Other Tapu Winti/Gods of the sky are Sofiabada/Gisri Koramanti, Tando Koromanti, and Dyebri or Dyani. According to Wooding, the Gods of the sky pantheon are all high Gods, "Black Royalty," who love to see their favorites, their *asi*, i.e., the people they choose to descend, ride on, abide by cleanliness. The colors that are associated with the Gods of the sky are white, blue, and black (Wooding 1988 [1972]:87).

Mama Aisa, the Mother Goddess of the earth, presides over the earth pantheon. She is the highest of all the Gods. Aisa's personality is construed as a typical mother's personality: she is sweet, she cooks, plants, loves to nurture, often wears *koto*/the traditional Afro-Surinamese dress of many-layered wide skirts when she visits people in their dreams, is fond of beautiful clothes, jewelry, gold, and copper basins and pots. Other Gron Winti/deities of the earth pantheon include Aisa's husband Loko, who can be recognized by his white uniform, Luango (male and female), and the pair Leba (Elegba, who is female) and Afrekete (male). Interestingly, in Africa Elegba is male and Afrekete is female. Thus in Suriname a reversal of their genders has taken place. I will return to this aspect later in this chapter.

The deities Gron Ingi, Papa Winti (Dagwe), Vodu, Akanta(ma)si, Apuku, Bus' Ingi, and Bakagron Aisa (Busimama) are reckoned to be members of the forest pantheon, according to Wooding, but many of my informants considered them to be part of the earth pantheon.[13]

The last pantheon is that of the water deities, which include Watra Mama (Mama Bosu), Watra Papa (Tata Bosu), Watra Apuku, Watra Koromanti, Watra Ingi, Watra Aboma, and Sefari (Zeekoning Balinsa/King of the Sea Balinsa).

Within each group, say Ingi (Amerindian), there are again subdivisions of various kinds. Thus there are Watra Ingi (Water Indians), Bus' Ingi (Forest Indians), and Gron Ingi (Earth Indians). Several of my mati friends mentioned having Motyo Ingi (Whore Indians). The latter are deities who love to have a good time, drink, have sex, sleep around.

The deities are known by name because when they take possession of someone they will often identify themselves in their own language.[14] Thus Majanna, Anna Maria, Philippina, Theresia have made themselves known as *Ingi prisiri meid* (Amerindian girls who like pleasure). The presence of these Amerindian deities in Winti attests to the openness of the system to incorporating cultural elements from other ethnic groups: Amerindian deities, Javanese clothes, white uniforms of Dutch army officers, cloths of the Dutch royal family, all speak of the inclusionary spirit that is characteristic of Winti. There is no means of knowing at what time the Amerindian elements found their way into Winti, whether during or after slavery. From the inception of the colony enslaved and Indigenous people interacted, and it is probable that the enslaved added elements that they found in their new Surinamese environment to their evolving religious system. What strikes me as significant is the Creole spirit of additivity, regardless of the ethnic provenance of the added elements[15].

The Gods in Winti are neither geographically nor ethnically homogeneous. They also have different characteristics. Afro-Surinamers distinguish between Nengrekondre Winti, the Winti that accompanied the enslaved from Africa, and Winti who originated in Suriname itself. The Nengrekondre Winti are thus older. Another division that is made is that some of the Winti are *wroko Winti*, i.e., working Winti; they help people by giving them advice and warnings in their dreams or by telling the bonu the herbs and leaves that are to be used in the cure of a disease. Winti will only help people when the people honor them, pay attention to them: "Ef i n'e ter' den Winti fi'i, den n'e ter' yu"/If you don't take care of your Winti, they won't take care of you. Other Winti do not interfere in the affairs of human beings. They are just themselves, like the *prodo Winti*/fashionableWinti, e.g., *prodo Aisa*, who do not do anything much but be beautiful. In addition, there are the *sidon Winti*, sitting Winti, who do not like to dance but prefer to sit around.

Different explanations have been offered for the phenomenon of "possession." The phenomenon has often been interpreted as a sexual metaphor of human intercourse with the divine. Bourguignon's analysis of the functions of Voodoo on Haiti speaks to me more, in that the characterization of the human self implied in the cosmology as vulnerable, powerless, porous to all kinds of negative forces, in need of protection and of divine intervention to bring about a desired change, whether in the sphere of illness, love, success in work or conflicts in the family, goes right to the heart of how Afro-Surinamese working-class women perceive themselves. Bourguignon's analysis applies equally well to Suriname's Winti:

> In a world of poverty, disease and frustration, ritual possession, rather than destroying the integrity of the self, provides increased scope for fulfilment. ... In a world perceived as hostile, in which the individual is anxious and powerless, only the spirits appear to have the power to effect the required changes. And so the individual—partly in fantasy and partly through the acceptance of a collective fantasy by his peers—may become powerful by impersonating the spirits.
>
> (BOURGUIGNON 1978:486, 487)[16]

I read the subtext of "possession" as a collective statement that people need all the help they can get in surviving, in warding off dangers of various kinds, and in attracting success. Muriel, the woman whom I accompanied to the Koromanti Prey described earlier, had a son in his late teens who was sent a conscription notice from the army. As there was a civil war going on in the interior, which was palpable in the city at times, Muriel sought the help of a bonu to ward off this dangerous situation. The bonu "prepared" Muriel's son in various ways, also pinning the conscription in a *was'was godo*/bee's nest in the forest, and eventually Harry was "forgotten" by the army.

All the deities have their own specific personality characteristics, since they are conceived as resembling human beings. Ethnopsychologically, the person who gets possessed by a deity will, also outside the moments of possession, have the same characteristics as the deity. Someone who has Leba, for instance, the deity who cleans yards, will generally be very clean.

There is a certain amount of built-in ambiguity in the system, which, as I understand it, serves the needs of the actors. Certain characteristics can be part of a person's "I" rather than generated by deities. Cynthia Leeflang, a thirty-nine-year-old cleaning woman, explained: "Mi no ab' Leba, ma mi ik e lob' krin oso"/I do not have Leba, but my "I" loves to clean the house. Moreover, some traits have permanence, but others do not.

All these different deities, of whatever pantheon, have their own songs, the lyrics of which are said to have been composed by the Gods themselves, who then transferred them to humans. When people sing these lyrics at Winti Prey, they thereby invite the Gods to come and take possession of them. The songs are often difficult to understand for outsiders, because of the archaic lexicons and because different language varieties are used, like Koromanti, which is only spoken nowadays by very few, older Creole people.[17] A typical song for Aisa, the female upper Goddess, is this one, which is often sung at the beginning of rituals or Prey:

Wanaisa yu mu yere begi o
Mi gron Winti yu mu yere begi
Yu na mama, wi na pikin o
Wanaisa, yu mu yere begi

[One Aisa, hear our supplications
My Earth Goddess, hear our supplications
You are the mother, we are the children
One Aisa, hear our supplications]

This specific song expresses people's supplications for care and comfort to the Goddess. Before the Goddess everybody is equal: "You are the mother, we are your children." Generally, lyrics are often short and repetitive; driven on by the different drums, they take on an inescapable, relentless force in which people get enveloped. The songs have a number of themes.[18] Often the God will identify him- or herself and/or what (s)he does in the specific linguistic variety that is appropriate to that God. Sometimes the God will indicate that (s)he is not content with the ways people treat her/him, as in this Aisa song:

Pikin di yu nyan, yu no gi na gron (2x)
Pikin di yu nyan, yu no gi na gron san yu e nyan
Gron wani nyan, yu mi gi na gron, san yu e nyan.

(BLAASPIJP 1983:6)

[Children, when you eat, you do not give food to the (Gods of) the earth
Children, when you eat, you do not give the earth what you are eating
The earth wants food, you have to give the earth what you are eating.]

In other songs received wisdom is passed on, as in this Apuku song, which warns people not to divulge too much information about one's self.

Te mati kon na yu oso
Gi en nyannyan a nyan

Gi en watra a dringi
Ma no puru yu bere g'en.

(BLAASPIJP 1983:45)

[When a friend comes to your house
Give him food to eat
Give him water to drink
But don't tell him your inside story.]

The centrality of food in these songs is significant and the metaphorical use of food in many expressions, stories, and proverbs points to its status as a cultural preoccupation.

Oftentimes, too, a fragment from the (slave) past is recalled and retained in the oral tradition. Finally, the Gods are begged not to *mandi*/be angry with their children, but to be patient and help them. In the next song an interesting dynamic between Aisa and her children is revealed:

Mi no abi fu gi Maisa (2x)
Mi e go na den moniman go suku tusren[19]
Te a doro wan hondro, fu mi gi Maisa

(BLAASPIJP 1983:6)

[I have nothing to give my Aisa (2x)
I'm going to the people with money, to look for 32 cents
Till I have a hundred, to give my Aisa.]

Apparently, one of the ways to stay on good terms with Mama Aisa is for her children to give her money. Etiquette and ways of relating between humans mirror those between Gods and humans.

Humans

The children of the Winti, humans, are the third link in the cosmological system. Understood to be partly biological and partly spiritual beings, they are fully integrated into the cosmology and linked to the Gods (Wooding 1988 [1972]). The biological side of humans, flesh and blood, is supplied by the earthly parents. The spiritual side is made up of three components: all human beings have a *kra*/a "soul," *dyodyo*/parents in the world of the Gods, and a *yorka*/a "ghost," the entity that remains after a person has died. The *misi*/miss, the female part of kra and dyodyo, and *masra*/mister, the male part, make up the kra, whose seat is in the head. There are numerous other terms for the kra, of which the most frequently used one is *yeye*. The names of the misi and the masra are decided according to the day of the week on which a person is born. These names, which are used during ritual occasions when the kra needs to be consulted, are:

TABLE 3.1 Male and Female Names of the Kra

	Male	Female
Sunday	Kwasi	Kwasiba
Monday	Kodyo	Adyuba
Tuesday	Kwamina[20]	Abeni
Wednesday	Kwaku	Akuba
Thursday	Yaw	Yaba
Friday	Kofi	Afi(ba)
Saturday	Kwami	Am(im)ba

There is a definite distinction made between someone's "I" and her yeye, and, especially for ritual purposes, it is important to know what the yeye wants. As Renate Druiventak, a fifty-six-year-old pig farmer and activist, who is deeply involved in the culture, told me:

> *My sister Joosje came from Holland and she had to do something for herself, because she had all kinds of problems, with her health, her leg was giving her problems, and at work things were not right, either. Everything in her life was holderdebolder/a mess, confused. I told her we had to talk to her yeye, to hear what they wanted.[21] It was not Joosje's will that counted, but her yeye's. You have to put yourself to the side as a person and the yeye will tell you with the help of a calabash, filled with water, balanced on your hand. The bonu talks to the yeye and asks questions:*
>
> *"Mis' Yaba, san y'e wani? Y'e wan' nyan wan sani? Masra Yaw, y'e wan' prisiri?"/Misi Yaba, what do you want? Do you want to eat anything? Masra Yaw, do you want pleasure, to dance? Her yeye answered by making the calabash spill over, when they heard something they wanted: they did not want to eat anything, they wanted kawna nanga kopro t'tu/singing with drums and copper horns, i.e., brass instruments. Asked what clothes the yeye wanted to wear, the answer was that a masra f'en/"her man," wanted to wear red trousers, while a misi/"the woman," wanted a red dress with white flowers.*

It is important to recognize that Renate distinguishes between what Joosje's "I" wants and what her yeye want(s). Renate even indicates that it is possible to put "yourself as a person," that is, one's "I" aside, to listen to the yeye. Ethnopsychologically, a person clearly consists of different "authorities" who do not necessarily want the same things or have the same desires. From the color her yeye wanted to wear, red, one can infer that Joosje is "carried" by Watra Ingi/Water Indian. It took me a while to understand that kra and dyodyo, although both consist of a male and a female counterpart, are different entities. Together, they define a person's mind, intellect, consciousness, personality characteristics, and mentality (Wooding 1988 [1972]:70). A human being is integrated in the world of the gods by his/her godly parents, the dyodyo, who look out for and protect their child through life. The dyodyo bestow a kra, an immortal "soul," with its male and female components, upon a human being at birth. After death the male and female parts of the kra return to their respective male and female dyodyo (Wooding 1988 [1972]: 84, 289).

While the kra is and should be with the person all the time, except when they are being consulted by a bonuman, the dyodyo are itinerant; they come and go. The kra, moreover, can be likened to a gatekeeper who needs to give permission for Winti to descend on someone. Dyodyo are the godly parents who protect a person from the time of conception. Dyodyo is both a noun and a verb, so that people will say, for example: *Ingi e dyodyo mi*/Indian Winti are my godly parents, meaning that there are a female and a male Ingi Winti who carry me, guide me, take care of me, look out for me. Other terms for the female dyodyo are *kwekima* or *uma dyodyo*/the mother, woman who fostered me, and *kwekipa* or *man dyodyo*/the father, man who fostered me. These terms express the gender aspect involved.

To make these various ingredients of personhood clearer to me, my friends would draw an analogy with the Christian concept of "guardian angels." Lena Cairo, a fifty-six-year-old neighbor and market seller, told me what she had to do to please the dyodyo of her son Harold some thirty years ago:

Before Harold I had had a boy, Ruben, who only lived one month; then he was gone. Pretty soon after that, I became pregnant again. Do you know how many times I had to go pai a doti g' en?/to pay the (people of the) soil for him? The people of the soil do not trust you with another child anymore. Could be that they think it was my fault that the other one died. "Pe yè kis' a bere, d'ape yè mus go pai"/where you become pregnant, there you have to go and pay. I paid twice: I brought red and white swit' sopi/a sweet drink, orgeade, beer, pikin mis' finga bana/small finger bananas, red, white, and blue pieces of cotton cloth, fried manioc, and dried fish. I put it all in a big basket and left it for his dyodyo. After Harold was born, I went again and gave them more things.

Dyodyo live at the place where a person is conceived and it is there one has to go to pay them, honor them, so that they will keep protecting and guiding their child. This, certainly, is one of the reasons why transatlantic travel between Suriname and the Netherlands is so prevalent. Bad luck in a person's life is often attributed to not having properly looked after one's kra and dyodyo: "A sma no ben luk' en bakaman"/the person did not watch her "back" people. The kra or dyodyo are then considered to be dirty or weak. One's "people" can become vindictive and angry when they are not taken into account. Cynthia Leeflang, reflecting on the reason why her younger brother had become hooked on drugs and was now in prison, thought it was because her family had neglected to talk to the "people" of the plantation, from which they had moved to the city, about twenty-five years ago. Her brother's dyodyo were certainly displeased and needed to be paid.

Since dyodyo and kra are conceived to be like humans, with all their human caprices, they have to be fed and cleaned to remain strong. The word for food and for eating in Sranan is *nyan* and it is a key metaphor in Creole culture. Beside feeding the kra, by means of a *kra tafra*/meal for the kra, and feeding the dyodyo, by means of a *dyodyo paiman*/payment to the dyodyo, the kra also needs to be ritually cleansed. The following diary entry marks an emic understanding of an occasion when a *wasi*/ritual bath is in order:

Diary June 12, 1991
    Today Juliette said that since I had been far into the interior twice and to St. Laurent, French Guiana, that "mi mus pur' a hebi fu mi skin"/I have to get rid of the "heavyness"/problems in "my body." Walking everywhere, it could be that a Winti saw me, liked me, and "sat down on me." She does not think anything is the matter with me, but I understand that I had better be safe than sorry. When I had malaria, that was just datra siki/ *doctor's illness, but we want to take care that I do not get* nengre siki/ *negro illness. So we are going to do a ritual bath,* tek' wan hebi watra/ *take a heavy water, to get rid of any problems. After that she will wash "the people that carry me," my yeye and my dyodyo, with a* swit' watra/ *sweet water.*

This diary entry offers constitutive images of the Afro-Surinamese way of understanding the self and the world. Juliette's pointed knowledge of the source of different illnesses is central to this understanding. The self is vulnerable, porous, as it were, to dangers of many different kinds. For datra siki/doctor's illness, also called Gado siki/God's illness, one consults a doctor, as opposed to nengre siki/negro illness, for which one has to consult a bonu. So, too, is her knowledge of the necessary ritual ingredients. Hebi watra, literally, "heavy water," is made to clean the self and release it of its problems. It is also called tingi watra/smelly water. Its ingredients are rum for the ancestors, different kinds of herbs (aneysi wiri, korsu wiri, konsaka wiri), raw eggs, pemba, black pepper, seven pieces of temreman kreiti/chalk, sangrafu, and dried plantains. Swit' watra, literally, "sweet water," is made from a mixture of black beer, sweet-smelling concentrated mixtures like Florida water, Pompeia water, and seven essences, seven geesten, red swit' sopi and white swit' sopi/sweet drinks, and flower petals.

The third spiritual part of the human trinity, the *yorka*/ghost, is the aspect that, when the person dies, goes to the realm of the dead where it joins its ancestors and kin. The yorka retains the experiences the human being has acquired in life and goes on living in the realm of the dead. Yorka, also, have the power to punish or protect their family members. Somebody who was good in life, has a good yorka; someone who was evil, an evil one. People generally are afraid of yorka, who are sometimes observed, exactly like the person was, when still living. Yorka are believed to be the deceased who are not able to reconcile themselves to death and, therefore, they come to participate in life. Misi Juliette has taken her precautions:

> *I always lived well with all my mati. When a relationship ended, natuurlijk krutu ben de/of course we quarreled. But, after a while, when time had passed, we would say hello nicely when I met one of them on the street. That is the way I want it, because I do not want any of them bearing a grudge against me: "Mi no wan' den yorka f' den kon lul mi"/I don't want their "ghosts" to come and trouble me.*

With this statement Misi Juliette shows how she imagines that yorka go about their business: the ghost of the deceased that has not come to rest visits people and troubles them. That is the reason one had better make peace with family members and mati during one's lifetime.

Takru Sani

Finally, the fourth category in the cosmological system of Winti are *takru sani*, literally, "evil things," beings that mean people harm. Often a *wisiman*, a worker of "evil magic," plays a part in sending takru sani on to someone. Takru sani can take many forms, e.g., *wroko dagu, wroko sneki*, literally, "work dog, work snake," i.e., creatures that are under a spell. Legendary are stories about men sending takru sani onto a woman who refuses their sexual advances. A special form of takru sani is *bijkracht*, literally, "coforce," which people seek to guarantee success in various endeavors to others' detriment. My neighbor Lena Cairo told me that her colleague at the marketplace,

Vrouw Melie, uses bijkracht so that only she will sell all her wares, while making sure that her colleagues do not sell theirs. All other market women working close to Vrouw Melie's stall are left with their merchandise, because she sought the help of a wisiman. When I asked Lena how she noticed this, she said that early in the morning she saw trails of powder around her stall, indicating that someone had been busy there. Lena had taken her own measures, however, and contacted a wisiman who was reputed to use even stronger powers. Takru sani may cause illness, loss of money, death even, in other words, it is a dangerous practice that courts punishment for those who invoke it and their children. It may ultimately become *kunu*/an eternal curse that haunts a family for generations. The consciousness of takru sani forms a real part of the behavioral environment. In conjunction with the ill feelings that Winti may harbor toward humans, it contributes to the widespread perception of imminent danger hanging over one's head, especially if one becomes too successful. It also helps to explains why *big' ai*, literally, "big eyes," i.e., envy, greed, is mentioned as the main explanation for other people's behavior.

Reciprocal Relationships

It is not surprising that the religious cosmology seeps through in people's understandings of intimate relations, since, as we have already established, the understanding of Winti is thoroughly anthropomorphized. To start with, there is a striking mirror relationship between the ways Winti interact with people and the behavioral conventions among people. Nana Burgzorg told me about a dream in which Akantasi, a God of the sky pantheon, appeared to her:

> I was very young, I did not have children yet. I had gone out of town, with some family members to work at a fis' kampu/fisherman's camp. There I had a dream that a Maroon woman, her hair was not braided and she was wearing a long dress, came to me. She had seen me and liked me. She came carrying three white bowls. One was filled with white rice, one with stof' taya wiri/simmered green vegetable, and one with butter. She gave me a new dime. Later, I told some older women about my dream and they said: "She came to pay your yeye, before she is going to bar' na yu tapu" /scream on top of you, take possession of you. Since then, I have had Akantasi and she is causing me a lot of problems. When she comes she dances so heavily I do not have any breath left inside me. I do not want to thank her, send her away, but if she would go to someone else it would be fine with me.

In this statement it is striking that the Maroon woman in the dream "pays" Nana in two ways: with food, rice, butter, and vegetables and with money.

The centrality of food, which I have noted before as a cultural preoccupation, shows up here again. Just as Winti "pay" people to take possession of them, so, in reciprocal fashion, it is with humans: people have to "pay" their own Winti, or those of a lover or a child, in order to placate them. There is a very strong connection for women between taking care of a man, having sex with him, and receiving money from him. An expression like "a man no kan gebruik mi fu soso"/the man cannot use me, have sex with me for free, is uttered frequently. The thought alone scandalizes women: to go along in such a one-sided relationship would underscore the lack of reciprocity, the lack of respect for all one's "people." The same principle of reciprocity also applies in mati relationships, where the women have mutual obligations toward each other, in the economic sphere but also, as important, in sexual and emotional domains.

Furthermore, it is necessary that there be some kind of understanding between the Winti of people who have a relationship. There is an array of expressions that stresses the importance of the congruence between the yeye of two persons: "den mus' lob' den srefi"/they have to love each other; "ala den tu yeye mu' de eens nanga den srefi or den mu' agri"/the two yeye have to agree with each other; "den yeye mu' miti makandra"/the yeye have to meet each other; "a yeye mus tek'a trawan"/the yeye has to take the other. When Gonda Burleson, a forty-six-year-old nurse and broker for a department store in town, first met Remy, it was not so easy for them to be together. She recalls how they started out:

> We had many problems in the beginning, where we could not "live together,"
> i.e., have intercourse as man and wife. When I had my period, it would stay
> for three or four weeks. So I finally went and consulted a bonu and she told
> me that I have a male Apuku na fesi/"on the front row," and that Remy had to
> pay him. So he bought Him a silver ring and gave Him black beer and pemba
> and pangi.[22] Because I had four "people," he gave them something to drink,
> too, and talked to them. After that we were all right.

After a while Remy began to *wakawaka tumsi,* literally, "walk around too much," with other women. It was not so much the fact that he had other women as the way he went about it that disturbed Gonda: too visible, which implies no respect. Pretty soon, she had a dream in which a black man, her Apuku, was carrying a calabash with a rotten egg in it. It meant that the relationship was spoiled, predicting separation. Gonda went to see the bonu again:

> The woman said: "No mek' grap nang' i skin. A Apuku san ye abi ne verdraag
> a man moro"/Do not joke around with your "I"/"self." The Apuku you have

does not tolerate that man anymore. You are going to leave him. Even if you yourself do not see everything that is going on, your "people" see it. Then your "people" have a "conference" with his. Yours will say: "Look, we don't want our child with yours anymore." Then they agree we have to split up. That is the reason why I never gave a thought to Remy after that: I left him and I never grieved, because the Winti themselves separated us.

Congruence between yeye is needed both in cross-sex and in same-sex relationships.

The Lexicon of the Self

The gallery of significant beings in Winti begin to fill in the contours of how a person is imagined in this universe: vulnerable, in need of protection in a world that may be envious of your success. An additional window onto subjecthood was opened at a crucial moment in 1990, when I realized that the women with whom I spent time daily had a sheer infinite number of terms at their command to make statements about themselves. I recall this particular moment vividly; it happened at night while I was transcribing notes taken during the day. Muriel Tevreden and I had been selling newpapers and magazines in the rural district of Groningen. Muriel predominantly speaks Sranan Tongo. I had been scribbling down her answers to my questions about a particularly difficult period in her life and, at night when I wrote them out, I suddenly saw the multiplicity of expressions she used to talk about herself. I jumped up and ran to Juliette's house, across the yard, beside myself with what I had just "discovered." Juliette, not in the least excited by my newly found insight, reluctantly interrupted watching the news on TV and affirmed that all those terms said something about "I."

I want to compare the use of the personal pronoun *I* in English and in Sranan Tongo. Language is both a mirror of the world particular people inhabit as well as a building block for that world. Different languages are different ways of being in the world; the speakers of American and British English, however close those language varieties may be, inhabit different worlds (Wekker and Wekker 1991). Western thinking about personhood is, postmodernity notwithstanding, still characterized by two important commonsense assumptions, which also inform academic studies. In the first place, there is the assumption that a "normal," healthy individual has a fixed core to herself or, more typically, to himself. Even though the situations in which this individual finds himself or herself change, he or she remains the same person. Individuals, in other words, are seen as fixed, static. The second assumption about the self is that it is bounded, that there is a clear and "natural" distinction and juxtaposition between the individual and society. The preoccupation with an essential interior "I" keeps the boundaries between this inner "I" and the outside world intact. Thinking in terms of these two assumptions is not only deeply rooted, it is still often projected unto selfhood in other societies. The person-as-an-island approach constantly reproduces notions of uniqueness, unchangeability, and boundedness.

In English *I* is a significant repository of personhood, agency, and personal identity (Kondo 1990). There is really only one term to express subjectivity by means of a personal pronoun; there are no synonyms, i.e., I is monolithic, indivisible, irreducible, transsituational. In other words, I stands like a house and in that house there are no chambers. The white, masculinist fort to which Harding (1991) refers when speaking about Western subjectivity masks femininity, layeredness, and ambiguity.

In Sranan Tongo, however, there is a plethora of terms to make statements about "I," pointing to the multiplicity and malleability of self. After my conversation with Muriel, I systematically set about collecting the lexicon of "I." In table 3.2 I have plotted the most recurrent terms to speak about "I" in Sranan Tongo:

TABLE 3.2 Personal Pronoun "I"

Mi ik, mi ikke	I
Mi kra	My "soul"
Mi yeye	My "soul"
A misi (f' mi)	That miss (of mine, my female part)
A masra (f' mi)	That mister (of mine, my male part)
Mi misi nanga mi masra	My miss and mister
Mi dyodyo	My godly parents
Mi ma dyodyo	My godly mother
Mi pa dyodyo	My godly father
A sma f' mi	That person of mine (singular)
Den sma f' mi	Those people of mine (plural)
Mi skin	I, my body

One of the striking features of this scheme is that it is possible, irrespective of one's gender, to make statements about self in one of three ways: first, in singular and/or in plural terms; second, in male and/or female terms. Thus, a man can talk about his "misi," for example Aisa, and a woman can indicate that her "mister" does not want her to cut her hair. When my friend Renate poured herself a drink, she said happily: "Ai, mi misi nanga mi masra e opo now"/Yes, now my woman and my man are getting up: "I am waking up." One day Mis' Juliette told me about the long-term relationship with her mati that she, at age eighty, finally and definitively put to an end: "Te a misi nanga a masra f' mi e kis' de pest, dan a san' kaba!"/When my female and my male part, "I," are sick and tired of it, then the thing is over! It is essential to know what it means when someone tells you *mi yeye e go g' i*/my soul "goes for you" or, as Juliette said to me sometimes: *mi yeye ben tek' di f yu*/my soul took yours. A deep declaration of love. The fact that people of either gender can make statements about self in terms of their "own" or of the other gender indicates that gender is not conceived as strict and rigid, based on biological sex, but that it is a system of possibilities.

In addition to these different terms, there is a third mode to make statements about self in terms of third-person constructions, i.e., in terms of one's Winti: "Mi Aisa e wan' a gowt' linga dati"/My Aisa wants that gold ring. A man who had drinking problems told me: "Mi ben aks' den Winti fu no dring' moro"/I have asked the Winti not to drink anymore.

Clearly, this is a radically different conceptualization of self and gender than the more rigid, hierarchical, exclusive Western system or the fragmented self postulated under postmodernism. All the different manifestations of "I" are, in an etic sense, deceptively close together. In an emic sense they are not. Here we are confronted with the epistemological problem that is so characteristic of anthropology, that is, how to do justice to an emic system when it has to be described in terms of another, normative, etic system. The source language and the target language embrace different cosmologies where subjectivity is concerned. A multiplicitous, dynamic I-system has to be described in terms of a unitary, static whole of conceptions about "I." It makes a world of difference when one says: *Mi no wani*/I don't want to, or *A yeye no wani*/the "soul" does not want to, the latter being unassailable, most deeply felt, no discussion possible. To do something when your spirit does not want to is tantamount to invoking deep disaster upon oneself and one's environment. Suppose that somebody has died and your relationship to that person has been such that everybody expects you to go to the funeral and *dede oso*/the wake, the ceremonial singing, praying, and storytelling that occurs eight days after a death or a funeral. But if "your soul" does not want you to go, then that is the end of the affair. Strategically, conceptualizing the self as multiplicitous opens a wider behavorial repertoire. Since everyone recognizes the difference between *Mi no wani* and *A yeye no wani*, the ambiguous possibility is created that the person would have wanted to do something were it not for the fact that the "soul" did not want it. The multiplicity of the self thus helps to deflect resentment.

On the other hand, it is also possible that the "I" does not want something that the yeye does, as in the example of Cynthia Leeflang, who further clarifies the difference between "I" and yeye:

> When I became a big girl, i.e., started to menstruate, my father gave me a gold taratey keti/a chain with different beads. I did not love that chain at all, so I lost it or misplaced it. Years later I was at a kra tafra for a friend. An old man was present, I did not know him and he asked me: "Where is your taratey chain"? I said that I did not have one. Then he said that I should buy one. Girl!!!! I went right away to buy one, because that old man wanted to tell me something. "Mi no ben lob' a keti, m' a Ingi f' mi ben wan' en"/I did not love that chain, but that Amerindian of mine wanted it. So I had to have it.

The chain referred to here is meant to placate and honor different Winti. It consists of three beads that are connected to each other by pieces of gold chain that have been forged in different motifs. There is an orange bead for Mama Aisa, a red bead for Amerindian, and a black one for Apuku.

Just as in the example of Joosje, Renate's sister, whose yeye wanted something different than "I," it may not always be advantageous to the individual or to her family to carry out the wishes of all the different "instantiations," which need to be held in harmony. Yet, when the yeye want(s) something, it needs to be executed. Yeye is a higher authority than "mi." "Mi ik," "mi yeye," "mi kra," "mi misi nanga mi masra" carry approximately the same force. "Mi skin" has important bodily connotations. It may involve great costs, hardship, and even entail poverty to placate the Winti. Tales about families ruining themselves financially in these efforts are numerous. Some women said that to be in "the culture" does not mean that you have to ruin yourself; when you talk to the Winti and tell them that you cannot afford to give a Winti Prey right now, but you will when you are able to, they will not mind. They will still help and protect you. In the meantime, you should buy some smaller things to satisfy the Winti, e.g., a silver ring or a nice piece of fabric for one's "I." In that more balanced sense, where people place emphasis on honoring one's Winti, instead of serving them, placating many "people" is not experienced as a burden but as an opportunity to strenghten the self and expand behavioral repertoires.

It would be a misunderstanding to think that people unequivocally like having Winti. The attitude, generally, is rather: if you don't have them, if they do not bother you, do not bother them, do not go looking for them.

Gender During the Plantation Regime

As we saw in table 3.2, it is possible to make statements about self in male or female terms, irrespective of one's own gender. Gender occupies a relatively egalitarian space if one examines Winti from an ideological perspective. That does not mean that there is no hierarchy, since, as we saw earlier, Anana Keduaman Keduampon is imagined at the apex, as the aloof Creator, with lower Gods who are more powerful than human beings. But one critical difference from the African belief systems of provenance is that the singular African Gods have become multiplicitous Surinamese Gods (Wooding 1988 [1972]:107). For example, the ungendered Nsambi-Ampungu God from Congo-Angola has become the Surinamese Apuku, who has both male and female manifestations.[23] Wooding does not explain this phenomenon, but it is tempting to interpret the transformation from genderlessness to masculinity and femininity in the framework of general processes of acculturation to plantation life.

Due to the lack of data on the gender system among the enslaved, my argument here is speculative, but one can assume that complex processes in or impacting on the gender domain were at work. Slavery, as a system, generally deemphasized status differences among the enslaved, for example, the differences between African royalty and ordinary citizens. There are indications, however, that individual colonizers and the enslaved sometimes honored status differences, as we will see in the case of Princess Apïaba in chapter 4. Her story was kept alive in the oral tradition. Differences between black men and women were in any case stripped of the significance that was attached to gender in the white segment of society. The gender ideology in the planter class, which constructed white women as possessing a less sturdy constitution to do physical labor, was racialized and only pertained to white women. This not only happened in Suriname, but it was generally the case in slave societies (Gray White 1985; Beckles 1989; Bush 1990). Until the abolition of the slave trade, in 1814, and for some years after, it was more efficient in the eyes of Surinamese planters to work their slaves to death and import new ones than to create circumstances that were bearable and that led to reproduction. The labor power of slave men and women was paramount. Enslaved women as well as men did heavy manual labor on the plantations. Another practice, the handing out of food to individuals, and not to families or to men as heads of households, contributed to the deemphasizing of gender differences. That does not mean that within the slave quarters all differences, gendered or otherwise, were absent. The most responsible and rewarding positions in white households and on the plantations were almost invariably given to black men. Mintz and Price (1992) point out that in a world where uniformity was so strongly enforced from the outside the slaves especially valued those elements of behavior, dress, and personality in which they could distinguish themselves from each other. The emphasis on those personal differences did not necessarily foreground gender but found expression in other ways that men and women shared. When one looks at paintings and sketches from the time of slavery, one is impressed by the finery, the striking colors of the clothes that both men and women are wearing on special occasions, as going to church or to a festivity, and the personal touches that the enslaved managed to convey in their presentations of self.[24]

Another example that may point in the direction of distinguishing oneself, albeit not necessarily by means of gender, is the practice, well known in other black diasporic communities, of giving each other personal nicknames to express the uniqueness of persons. This practice was already present during slavery in Suriname (van Stipriaan 1990).

Research among working-class blacks in the U.S. indicates that, due to the structural limitations of slavery and the characteristics of the labor market after that period, black men and women show a remarkable degree of similarity in personality traits. Both are autonomous, display expressive and "mothering" behavior, individualism paired with strong interpersonal connectedness, independent sexual initiative, and a strong self of self-worth (Lewis 1975; Stack 1986). The fact that women are allowed to be sexual personae, who have their own sexual desires and needs and can take initiatives in this domain, is noteworthy. Different historical configurations constructed these parallel definitions of personhood in Afro-Suriname and in Afro-America, but in my understanding the common cultural heritage—the "grammatical" West African principles—provided the foundation for this outcome. Different forces were thus impacting on the enslaved in the domain of gender, but their own cultural capital predisposed them toward egalitarianism.

Where independent behavior of women was, unintentionally, stimulated by the equal labor that women had to perform, strengthened by the individual system of food provision, and where the West African behavioral principles already opened a window on egalitarianism in the ideological sphere, gender egalitarianism was probably an important way for the enslaved to be in the world. This would also explain why, if originally there were hierarchical differences between Gods, these were deemphasized. One effective way of expressing egalitarianism is to create male and female manifestations of Gods who were before genderless or male. The transformation of the Gods fits well with an egalitarian gender system and also corresponds with a multiplicitous malleable subjectivity.

Egalitarianism on this "theoretical" level, as a general principle that applies to different kinds of relationships, e.g., those of gender and class, is apparent in a number of features. First, the anthropomorphic qualities of the Gods make them "experience near." They are talked about as if they were humans. In fact, that is what people say: they are like us, they like to "whore around," to drink, to have sex, to make children; others have a bag full of tricks or like to dress up or are extremely fond of cleanliness. There is a marked degree of parallelism between the world of the Gods and that of humans. Second, egalitarianism in the gender domain is apparent in the fact that every human being is made up out of male and female elements. It is not the case that male Winti are valued more; if anything, Aisa, the upper Goddess, is extremely popular, and almost everyone, females and to a lesser degree males, and most emphatically male mati, would like to be carried by her. Third, another indication of gender egalitarianism is again found in the Afro-Surinamese lexicon. For instance, the word *bonuman,* often shortened to *bonu,* is applicable to both men and women. There are various words in Sranan ending in *man*/-man, that do not carry masculine connotations. The most striking example might be *futuman,* a menstruating woman. This feature of the language, again, points to the relatively egalitarian gender ideology present in the working class. This feature of ST clearly correlates with the West African heritage and principles , because as Oyeronke Oyewumi reminds us, many African languages do not have gender-specific codes and there is a lack of gendered notions of power and hierarchy in African cultures generally (2001:6). Fourth, as in African cosmological systems (Mbiti 1969), there is an intense unity between the world of the living and the dead. No opposition between these worlds exists; one is an extension of the other (Wooding 1988 [1972]: 290).

Of course, there are status differences between people in the religion. Although we are all children, those with more knowledge in the ritual-cultural domain, having been elected by the Winti, enjoy more status.

On the basis of what I have presented thus far, it is appropriate to conclude that the cosmological system has a marked degree of egalitarian potential, which has consequences for constructions of subjectivity and the gender system.

Self-Representations and Ideal Self-Representations

Successful cross-cultural studies of the self pay thickly descriptive attention to the textual, to local linguistic complexes and understandings in the domain of self. Still, in many handbooks about psychology and anthropology the beginning researcher is told that there is great danger in rashly believing what it is that people say about themselves. People like to give socially desirable answers; it is therefore important to find out in many different, preferably unobtrusive ways, whether their answers are "right," valid. That difference between how people are and how they say they are is indicated by the terms *self-representation* and *ideal self-representation*. Self-representations are the ideas and images one entertains about oneself and are elicited, in a Western context, by statements like "I am the type of person, who … " During my research I noticed that this type of question hardly quickened Afro-Surinamese women's imaginations. The question springs from a unitary, static self concept: the person is more or less forced to fix herself once and for all. Moreover, the question presupposes that it is possible to separate the self from its environment.

The ideal versions of self-representations have to do with how a person ought to be: these entail normative statements about which characteristics a "good" woman or man ought to display in their own behavioral environments. The issue of the relationship between self-representations and ideal self-representations is a rather thorny one over which there is no real consensus. Hallowell (1960) assumed that the individual's mental self-representation and the culture's ideal representation were the same. Spiro (1987), on the other hand, argued that there is a universal tension between the two.

This issue and the amount of attention it has received find their origin in the dominant Western conception of persons. Cultures may vary in the latitude allowed or deemed necessary between self-representations and ideal self-representations, and that is an empirical question. In cultures where a lot is invested in ignoring the fact that "we are all wearing masks all the time, through all the changes of social morphology" (Geertz 1984:15), where there is an emphasis on a "fixed, authentic, true self," people will be interested in bridging the gap between self-representation and ideal self-representation. Having only one true self to go around, the (cognitive) distance between self-representation and ideal self-representation may possibly be enormous and will *have* to be bridged if individuals are not to experience severe problems with self-esteem. In cultures, on the other hand, where subjectivity is conceived as multiple, layered, multiplicitous, where particular aspects of selves, as it were, rise to the occasion, without pinning one down to one "true" self, there will be less tension and thus less cognitive dissonance between the two forms of self-representation.

The Current Creole Gender System

There are, of course, class and gender elements to self-representations, and considerable attention has been paid in anthropological literature to define the parameters of being a "real man" in black communities in the New World (e.g., Liebow 1967; Hannerz 1970; Keil 1966; Wilson 1973; Brana Shute 1979). For the English-speaking Caribbean working class, Wilson's (1973) analysis tried to capture what it means to be "a real man" by juxtaposing a "respect" and a "reputation" system. This paradigm, which has been influential for a couple of decades, comes close to what Trouillot calls a "gatekeeping concept": a maneuver to block the full investigation of complex systems, which reflects the West's ranking of Others (1992:21). According to Wilson, Caribbean men subscribe to the egalitarian value system of reputation, an indigenous counterculture based on the ethos of equality and rooted in personal as opposed to social worth. Caribbean women, on the other hand, are portrayed as the bearers and perpetuators of inegalitarian, Eurocentric respectability because of their closer association with the master class during slavery when they had roles as concubines and domestic slaves.

Although we have not exactly been spoiled with paradigms taking account of women, whether in the Caribbean as a whole or in Suriname in particular, Wilson's scheme does not do much to help us in understanding working-class women's culture in Suriname or elsewhere in the Caribbean (Besson 1993). It has by now been amply demonstrated that Afro-Caribbean women participate in the main dimensions of reputation (Yelvington 1995; Wekker 1994). There is far less descriptive material on what characteristics constitute valued female personhood. Rosemary Brana-Shute (1993) has captured an important part of the emic system of valued female personhood, which she calls *lespeki*/respect:

> She must be "respectable" … an important aspect of her reputation. This will mean that she is recognized as courteous, cooperative, trustworthy and as leading a scandal-free life. The latter is not correlated with being legally married; so long as she is not regarded as promiscuous, the civil status of her intimate relationship[s] is not an issue. Good humour and an ability to wield traditional Creole proverbs and Sranan Tongo is a plus. If she is thought to be greedy or stingy, to have a malicious tongue, or to appear to move in on other women's spouses or mates, she is unlikely to be appraised either as respecting herself, or being worthy of respect.
>
> (1993:136)

I almost totally agree with this portrait of working-class Creole women, except for the elements of the desirability of "scandal-free living" and non-promiscuity. The parameters of these terms are not self-explanatory and cannot be supposed to have universal, unproblematized content. It is important to specify which women we are talking about.[25] To have many partners is not taken by the women with whom I worked, members of the working class and underclass, as a criterion by which to judge their value, as the well-known odo "I am a gold coin" illustrates. This is a good moment to analyze the odo as its significance can now be appreciated more fully.

The entire text of the odo is "Mi na gowt' moni, m' e waka na ala sma anu, ma mi n' e las' mi waarde"/I am a gold coin, I pass through everyone's hands, but I do not lose my value. Working-class culture, like other cultures in the black Diaspora, is an oral culture, replete with proverbs, verbal arts, storytelling, riddles, and songs. This particular odo precisely sums up the main parameters of Afro-Surinamese working-class women's lives. Insiders usually do not utter the full text of the proverb; the clipped version, "Mi na gowt' moni," suffices for members of the in-group.

Odo serve multiple functions: first, they encapsulate orally transmitted wisdom. Second, they were used in the communication that women had with each other by means of the *angisa*/headdresses they wore. As I will explain, this odo is an answering cloth. Third, they promote living memory in an oral culture, and, fourth, they provide a subordinated group's perspective on the world, which is often a contestation of society's dominant values. Odo are a women's art form, transmitted through the female line in families.[26] Especially working-class women have been the vigilant treasure keepers of the cultural heritage forged in the crucible of this Caribbean society.

Besides being an odo, "Mi na gowt' moni" also is the name of a particular design of fabric that women use for headdresses and skirts: diagonally rising rectangles with a little circle in them (as illustrated on the title page of this book). The circles are reminiscent of coins. I have seen the fabric executed in red, purple, and yellow. Seeing that particular pattern on fabric immediately calls up the odo for insiders. Continuing the West African tradition of naming fabrics (Ross 1998), women in Paramaribo conjured names for the new bales of cloth imported by merchants (van Putten and Zantinge 1988). It was women who occupied themselves with naming; they were, after all, the ones wearing angisa,[27] the traditional, intricately folded headdresses that mainly older Afro-Surinamese women wear nowadays, and *koto*, the multilayered Creole skirts. In their naming of the cloths, women were often inspired by events in everyday life. Numerous names of fabrics survive in the oral tradition as odo, proverbs that contain oral wisdom.

Several versions of the story behind "Mi na gowt' moni" circulate. In one account van Putten and Zantinge explain the proverb as a so-called *piki duku*/answering cloth. They situate "Mi na af' sensi"/I am half a cent and its answering cloth "Mi na gowt' moni" in a prostitutes' environment. "Mi na af' sensi, no wan sma kan broko mi"/I am half a cent, no one can break me, is the *opo duku*/the opening cloth, formulated in this narrative by a woman who looked down upon prostitutes. They subsequently responded with "Mi na gowt' moni." The period in which these odo came into being is probably somewhere between 1900–1930, when there was a lot of money circulating in Creole circles because men were working in the burgeoning gold and rubber industries in the interior. Prostitutes did good business, too, and many coins were gold plated as adornments for "the self."[28]

Another frequently heard version is that a woman who had not been very fortunate in her relationships with men, trying to find her happiness, i.e., material security, with one, then another, finally found a good man. He "lifted" Matsi, as I will call her here—her name is still known in the oral tradition—by buying her a house. Matsi, her financial worries over, then came up with this meaningful odo, summarizing her personal history and her view of self. Several features of her self-assessment, particularly its uses of cultural ideal representations, suggest something more than mere personal biography.

There are several proverbs in which self-identification with money occurs,[29] but this particular one typically arouses much resonance with Afro-Surinamers, men and women alike. Everyone likes the expression a lot, it elicits much empathy. Moreover, it is a gendered odo, i.e., it is typically women (and male mati) who use the proverb. It is used both by women who are in same-sex relationships and those who are involved with the opposite-sex. Its centrality to an Afro-Surinamese working-class women's worldview is further attested to by the fact that it was this proverb that was most often mentioned when I asked women to name an odo that said something meaningful about themselves. The entire odo points to working-class women's embeddedness in a discourse that differs from that of the middle and upper class. Working-class women are—sometimes explicitly, sometimes implicitly—aware of a sexual double standard as part and parcel of the dominant ideology.

Analyzing the odo, we see, in the first place, Matsi's identification with a gold coin, with *money*. Money, far from being filthy or something to luxuriously imagine oneself "above," is the standard by which women measure men's seriousness of intent. The extent to which a man is forthcoming with money often determines whether a woman will enter into or continue with the relationship. The more a man spends on a woman, the more secure her financial position becomes. Her status, too, will be raised, both in her own eyes and in those of other women (see chapter 4). Implicit in the odo, furthermore, is the exchange relation many working-class women perceive between money and sex.[30]

Second, Matsi's identification is not merely with money, but with *gold* money. This indicates that she considers herself excellent, top of the bill.

Gold, a metal found in Suriname, is the most precious, enduring, and desirable object for people from different class backgrounds. It is much desired by many working-class Creoles, male and female alike. It is used to adorn the self with elaborate, heavy jewelry, rings, necklaces, bracelets, and inlaid teeth. There is a characteristic gesture working-class women use to indicate that another woman is loaded, up to the elbow, with jewelry: one arm is bent and is slapped, at the elbow, with the other hand. Jewelry and gold bracelets are favorite conversation topics among women at parties; their abundance a marker of sexual competition.

Gold is not only important within the context of daily material life but also in the Winti religion, where people place far greater value on gold than on silver jewelry. The latter will do as a temporary gift to the self, *fu houden bij*/to temporarize, until the moment when the individual is able to afford gold jewelry. There are certain occasions when gifts of jewelry to self or to others are in order: e.g., when a baby is born or "bought,"[31] when a girl starts menstruating; lovers also should give each other jewelry, in order to win the "soul" of the loved one. Certain Winti/Gods love silver, but many prefer gold. Wooding notes that the custom of giving gold jewelry to one's *kra*/soul is also to be found among the Akan peoples of the Gold Coast: "Ashanti consider gold the symbol of the kra of the Upper God, the eternal soul of the sun" (1988 [1972]:74). Gold, finally, is a versatile object, because it can be readily transformed back into cash in dire times by taking the jewelry to a pawnshop.

Third, while Matsi, in the middle phrase of the odo—"I pass through everyone's hands"—admits to having been in many relationships, whether with men or with women, she ends on a defiant note: "but I do not lose my value." Numerous women impressed upon me that multiple partnerships had more to do with survival than the loss of their integrity or the measure of their worth. They did it to keep their heads above water: "Mi ben suk' mi libi"/I was looking for my "life," I was trying to survive. Again, a window is opened here on the worldview of a subjugated group resisting a dominant discourse that would have women be monogamous and asexual. This book is an attempt to lay out the value structure of working-class women that underpins their constructions of sexual subjectivity.

Let's return now to valued working-class female personhood, which is pertinent to all women, regardless of the sex of their sexual partners. To be knowledgeable in cultural ways is important. This includes, but is not limited to, being versatile in odo and other received wisdoms, but also to know how to make a *swit' watra*/sweet water for a ritual bath, how to cook *wan bun peprewatra*/good pepper soup,[32] how to *tak' wan mofo*/conjure up, talk with Winti. Mis' Juliette was often called upon by neighbors and family members to preside over ritual activities or to explain their dreams. In addition to the features Rosemary Brana-Shute mentions, I have found that presentation of self in, especially, a female Creole universe begins and ends with a well-tended exterior: preferably straightened hair, elaborate jewelry, and having a clean and varied wardrobe. Since a woman's children reflect her personhood, they are also scrutinized as to how they look—freshly washed, ironed clothes without holes is an absolute minimum. Another feature that is stressed by many women, either when they are describing themselves or their best friend,[33] is that they are content with what they have, not envious of other people, do not seek cultural ways, i.e., through wisi,[34] to harm others. This is a significant theme in an environment that attributes bad luck or lack of success to envy.

An additional quality of women is their ability to set' den libi/arrange their lives, take care of business. This is a rather wide, amorphous category in which competence along various, but prominently economic, lines plays a major part. Certainly women can be called brokers,[35] mobilizing their various networks to command goods, services, money, information, and, as the case may be, sex. Being wan kankan misi or dyadya uma/a plucky woman includes being able to be counted upon when something major needs to be organized, e.g., cooking for a hundred people or canvassing for one's political party. It means being able to come up, weekly, with the agreed-upon amount in the kasmoni circle,[36] a rotating credit association. One should have the savvy to save that money and not spend it immediately or completely and certainly not tell one's man about it, otherwise he may want it. Most women use the money to settle a big expense, such as the purchase of a refrigerator or a washing machine or to finance a big birthday party. A distinct symbol of success, too, is to own one's own home, however modest. A woman should not only strive for economic independence, i.e., raise her children so that they bring in money, at some point, rather than keep taking it from her, but she should also have the insight and initiative to take action when she or one of her close family members is in "cultural" trouble, e.g., by consulting a bonu. To be bruya(dor)/messy, confused, not being able to set one's priorities, is a serious indictment.

Mostly, Creole womanhood is epitomized by having children and grandchildren. For older women, having a large bere, literally, "belly," group of descendants, is a source of great pride. Especially for these women, there is a clear economic aspect, too, to having children. Mis' Juliette and I were talking one day about one of our neighbors, Hilda, who had to be admitted to a home for the elderly. Hilda had raised quite a few children, who are all in the Netherlands, but had had none of her own. Juliette's concise comment: "We, grit' na mi ben griti, ma mi ben gebruik mi ferstan. San mi b'o waard now, ef' mi no ben abi den pikin?"/Well, I "really rubbed,"[37] but I used my brain. What would I be worth today, if I did not have the children?"

Having children is also highly appreciated by and for men. Some men in older generations had twenty or thirty children, but younger men reject this behavior as irresponsible (Terborg 2002). One of Juliette's sons, Simon, was such a man; he was *mek' futu*/very fertile. As far as Juliette knew, Simon, who was in his early sixties, had fathered at least thirty-five children. She talked about it, shaking her head, but she also chuckled. She was proud of him, because he enlarged her kingroup, and she made sure, on her birthdays, that all the grandchildren would be invited so that they could meet. Mek' futu is an ungendered, old Sranan Tongo concept, used for men as well as women, who have made a lot of children. Mek' futu points to the importance of having children and I regard it as one of the West African grammatical principles for behavior. The fact that the concept is ungendered points, again, to the, in important respects, egalitarian character of the gender system.

Compared with the often brittle nature of their relationships with men, women have their children and long-standing relationships with women, oftentimes spanning decades. While men, as long as they have money, are powerful and can have multiple simultaneous relationships with women, for many women their relationships with men are largely predicated on money and their real meaningful ties are with her children and (an)other woman (women). For both genders having children is an essential component of their self realization.

The Creole working-class gender system potentially is a system of relative egalitarianism and possibilities. Under the influence of West African grammatical principles and tendencies during slavery and after, the ideology, embedded in Winti, considers men and women to be complex, multiplicitous beings who are not in a hierarchical relationship to each other. Masculinity is not superordinate to femininity and every person combines aspects of both in her-/himself. In the working class there is considerable latitude to "choose" one's gender role without severe sanctions from the environment. While there are clearly identifiable roles and behavior patterns that go with one particular gender, people so disposed can take the gender role "belonging" to the opposite gender. Men make that choice more often, and more openly and flamboyantly, than do women.

Feminist conceptions of gender, in which gender is not seen as a stable identity but as an effect that needs to be produced continuously like a performance (Butler 1990), also fit well with the open nature of the Creole system. Men whose Aisa is foregrounded can choose to take the female gender role. At mati parties there are invariably men who wear koto and display typically "feminine" behavior. Performances by male transvestites are among the most popular parts of plays at the NAKS theater.[38] One of the colorful personalities around town is a male who only cross-dresses. He had, at one time, been a high-ranking civil servant, also in feminine attire, and most of my middle-class acquaintances referred to him as crazy. My working-class friends understood him as having a prominent Aisa.

It should be acknowledged that in practice there is a certain asymmetry in the liberty that women have to publicly assume the role of the other gender. Although it occurs, women "genderbend" less frequently in public.[39] Public space is, here as elsewhere, more often claimed by men. It is understood that women who dress and act like men have a strong male Apuku.

The Afro-Surinamese Winti religion, with its gallery of active, meaningful beings, holds within itself a multiplicitous conception of the self and a gender ideology that permits people to "choose" between roles regardless of one's biological sex. I have characterized the gender system as relatively flexible and nonhierarchical: a system of possibilities. Certain aspects of self become contextually salient without laying claim to a core, essential, transsituational self. This is true as well for sexual subjectivity, as will be investigated in chapters 4 and 5. Selves are transactional, malleable, and multiplicitous. I have showed that this multiplicitous conception of self opens up a wider behavioral repertoire in an environment that is experienced as hostile, offering few chances for fulfillment. Sexual relationships are constructed against this background.

In the next chapter I will examine the dynamics of female-male relationships against the backdrop of the Winti worldview.

"Kon sidon na mi tapu, dan a n' e tya' mi sensi kon. Dan m' e law."/Then he comes and sits down on top of me[1] and does not bring me my money. Then I must be crazy.

ANDREA ZORGZAAM, THIRTY YEARS OLD

4

Kon Sidon na Mi Tapu / Then He Comes and Sits Down on Top of Me: Relationships Between Women and Men

Sex in a male-female context can seldom be captured in romantic metaphors of the sort that have kept generations of Western women enthralled. "He came and swept me off my feet…" is typically not heard from Creole working-class women. Sex is, broadly speaking, what men are after and women who have some savvy cannot afford to give it away lightheartedly. The statement by Andrea Zorgzaam that serves as epigraph to this chapter captures the politics of passion of many working-class women much better: when he thinks that he can have sex with me without giving me any money, then I've got to be crazy. Carrying the main and often exclusive economic responsibility for their children, working-class women have to struggle to keep their heads above water. Andrea's statement points to the transactional way in which she conceives of sex with men: without money, no sex.

Sex, then, becomes one of the strategic assets women can control and use for economic gain. It is a matter of deliberation and negotiation from a position that the woman herself often implicitly perceives as relatively weak. Some women are more adept, more prepared in terms of resources, e.g., looks, experience, smartness, to play the high-powered and high-risk games that entering into and keeping a relationship with a man often entails.

This chapter deals with the ways Creole working-class women in Paramaribo, at the end of the twentieth century, constructed their sexuality in their relationships with men, the discourses and social arrangements in which sex was embedded, how women experienced sex, the extent of their sexual knowledge, and the language they used to talk about sex. In addition, I explore notions of female personhood that are implied and articulated in this specific configuration. Finally, reading existing sources against the grain, I wanted to uncover values that have historically guided working-class women in the cross-sex relational domain. The discussion will focus on a complex conglomerate of values in which women want economic independence from men, trade sex for money, and prefer, generally, not to be tied to a man in the form of marriage.

The subject of this chapter is not the etic category of heterosexuality, but, in keeping with women's own worldview, it does concern sexual activities with men: mati are also active in this domain and present in this chapter. One of my central understandings is precisely that the particular distinction entailing the carving up of sexual identities in hetero-, homo-, and bisexuality, which appears to be so "natural," precultural, in many Euro-American contexts, has historically and emically not been salient. In an Afro-Surinamese working-class universe it is sexual activity and sexual fulfillment per se that is significant; it is not the sex of one's sexual counterpart that carries the most meaningful information. I understand this principle as expressive of the West African cultural heritage.

There are several connected themes that I will deal with in this chapter and the next one on the mati work. First, I want to highlight that a relatively egalitarian gender system comes into conflict with economic inequalities between men and women. Apart from the everyday realities in which gender is constructed and ordered, in turn, by it, gender also is fueled by and resonates with deep notions in the spiritual domain. One of the operating principles in Winti was, as we saw, that reciprocal relationships should characterize the ties between the Gods and humans as well as the relationships between humans. The "theory" or ideological level of gender relations, which forms part of the deep plane of the ordering of the world, contains, so I argue, thick West African "grammatical principles." In the ideas about how gender relations should be, about what is good and right in this domain, notions of reciprocity and egalitarianism figure prominently. In practice, however, the tensions between relatively egalitarian ideological notions about gender and unequal economic circumstances are enacted in sexual domains where women perceive an exchange relationship between sex and money, primarily in their relationships with men. There is historical evidence that black women already made this connection during slavery. The connection between sex and money, also evident in the words of the odo discussed in depth in the previous chapter, "I am a gold coin ..." speaks to a cultural preoccupation that, however, is by no means typical for Afro-Suri-namese working-class women.[2]

The second theme that I want to foreground is that working-class women, both mati and women who engage exclusively in cross-sex connections, are embedded in a shared discourse regarding sexual subjecthood. The centrality of motherhood, full sexual subjecthood of women, a preferred independent status from men and sex, seen both as a strategic asset and as a relational activity, figure prominently in this working-class discourse. Many women consider sexual activity as healthy, joyful, and necessary. The organization of the fulfilling of passion in this Creole universe shows that there is no one "natural" way of going about one's sexual business. This does not mean that there are no differences between those women who are involved exclusively with men and mati. Mati had more extensive sexual knowledge and, as they conveyed it to me, enjoyed sex with other women to a far greater extent than women in cross-sex relationships. From the perspective of the dominant gender discourse, mati engage in unruly and unrespectable behavior, but I will argue that mati have more independent understandings of sex than do women involved exclusively with men.

Third, taking a diachronic perspective, I will make the attitudes of work-ing-class Afro-Surinamese women and their foremothers, enslaved women, toward different relational arrangements with men a central focus of atten-tion in this chapter. Reading existing historical sources with this interest in mind, the undesirability of marriage comes to the fore. It is accompanied by a host of other features in the relational and social structural domain, which all demand attention in trying to come to terms with Afro-Surinamese relational patterns: the Creole kinship system with its greater stress on con-sanguineal bonds than on the conjugal relationship; matrifocality, the system in which women as mothers are economically and psychologically central in their households, while men in their roles of husband-father are rather mar-ginal to domestic affairs; the institutionalization of the *buitenvrouw*/"outside" woman; the thick distribution of particular masculinities and femininities; and, as I will argue in the next chapter, the mati work. This last has in the standard literature on the Caribbean not been considered an integral part of relational and kinship formations. Central in my historical discussion in this chapter will be the foundational question that too many scholars of the Caribbean have shied away from, either because of methodological difficul-ties involved (Barrow 1996) or because the sheer possibility of the African provenance of features in the relational domain was for a long time not wel-comed (Sudarkasa 1996): how can the dual marriage structure (Smith 1996), the hegemonic organizing principle in Caribbean societies whereby white males had sexual access to both white and black or Creole women—marrying

the first and living in concubinage or in a visiting arrangement with the latter—be reconciled with West African cognitive and behavioral principles in
the cross-sex relational domain (Mintz and Price 1992 [1976])?

Mintz and Price (1992 [1976]) reopened the old debate between Melville
Herskovits and E. Franklin Frazier by claiming that the enslaved, in various
locations, had varying opportunities to redevelop culture and that in recon-
figuring family forms they drew on West African principles: "An African
cultural heritage, widely shared by the people imported into any new colony,
will have to be defined in less concrete terms, by focusing more on values,
and less on sociocultural forms, and even by attempting to identify unconscious 'grammatical' principles, which may underlie and shape behavioral
response" (1992 [1976]:9–10).

In the next chapter I argue that underlying the mati work are West African principles in the domain of sexual subjecthood, which underwrite full
sexual subjecthood for women and take it for granted that women have sexual desires and can act on them. In this chapter, at its heart, I want to engage
in the task of uncovering which West African principles might have been
operative, especially in cross-sex relational spheres, and how these could
be reconciled with the overarching template that was laid over Surinamese
society by the dual marriage structure (Smith 1996). This ordering principle
at the root of Caribbean societies considers sexuality as central to the colonial enterprise, reserving marriage for white men only to status equals, that
is, white women, while other forms of sexual access, visiting relationships
and concubinage, were deemed appropriate to status unequals, enslaved
and freed women. The system of plantation slavery was the meeting ground
between "two opposed yet interdependent cultural and ideological systems
and their attendant conceptions of reason, history, property, and kinship.
One is the dilute product of Africa, the other is the antinomian expression
of western modernity" (Gilroy 1993a:219). Even though it is difficult meth-
odologically to pinpoint the West African provenance of particular features
in Caribbean family forms and relational patterns, because the necessary
data simply are lacking, it is important to understand the articulation of
those two opposed systems. It is a question that has not yet been dealt with,
and it entails making sexuality a central concern and even though the data
are unclear it is worth hypothesizing about. If it is speculation, as some
undoubtedly will call it, at least it is informed speculation. What is important is to develop a new, more complex way of looking at the Caribbean past
and present that takes the different systemic influences into account, which,
in time, might be uncovered more fully.

My approach here is novel in a number of respects. In trying to understand the Afro-Caribbean relational configuration, it brings to the fore sexu-

ality as articulated by subaltern voices both in a male-female and in a same-sex context. In general, in the many studies about black family life in the "New World," attention has been paid to forms of mating and to kinship, but hardly any attention has been given to sexuality per se. Sudarkasa correctly points out that in some areas of their lives early enslaved blacks behaved toward each other as Africans: "Their Africanity was manifest in their family and community relations; in their music and their recreation; in their spirituality; and in their rituals and rites of passage (most especially in the way they mourned their dead" (1996:113).

It is remarkable that she does not add sexuality to the list of domains in which the enslaved lived their lives as Africans, which points to the blinders that have characterized studies of the African American family. The study of (hetero-)sexuality in the Caribbean as well has by and large remained a black box, either as a subject in itself, connected as it is to many other features of the social system, or as a tool for understanding Caribbean realities, past and present (Wekker 2001). It is still tantamount to heresy in many Caribbean and African American contexts, scholarly or not, to suggest that deeply complex and unnatural processes go into creating gendered and heterosexual subjects.

In Caribbean scholarship discourses and structures constructing "race" and class have traditionally been privileged overwhelmingly, while gender has only in the past three decades been taken up as an indispensable explanatory set. This has led to a by now impressive body of work. But studies that explicitly focus on sexuality have thus far been few and far between. Beside a system to extract labor from the enslaved, slavery was nothing if not a system to organize and order incommensurate sexual access for white men to women. Sexual domination was the substance of imperial policy (Stoler 2002), so it is important to ask what the enslaved female population made of this system—what room did they find to maneuver and to express their own principles operative in the relational domain? Curiously few studies of the construction of heterosexuality have been undertaken in a Caribbean context[3] (but see Beckles 1999; Terborg 2002; Tafari-Ama 2002; Kempadoo 2004).

Looked at from the perspective of the blossoming field of sexuality studies, this study also takes a different route than the usual one. Instead of solely traveling in the by now thick forest of glbtq studies, *The Politics of Passion*, in keeping with emic constructions of sexuality, addresses sexuality in its same-sex and cross-sex manifestations. In the past three decades we have seen a swelling tide of studies of sexuality as a historical and relational category. In opposition to deeply ingrained essentialist notions that assumed existing social and sexual arrangements between women and men were natural, normative and inevitable (Peiss, Simmons, with Padgug 1989), these studies have convincingly shown that all sexualities are socially constructed. Insightful work has been done on the construction of heterosexuality in Euro-American contexts (Katz 1996), tracing the history of the concept that so skillfully organizes immutability, normativity, and ahistoricism in our thinking about sexual identity. The concepts of hetero- and homosexuality did not arise until the late nineteenth century in Europe and although reverberations of these ideological developments, like eddies in a global pool, made themselves felt in Suriname, e.g., through medical doctors and clergy trained in Europe, that is not my focus here. Instead, I am focusing on the subaltern cultural and ideological system and the ways in which it intermeshed with the dominant sexual system. Reading against the grain, the goal here is to follow the ideas and practices of the female enslaved population concerning male-female relationships and to ascertain whether these can be traced to a West African heritage.

The approach I offer is also novel because this study foregrounds Suriname. The genealogy of Suriname was extraordinary because of a specific constellation of demographic and cultural-political circumstances. The African contingent among the slave masses was continually replenished until about 1830, whereas the cultural policies of the colonizer dictated that, excepting the sexual domain, slaves be kept as far away from them—linguistically, spatially, culturally—as possible. Surinamese slaves were very much left to themselves, allowed to develop their own ways of being in the world, their own languages, cultures, and relational arrangements. It is my contention that the West African cultural archive was excellently kept and elaborated on in the lower strata of the Afro-Surinamese population. Thus, the study of relational arrangements in the Afro-Surinamese working class offers a meaningful configuration within the framework of relational and familial patterns in the black Diaspora.

In this chapter women who operate in the cross-sex relational domain and who are at different points in their life cycles speak about their experiences with men and with sex. They also talk about their views with regard to marriage. Prominent will be Andrea Zorgzaam, a thirty-year-old administrative aide, who had upwardly mobile aspirations. She hoped to find a man for herself alone, even to get married, but she was forced to make certain compromises. Offered the choice of making do on her own or becoming someone's buitenvrouw, she chose the latter. Nana Burgzorg is sixty-three, a cook, who had eleven children and relationships with numerous men. She was sexually active and hoped that it would be possible to go to the Netherlands, "to check out the men there." Reportedly, Dutch men are more secure financially and less fickle.

I have chosen to focus on these two women because they are in significantly different age brackets, thirty and sixty-three years old, and while I do not want to make a claim about their being representative for their peers, they do illustrate two different positions in the ways in which they defined their positions in relationship to men, independence and marriage. During the nineteen-month period in which I regularly interviewed Andrea in 1990–1991, her position shifted from a discourse of self-reliance to one in which she, due to her dire economic straits, wanted a man to support her, even if she would have to take second-quality, "waste," from him, being his outside woman. In 2001, when I last had an in-depth conversation with Andrea, she had shifted again to a discourse of taking care of herself and her children. I last saw Nana in 1996. She died in 1997, from high blood pressure, without ever having made it to the Netherlands.

Andrea Zorgzaam

Andrea lived with her four-year-old daughter, Alexandra, in a housing project outside the center of Paramaribo. The rental house, which was soberly furnished but clean, was in the name of her mother, who was in the Netherlands. The refrigerator had broken down a while ago and the black-and-white TV mainly showed snow. Andrea was a proud and pretty woman, plump but staying well within Creole beauty standards. She had definite aspirations for upward mobility. The poverty line in 1990–1991 for a family of four persons was sf 1,300 a month. Andrea's ambitions were to be economically better off. Out of her meager fixed income of sf 350 a month, equaling about $17, she saved sf 50 a month for a fund that would amount to sf 20,000 or $500, in the end. Alexandra would come into it when she would be twenty-one years old. Since then inflation has taken such astronomical forms that sf 20,000 was only worth about $100 in 1994. By 2001 the amount had shrunk to $10. In view of Andrea's hardships to save, it was painful to acknowledge that it did not make any sense to do so. Andrea had an additional irregular income catering for middle- and upper-class parties. Her most profitable economic activity was working as a waitress, on an on-call basis, at a hotel-restaurant that mainly serves tourists from the Netherlands.

Andrea hoped that Alexandra would be able to study. Even when Andrea was extremely worried about her financial situation, she would not show it to outsiders. Except for regularly interacting with a sister and an aunt, she mostly kept to herself.

She finished the sixth grade and, while on her way through the administrative stream in secondary school, she met Romeo, who was then twenty-seven years old. She was nineteen at the time. He convinced her that he was going to take care of her, so she discontinued her education, which has remained a sore point to her—so shameful that she felt compelled to hide it from prospective suitors. She felt that she had been reduced to less attractive, less promising partners because of it. Andrea mostly spoke Dutch, the official and high status language, and only when she got excited, or when she did not want Alexandra to understand something, would she turn to Sranan Tongo. She did not want Alexandra to speak Sranan, which to Andrea would mean a certain working-class future, under any circumstances. Alexandra sternly corrected me with regularity when I was over at their house and said something in creole.

After taking a course in typing, Andrea found work as an administrative aide at a private foundation in the welfare sector. When she was twenty-three she moved in with Romeo, and pretty soon problems began around his seeing other women. Additional problems resulted from the fact that his mother and sisters did not like Andrea, finding her spendthrift and stuck-up. Fairly soon after she got pregnant, Romeo left her, never legally acknowledging the child. He stopped supporting them financially when he found out that Andrea had a boyfriend. Fortunately, he did not take away their health insurance card that entitled Andrea and Alexandra as his dependents to free medical care.

Apart from Alexandra, Andrea lived with and cooked for three younger brothers, twenty-seven, twenty-five, and twenty-three years old, none of whom worked regularly. In the four years since Alexandra's birth, she had had two short-lived affairs with men. When I met her in August 1990, Andrea was on the verge of losing her job because of the foundation's lack of funds.

Nana Burgzorg

Nana was a sixty-three year old cook at a hospital, where she made sf 420 a month. Rather heavyset, her legs and high blood pressure gave her problems, but she looked very young and was attractive with her flashing gold jewelry and her radiant smile, which put dimples in her cheeks. Nana's days started early: at 4:30 A.M. when she got up to start cooking for the entire household. There are six children, three daughters and three sons, still living with her. The household consisted of ten people including three toddlers, Nana's grandchildren. From 6.30 A.M. till 2.30 P.M. she worked at her job, and in the afternoons she joined a group of colleagues and other men and women, at a nearby club, to play *pesepese*/a game of cards and bingo. Nana considered this part pleasure, but part work, too, because she intended to make money out of the game. Although she sometimes was lucky, most of the time she was not and she had to find short-term loans or gifts. With the music, the drinks, the joking and laughter, Nana said she preferred to spend her time there rather than at home, where she only found worries. She often did not get home until 10 P.M., getting a ride with her current lover, Humphrey, a watchman. The relationship between Humphrey and her adult children, especially her sons, was not very cordial, and it was problematic for Humphrey to sleep over at her place because one of Nana's sons had beat him up.

Nana was disappointed in her children: five of them were in the Netherlands, but they rarely sent her money, while her other children "used the house as a hotel," not bringing in any money, only more mouths to feed. The two eldest daughters were cashiers in a supermarket, but it was a constant battle to have them contribute to the household. The three sons had been in the army, two of them becoming addicted to drugs during the Civil War (1986–1992). Their creativity and frustration went into redesigning the house, an ongoing project. The interior of the house was dismal: three TV sets, which together had the properties of one functioning set, played constantly; two dogs and three cats roamed the house, which was unusual because pets are mostly kept out in the yard. She kept her bedroom with the phone and her clothes and jewelry locked because her sons had sold some of her possessions in the past.

Nana felt that she had been unlucky with the men in her life and with her children. Six men fathered her eleven children, and Nana blamed some of these men for saddling their children with bad Winti, meaning that they had to consult a bonuman often, which cost her a lot of money. Nana irregularly received packages and Dutch guilders from two sisters in the Netherlands, who kept helping her after their mother had died. She often said that if she had the money today she would leave for *P'tata*/Holland tomorrow. Her ray of hope was that a male friend there might send for her.

Paramaribo as Context

The immediate contexts in which women like Andrea and Nana live are complemented by wider contexts, like the layers of an onion (Geertz 1973; Ross and Rapp 1997), that are pertinent for an analysis of sexuality in Suriname. I will describe two features of that wider public context: the ubiquity of sex and the master metaphor of greed.

Sex is without a doubt a subject that holds a lot of interest for Surinamese people in general and for Creoles in particular. The fabric of everyday discourse between men and women, as well as between mati, is to a large extent replete with sexual innuendo, sexual metaphors, and with general topics of conversation that are construed as sexual.[4] During a political debate that was nationally broadcast on radio and television in February 1990, the representative from the Nationale Partij Suriname, NPS,[5] the Creole block, threw his hands up in the air and exclaimed: "Mr. Chairman, governing in Suriname is like a coitus interruptus. You start the job but you never get to finish it."[6] This statement, which was received with much acclaim and laughter in the National Assembly, is saturated with gendered, heterosexist imagery. The imaginary subject of this imagery is masculine. Obviously, the governance of Suriname is envisioned as a masculine enterprise; thus women are discursively evacuated from active involvement in processes of governing. In addition, when the appropriate masculine role is active and penetrating, Suriname itself is envisioned as passive and feminine. Hence, within this dominant discourse, women are twice shown their appropriate places: having no place in the governing of the nation and, sexually, being imagined as passive and prone.

Another important arena where thinly veiled sexual content is abundant, where templates for the relationships between men and women are rehearsed, is in the lyrics of *kaseko*, a very popular musical style, mainly but not exclusively performed by men. Drums are the propelling force in this genre. One of the most popular songs, in 1990–1991, was "Didon Fisi"/Flat Fish, which would send people, young and old, male but mainly female, into raptures of delight. Little children in my neighborhood knew the lyrics without fail, accompanied by the appropriate sexual postures and gestures. The song is apparently about a man who is selling fish door to door, and the chorus, which is repeated over again, goes like this:

> Ma didon fisi-eee zevenvijftig
> Oh mi mama
> Afu skoynsi wan   drievijftig
> Oh mi mama
> Baka pataka nownow   wan dalla
> Luku fa mi e taigi yu, mi brada
> Na so a tori de
> Zevenvijftig, drievijftig, wan dalla.

The lyrics of the song did not make too much sense to me. It was only when I saw the accompanying performance by children that I understood the song to refer to different sexual positions and their corresponding cash values:

[But flat fish is seven fifty
Oh, my mother
A half slice is three fifty
Oh, my mother
Pataka-back is now one dollar
Look what I'm telling you, my brother
That is how it is
Sevenfifty, threefifty, one dollar.]

At the first line, *didon fisi*, both hands were put behind the neck and the body was bent backward as far as possible, suggesting a lying down posture: the rate for a sexual transaction, lying down, was sf 7.50. At *afu skoynsi wan*, the children put an elbow under one side of their heads, slanting down: lying down askance would cost sf 3.50. Finally, on *baka pataka*, which referred to a particular fish, pataka, they would bend through their knees, jutting up their butts: explanation superfluous at this point. Several women and women's organizations have tried to alert people to the sexist character of these songs, but generally there is little concern about these matters.[7] In the summer of 2001 the most popular song was Bossé Krioro's "String in de Bil," which sought to inform listeners that nowadays women do not wear big underpants, as in grandmother's day, but just a string in between the buttocks.

It is not only men, however, who initiate sexually laden discourse. Through the work the women did, selling products on the market or in the streets and oiling their business with a short conversation, I was able to observe that sales went better if women gave a sexual turn to their pitch. Even women who had trouble talking about sex with me or who did not seem very savvy in the management of everyday life were adept at this practice. Sexually construed gender is, next to ethnicity, the favorite folk explanation for differences between people.

When starting a new relationship or carrying on an existing one, a woman has to pay attention that her good name is not spoiled in the busy little beehive of Paramaribo. There are few actions that escape the interested eye and there is incessant talk about everybody's business. Different women have different stakes in protecting their names, but nobody is interested in being the talk of the town. The often merciless and injurious talk, which functions as an extensive system of social control, is the subject of numerous kaseko songs.[8]

Coupled with what may be the master metaphor in Creole culture, *big' ai*, literally, "big eyes," greed, jealousy, a picture of the context emerges in which one should tread carefully. There is more than one paradox here: on the one hand, there is a strong preference for conspicuous consumption.

On the other, one should take care in displaying one's good luck and riches, lest jealousy be aroused. Greed and envy are often invoked in explaining the behavior of other people. While in reality resources are often readily shared and exchanged between households and individuals (although less so than used to be the case, according to most informants), there still exists a paradox in that the deployment of the *metaphor* of greed is extraordinarily strong. At the same time, the lyrics of many songs can also be understood as an expression of a defiant, almost provocative attitude, along the lines of "let them talk; only I know my own business." This attitude is also present in the proverb "Mi na gowt' moni ... " Both attitudes, the fear of being the object of gossip and the provocation, are present, often in one and the same person.

The impressive explanatory power that is attributed to greed is tied to the evil side of *kulturu*, of Wisi. There are ways to be successful in attracting success in life and there are ways to ward off the jealousy one may invoke in other people because of that success. Both modalities can be subsumed under the concept of *bijkracht*/"coforce," as we saw in chapter 3. Two concrete examples may clarify the way in which these insights work in everyday life. When Anthony Nesty, the Surinamese Olympic swimming champion, was welcomed in Paramaribo after his victory at the Goodwill Games in August 1990, my neighbors were immensely proud and elated. At the same time, they explained to me how worried they were that somebody would "harm" Anthony now that he had become the world champion. They felt strongly that he should consult a bonuman to protect himself. Another instance of using big' ai as a master metaphor happened to me. When I went to Suriname for my first fieldwork period, I had taken a new laptop as well as a software package with which I was only marginally familiar. I regularly ran into problems, losing and fragmenting files because I had not taken the trouble to read the manual. I publicly complained about my bad luck and sometimes even added that I must have the evil eye on me. This was not really a joking matter, because Mis' Juliette, who was intensely empathetic, advised that we should go *opo luku*, have a *lukuman*/diviner look at my case: maybe people were trying to make my work go badly or maybe I had not looked after my Winti. Given my line of work, my desire to get ahead and my not having children, which meant that I had to take care of myself in old age, it was important to ascertain whether anything was wrong. Whereas for me the solution to my problem rested in consulting the manuals, Misi Juliette's worldview suggested that something quite different, a spiritual imbalance or bad luck caused by jealous humans, was the matter. The notion of personhood that emerges from the two previous examples is one that is "embattled," endangered by its environment. Beings around one, both visible and invisible, may be out to get one, to do one harm, to envy or even be angry with one. The person who is brought up in the culture needs to *luk' en baka,* literally, "watch one's back," i.e., take care of the needs of one's Winti, keep them satisfied.

Within a universe that shows itself at times as distinctly adversarial even in the sphere of intimate relationships, it is not surprising that relationships are fraught with excitement, fears, and tensions. There may be "girlfriends" who threaten to divulge an outside woman's story to his "inside woman";[9] one has to deal with one's own fears that what one is doing is asking for cosmic punishment in the form of *kunu*/a curse. Many people are plagued by a mixture of Christian and deeply cultural feelings of guilt around "San i no wan' f' i srefi, no pot' en in' yu mati saka"/Do not do unto others. The paramount justification women gave for their behavior in the relational domain was that it was not the sex, the pleasure, or the companionship but sheer economic necessity: *M' e suk' mi libi*/I am searching for my life, i.e., I am just trying to keep my head above water.

Searching for One's Life

> *"Uma na lep' bana, a no man pori"/*
> *A woman is like a ripe banana, she can't spoil.*

A standard expression women used when they were talking about their, sometimes successful, but often failed attempts to establish a satisfactory relationship with a man, was "mi ben suk' mi libi"/I was searching for my life, i.e., financial security. Thus women made a clear connection between relationships and political economy. The moral and emotional tone of this expression comes close to that of the odo "Mi na gowt' moni ... " in that the subtexts of these and various other proverbs insist on a benevolent attitude toward women, who in their often lone responsibility for the survival of their families have to engage in various attempts in the cross-sex domain to find a "good," i. e., a financially sound, man. Other such odo are "Uma n' e abi fadon"/Women cannot fall or "Uma na lep' bana, a no man pori"/A women is like a ripe banana, she can't spoil. These odo reflect working-class women's consciousness that pertains to the difficult conditions under which they have to survive: no matter how active they may have been in the cross-sex relational sphere, they did it to keep their heads above water. At the same time, the odo construct the world around them.

Although it would be erroneous to think that all male-female relationships are transactional, exchanging sex for money, the pattern is fairly widespread. The male-female domain of relationships can be thought of as an arena in which each person enters, wanting to get the most out of the other without incurring too much loss on his/her own side. Time is an important variable that seems to work in opposite directions for the people involved: while it is to the man's advantage to "score" as fast as possible, it is to the woman's advantage to postpone that moment while holding out a promise and collecting what she can from him. What men want, according to women, is sex. Conversations with men taught me that an additional benefit to them, if they have the income, is status in their own peer groups, which derives from their "keeping" two, three, or more women. A connection need not result in pregnancy, but it is rare, according to women, to come across men who are willing to actively do anything to prevent it or who inquire whether a woman is using contraceptives. Among older men, it is not unusual to encounter men who have made twenty-five to thirty or more children.[10] Several men indicated that they had the income to keep more than one woman happy and represented their exploits as a form of social work. And it is true that goods and money rapidly change hands and are circulated and distributed through relational networks.

The woman enters the cross-sex arena with her personality and wits, her beauty and sex appeal, a varying number of children, and, in the back of her head, the perception that there is an uneven sex ratio. Preferably the financial security that women seek should be long-term, but even if the relationship is temporary it is important to get something out of it. Maureen Fernandes, forty-four years old and the owner of a beauty parlor, is the oldest and the most successful of her seven siblings. With only a grade-school education, she managed to find some economic security through her good looks, smarts, and her own initiatives. Beside running the parlor, her manifold income-generating activities consisted of raising chickens and dogs for sale and selling mangoes and preserves from her yard. A smart move had been that she first had her own house built and later added an annex to it, which she rented to tourists from the Netherlands, giving her access to Dutch guilders. But the best foundational move had been her choice of a man "who was capable of making something of her." Tonko, her partner, was appreciably older, sixty-seven, and had a Dutch pension. Maureen had been in a visiting relationship with him for fourteen years and they had two daughters together, twelve and thirteen years old when I first met her in 1990. Tonko had been living with Agnes for over thirty years, but they had no children. Agnes was aware of Tonko's relationship with Maureen, his buitenvrouw. Asked how the three of them managed the relationships, Maureen said:

> As long as she stays in her yard, I will stay in mine and I am not going to
> bother her. Sometimes we have to call each other, when I am looking for him

or the other way around. We are civil to each other. You hear so many stories about the buitenvrouw going to his house and cursing his wife. I am not going to do that. She would be crazy to let him go with everything she has got and his pension. So I have to take care of myself.

When I visited Maureen in 2001, her insight about taking care of herself had been a realistic assessment. Tonko had suddenly become unwell, in 1998, and had died at her house. Maureen and Agnes agreed that he had to be transported to Agnes's house, under cover of night, where he was laid out in the living room. Maureen did not attend his funeral and wake. She felt that he took good care of her and the children and, even though Agnes had the pension, she owned the parlor and her house. Both during her relationship with Tonko, but more frequently after his death, Maureen had had relationships with women.

In Andrea's case a successful exchange was accomplished when she got acquainted with Roy Hemelrijk. For some time, she had been extremely worried about the prospects of being able to keep her job at the foundation and about how she would be able to make ends meet against the backdrop of the ever faster devaluation of the Surinamese guilder. One day in the fall of 1990 she confided in me:

Lately, I have started thinking.... Around the end of the month when I get my salary, before I know it, it is gone, paying just the regular bills—rent, gas, electricity, insurance. I am going to find somebody who will support me. I would like somebody who would take care of me, so that I could save my salary, I would not even have to touch that. That person would have to understand himself what I need. Even though my salary was never great, I had my pride and was not waiting for a man to take care of me. Nobody is going to support me out of sheer kindness though; I am going to have sex with him.

Here is a moment where Andrea admitted that the traditional set of values around being self-reliant, which she is well aware of, no longer sufficed. Growing up, her mother, like so many other Creole mothers and grandmothers, had told her that (SD) *je diploma is je eerste man*/your diploma is your first husband, meaning that she had to finish her education so that she would be able to take care of herself. In the economic situation at the beginning of the nineties, where she could not count on her three brothers, she needed another strategy to survive. She made an assessment of her situation in which she described herself as "a woman who has no great education, who is not ugly, but is not a rose either, and whose skin color is a little too dark." Even though she did not think that it was impossible to have a man of her own, she decided that she needed to put some of her values on hold until he presented himself. At that moment her only income came from her regular job at the foundation. Her other side job, cooking and baking for parties, dipped because of the expenses she had to make to get the ingredients, leaving her profit margin virtually negligible. Let's look at the costs of baking a typical Surinamese birthday cake, a *viado*, and the price at which she could sell it. The price index is that of the beginning of 1991.

TABLE 4.1 The Costs of Producing a Viado, 1991

1 tin can of butter	17.50
4 ounces of fruit	16.00
(raisins, cherries, currants)	
1 kilo of flour	2.50
1 bottle of almond essence	3.00
1 bottle of vanilla essence	3.00
1 kilo sugar	10.00
Yeast	2.00
Cinnamon powder	2.00
8 eggs	10.00
Milk	2.00
Total ingredients	68.00
Gas cannister[11]	+20.00
GRAND TOTAL	Sf 88.00

One big viado was cut up in twenty-four little pieces, which usually sold for sf 2. So that this viado would get Andrea sf 48, which clearly was not enough to make it an economically advantageous endeavor. When she asked people who ordered a viado to buy the ingredients themselves, they did not like it. And they complained that she was too expensive when she asked sf 150 for a viado. She had become tired also of dealing with people, often acquaintances, who ordered a viado on credit and then neglected paying their debts. So for the time being she gave up on cooking and baking.

In 2001 I looked up Andrea again and also met fifteen-year-old Alexandra and a seven-year-old son, Marco. She now worked as an administrative assistant at the Ministry of Social Affairs, where she was having a hard time because of her supervisor, who felt that she was not behaving as submissively as someone with her skin color should. The relationship with Roy ended in the fall of 1991. His woman had found out about it, so it had to stop. Andrea did not want a screaming Norine in front of her door, which would make her lose respect in her neighborhood. A couple of years later Andrea struck up a relationship with forty-seven-year-old Igor de Freitas, *een heer uit Nederland*/a gentleman from the Netherlands, a Dutch Surinamer. Igor lived half the time in Suriname and half in the Netherlands and had a Dutch social security income, which made him an absolute catch.[12] Moreover, he drove a taxi in Suriname. Pretty soon, Andrea and Alexandra moved in with him and she became pregnant, but the relationship did not survive. Igor denied his paternity, which put the baby in her womb in jeopardy. This is referred to as *fyofyo*/an affliction targeting babies in the womb or newly born whose biological parents live in disharmony. Igor also had relationships with other women. Andrea's yeye did not want to have sex with him anymore, so eventually she had to move back to her mother's house, where now only one of the brothers still lived. Another change in her life was religion; Winti had become important to her. She consulted a bonu on a regular basis in regard to her health and for explanations of her dreams.

Andrea felt that she had become harder, less trusting of men in the past ten years, more convinced that she herself had to make things better for herself and her children. Financially she was doing better than ten years ago. And this gave her pride. She had bought a freezer, a TV-set, a video, and a wardrobe. She was saving for a refrigerator and a new gas stove. She was no longer counting on a man—but see Igor's contribution—to solve her problems; men, these days, she said, are more like *kaiman*/crocodiles.[13] She could start something with a younger man; they were often attracted to her, but she quickly dismissed that possibility: "I have built myself up now. I have got almost everything I need. Then he would just profit from me." This last utterance pointed to the inappropriateness of an older woman in a relationship with a younger man, helping him to build himself up; Andrea conceived of it as him taking advantage of her. The other modality, an older man who is well off helping her was the one culturally approved.

She now earned sf 165,000 a month at the ministry and got 150 Dutch guilders from Igor,[14] who finally had come around and admitted that Marco was his, which together amounted to a little less than sf 300,000 a month. The poverty line for a family of four, at the end of 2000, was sf 447,000 (ABS 2001), which put even middle-class women, e.g., teachers, nurses, lawyers, in severe jeopardy. After the middle of the month, Andrea's sources were depleted, so she still had to find additional income. Since people like spicy food, and there was no snackbar in the neighborhood, after work Andrea prepared snacks like *telo*/fried cassava with salt fish or French fries with drumsticks and a sweet-spicy sauce. The costs and profit from Andrea's new source of income, selling chicken and french fries from her house, are apparent in the next chart, which in comparison with her earlier viado activities also shows the dazzling inflation of the Surinamese guilder, between 1990 and 2001. Note, for instance, the price of the same gas canister rising from sf 20 to sf 650.

TABLE 4.2 French Fries with Drumsticks, 2001

Package of 12 chicken legs	11,000.00
1 bag of potatoes	3,500.00
Peanut sauce	3,000.00
Mayonnaise	2,000.00
Ketchup	5,250.00
Baking oil	1,500.00
Spices (sieuw, chinese powder adyinamoto, onion, and garlic)	1,000.00
1 bag of charcoal	1,000.00
Gas canister[15]	650.00
GRAND TOTAL	sf 28,900.00

Andrea sold large portions for sf 5,000 and half portions for sf 2,500. When she sold 12 full portions, she received sf 60,000, which gave her a profit of sf 30,000. She worked hard at her hustle seven days a week, starting to prepare the food at five in the morning and closing off at midnight. She made more money selling chicken than working at the ministry, where she stayed because of the health insurance. Andrea was doing better financially in 2001 than in 1990–1991, but the improvement was also due to her access to Dutch guilders via Igor.

Some major themes in the cross-gender relational sphere are transparent in Andrea's words:

If I do not work at my hustle so hard, I will be a burden on somebody. Then I will have to live with a man. (Disdainfully): "Dan i kon gi mi wan sf 50,000 or 75,000, te mun tapu. Te a hossel e go so, dan trawan e prakseri, dan mi n' a f' gi yu sensi kwet' kweti"/Then you give me sf 50,000 or 75,000 at the end of the month. When my hustle is going so well, some men think: well, then I do not have to give you any money at all. I can walk around with my head held high, you hear?

Contemporary Relational Arrangements with Men

"If I do not make enough money, then I will have to live with a man." Thus
Andrea summed up her predicament, and it was clear that, at this point,
she would not want to be caught in such a situation. In 2001, when she had
reached a somewhat secure economical position, living with a man was not
attractive to her anymore. Earlier in our conversations she had expressed the
wish to be married, but generally marriage has not been an attractive option
to most working-class women. Although marriage carries more legal protection for a woman and her children, this form has never found widespread
acceptance within the Creole working class. The narratives of the women
who are central in this chapter show that there are different relational
arrangements with the men in their lives. The three main types of relationships mentioned in the literature are a legally sanctioned arrangement, that
is, marriage; concubinage—cohabitation outside of marriage, also indicated
in the literature as "common law marriage" or "Surinamese marriage"—and
a visiting relationship.

The relational situation of the group of twenty-five women I worked with
most closely, ranging in age from twenty-three to eighty-four years old, is
somewhat complicated, because their personal situations changed in the
course of the research. At the start of the first research period in February
1990, six women lived with a man, two of which were legally married. Seven
women had a visiting relationship with a man, while twelve did not have
a relationship with a man. At the end of the research in August 1991, nine
women had no relationship with a man, thirteen had a visiting arrangement,
and three lived together, none of whom were married. Of the two married
couples, one man had been killed during a fight and one couple had separated. It was even more complicated than this, because within the categories
of "visitors" and "concubines," there were changes in the makeup of the couples. Thus, a woman who was living together with a man at the start of the
period might still be in concubinage at the end, but with a different partner.
Several women had more than one male partner. Marriage did not occur in
the circles in which I moved and only very few younger women mentioned
it as desirable. A new phenomenon in 2001 was that women's siblings and
parents, living in the Netherlands with their long-term concubinage partners, came to Suriname to get married, legally and in either the Catholic or
Protestant Church, and celebrated it in the family circle.

As one of the few national research results, the *Suriname Contraceptive
Prevalence Survey* (Jagdeo 1992) presented data about the frequency of marriage, which are differentiated by ethnicity. The survey showed that family
structures vary significantly with ethnicity. Among Hindustani and Javanese

women with a steady partner, marriage is the dominant relational form. Respectively 74 percent and 58 percent of these women were married. Only 9 percent of Creole women with a steady relationship were married, and, among Maroon women, this percentage dropped to 3. Terborg found that Creole men and women preferred, for different reasons, to live in concubinage or in a visiting relationship (Terborg 2002). Men of all classes idealized marriage, looking upon it as a symbol of social status, prosperity, stability, and a good relationship with the partner, which they deemed only attainable when they had acquired certain material goods, i.e., a house, a car, and other status-enhancing possessions. For working-class men, a spiraling configuration, of him wanting to control his woman's sexuality, while not having the economic means to enforce her fidelity and always harboring the fear that she might leave him for an economically stronger male partner, resulted in a tendency to postpone and be wary of marriage (Terborg 2002:256–257).

Buschkens, who studied the family system of Paramaribo Creoles in the mid sixties, concluded

> that the notion that legal marriage is a form of union which only the socially successful—or more particularly, people who are able to give evidence of this by holding a lavish wedding feast, being able to afford a comfortable home and furnishings, and arranging their lives in such a way as to obviate the necessity of the wife going to work in the category of menial jobs (at the very least as teachers or clerks)—may enter into is still very much alive in broad groups of the lower-class Creole population.
>
> (BUSCHKENS 1974: 267)

The terms in the literature for these different arrangements, mentioned above, are etic terms. The women themselves have a partly overlapping, but a partly very different repertoire. To be or to get married in Sranan Tongo is *trow* and covers the same territory as the legally sanctioned form. Legally sanctioned marriage among Creoles was and is a rare phenomenon. As may be recalled, Juliette was adamant in chapter 1: "Trow? Suma? Mi? Noit' mi ben wan' trow!"/To be married? Who? Me? I never wanted to get married! With *trow* she was indicating the legally sanctioned form, which until 1982 also meant legal minority status for women. During the period of the military regime the legal obstacles oppressing married women were repealed in "Rechten van de Vrouw, Rechten van de Man"/The Rights of Women, the Rights of Men. The decree C11, 1981, recognized women's full legal capacity. Later *A Statute of Basic Rights and Duties of the People of Suriname* (Paramaribo 1982) was adopted. These and other basic rights were incorporated into the 1987 constitution. These measures were taken by the military regime so as to mobilize women behind "the Revolution." Marriage was very much irrelevant to the discussions I had with women, unless I introduced it. Nana indicated that she never really thought about marriage and is referring to some of the impediments for women, which by then had been repealed but were still very much part of women's consciousness around marriage:

> *I don't see the point of getting married. All married men have their outside women, anyway. You don't profit from marriage. You have more obligations, you have to bring him into everything you do, whether it is taking out a loan, buying a refrigerator, or going to a government office. They will tell you: your husband has to sign. Suppose I want to leave him, then maybe he does not want to separate: it's going to be one headache. Some men are so pertinent/insolent, even when you are separated, and you are with another man, they will still come to you and demand all kinds of things. No, let me stay by myself, it is better that way!!!*

Mis' Juliette also had quite distinct ideas about the undesirability of marriage:

> *I never wanted to marry, or make verbontu/union*[16] *with a man.... . Even when a man is beautiful, I cannot put beautiful in my pot to cook. "Mi kan or' nanga man, ma dan a mu gi mi sensi. Mi no law"/I can have a sexual relationship with a man, but then he must give me money. I am not crazy. When I am with a man, I do not tell him all my business, for example, that I am playing kasmoni. I always rented my own house; the contract was in my name. "No wan mannengre*[17] *sa kis' mi oso na tap' en nen"/Not one man-negro [man] will get my house to his name. Then he is going to send me away and start living there with another woman.*

Juliette made the impression of having been very self-possessed, ready and willing to be in control of her own life, not given to behavior that would have made her beholden to a man. Marriage clearly was not for her. To Nana and certainly to Juliette, it was more important to be able to count on a man to contribute money regularly than to be in a legally sanctioned union.

Concubinage is indicated with: *m'e lib' nanga man*/I am living with the man. When referring to a visiting relationship of a more than incidental sexual nature, women might say: *m'e or' nanga man*, literally "I am 'holding' with the man." By contrast, *mi de nanga man*/I am with the man, indicates a more steady relationship. Thus a woman might say "Mi de nanga Johnny, ma m 'e or' nanga Freddy"/I am with Johnny, but I have something sexual going on with Freddy. But it is significant that in the emic realm the nature and the modality of the relationship are referenced and not so much the location of the partners, that is, whether they are living together or in separate households. The cultural salience of the nature of the relationship is borne out by the fact that *mi masra*/my man pertains to a steady male partner both in a legally sanctioned marriage and in a steady concubinage arrangement. Thus, whereas in the eyes of most outside observers the "juridical" status of the couple—living with or without legal sanction—and the location of the couple have been paramount, the emic ordering puts emphasis on the quality, the steadyness, and the sexual character of the relationship without privileging joint location. There is a wide array of terms women use to refer to the man in their lives: (SD) *de vader van die kinderen*/the children's father, *mijn vriend*/my friend, *mijn vent* or (ST) *mi ke'l*/my guy. Of course, there are many idiosyncratic expressions circulating: (SD) *mi lollipop*/my lollypop, *mi sterappel*/my star apple. An older woman called her significantly older male partner *vader*/father.[18]

A special institutionalized form of the visiting relationship is that of the buitenvrouw, which, as we have seen in the cases of Maureen Fernandes and of Mis' Juliette, is ordered by unwritten rules. The form is historically so institutionalized that the women I worked with hardly found it worth mentioning, nor has it accrued hints of inappropriateness or undesirability. Not many women had strong negative feelings about it, although this does not go to say that it does not cause feelings of hurt to either the inside—or the outside woman. One should not flaunt being someone's buitenvrouw, but it is understood that in a situation where women have to hustle to survive, it is better to have a man who is already tied to another woman. He should be able contribute to the second household. The institution is further anchored by the preference to have a partner of the same ethnic group.[19] By the perceived lack of suitable working-class partners, Creole working-class women are more likely to begin an outside relationship with a well situated Creole man who is already "taken" than to consider a relationship with a working-class man, whether of Creole or of another ethnic background (Terborg 2002). The unwritten rules center around respect for the *oso vrouw* or *getrouwde vrouw*/inside woman. She should not suffer from her man being involved in another arrangement. The man should preferably not appear in public with his outside woman, who, moreover, should not be harrassing the inside woman in public. In addition, as we saw in Juliette's deportment toward her two "co-wives" it was part of her code of honor that the other women would not suffer financially from her having been favored as Dorus's binnenvrouw. She urged Dorus to give them the money that was due to them. An honorable buitenvrouw, also nowadays, even though she is searching for her life, walks a fine line between looking out for herself and her children and the interests of his getrouwde vrouw. The male partner should observe his responsibilities at home, whether sexual or financial, fully. He should not be withholding too much money and goods from his inside wife and family. In Maureen's case, we saw that when Tonko died at her house, it was understood that he should be at his inside woman's house and that Maureen did not attend the funeral service. In the central guiding principle of respect that is due to the inside woman, there are reminiscences of Juliette's values in my relationship with her. I withheld respect that was due to her, as the first or inside woman, when I met Delani. This, again, points to working-class women being embedded in a common culture that upholds the same values.

Historically, it was middle and upper-class men who were capable of keeping an outside working-class woman and their possible children. With the generally deteriorating economical conditions over the past decades, it has become impossible for the average man to keep an outside family, but those who have access to foreign currencies or who have a good hustle, e.g., driving a taxi or being involved in the drug trade, are still capable of doing so. We will see later on how Andrea dealt with becoming Roy's buitenvrouw. One of the reasons women consistently offered for their lack of interest in marriage was that the man would have his buitenvrouw anyway. Terborg, in her excellent study, points to a new phenomenon, the "modern buiten-vrouw" who is of middle or upper-class background and does not want a man for his financial contributions but for his emotional and sexual companionship. These relationships are often short-lived, and children are not part of the design (2002:234–236).

Looking for Mr. Right

In a series of conversations during the course of 1990—1991 Andrea kept me abreast of her desires and plans regarding a man in her life. This is a different story than we have encountered among older women. When she talked about her personal goals, Andrea was rather exceptional when she said that she aspired to marriage:

> *You know, every woman wants to be happy, wants the best for herself. I would like to be married, have somebody for myself, have more security. I know that not everybody gets so lucky to be married, but I would really, really like it. Financially it is important, of course. But I also abhor women who make children here, there, and everywhere. Sure, I would like to have one or two more children, but only when I am married.*

Suppose I would win the lotto, I would immediately buy a piece of land and build a house on it. If I had a good income, let's say sf 2,500 to 3,000 a month, I would not put up with any nonsense from a man. If I did not like his ways, he would have to go!

In this narrative there are two seemingly contradictory discourses between which Andrea commutes. On the one hand, there is marriage with its benefits of economic security, elevated status (the best for herself), and legitimacy for her future children. On the other hand, she desires an independent economical position that would insulate her from the hazards of having to put her eggs in the first basket. In Andrea the traditional working-class pattern of the undesirability of marriage and independence from a man and a dominant pattern of its desirability, which is also very palpable in society, are waged against each other. In some important respects the working-class configuration is an antithesis to middle-class ideology,[20] which, however, has forceful ways of making itself felt in the working class, e.g., through media images, popular U.S. and Dutch television shows, legal and financial regulations designed by the state that construct the nuclear family as the universal model, and by the content of Christian education. In the dominant middle-class gender ideology there is, for women at least, a rather strict prescription that combines love, marriage, monogamy, preference for one progenitor, who is also pater, with the male as breadwinner and head of household. Younger working-class women, like Andrea, have had more exposure to elements of the dominant ideology in the realm of gender relations and have "bought into" some of its ideals.

Ultimately, Andrea wants economic security, and, if marriage is the way to get it, she will get married. With the disastrous economic situation, which steadily deteriorated during the eighties and nineties, with a Structural Adjustment Program (1993–1996), the preferential relational pattern in the working class was put under increasing pressure. Andrea's desire to be married corresponds with findings by Terborg, who notes that marriage appears attractive to younger women who have not yet had a lot of experience. As they get older and they amass negative relational experiences, their rejection of marriage grows (2002:213).

Let's see what the characteristics are that Andrea's kind of man should have:

I first look whether he is going to be able to take care of me, does he have a regular income? I cannot stand it when a man is stingy. When a man who shows interest in me does not have any money, I do not even give him the time of day. He may love me, but I have to eat, too. "Kon sidon na mi tapu, dan a ne tya' mi sensi kon. Dan m'e law"/Comes and sits down "on top of me" and does not bring me my money. Then I must be crazy.

Besides that, he will have to love my child. And he must have plans for the future, must want to build himself up, so that I can stimulate him. Finally, we should trust each other, respect each other, and be able to talk together. He must be able to accept that I have an opinion, too, and be willing to listen to me. I really pay a lot of attention to that, whether he has respect for me.

This passage is a microcosm of values regarding relations with men. First, it is not a tall, handsome man with brown eyes that is at the top of Andrea's list, but a man who has regular and preferably more than average income which he should want to spend on her. This notion ties in with imagery that has often been used to represent spending patterns among Caribbean and North American blacks—clothes, jewelry, food, drinks, nice cars—the good things in life are valued. As with any stereotype, there is a kernel of truth hiding in the imagery. In the Caribbean, specifically, the pattern has been identified as *conspicuous consumption* (Hoetink 1958). Men themselves are well aware of this pattern, too. Hesdy Pocorni, a twenty-nine-year-old neighbor who does odd jobs, regularly complained to me that he was not able to find a woman, because most of the time he did not have any money. He liked to fantasize about what he would do if he did have money: he would take the imaginary girlfriend to a boutique and just stand by while she picked out all the clothes, shoes, and jewelry she fancied. Hesdy here makes implicit reference to a valued representation of successful manhood, which cuts across all ethnic groups and classes: the "big man syndrome," in which big spending, boasting, bragging, making promises one cannot possibly keep, all play parts.[21] Hesdy's unfavorable position in the relationship market illuminates a pattern with remarkable historical tenacity. As we will see later on, the fate of enslaved men who did not have a penny to their name was that they could not find a female companion.

To somebody with Andrea's ambition level, Hesdy is not a potential mate. She feels she has nothing to gain by beginning a relationship with somebody who is in the same or even a lower income bracket than herself. The widespread perception among women of an unequal sex ratio, i.e., that there are not enough men to go around, may say more about the eligibility profile for men than about men's factual scarcity. But the fact remains that men like Hesdy just do not qualify as a steady partner for many working-class women, upwardly mobile or not. Only incidentally, when he is capable of showing that "he can move decently," i.e., that he has money, will he have a chance to have a date. Several of Juliette's grandsons were in that same position, and though she would regularly feed them and give them some money, she made it no secret that she would not have given any of them the time of day as a potential partner.

Economically, a budding relationship is conceived in reciprocal fashion. Many working-class women do not conceive of love as an entity that can be bestowed, regardless of the economic position of the beneficiary. Frankly, they think it is foolishness to love somebody who does not have a "copper penny" to his name. Men are there to help you reach a more stable economic situation, and if they are not able or willing to do that, there is no point in beginning or continuing a relationship.

Another value that emerges from the passage above is respect. It is not only in her interactions with men that Andrea demanded respect, but it is present in her attitude to the world at large. In self-descriptions it was one of the first characteristics she mentioned about herself. She gave respect to others and also wanted it for herself. She hated the feeling of being belittled, of not being properly treated, of being underestimated. Her recent work history illustrates the importance she gave to respect. In the evenings and on weekends she had a job as a waitress at the poshest hotel-restaurant on an on-call basis. Her income there, based mainly on tips from foreign guests, was at least three times the amount she made at her regular job. One bad evening the manager reprimanded her in the presence of guests and colleagues. Andrea immediately quit the job. When I tried to persuade her to go back, she said it was too humiliating *fu go begi-begi*/to go begging. When I asked her what she would like people to say about her, she spoke about respect, having good manners, speaking in a decent way, not using curse words, not mistreating people, whether they were whores or thieves. It is a consistent red thread through her discourse. Respect may well be one of the core African values inscribed in the cultures of the black Diaspora (Wekker and Wekker 1991). Just as Aretha cries out for R-E-S-P-E-C-T, so does Andrea.

Last, in positioning herself vis-à-vis her prospective man, Andrea clearly envisioned a derivative situation: she would encourage him to attain his goals, he would have his opinion but should be willing to listen to her. There was minimal reciprocity or equality envisioned here. Even though Andrea's mother had taught her the central lesson that (grand-)mothers transmit to their female offspring, that "a diploma is a girl's first husband," the deference to "Mr. Right" which she apparently was prepared to give was impressive. This is a striking transformation of an earlier emotional, psychological, and financial economy between men and women, with older women roughly in their fifties and up. It is hard to draw a firm and fixed age line here, since there are younger women who have the "traditional," independent pattern, while there are a few older women who aspire to the "middle-class" configuration. But I am describing a tendency, which older Creole women themselves see also. While older women displayed characteristic independence in emotional and financial matters, some younger working-class women evidently have internalized more middle-class ideology as far as their inter-actions with men are concerned. Although these younger women may, as they grow older and accrue more experiences, revert back to the traditional pattern, as also happened with Andrea, still the different, globalized land-scape which surrounds younger women and transmits messages about the normativity and desirability of marriage and the position of housewife is a different environment than the one that their (grand-)mothers survived in. Internalizing these ideologies amounts to an appreciable loss of power for younger women. Nana, like Juliette, operated from a different set of prin-ciples when she explained:

> *I have always thought: whatever is your (i.e., a man's) right to do, is mine too. For example, I have this friend in Holland who is very fond of me: He calls me often and sometimes sends me money. When he comes here on vacation, I spend a lot of time with him. Humphrey cannot stand it, but I told him: Look, what this man is able to do for me, you can't do. Besides, you profit from him too by being around me.*

Women and In-laws

Having a relationship with a man also entails managing relationships with his family, notably his mother and sisters. Those relationships figure promi-nently and contribute substantially to the well-being or the demise of a rela-tionship. The Creole kinship system is formally bilateral, but much greater stress is placed on the relatives on mother's side, mother's mother and her siblings, especially mother's sisters, one's own siblings and the children of those siblings, especially of one's sisters, involving extensive obligations of mutual help, loyalty, and allegiance. Striking in women's stories was the fre-quency with which conflicts with in-laws, mainly the man's mother and sisters, were reported. In recounting the history of a relationship, one of the recurrent features women addressed was men's support or taking sides with their mother and sisters, in a way that left their partners unsupported. Complaints of in-laws centered on the wife of their son or brother being spendthrift, blowing away all the man's money on clothes, shoes, and jew-elry, his allowing her to spend money on her own family, and, on top of that, possibly, her *uitlopen*[22]/giving him horns.

Adult men are often closely involved with their families of origin, and many women complained about the roles their mothers-in-law play in alienating their son from his wife. When Gonda Burleson, a forty-six-year-old nurse's aide, broke up with Remy, she became engaged in a vicious communicative exchange with her mother-in-law, called *tya' boskopu* /carrying the message. In the next chapter we will encounter this institution again in a mati context, where it is deployed in a festive way at parties, exchanging odo. Of course, the exchange may also become quite sharp and bitter in a mati setting; but here it is worth noting that the institution is part of working-class women's culture, whether in a same-sex or cross-sex context. Older women are especially adept at tya' boskopu, which, in this case, is carried out through instructed intermediaries, who in flowery, metaphorical language, again often by means of odo, give the adversary a piece of the sender's mind. In Gonda's case, her mother-in-law let it be known that Gonda was only half a woman and that cockroaches had eaten her uterus since she had not been able to give her son children. Gonda's response was quick and equally poisonous:

> *I found a friend to send her a message back. She went and said: "Ai, Mis' Joosje, mi ab' wan boskopu g' i. Kalaka ben nyan Gonda muru, no? We, Gonda bi 'o sen wan snoep gi' i. Ef' i wan' ferter' pe a kalaka de, dan a sa pot' wan gowt' keti f' en drape"/Miss Joosje, I have a message for you. Cockroach ate Gonda's uterus, no? Well, Gonda was going to send you some sweets. If you want to tell where the cockroach is, then Gonda will put a gold chain there for him. The woman was seventy-something, she almost died of anger, but she had asked for it!*

This lethal message had several layers. First, the friendliness implied in Gonda's plan to send Mis' Joosje some sweets was only apparent. The underlying message was if there is something in Mis' Joosje's mouth, at least she could not use it in badmouthing Gonda. Second, there was the juxtaposition of "a sweet thing—a gold thing." Mis' Joosje would get some sweets, but the cockroach would get a gold chain. The relative worth of sweets versus gold reflects unfavorably on Mis' Joosje. Third, the cockroach was valued and rewarded because he made sure that Gonda did not get children from Mis' Joosje's son. Who would want children from the son of somebody who is worth less than a cockroach?

The open animosity in this exchange illustrates that the matrigroup, the group of consanguineal relatives on mother's side, cannot afford to let go easily of the contributions of one of its members, and thus a pattern that has been described for other matrifocal societies such as East London (Bott 1957; Young and Wilmott 1957) and urban working-class U.S. blacks (Stack 1974) is applicable here too. Women perceive that as wives they are expendable, but not as mothers and sisters (Sacks 1982); in other words, conjugal bonds are weaker than consanguineal ones. This is one of the persistently noted Africanisms in black diasporic family life (Sudarkasa 1996). Since a woman can expect that the odds are that her relationship with a man is likely to be short-lived, she acts in her best interest to "collect" as much as possible from him in the time that is given her.

The Tactics of Keeping a Man

> *Everyday you are eating rice, one day you are*
> *going to want to eat some saltmeat, too.*

Andrea looked down on women who *ser' den skin*/sell their bodies to come by money fast. There were emic degrees to this, however. Standing on Watermolenstraat, the "red light district" of Paramaribo, clearly was beyond the pale. But one of her colleagues regularly came into the office without a dime to buy food that day. She got on the phone to male acquaintances, made a lunch date, and, when she returned after lunch, waved sf 200 in the air. Andrea had a mixed attitude toward this behavior, which is variously called *stukwerk*/piecework or *piki man*/to pick men. While she said that she would never consider doing that herself, she also admired the woman for taking care of business so efficiently. At the office there is a constant flirting game going on between male and female colleagues. Andrea has problems with this:

> *I never accepted it when a man offered to buy me a roti or a portion of fried rice. The other girls have no qualms about it, but if I do not know you, I am not going to accept it. I will get my purse right away and ask you how much it costs. Nobody is going "to buy my yeye" with roti or fried rice!*

Andrea noted that "nobody is going to buy my yeye with a roti or fried rice." Here we are deep in Creole working-class culture, staunchly underpinned by notions from Winti, where "to buy someone's soul" literally alludes to the act of paying, often symbolically, only ten cents, for somebody whom you then own. It is often done with children who are sickly; the mother will offer the child for ten cents to an acquaintance or a relative who is "in the culture," too, thereby averting the "evil gaze" that has made the child sick. Lovers, both in a male-female context and in an all-female context, may buy each other, too, one to spiritually protect the other. "Buying someone" in this sense is a cherished and profound gesture in the culture. Beside the positive

connotation, "buying someone" can also be done in a negative context, sub-
jugating a person, *broko sma yeye*/breaking someone's will, making someone
totally dependent for the price of a roti or a portion of fried rice. Surely,
Andrea was saying, she was worth more than that!

What had become acceptable to Andrea in the then current circumstances
was to find a man who would support her in return for which she would
have sex with him. The sex would be embedded in an ongoing relationship;
she would become his buitenvrouw. Roy Hemelrijk was living with an other
woman with whom he had two children. During the day he worked at a low-
management level at a ministry; at night he drove a taxi. She described the
tactics of what to do and what *not* to do to keep him:

> *What you do not do is ask him, hey, listen, what is the story here: you have
> a wife and two children, what do you want with me? You also do not tell him
> too much about your story. I pamper him a little bit, I cook something special
> that he likes, sowt' meti nanga bitawiri/salt meat with bitterleaf.*[23] *I also fuss
> over him. I have to admit, I am dissembling a bit, because I do not care that
> much for him. I am not sure that I am going to love him; he wants to look a
> little bit like a bonkoro/very light-skinned Creole.*[24] *I don't feel an obligation
> to sleep with him now: he came running after me, it was not the other way
> around. So I never sit next to him on the couch and I do not let him touch me.
> I tell him: "Don't touch me. I'll decide when it is the time for that and you
> have to wait patiently." He cannot expect to profit from me, from one day to
> the next. I think that I can stall for two to three months, but one day I am
> going to have to give in.*

The expression that Andrea used to sum up Roy's objective in the enterprise (Surinamese Dutch), *van mij profiteren*/to profit from me, is telling.
It is a euphemism for having sex with her, and it showed the transactional
aspect of the affair as Andrea experienced it. The foundations were being
laid for a more serious, long-term relationship as Roy had asked Andrea to
be honest with him and not to see other men in the evenings when he was
not around. She had assured him that she was not going to see anybody else.
She had also announced that she was not a cheap woman, clarifying that her
last boyfriend gave her sf 500 a month and that she would be expecting at
least that amount from Roy. She did ask him at some point why he wanted
another woman on the side, and he answered that he had the income to
take care of two women. This was a satisfactory answer to Andrea and she
commented to me that he had said a lot with it. When I did not understand
what was implied, she explained that in the future, if all things went well, he
would have to give her the same amount of money as he was giving Norine,

his *binnenvrouw*. If Norine got sf 1000 Andrea would expect as much or sf 750 at the least.

There is a wide array of expressions that bespeak the elaborate art of feeling and displaying sexual interest in someone and the concomitant responses (Wekker 1992b). Andrea's behaviors toward Roy were an interesting mixture of teasing him, showing him discontent over what he brought her, aggravating him, "harrassing" him, giving him good loving, all of it embedded in a sweet sauce of making him feel special. In Sranan Tongo this is referred to as *kot' pangi gi wan sma*/to go out of your way for someone, treating someone as really special or *mek' meki gi wan sma*/to spoil, pamper someone.[25]

Returning to the pertinent question raised by Elliston (1995), "what is to count as sex?" in different cultural settings, I want to note the elaborate set of expressions in Sranan Tongo that fill in the landscape of passion for another person, irrespective of her or his sex. Like other creoles, Sranan Tongo makes use of verbs rather than of nouns in structuring this interpersonal domain, lending it an aura of activity. These expressions include *kor' kori wan sma*/to charm someone, take someone in; *prey nanga wan sma*, to play with, to caress someone; *suku wan sma*, to have one's eye on, to try to seduce someone; *fir' switi gi wan sma*, to be in love with someone; *tyallans wan sma*, seriously seduce someone; *tya' sma ede gwe*, to take someone's "breath," literally head, away; *go gi wan sma*, to go for someone; *pot wan sma volledig*, satisfy someone completely. Let's see what behavior Andrea was referring to:

> It is not good to show a man that you are really content, you have to keep him dangling a little bit. When he just gives me sf 75, I will tell him: "I am not going to take it, it's peanuts." M' e tanter' en strak! I am really tormenting him! This past month, he gave me close to sf 650, but he does not give it all at one time, but in smaller sums. So I always find a chance to tell him: "You are only giving me this?" I do not show him how glad I am. He should not think that I am content with just any old amount.
>
> But from the way I act toward him, he should know that I like him. I do not love him, but I do not like to say that out loud, because I am afraid God is going to punish me for it. And even if I did love him, I would never tell him, because a man should not have that kind of security. So I caress him, I am talking sweet talk with him, I pamper him. When I am bringing him a glass of milk, I will say: "Gudu/Sweetie, drink this. You are spending in two places now, so you need to keep up your strength.

In the latter example, involving the glass of milk, there was a clear double entendre intended; Roy's spending in two places referred to his spending money, but also to his having sex with two women. This in itself was a matter that could not be dealt with spontaneously as it came up. Each participant had private sources of worry in this domain. Andrea did not want her daughter and brothers in the house when she was having sex, which practically meant that she was only available during certain times of the weekend when she could bring Alexandra to her sister. Roy did not want his woman to have suspicions that he might be less forthcoming toward her, so he told Andrea in so many words that he could only be available to her when he had taken care of business at home. Although Andrea protested against her having to take "second quality," "waste," all the time, she admitted to me that Roy really had a point. The best policy for her was to be accommodating. Her protests fit within the discourse that was socially desirable at that point. She admitted that she had to play at being jealous. The friendly, teasing "harrassment" of Roy and the feigning of jealousy stood out as markers in the emotional atmosphere that Andrea was creating. When Roy had to go to Trinidad for a week in the context of his work at the ministry, he allegedly tried to call her several times, but—not surprisingly in view of the state of telecommunications in the region—did not succeed. After he returned, Andrea gave him a hard time, claiming that he had not gone away at all but had been running around with another woman. In private she explained to me that she believed him, but she just did not want to make it too easy on him.

This pattern seems fairly general for what takes place in working-class relationships, whether the object of love is male or female. One does not deny the accusations much less become argumentative. Jealousy is expressed and taken as a measure of commitment and as such is often welcomed. The typical reaction to an expression of jealousy, as I watched Roy and others display on several occasions, was to smile shyly, enigmatically, pleasantly. Andrea's offstage comments illuminated her position:

> *It should not be so that he can have sex with me every time he wants it. A no mu kon rampeneer mi skin ala neti /He should not come and mess my body, me, up every night. One of the things I hate most is when a man is misusing a woman; he wants to have sex with her all the time, knowing he supports her. It gives me a feeling of hate, when I do not have any choice but to spread my legs.*

Kamra Prikti / Chamber Obligations

In real terms Andrea really was not too unhappy about the arrangement in which Roy was not "messing up her body" every night. Another fac-

tor that Andrea also took into account was that she was not taking care
of Roy: she did not do his washing, ironing, nor major cooking, meaning
that she might have to give him a little more in the sexual domain than she
might otherwise. Implicitly here we have again come into the domain of
kamerplichten/"chamber obligations."[26] By this concept women indicated
the sexual obligations a woman has toward her partner, be the partner male
or female, in return for the goods, services, or care that that person bestows.
The historical literature shows that obligations between men and women are
historically anchored. During slavery men brought in fish, hunted for meat,
and chopped wood, while women had to cook and wash. If one of the partners was not able to meet her or his sexual obligations, for instance because
she or he had become too old, it was considered a valid reason by both partners to end the relationship (Everaert 1999).

Every working-class woman I asked knew what kamra prikti meant
and had ideas and standards of fairness associated with it. Although some
women indicated that they really detested the implication of kamra prikti,
practically everyone accepted the basic premise of the concept: "ef' i tek' a
sensi, dan i ab' verplichting, dan na wan wroko"/when you take the money,
then you have obligations. It is tantamount to work.

Women thought that the extent to which one has to give sexual favors is
subject to unwritten rules. What is fair depends on the context of the relationship. If one is doing his laundry, shopping, and cooking for him, then one
has fewer sexual obligations than when there is a servant in the house to take
care of the daily drudgery. This would not be the case in many working-class
households. Also, when you are bringing in money yourself, which all the
women I talked with did by their labor, one has fewer obligations than would
be the case if the man were the sole breadwinner. In view of the arc of possible
gender arrangements between men and women, we should not underestimate
the personal factor in this obligatory exchange. Despite the sometimes striking
dominance that women had in their relationships with men, in the end even
someone like Juliette knew the rules by which she had to play. Several women
said they did not like the obligatory character: *a no musu mi musu*/it is not that
I must, but the other side of the coin is that the partner is going to stop giving
you money at some point, or might *uitlopen voor je*/run off to another, with the
same result in the end. The moment a partner stops giving money is generally
taken as a symbolic announcement that the relationship is in trouble and that,
if no measures are taken, the end might be in sight. From a woman's standpoint
that same statement is made by refusing to cook, wash his clothes, or otherwise
take care of her man. Refusal to cook is especially fraught with meaning.

In general, women who are involved with men talked about sex in a quid
pro quo fashion: when he gives you money, you give him sex. Yet while
women construct themselves and are constructed by men as sexual beings,

sexuality is not a domain that can be kept apart from the harsh economic realities. Sex is "what men want" and one of the few strong negotiating bases that women can command. Sex, then, often becomes a means to an end; there is little room for women to experience sex as pleasurable.

Experiences with Sex

It was not always easy to talk about sex with women who are only operating in the cross-sex market. Often they, and I in turn, were ill at ease about it, groping for words, giggling nervously. For many, it was the first time they talked with another woman about sex. Others liked it and had no problems sharing their experiences. These experiences run the gamut from very pleasant to abominable. Witness Andrea's account:

> Roy is good. Some men really do not know how to sex you. They just want to get on top and that is it. First, a man has to freri yu[27]/kiss and pet you, before a'e nai yu/he screws you. I do not come every time, sometimes when I do not really feel like it, I just pretend I have come.
>
> What I basically like about sex, is the way he looks at me, so intently, the way he kisses, the way he talks to me, his tollie/penis, and the movements he makes. I really liked having sex with Alexandra's father, because while he was inside me, he would also play with my poentje[28]/pussy, with his hands. It drove me wild. Roy does not do that, and I do not ask him to. The same with nyan blik, literally, "to eat tincan," oral sex. I do not ask him, because when he does it I am going to have to do it to him too. And I do not want that, because a e saka yu yeye/it lowers your "soul." If he wants to do it to me, it is his business, I will not stop him.

A noteworthy pattern that emerged from women's accounts was that an appreciable number of women had a preference for being with a significantly older man. Different reasons were given for this pattern. An older man is likely to be more stable financially. Preferably he is a widower, but even more important, he is somebody who has a pension in foreign currency. It is typically a male prerogative in the gender-segmented dual labor market, as we saw in chapter 2, to have access to foreign currencies. But there are other reasons why older men are sought. Cynthia Leeflang (thirty-nine), a cleaning woman, put it this way:

> Mang!! Man!! I am really tired of men my own age. The man I had my three children with, and with whom I had been since I was seventeen years old,

walked out on me and started with one of my best friends. You cannot trust any man. If I start another relationship, it will have to be an older man. He has made his children already and has proven that he can. May be he does not feel like sex so much anymore or he has broko neki, literally, "broken neck," suffers from impotence, which suits me fine, too. Then he won't pester me too much, either.

But there are also women for whom sexual pleasure comes first. Nana is one of them. Embedded in a cultural context, sex was important to her; she considered it necessary for her physical and mental well-being. The money a man brought her was important but secondary to her pleasure, which was evident from her words:

You are not only on earth to work: "down there" also has to find something. "Te m'e taigi fa m' e lob' a sani! M'e taigi krin, mi gudu, m'e lob' a lekker ding. A bun gi a insey en a switi ooktu. Te y' e du en so, a tra manten f 'en, a er' skin fir' lekti so, a er' ede fir' lekti so, ala san' krin so. Kan de mi baka broko, ma dat' n'e bis' mi. M' e prakser' nomo: Oten m'e sa fen' so wan switi baka?"/ When I tell you how I love that thing! I am telling you honestly, my sugar, I love that sweet thing. It is good for your insides and it is sweet, too. When you are doing it, your body feels so light, the next morning, your whole head feels light, everything is clean. Maybe my back is hurting me, but that does not bother me. I am only thinking: when am I going to find such a sweet thing again?

Nana had some good experiences with men and knew that when a man is sexually *een slapperdje*/whimpy, one had to build him up. The recipe: strong soup, broth of beef, milk, raw eggs with cognac. This would do wonders for him. There are a great deal of *oso dresi*/home medicines to help in this case. At certain strategic places in town, on the markets but also at the office of the foreign police, where Dutch Surinamese "tourists" had to go shortly after their arrival in Suriname, there are booths with people selling bottles with concoctions to make people, men and women, perform better sexually. Having had so many men in her life, Nana knew the difference between a good lover and a lousy one, but she would never tell a man what he should do. Many women do not find it commensurate with their gender role to indicate their own pleasures to a man.

The opinions among women were divided as to whether sex with men is culturally prescribed. A group of women thought that sex is good and necessary for one's physical and mental well-being, that the "insides" of a woman ask for "that thing" and that the long absence of sex with a man will result in disease, ailments, and madness (Lenders and van der Roer 1983). But others found this nonsense. Renate Druiventak, a fifty-four-year-old pig farmer, laughed uproariously about that idea.

Few women with whom I talked could be called really "enthusiastic" about sex with men. Sometimes it took considerable probing to find out more about what women felt or thought on the subject. Mildred Jozefzoon, a forty-three-year-old hairdresser, told me about her relationship. She had never lived with her man, the father of three of her four children, because he lived with another woman. The visiting arrangement they had had been going on for fifteen years, interrupted by Mildred's stay in the Netherlands for four years. Johnny had a Dutch army pension and came to see her every week:

> Mostly he comes around 11.30 A.M. and has to be out of my house by 1.00 P.M. He wants it to be quick-quick. The way I feel about it is that somebody has come to take something away from me and then he leaves. I feel misused, taken in, even though he gives me the money. I get sf 100 or 125 from him a week.
>
> It goes like this: every week he pretends that he is warm. He takes off his shirt and his trousers, lies down on my bed. Then he wants me to come lie down beside him. Sometimes I sabotage the whole business by being agonizingly slow in taking off my clothes. Then we can't do it, because he does not have enough time. Sometimes I say that I do not feel like it. Then he says: I will make you feel like it. What can I do? He wants it so often and I need the money.
>
> Then afterward, he asks me to pour him a glass of soda pop in the kitchen. Then he puts down the money. All the time, he keeps saying in how much of a hurry he is, he looks at his watch, he has to go. The thing that I can't bear is that he always wants to leave right away. As a woman, you still would like to lie down a bit and stuff.

I found it impossible to construe any kind of pleasure out of this account. Since Mildred had not had a lot of other sexual experience—getting pregnant at seventeen, the first time she had sex, and the relationship did not develop—she knew that sex was not pleasant to her. She did not know, however, how to make it different. One of the most memorable conversations between us was our conversation about the role of sex in building a relationship and the experience of orgasm.

Another woman, Lygia Nelom, a factory worker who was thirty years old, told an even more distressing story. Living from age eighteen with the father of her three children, her personal life had been on a downhill course for years. Marcel Muringe, her man, had become involved in drug use and trade. He did not bring any money into the household anymore and was exceedingly jealous and violent. Though Lygia tried to leave him several times, she was not successful at this because he always was able to locate her and the children again. The police had been seriously defective, because their typical reaction had been to say "Oh, little lady, in every household the husband will have to assert his position sometimes."[29] Lygia's sexual life consisted, in her own words, of the following:

> *I try to go to bed after he has left the house at night, to hang out with his bud-*
> *dies. But when he comes home at four or five in the morning he always wants*
> *to have sex. I have to get up at six to go to work and he does not do anything*
> *all day but sleep. He just basically uses me—I do not feel anything. I want to*
> *get it over with so I can sleep another hour. He is not interested at all in what*
> *I feel or think. I just lie there, thinking: Please, let him come soon and hope-*
> *fully he will not want to do it twice tonight. Sometimes we fight, but I am*
> *tired of that too. The only way out of my situation is to leave for Holland. I*
> *am working on it.*[30]

It was somewhat paradoxical that when Mildred and Lygia were in merry, mixed-sex company they would follow up on and laugh heartily at sexually laden discourse. Their public personae were distinctly different from those they projected in private. The public impression given was that sex with men was an activity that was thoroughly enjoyed and known. Of course, there are many instances where people will present a different public front than the one that is private.

I have understood this discrepancy between public and private in the sexual domain as the locus of power in determining the content of cross-sex sexual discourse and behavior lying with men. Women who are only involved with men will, unlike mati, seldom discuss sexual activities, thus expanding on their sexual knowledge. Unless women in this category are really good friends, which seems preciously rare in itself, sex is a nontopic. Women with opposite-sex sexual preferences do not see each other easily as trustworthy. They are operating in an ostensible buyer's market, where desirable men are scarce and their own position is perceived as relatively weak. They tend to see each other as competitors. For a number of these women, too, sex is not a topic to be discussed. In aspiring toward upward mobility, respectability demands silence in matters of sex. Whereas the baseline for all working-class women is more or less the same, namely that sex education in the home is virtually nonexistent, mati work themselves out of that situation by actively exchanging sexual knowledge. This is a situation, where there is a dominant public discourse about sexual realities, namely, that of males. The many kaseko songs with negative sexual imagery constructing women and the many allusions to sex in the public arena attest to this discourse. Then there is another, embryonic discourse that remains mostly cloaked but that could potentially be challenging to the public discourse. The latter is mostly engaged in by females. The former discourse is hegemonic. Since women, either individually or collectively, do not perceive it to be in their interest to challenge men on their abominable sexual behaviors, men are allowed to get away with the habits described in Mildred's and Lygia's accounts.

Furthermore, under the pressing economical conditions, a downhill course having been set in 1980 when the military took over, the negotiating space of women in their relationships with their male partners has declined even more. As the economic situation got grimmer, women saw their chances of eking out a livelihood by working "decent" jobs become increasingly smaller. Older women I have interviewed, those in their fifties and over, said that even though they had their kamra prikti, a man should not make it *tumsi beestachtig*/too animal-like, and they were well aware of their rights and their alternatives.

Many younger women find the independent position of the older generation unattainable and untenable. First, there is the perception that there are three times as many women as men, so that once one has a man one is unlikely to ignore what it takes to keep him. Second, within a sharply gendered division of labor, men make more money for the same labor, as we saw in chapter 2. The position of women who overwhelmingly have to seek employment in the informal sector and in the lowest echelons of the bureaucracy is consistently worse than that of men. Third, it is women who carry the burden of keeping their families' heads above water, while men are often dodging their financial responsibilities. Thus, men, earning more and having fewer responsibilities, end up with more free-floating spending capital. Fourth, whereas it is mainly younger women who have dependent children and are thus most in need of additional cash, it is also precisely this group that is more exposed to middle-class values which, to the extent that they stress traditional "feminine qualities," like dependency and passivity, are disadvantaged. The gap experienced by this group of women between their own reality and the "good life" was thus more acute than that for older generations, who already have older children, some of whom might be in the Netherlands, able to support their mothers.

Notions Around Oral Sex

The "pleasure and danger" attached to oral sex, which is operative both in a same-sex and in an opposite-sex domain, still needs to be excavated. While

Andrea knew very well what felt good to her in having sex with a man, she did not get all of it with Roy and she was reluctant to ask for it. Asking him to play with her clitoris was embarrassing to her. Oral sex, on the other hand, was altogether of another nature. It involved a debt she did not want to repay because it would lower her "soul." This is a deeply cultural notion, which again spans the gamut of male-female and female-female sexual interaction. The oldest women, in their seventies and eighties, told me that oral sex is culturally unclean, polluting, so powerful that it is fraught with ritual danger. This does not go to say, of course, that people actually refrain from it. Oral sex between two partners, for example, formed part of a ritual, *sjweri*/oath, in which they promised sexual faith to each other. If one of them broke the oath, people believed that misfortune, disease, or even death would ensue. When two people mutually and willingly engage in oral sex, there is no problem of sanctions of the Gods involved. My impression is that most people will not engage in it lightheartedly or casually.

When only one person does it to the other, it carries ritual danger and psychologically and morally it means that that person has lowered her or his yeye before the other. As we saw in the chapter on Winti, notions of reciprocity characterize the relationships between Gods and humans as well as those between humans. To engage in an intimate sexual practice that is not returned by the other person is damaging to the "soul." It is interesting to note, first, that one of the most serious and deadly dismissals of a person, man or woman, occurs when it is said: *A' e nyan blik*/(s)he engages in oral sex. It is tantamount to pointing to a case of entirely spoiled identity (Goffman 1963). Even when the oral sex was mutual, an agressor will maintain that it was only a one-sided affair. Again, Paramaribo being as small as it is and quarrels, for effect, preferably being brought out in the open, "script-like" stories of this nature abound. Obviously, it is a way for a woman to get revenge, when a man has left her, to yell at him, when he is standing "under the market" amidst his buddies on a Saturday *brekten*/around noon, when everybody is up and about: "Jouw zaagsel, nownow de fa i n' e sab' mi moro, ma di yu ben nyan a blik f' mi ... "/You sawdust, now you don't know me anymore, but when you were eating me out ... Instantly, the man is reduced to being *een vriendje,* literally, "a little friend," a wimp.

Second, and by no means peculiar to Suriname's Afro-Surinamese alone, is the negative terminology and conceptualization attached to female sexuality and sex organs. *Nyan blik* refers exclusively to the eating of the female parts.[31] Indeed, one only has to listen randomly to a small sample of kaseko texts to have the negative imagery fully impressed upon one's consciousness. Recall the text of the kaseko mentioned earlier in this chapter, "Didon Fisi," where a parallel between female sex organs and fish was drawn. Women themselves also use expressions like nyan blik, which could be interpreted as the claiming of negative terminology to reappropriate the female body and its functions. But there are more arguments to support the contention that certainly in the group of women who mainly or exclusively engage in sex with men there has been an appropriation of male values, ideas, and orientations by women. Witness what Andrea has to say in this respect:

> I never have sex during and after my period. At least a week has to pass before I want to do it again. It is not clean, you know? It might make a man sick.
>
> Roy feels that he should be the one to indicate that he is interested in intercourse. When he gets home at midnight, Norine does not want sex 90 percent of the time. To me, that means she is seeking the troubles she is in now. She should not neglect her man so, it is asking for him to "walk out" on her. Married women, or women who are in a steady relationship with a man, get too confident. It is really their own fault that the men run around. He likes it with me, he never has to beg me for it. What can I do? The only thing I have to give him is that.
>
> You know what else he told me? This is kind of embarrassing, but I am also tickled to death by it. He told me that the way I can sex him, Norine can't, because I am so tight down there. It made me think: "Aaai, everyday you are eating rice, one day you are going to want to eat some saltmeat, too."

It is disturbing that however well Andrea in general is able to oversee her own situation and look after her own interests, there is a gap in the more narrow sexual domain. The above passage reads like a study in displaced subjectivity. Her pleasure in sex seems less direct and abundant, more instrumental than that of some of the women we will encounter in the next chapter. One of my fundamental contentions is that working-class women who mainly operate in the cross-sex domain have a less clearly defined picture of what their pleasures are, and what to do to get them, than women who are active also in female-female dyads. The latter group has extensive sexual knowledge, skills, terminology, and experience as to what feels good and what does not, and in general they convey a more definite sense of how fun sex is to them in itself rather than merely as an instrument for economic security. Put differently, those who are furthest removed from female "respectability," according to the dominant gender regime, in terms of their class status and sexual behavior get the largest share of pleasure.

This insight ties in to longstanding debates in the social sciences on the nature of the consciousness of oppressed groups: working class versus middle and upper class, people of color versus whites, women versus men (duBois

1982 [1903]; Leavitt, Sykes, and Weatherford 1975; Bookman and Morgen 1988; Martin 1987; Ladner 1971 Gwaltney 1980; Hill Collins 1990). Roughly two positions have been taken in these debates: as one goes down the hierarchy of class, race, and gender, the possibility of an alternative consciousness or resistance to the status quo is understood by some to diminish, by others to increase. To the triad of class, race, and gender I would like to introduce a fourth variable, sexual behavior, which I contend heightens alternative consciousness in its "unruly, unrespectable" version. Mati know how to perform in the cross-sex sexual domain, and while they, too, might not get there what they would like and will likely be as hesitant as other women to ask for it, they have another domain for sexual activity in which they do experience abundant pleasure. This resulted, as we already saw in Juliette's narrative, in a sharp consciousness of the differential pleasures that sex with men and with women brings them. Other mati, belonging to different age categories, exhibited the same sensibilities. This heightened knowledge about sex has not led to collective efforts on the part of mati, or other women, to have a public conversation with men about sexual pleasure. Within the dominant gender regime, men, to a large extent, own the public sphere, and it is their voices that are represented in the dominant discourse, kaseko music, and other cultural artifacts. In women's own expressive media, however, e.g., in odo and lobi singi/the songs women sing for other women, we can hear their own voices, their outlook on the world and hardly veiled criticism of the sexual standards held up as normative. In women's insistence on their inherent value, no matter how many relationships they may have had, in their dismissal of a dominant understanding that considers women who are sexually active as *pori*/"spoiled," odo project statements "in defense of themselves."

Attitudes Toward Mati

Andrea, like every other working-class person, was fully aware of the mati option but strictly rejected it. In effect, she had been propositioned several times by women, but so far she has not taken that route:

Of course, I know mati. It seems like a craze, these days. Everyone is getting into it, out of curiosity or because they are disappointed in men. It starts out at the Winti Prey, there they meet each other and learn how to "rub." Several women were after me, den ben suku mi strak/they were really into me. I am not saying that I will never do it, but from what I hear they are really into nyan blik/eating each other and rubbing. I frankly think it is filthy. And then these ladies are incredibly jealous. Roy also told me not to do it, because it does not look nice for a woman to do that. If I would do it with a woman, she would have to take care of me financially, twice as well as a man would. "A sma dati ab' fu fur' mi anu nanga gowtu, m'e taig'i!"/She is going to have to fill my hands with gold, I am telling you! I would never do it with a poor, dark-skinned woman like myself. "A sma dati e mus' fu pot' mi"/That woman would really have to satisfy me sexually. But imagine the talk! If you have that stain to your name, not even bleach is going to wash it away.

Illustrated here are some of the negative feelings that surround the institution of the mati work, prevalent among those who aspire or are heirs to middle-class lifestyles and value patterns. Noteworthy in Andrea's words is that the same intimate relation between sex and money characteristic of male-female associations features in her evaluation of the mati work. The majority of women with whom I worked did not share her views. When I asked Nana about mati work, she said:

Alasma ab' den lobi/Everyone has their love. It would be vrijpostig/insolent to say what others should do or should not do. I myself never did it, but when I go to Winti Prey I love to sit with mati and have a good time. I love the teasing that goes on. My aunt and her mati have been together for more than thirty years.

Most other women I talked with who relate sexually to men shared Nana's views.

Historical Attitudes Toward Relational Arrangements with Men

Who bedded and wedded with whom in the colonies of France, England, Holland and Iberia was never left to chance.

STOLER 2002

The descriptions above, offered by Creole working-class women at the end of the twentieth century about their cross-sex relational arrangements, showed the variety and the distribution of patterns in the working class. Legal marriage clearly was not the preferred modality; women generally preferred arrangements in which they had more freedom, either living in concubinage or in a visiting relationship. In their own terms they stressed the quality of the relationship, not its legal status or the locality of their partners, which have been such obsessive anchoring points for academic observers. According to most current views, these patterns have shown remarkable continuity and tenacity over time. In addition, even though few in-depth, qualitative studies comparing middle- and working-class relational patterns have been undertaken in Suriname or in other parts of the Caribbean, the main position currently is that "one finds unions of all types among all classes and racial groups (though the incidence of occurrence certainly varies)" (Smith 1996:47; Barrow 1996; Terborg 2002). I agree with this position and the understanding that underlies it: since the dual marriage system was operative in Suriname it conjugated relational arrangements among the entire population along racial, gendered, and class lines and produced an ideology and practices that share main features across different layers and segments of society. Still, it would be premature to conclude that middle- and working-class configurations are entirely overlapping and interchangeable and that the cultural archives fueling attitudes and values in each class setting contain the same material. We are a far way off from having a full grasp of the dynamics that were and are operative within each class as well as in society as a whole. I am working on the assumption that the working class has historically been more insulated from hegemonic norms and values and that women especially have acted as important conservators of the West African archive. My emphasis in the argument that follows will be on historical data concerning working-class relational patterns.

In order to bring more clarity to the question I posed at the beginning of this chapter, that is, which West African grammatical principles were operative in the cross-sex relational domain, it is necessary to revisit the debates about family forms and kinship in the Caribbean. Without wanting to rehearse the extensive debates, which started in the 1930s, in much detail, in my—simplifying—reading three phases can be distinguished. In the first phase, the debate centered on the origins of Caribbean families: were they characterized by African "retentions," as Herskovits (1941) maintained, or had the cultural heritage of the enslaved been so thoroughly destroyed that, as E. Franklin Frazier (1939) and later Orlando Patterson (1967) argued, family forms had to be remade from "scratch," resulting in largely dysfunctional, unstable units (cf. Moynihan 1965). Deemed paramount in family dysfunction was the position of the men/fathers who, because of their precarious economical positions, could not take their rightful place as heads of household, which again was complemented by the too powerful position of women matriarchs. These "grand theories" stayed away from questions concerning the lived realities of the enslaved, hardly granting them the position of agents. Family was often unproblematically and universally understood as a conjugal pair with children living together under one roof, thus defining Caribbean forms, from the start, out of the range of normality. In the second phase, when the historical debate could not be resolved conclusively, the emphasis shifted to the question of how contemporary families functioned in society. Mainstream anthropologists and sociologists who studied famil-ial and mating patterns believed that these patterns mimicked middle-class value systems; that is, couples either preferred marriage (Wilson 1973) or, in view of the impossibility of attaining those values, they stretched their values to emulate those of middle-class families (Rodman 1963). The latter would mean, for instance, that a couple's long term cohabiting arrangement would count as marriage for them. In these models we do find some atten-tion for the lived experiences of men and women, with women often being the ones who strive for upward mobility and willing to take over normative values in the familial and relational domain. In Wilson's model, for instance, it was working-class women who, historically through their closer ties to the planter class and the Catholic Church, supposedly fully subscribed to middle-class values in the relational sphere, i.e., preferring marriage. Femi-nist researchers have convincingly shown that women, too, partake in the "reputation" culture in which supposedly men alone were embedded (Bes-son 1993; Wekker 1994). In the third phase we see that a variety of new and old perspectives are engaged, with in general a renewed interest in his-torical formations; Herskovits's position has been reformulated along more dynamic lines (Mintz and Price 1992 [1976]); of critical importance, gender perspectives have been introduced (Bush 1990; Shepherd, Brereton, and Bai-ley 1995; Beckles 1989; Barrow 1996; Terborg 2002) and a perspective that does not rigidly binarize class experiences in the familial domain is now more broadly accepted. Along methodological lines, people themselves are asked for their ideas about relationships instead of yesterday's large-scale household surveys, which were largely informed by etic perceptions of fam-ily (Barrow 1996).

The legacy of these different debates is that they have left behind a num-ber of persistent biases: an ethnocentric, a gender, and a heteronormative bias are among the noteworthy features. The research has contributed to the labeling of families, which diverge from the traditionally gendered roles of the Euro-American family, as deviant. The persistent usage of terms like male absence/marginality and the characterization of matrifocal households as lack and pathology rather than as productive social relations point to a gender bias. The gendered sexual images that can be culled from the pro-lific literature on matrifocality position men as sexually hyperactive high performers, while women are positioned as waiting around passively for the hunter to bestow his sexual favors upon them (Wekker 1999). In addition, a heteronormative bias has been operative in kinship studies (Blackwood 2005). This latter bias is evident in the unquestioned assumption that it is heterosexual relations that form the basis of families and domestic units. The study of heterosexual relations has consistently been privileged over other kinds of relationships, e.g., the relationships between women, as (grand-)mothers, sisters, neighbors, mati, and meti. Same-gendered sexual arrangements have not been considered to be an integral part of the way that Surinamese or Caribbean kinship systems operate.

Instead of this gender-biased, heteronormative, hierarchical structure, I want to propose that Afro-Surinamese working-class culture in the relational domain can best be understood as a combination of the templates for relational behavior that were laid down by the dual marriage structure in the formative years of the colony (Smith 1996)[32] and "West African grammatical principles" (Mintz and Price 1992 [1976]), which endowed women with full (sexual) subjecthood.[33] Smith stresses that in order to understand Caribbean societies one needs to understand the family and mating patterns and relate them to other factors in contemporary social systems as well as to the cultural traditions of the people concerned. Let's look from such a perspective at Creole relational patterns during the Dutch plantation colony, which was formed in Suriname in 1667.

Surinamese society was, from the beginning, characterized by sharp stratifications in which race, gender, and class were the main parameters.[34] Gender-specific sexual sanctions and prohibitions not only demarcated positions of power but prescribed the personal and public boundaries of race (cf. Stoler 2002). My description of Surinamese colonial society starts with the sexual configuration that took shape in the European segment of society, tying in, from the start, the female slave component. After an early settlement period during which white families came to Suriname, until about 1775, mostly single men settled in later centuries. The *animus revertendi*, the spirit to return to Europe, after having amassed riches, was strong among the colonists. They were Dutch, but other European men, German, British, French, and Portuguese, unaccompanied by a white wife (*misi*), came too. In the colony they took a Creole housekeeper/concubine (*sisi*). This institution of concubinage, so-called Surinamese marriage, entailed sexual access to a black or Creole woman, enslaved or free, as well as demands on her housekeeping labor. After 1775 it was the most frequent relationship in the white community and was quite openly lived during the nineteenth century (van Lier 1977 [1949]).[35] As late as between 1850 and 1900 at least three Dutch governors openly lived with a colored concubine. The same was true for clergymen. The open concubinage of upper-class men with lower middle-class colored women, gradually became less accepted in Dutch circles after 1900 and as a result became more secretive in character. The Surinamese Jewish population and elite Creole families gradually also became part of this upper class. Many of these men, mainly civil servants, conformed to the same pattern: they had one official family, formed with a wife from their own ethnic group and, in addition, they had a "Surinamese marriage." Ultimately, one might argue, in much the same way as Stoler has in the case of the Dutch East Indies, that sexual domination was the substance of imperial policy.

Raymond Smith refers to this asymmetrical system as the dual marriage system, and he argues convincingly that this Creole kinship structure was established in the formative stage of West Indian society. The operative rule was everywhere the same: men married status equals but had nonlegal unions with status inferiors. One of Smith's illuminating insights is that

> (the dual marriage system) wove a complex tapestry of genetic and social relations among the various segments of Creole society. Once established … it was capable of ordering conjugal relations outside the simple black-white conjunction; it could generate the forms of sexual and conjugal behavior appropriate to equals and unequals of all kinds.… . The West Indian system of kinship and marriage was an extension in cultural logic and social action of the dominant structural element in Creole society, the racial hierarchy—an element that pervaded every aspect of social life: economic, political, religious and domestic.
>
> (1996:70)

While Smith positions only race as central in this system of hierarchy, we should position race, gender, and class as simultaneous axes of power ordering the system. Racial, gendered, and classed inequalities were essential to the structure of colonial racism, resulting in a systemic pattern of unequal sexual access. Being white was not enough to consolidate this structure; this sexually asymmetrical system was built on the combination of whiteness, which automatically entailed higher class status, and maleness. White men were constructed as being highly sexually active, needing more sexual freedom and gratification than white women. While it is only their offspring with white women that counted as legitimate, they accorded themselves free access to black and colored women. It was thus the *combination* of one's gendered and racialized positions that determined one's prerogatives and limitations in the dual marriage system (Wekker 2001).

For the few white, Jewish, and light-skinned Creole women in Suriname it was unthinkable to have a sexual relationship with a colored or black man. This possibility presented a serious transgression of racialized sexual boundaries. An unmarried white women having "carnal conversation" with a black man would be tortured severely and banished from the colony, while a married woman would undergo the same fate in addition to being branded. The black man would be killed (Schiltkamp and de Smidt 1973:227). White women—and Jewish and light-skinned Creole women—were seen as sexually innocent. Put on a pedestal of being nonsexual, they embodied the Surinamese version of "the cult of true womanhood." Being identified with the longevity of the nation, it was essential that their sexual activities be policed and that they be offered protection: their offspring should be white or, in the case of Jewish and Creole women, as light skinned as possible. If this interpretation holds any validity, it would explain, what has always seemed to me, the disproportionate number of unmarried, upper-middle-class Jewish, Creole, and Chinese women, a situation still prevalent in the first half of the twentieth century.[36]

A dominant racist gender ideology and a gendered racial ideology both pointed to the obvious: various actors in the system had different sexual positions. This ideology amounted to a pattern of unequal sexual access favoring white and light-skinned men, which corresponded with a high class position. In the course of later centuries the basic pattern has not only been adopted by prosperous men of various ethnic groups, it has also increasingly found its way to men of different classes, producing a dominant variety of Surinamese masculinity. A dominant Surinamese male script has arisen, which holds that men should have sexual access to women, regardless of ethnic group. It has become *gesunkenes Kulturgut* (Hoetink 1958) or it can be understood in terms of Homi Bhabha's mimicry, a male strategy whereby the disempowered appropriate a flawed identity that has been imposed on them by the colonizer. The colonized are obliged to mirror back an image of the colonials, but in imperfect form: "*Almost the same, but not white. Almost the same, but not quite*" (1984: 130).

When we shift the focus to slave men and women living under this constellation, historical knowledge is still fragmentary. We know that formal marriage was forbidden to slaves and that contemporary colonial sources construct both genders as hypersexual. But there are gendered differences: slave men were conceived as sexually potent, dangerous to white women, and were accordingly severely circumscribed in their sexual activities toward white women. Slave women were depicted as sexually interested, excessive, insatiable, and always available. But if we are concerned with the internal contours of slave beliefs and practices regarding relational life, as we must be, we are still groping in the dark. These internal contours must be of interest to us because we need to answer the question whether there are elements in slave relational arrangements that can be understood as elaborations of West African behavioral principles in the meeting of the "two opposed yet interdependent cultural and ideological systems" on the plantations. In addition to the dual marriage structure, the strong African rootedness of Afro-Surinamese working-class culture needs to be taken into account when trying to understand attitudes of the female enslaved toward relational arrangements with men. The Surinamese slave population was continually replenished from Africa until the abolition of the slave trade (1808), but the replenishment persisted actually even longer because the slave imports from Africa only ended around 1830 (van Stipriaan 1993). Because most written sources originate with whites, different sources and reading practices are necessary. Reading existing sources against the grain, some insights as to how slave women thought about relationships with men may be gained.

There are a few studies that are specifically devoted to the nature of Surinamese slaves' family lifes, using demographic data on a limited number of plantations (Lamur 1985; Everaert 1999). These and other studies (Oostindie 1989; van Stipriaan 1993; Beeldsnijder 1994; Lenders 1994; Klinkers 1997) have laid to rest contemporary sources that had depicted slave life as chaotic, licentious, immoral, unstable, and noncommittal. Women especially had been portrayed in those early sources as extraordinarily lascivious. The consensus on slave relational life is now that there were several types of relationships in the slave community: polygyny and monogamy, two-parent and one-parent families next to each other and a probably high measure of stability of unions. In addition, sexual morals were probably looser than in Europe (Lamur 1985; van Stipriaan 1993).

Everaert's study, covering the period 1836–1863, but with special quantitative focus from 1850–1863, is concerned with the stability of slave unions and is based on the slave registers of four sugar estates. It has to deal with the built-in bias of the sources of the Moravian Brethren (EBG) who came to Suriname in the early nineteenth century to preach the gospel among slaves and to encourage stable unions among them. In the *Specialien*, the extensive written records of the slaves in their care, kept from 1836 on, the brethren only recorded the troublesome cases, reprehensible behaviors with regard to mating; moreover, they only dealt with slaves who had been converted to Christianity.[37] Everaert supplies data about slave mating patterns in terms of place of birth, class, and gender. Interestingly, African-born men and women had fewer partners than Creoles; they were less often polygamous and their unions lasted relatively longer. Both African-born and Creoles seemed to prefer people from their own group as partners (1999:122–124). Everaert understands these differences in terms of the greater status that Creole men and women had accrued on the plantations, their command of the language, and their accommodation to plantation life. Africans were the lowest in the plantation hierarchy, given to despair, suicidal behavior, and running away. Creole men and women more often belonged to the slave elite and held the more prestigious occupations, like domestic servants, artisans, and basya/overseers. I am tempted to conclude that the longer exposure of

Creoles to the plantation regime resulted in creolization, in accommodation to the dual marriage structure and its attendant characteristics in the mid-nineteenth century. It would be too quick to deduce, however, that Creoles had abandoned West African principles in the domain of relationality.

While men with a high occupational status were more often polygamous and less often without a partner than men with a low occupational status; women present a different picture. Women with a high occupational status tended more often to live without a partner than women with a low occupational status. Polyandry was rarely seen, while polygyny occurred more often. It was not exceptional that a woman sometimes was much older than her partner. Women with a higher status tended to have younger partners more often than women with a lower status. Everaert concludes that "just like men, women could break up relationships. Women tended to break unions as often as men. This can be seen as an indication of the independent position of the woman" (1999:222).

In the framework of uncovering the internal contours of the slaves' belief systems and practices, the differently gendered patterns are intriguing because they point to different ideal situations for men and women. Women preferred an independent status; if they could afford it, they did not want to be subjugated to a husband, and if that modality was not possible and compromises to independence had to be made, then at least the partner should be able to furnish goods and money. This in its turn is a proposition that was prefigured and reproduced in the ideology inherent in Winti. The undesirability of marriage and the connection between sex and money that slave women perceived is borne out by diverse data. Oft-cited is the following quote from Teenstra (1842) to illustrate the attitude of Creoles toward marriage:

> Some colored people consider marriage as very oppressive, through which crushing links they do not want their daughters tied; one even has examples, that colored parents who, living together for better and for worse in unmarried state (like most colored people) and having produced children, absolutely refused their daughters to enter into a marriage contract. A certain colored father answered a white man, who asked for his daughters's hand: "Get married, get married immediately? No! It does not go like that; should you want to live together first with Louisa, you can do that, then one can see how things go, but my daughter has to be free and will not permanently commit herself blindly.[38]

(48–49)

Regarding the connection between possessions and starting a relationship, van Stipriaan cites a white carpenter, Röman, who for years lived as an outcast among the slaves and wrote in 1827: "when a slave does not possess anything, he cannot get a woman" (1993:381). The historical continuity of this attitude is striking, as we have seen earlier in this chapter. Everaert cites the slave Maria Henriette of the Breukelerwaard Plantation, who says , in 1847, that there are many women without a man, but "they prefer not to have men from the plantation. They prefer white men or basya.[39] The slaves on the plantation are poor and the young girls like gold chains, rings and beautiful clothes. Those brothers of ours (i.e., Christianized slaves) are poor" (Everaert 1999:127).

There is another source, a rather disregarded but rich oral source, that alerts us to the attitude of a prosperous female slave regarding relationships between men and women in general and her own habitus in this regard specifically. Master storyteller Aleks de Drie bases his oral knowledge on the stories of his *uma afo*/mother's mother's mother, born around 1837 (de Drie and Guda 1985:16).[40] In one of his fascinating stories, *Prensés Apïaba*/Princess Apïaba, de Drie introduces us to an African princess who had been sold into slavery. The story should be situated in the second half of the nineteenth century.[41] The governor treated her with special attention, because of her status, and gave her a house and a yard. She loved to dance Winti, on top of a sheep; she would cut its head off and drink its blood. Apïaba had a well in her yard from which she not only got water but also money. A light-skinned man, watching the princess dance, fell in love with her. He proposed to her, but Apïaba, who liked the man well enough, had little use for him:

> "Wel kijk, wan libi fu yu seti anga mi a no noti, a no wan trobi sani. Ma mi no abi noti fu wan mansma fanowdu. Want luku, i no syi mi saka wan embre go nin a peti, di mi hari kon, mi hari wan embre moni. We na umasma, na moni a abi fanowdu. En dat mi habi keba. Dus mi no abi yu moro fanowdu. En mi winti di e kon a mi tapu, mi no makandra nanga mansma. Y' e kon dyaso, mi kan meki den bediende f' mi poti moy nyan gi yu nyan, maar verder niets."
> Well look, for you to set up life with me, that is not nothing, it is a sweet thing. But I do not need anything from a man. Because look, did you not see that I lowered a bucket into the well and when I hauled it up, the bucket was full of money. A woman, well, she needs money. And that I already have. So I do not need you anymore. And my Winti, when they come on top of me, I cannot be with a man. When you come here, I can make my servants put something nice for you to eat, but nothing else.
>
> (DE DRIE AND GUDA 1985:129)

From this oral source several important themes emerge: first, again, we are confronted with the importance of food, that sign of hospitality, sharing, and cultural preoccupation. Second, there is Apïaba's relationship with her Winti and the money they provide her, in return for her honoring of them. In the juxtaposition of those relationships and one with a real life man, she makes clear the greater significance of the first type of relationship to her. Third, and important, the story shows that women made a firm connection between being in a relationship with a man and money. Having money made a relationship with a man questionable. The desire for an independent position points to the agency of slave women. It was the preferred mode by women, facilitated by the equal work burdens men and women carried and the independent food provision.

Still, the question whether rejection of marriage was a product of the dual marriage structure or an elaboration of West African principles in the domain of subjecthood needs to be answered. Women's desire for independence was equally operative in relationships with white men as in those with enslaved or free men. It is noteworthy that the dual marriage structure, which did not offer marriage to slave women in their relationships with white men, but did produce mobility in terms of status for themselves and their children and a varying measure of freedom,[42] coincided for slave women with their own negative feelings toward marriage. I read the longevity and tenacity of the rejection of marriage as a testament to this coincidence, but it certainly does not point to the equivalence of the two organizational systems. In other words, enslaved women had their own reasons, based on the West African archive, to want an independent status from men, and this wish dovetailed with the structural position offered to them by the dual marriage system. Thus a system that was inherently saturated with inequalities, the dual marriage system, could in practice be reconciled with a subjugated but relatively egalitarian system that fueled enslaved women's own understandings of relationships.

While, from the worldview of the dual marriage structure, the emptiness of the category of marriage, with someone of an unequal status, was a way of creating and expressing racial, gender, and class inequality, from a West African perspective the point to be grasped is that enslaved women preferred to be in a relational arrangement that granted them as much freedom as possible and considered conjugal relations to be less prominent than relations with consanguineal, uterine kin. It was and is not wifehood that is paramount in African household and family organizations but motherhood (Oyewumi 2001; Amadiume 1987). I would like to propose that the centrality of motherhood, a reliance on uterine kin as opposed to consanguineal relations and forms of femininity that stressed independence from men, which various enslaved took with them to the "New World," different though their provenance and cultural archives were, became part of the organizing principles upon which life was based. I have established that

West African principles in the domain of subjecthood and relationality find expression in the conglomerate of notions around full sexual subjecthood for men and women, the necessity of regular sex for one's inner well-being, the active sexual roles that both men and women can play, the centrality of parenthood for both genders, the fact that sexual fulfillment per se for both men and women is more important than the sex of one's sexual partner(s), and a preferred independent status by women from men.

In this chapter I have shown, first, that a relatively egalitarian gender system, which the enslaved shaped on the basis of the West African archive, has historically been in tension with inegalitarian overlaying systems. During slavery the dual marriage structure militated against egalitarian relationships between white men and black women and during, but also after slavery, unequal economic circumstances between Creole men and women were enacted in sexual spheres, where women made an equation between sex and money. There are strong indications that this connection was already made during slavery. At the end of the twentieth century starting a relationship with a man had the character of a contest. Both contestants knew that relationships are brittle, and they wanted to get the most out of them without investing foolishly. The nature of what men and women wanted primarily from the relationship was different. Men, according to women, wanted sex. Their status and feelings of manhood were perceived to be enhanced by "keeping" other women apart from their steady relationship. Women mostly wanted economic security and could not afford to give sex away lightheartedly. There was a strong relationship for most women between a man's solvency and her willingness to be intimately involved. The bottom line was without money, no sex. To act differently would be foolishness.

Second, taking a historical route, I have developed an argument concerning the contribution of West African grammatical principles in the domain of sexual subjecthood. These principles could be elaborated upon rather freely, due to Dutch colonial policy, which left the enslaved as much as possible to themselves. To begin with, this conglomerate of guiding principles does not foreground the sex of one's sexual partners, thus avoiding a worldview that distinguishes between hetero-, homo-, and bisexuality. In addition, it finds expression in the understanding of full sexual subjecthood for both men and women, the active sexual roles that both men and women can play, the fact that sexual fulfillment per se for both men and women is important, the necessity of regular sex for one's inner well-being and to an advanced age, the centrality of parenthood for both women and men, a preferred independent status by women from men, and a transactional conceptualization of relationships with men. Conjugal and affinal relationships were and are considered to be less important than consanguineal ties. Thus many women, including Nana, relied on the help of their mother and sisters rather than on the help of her male partners to bring up their children.

Third, women who engage exclusively in cross-sex relationships are embedded in a working-class discourse and value structure, which they share in important respects with mati. In this working-class culture, financial and emotional independence from men was deemed very important and led to a preference for relational arrangements that allowed relative freedom, i.e., visiting or concubinage relationships or being someone's outside woman. Most working-class women have historically found marriage and monogamy undesirable, with the limitations they bring in terms of independence. The dual marriage structure and various West African principles in the domain of sexual subjecthood and relationality coincided to shape this social formation in which women who could afford not to have a steady live-in male partner preferred such independence. If this modality was not possible, then a man had to contribute financially in return for sex. Other prominent features shared by working-class women alike, regardless of the sex of their partners, were institutions like tya' boskopu, in which another woman's behavior is criticized or praised, the jealousy and violence accompanying relationships, the importance of kamra prikti, the understanding that one has sexual obligations toward one's steady partner, and negative attitudes toward oral sex. The ideal typical attitude required of the outside woman toward the inside woman invoked the same principle that is used in mati relationships where one of the partners has an outside relationship: respect is due to the partner who was there first. All these "intangible" features of the ways in which relationships are conceptualized, the ways in which they should be handled with care and respect, point to a shared West African cultural archive.

Fourth, a male ideology is hegemonic in the cross-sex sexual domain because women have scant sexual knowledge and perceive each other, especially when they are nonkin, predominantly as competitors for men's contributions, a situation that is aggravated by a perceived unfavorable sex ratio. This has led to diminished sexual pleasure on the part of women and allowed men to get away with abominable sexual practices. Due to the deteriorating economic situation, the negotiating space of women in their relationships with men declined over the past decades. Many women felt forced to start or to continue a relationship with a man because of their dire economic straits, not because the relationship was gratifying in itself. Some younger women, like Andrea, looked upon marriage as an ideal, but as they grew older they too preferred to be independent. Younger women have been more exposed to middle-class values through the media, through their dealings with government regulations, through educational institutions and the teachings of the Church. Creole working-class culture, in its traditional manifestation, does not have a double standard concerning the number of partners a woman was supposed to have, as is evident in odo like "I am a gold coin" and others. These other standards are imported from hegemonic, male-dominated value patterns and are indicative of the loss working-class women incur in terms of personal worth, interdependence, integrity, and negotiating space in the relationship when they buy into this "foreign" pattern.

Lena pikin
I mu teki wan man (2x).
No no mama,
Mi n' e wani no wan man (2x).

[Lena child
You have to take a man (2x).
No no mama,
I do not want any man (2x).]

ANONYMOUS KASEKO

5

The Mati Work

In focusing on female mati in this chapter, I embark on a much overdue project in a Caribbean or a wider Black diasporic context

> to theorize from the point of view and contexts of marginalized women not in terms of victim status or an essentialized identity but in terms that push us to place women's agency, their subjectivities and collective consciousness, at the center of our understandings of power and resistance.
>
> (ALEXANDER 1991:148)

Mis' Juliettte's life history in chapter 1 challenged several central anthropological articles of faith. In the domain of family formation, her narrative illustrated the establishment of kinship ties through women, her mati or meti/cowives. As far as marriage was concerned, contrary to theoretical beliefs that have been circulating for decades according to which working-class Caribbean women see marriage as highly desirable but virtually unattainable, Mis' Juliette and many of her younger sisters strongly rejected this form as not giving them enough autonomy. In the domain of sexuality Juliette's behavior unhinged the certainty that the core of sexuality is reproductive heterosexual intercourse. Even though there was no dearth of the offspring she produced, her sexual joy was overwhelmingly located in her connections with women. In addition, it was abundantly clear that her sexual activities with women were not passive and nongenital. Finally, new light was thrown on the contours of a black diasporic sex/gender system, which will be fleshed out further.

In this chapter I will contextualize Mis' Juliette's life and a key institution in it, the mati work, in more detail and complement her life story with the stories of other, younger mati. In section 1 I will present the data I gathered during different research periods in Suriname from 1990–1991 until 2002. These data pertain to the universe mati inhabit and construct, linguistically and culturally, to initiation into the mati work, jealousy and obligations, and the relationships between mati work and the Winti religion. In section 2 I will deal with some theoretical issues, reviewing the diverse explanations from the disciplines of history, sociology, and anthropology that have been offered for the prevalence of the phenomenon. Dominant approaches in the literature about the mati work have stressed negative factors such as the unequal sex ratio, unpleasant experiences and disappointments with men, the advantage of not having to worry about pregnancy, and the impossibility for upwardly mobile women (e.g., nurses, policewomen, and teachers) of finding a male partner of equal social status. In contradistinction to these approaches, I will propose a positive explanation that builds on the continuity of constructions of selves, genders, and sexualities in the African heritage in the Diaspora. My data will show that the dominant paradigms overlook a sizable proportion of women who make a positive choice to be emotionally, sexually, and economically most deeply involved with another woman. Growing up amidst a varied repertoire of sexual behaviors that do not carry pronounced stigma, it may very well be the case that women choose to be with women positively and not by default.

Women will speak in their own terms about their sexual experiences with other women. In an Afro-Surinamese working-class universe it is sexual activity and sexual fulfillment per se that is significant; it is not the sex of one's sexual counterpart that carries the most meaningful information. I understand this principle as expressive of the West African cultural heritage. Current manifestations and the history of the institution variously called *a mati wroko*/the mati work, *a mati libi*/the mati life, *a beweygey*/the movement, and, by older women, *a uma wroko*/the women's work and *a kompe wroko*/the kompe work will be the central focus of this chapter.[1]

Mati are working-class women who typically have children and engage in sexual relationships with men and with women, either consecutively or simultaneously. This, admittedly, is a minimal definition because mati certainly are not a unitary category; some women have relationships with men and women, while others are only involved with women. The latter are, in mati language, indicated with *effektieve mati meid*/effective, true, mati gal(s). We will explore other emic categories that the women themselves employ to order their world. While the percentage of Creole working-class women who engage in mati relationships must clearly remain a "guessti-mate," I would say that it is quite common, perhaps as high as three out of four women. Out of the twenty-five women with whom I originally worked in 1990–1991, ten told me they had engaged in the mati work at some point in their lives. The widespread occurrence of the mati work can be linked to a discourse about the self embedded in the Afro-Surinamese Winti religion, which is discussed in chapter 3. The mati work is seen by its practioners as varying, versatile sexual behavior: no real, authentic, fixed self is claimed, but one particularly strong, masculine instance of the multiplicitous "I," who loves to lie down with women, is foregrounded.

Showing the contours of continuity in this construction of female same-sex sexual activity is my first aim in this chapter. In addition, I want to con-tinue the argument I began in the last chapter that all working-class women, irrespective of the sex of the object of their sexual activities, are embedded in a gender ideology that stresses in(ter-)dependence, self-worth, and self-respect. None of this, in itself, is predicated upon the presence of a man in their lives.

The embeddedness in a common culture does not suggest that there are no differences between women who operate exclusively on the cross-sex relational market and mati. Mati, through their sexual styles and behav-iors, do incur the wrath of those who subscribe to middle-class values, but they gain decidedly in sexual pleasure and knowledge. In fact, I will claim that mati, with their "unruly," "unrespectable" behavior, have a more autonomous, "alternative" understanding of their own sexuality. Finally, I want to engage in a dialogue with contemporary Western feminist theories by showing a sexual configuration where women unabashedly enjoy sex, are active sexual beings, take sex seriously, can disengage sex from love, and, strikingly, talk about sex openly, using distinct linguistic expressions of their own. Mati work is good to think with (cf. Weston 1998). It under-scores that an earlier, influential concept, "compulsory heterosexuality" (Rich 1980) did indeed not have the proclaimed cross-cultural validity. The mati work also invites us to think about the relationship between sexual-ity and gender. We have come a long way from the supposedly simple and straightforward relationship that was hypothesized at an earlier stage of feminist scholarship. The mati work shows that it is apparently possible to have a female gender identity without a muted sexuality and without a fixed, cross-sex sexual orientation. Lewin (2002) summarizes the status quo in current gay and lesbian studies, with the first paying attention to

sexual behavior, while the latter is more interested in gender. In keeping with the universe working-class women have constructed I pay ample
attention to sexual behavior.

The mati work, finally, offers a radically different alternative configuration to the historical genesis of "homosexual identity" under capitalism
(D'Emilio 1984; D'Emilio and Freedman 1988; Faderman 1991), in conceiving of itself in terms of behavior: no homosexual self is claimed. Although
West-African data are scant, I will present an argument speculating that the
configuration inscribed in the mati work builds upon African continuities
in the construction of (sexual) selfhood. Among these continuities are a
notion of personhood in which the secular and the spiritual are intertwined;
the importance of fertility and parenthood for both men and women; the
full sexual subjectivity of women; sex as an extraordinarily pleasant part of
life, which does not need to stop with advanced age; sexuality as activity, not
exclusive identity; the disjunction of sex and gender; a flexible gender system and the conceptualization of women who like to lie down with women
as having a "heavy soul." I am aware that much more work will need to be
done on both sides of the Atlantic to corroborate my line of reasoning.

The Term *Mati*

At the outset I want to explore the possible provenance of the term *mati*.
There are two possible explanations for the term. First, mati could possibly
be traced to Dutch *maatje*, "buddy," the diminutive of "mate." Van Donselaar
(1989)[2] sums up two older meanings of the word *maatje*: 1. girlfriend and 2.
term of address for a housekeeper who is a slave. Those two meanings are
found in older sources from the first half of the nineteenth century. Thus A. F.
Lammens writes in his *Bijdragen tot de Kennis van de Kolonie Suriname: Tijdvak, 1816–1822*[3] about the proper terms of address to be used with slaves:

> "Baasie" (boss) and "sisa" (sister) are the general terms of address for slaves
> that are unfamiliar to you, but one's own slaves, one calls "booij" (boy), or
> like the female slaves by their first names;—the elderly people one calls Fata,
> father; Mama,—Mother: the children call their elderly papa, father; nene,
> mother:—when you are talking to a housekeeper, still a slave, then one calls
> her *maatje*, friend.[4]

(1982 [1822]:114)

August Kappler, a German soldier, adventurer, and explorer who founded
the city of Albina,[5] the border town on the river Marowijne that separates

Suriname from French Guyana, uses the word *mati*, too, in his *Zes Jaren in Suriname, 1836–1842* (1983 [1854])[6] When he describes the way of living on the plantations, he observes:

> Like I remarked above, marriages after European fashion, are not very pop-
> ular here; because free housekeepers or concubines replace the housewives
> almost everywhere and this is not deemed a disgrace at all. ... Thrift and order
> one searches for in vain in these households; because even if the man is not a
> squanderer, his wife knows to spend the money in such a way, that one is lucky
> when the expenses are covered by the incoming funds. Usually, these house-
> keepers eat alone or they invite *vriendinnen (maatjes)* over.[7]
>
> (1983 [1854]:23)

Dutch *maatje* could thus have become *mati* in the creole that was the linguistic vehicle between slaves and planters. It is impossible to pin down more precisely in which period a sexual connotation of the word developed among the slaves. Nor is it clear, of course, whether the female friends did or did not engage in sexual activity. It is, finally, in light of the second explanation, interesting that *maatje* also has maritime connota-tions, referring to a (junior) sailor. This common ground offered possibili-ties for convergence.

A second explanation of the word *mati*,[8] which speaks to me more, connects the term to the Middle Passage. Richard and Sally Price, in their *Two Evenings in Saramaka*, note about the mati relationship among Saramaka Maroons:

> *Mati* is a highly charged volitional relationship, usually between two men, that
> dates back to the Middle Passage—*matis* were originally "shipmates," those
> who had survived the journey out from Africa together; by the eighteenth cen-
> tury, *mati* was a lifelong relationship entered into only with caution and when
> there was strong mutual affection and admiration.
>
> (1991:396)

My understanding is that slaves arrived in Suriname with the concept of mati, referring to the special relationship of shipmates. This special relationship acquired a sexual meaning for both Creole men and women, apart from its general, affectively laden meaning of friend. In various parts of the black Dias-pora the relationship between people who had come over to the "New World" on the same ship had been and remained a special one. "Brazilian 'malungo,' Trinidadian 'malongue,' Haitian 'batiment' and Surinamese 'sippi' and 'mati' are all instances of that special, non-biological, symbolical connection between two people of the same gender" (Mintz and Price 1992 [1976]:44). On the ships men and women were kept apart, thus the special relationships were always between people of the same sex, and they were sometimes transmitted from generation to generation. Maroon and Creole history diverged when the Maroons started to run away from the plantations to form viable communities in the rain forest from the middle of the seventeenth century. Whereas among Maroons *mati* and *sippi/sibi* are gendered, among Creoles nowadays the term *mati* is used for both men and women, possibly pointing to the more egalitarian tendencies that were operative in the enslaved communities on the plantations than in the semimilitary Maroon communities in the interior who had to defend themselves against the colonizer.

Creole master storyteller Aleks de Drie (1902–1984), whose stories originated with his great grandmother who lived in the second half of the nineteenth century, recites several *banya* songs, in which the terms *mati* and *sibi* occur, that reference the significance of the special relationship among Creoles. Banya was a dance, accompanied by drums, performed by the slaves in Du associations. It was a female genre, with the women singing and dancing while men played the drums. The colonial government regularly forbade the Du associations, and one can thus safely assume that the prohibition was largely in vain. Mis' Juliette was, as we have seen, an indefatigable banya singer. Banya are not performed anymore nowadays, but there are several important collections of these songs (Comvalius 1935; Herskovits and Herskovits 1936; Voorhoeve and Lichtveld 1975; de Drie 1984). According to de Drie, the purpose of banya was to keep the memory of what the whites had done to the ancestors, who had come from Africa, alive. Their descendants were not to forget the atrocities. One such text is:

> A de a mi ede,
> Sibi a de a mi ede.
> A de a mi ede o,
> Sibi a de a mi ede.
> Kaba a tori di mi anga yu ben habi.
> Fu den Nengrekondre nengre
> A de a mi ede o,
> Sibi a de a mi ede (1984:41).

> [I carry it in my head,
> Shipmate I carry it in my head.
> I carry it in my head,
> Shipmate I carry it in my head.
> Let us stop that story[9] that you and I had.
> But the story of the blacks from Africa

I carry it in my head,
Shipmate I carry it in my head.]

Another banya song expresses the grief of an enslaved person, probably a woman, upon arrival in Suriname:[10]

Mi doro na lanpresi
Ma furu sibi mi no si.
Watra lon na mi ai.

[I arrived at the landing place
But I did not see many shipmates.
Tears welled up in my eyes.]

Comvalius, a connoisseur of music, writing about Surinamese song, dance, and folklore in the thirties of the twentieth century, brings up another instance of popular cultural memory in which the term *sibi—sien* in this case—is preserved. He analyzes a children's song, still sung in his day as well as in ours, "Perun Perun, Mi Patron," which children often accompany with a game where one child stands in a circle of others sitting down. While the child sings the song, she touches everyone's legs until the child whose leg is touched at the last word of the song is struck out. The song recounts the spotting in 1799 of a British fleet still far removed from Fort Nieuw Amsterdam, at the confluence of the Suriname and the Commewijne Rivers. This military post, under a commander called Peronne (Perun), was established to keep enemy ships from sailing into the Dutch colony from the ocean. The song, in archaic Sranan Tongo, starts with the following lines, uttered by a soldier standing guard:

Sien, san dee na mofo sien dee kom,
Peroen, Peroen, mie patron?

[Sibi, what is sailing there toward us from the mouth of the sea,
Peronne, Peronne, my commander?]

The guard addresses his fellow soldiers as sibi (Comvalius 1935). The song ridicules Peronne, who has a big mouth—"who wants to come, / make them come; / I will send those Englishmen back into the sea on wooden boards," implying that the ship would have been shot to pieces—but turns out to be an inept coward because he started negotiations immediately.

This special shipmate relationship, mati, that became one of the building blocks of the "New World" societies, creating kin for the enslaved, acquired a sexual meaning in the course of time, both for Creole women and men. The word *mati* now carries a general, sexually neutral but affectively laden meaning of "friend" (m/f);[11] but it also references someone who engages in sexual relationships with persons of the same sex and it is used for both women and men.[12] Which meaning is intended depends on the context and it stands to reason that this characteristic ambiguity was to the advantage of enslaved women and men who engaged in same-sex sexual behavior. It is quite conceivable that the two possible origins of mati, Dutch *maatje* and the African "shipmate," since they covered some of the same conceptual terrain, merged and converged. In the public domain the friendship and kinship element was stressed, while the sexual modality was in place for those who wanted to invoke that nuance.

Interestingly, at the end of the twentieth century, the term *mati* has traveled transatlantically and has in the Netherlands become part of the street language that youth, both boys and girls of diverse ethnic backgrounds—Surinamese, white Dutch, Moroccans, and Turks—use to designate "friend." In typical mixing and matching style, one can hear in many a Dutch rap song, too, texts referencing *die mati van me*/that friend of mine. The term does not carry sexual meaning in street language.

FIGURE 5.1 Suriname maties, female friends, 1920. *KITLV, Leiden, the Netherlands, no. 8829*

The Linguistic Universe of Mati

The importance of having command of the language a particular group uses to conceptualize and construct itself and the world cannot be easily overestimated. The special language, so rich in metaphors, used by mati is a case in point. As I noted in chapter 1, without the help of Mis' Juliette and my lover and collaborator Delani McDonald, I would not have succeeded in entering the world mati inhabit and construct. Although my command of Sranan Tongo was good, I noticed that linguistic competence was not sufficient. I missed the cultural skills and sensitivity to determine the circumstances under which I could engage in conversations with different people about sex. Juliette and Delani helped me to know which questions I could ask women and how they could most profitably be phrased. It turned out that my initial hesitant, roundabout way of broaching the subject would have to be abandoned. Using the appropriate linguistic terms, which were often quite graphic, was much more productive. I came to the point where I would ask women: "Ai, Hilda, i de in' a wroko, no?"/Hilda, are you in the work? i.e., doing it with women? If I knew the person really well, I could talk in terms of *griti* or *grit'griti*/"rubbing," i.e., tribadism, which is the most colloquial idiom used by mati themselves. With older women, Juliette told me, I had better ask: "Tant' Lexie, i ben vriendin ooktu ?"/Auntie Lexie, were you "girl-friending" too? I think that this direct, *sranti*/outspoken, way of questioning was allowed me because I was an "outsider within" (Hill Collins 1986).

This chapter is also a modest exercise in ethnosemantics. Mati have an extensive linguistic apparatus, lexicon, and idioms to talk about sex. Thus, in the second half of my first research period in 1990–1991, the "folk seminars" took on unprecedented momentum. I had acquired more cultural competence, and Delani often accompanied me when I was *tap' a veld*/in the field. Delani not only spoke fluent Sranan Tongo, but she had socialized frequently in mati circles. Folk seminars were one of the most vital instruments I used to gather information, to distill emic constructions of selfhood, gender, and sexualities. Anthropologist John Langston Gwaltney, who first coined the term *folk seminar* while doing research with residents of black American urban communities, described the seminar:

> Folk seminars were convened in locations as varied as churches and taverns. They were devoted to the exchange of views on recurrent themes in personal documents, the evaluation of some main premises of social science and the indigenous definition of core black culture. The complement of folk seminars ranged from three to twenty persons, who were, for the most part, well known to each other. Once I or some key consultant informant initially clarified the

purpose for which we were assembled, discussion was free and almost invariably civil, with no reliance on formal rules of procedure.

(1980:XXIV)

Before the seminar Delani and I discussed which subjects we would cover. During the seminar Delani did most of the talking, while I took verbatim notes on what was being said and body language. The central role Delani plays is obvious from the next fragment, part of a folk seminar. Talks about sex went best when we organized it so that a number of women who knew and trusted each other would sit down—feet on the table, beer, whiskey and rum coke at hand—and discuss the ins and outs of the matter. This particular conversation took place spontaneously.

Paramaribo. June 18, 1991. After Ligia de Freitas's lively forty-fifth birthday party, five of her guests moved over to Milly Pinas's porch next door. I had just met Milly today, but I had been friends with the others for varying periods and they all knew each other. The air was humid and heavy in the late afternoon, full of aromas and promises. Pretty soon siksi juru/crickets, started to announce that the sun was about to set. Milly, a fifty-six-year-old street sweeper and mother of two, told her son to get some ice cold beers and banana chips at Omu Snesi/the neighborhood Chinese store. We settled down under a roof of dried plantain leaves, discussing highlights of the party, the various guests and their inside stories, a favorite postparty activity. Delani was with me, which was reassuring because by now she and I had developed such a bond that she knew when I needed clarification. The idiosyncrasies of the rich language mati use made me walk a fine line between not wanting to interrupt the flow of the conversation yet not wanting to let the band march too far ahead of me. My friend Lydia de Vreede, a thirty-seven-year-old nursing aide, mother of five and former lover of Milly's, was there. Lydia was married and at this point it was not clear to me whether she still engaged in relationships with women. Milly has a female lover. Milly and Lydia have remained best friends and are each other's confidantes. The youngest in our company was twenty-seven-year-old Diana Doorson, a hairdresser and Lydia's niece, who according to Lydia in the domain of same-sexed sex "e bar' hip hip hoere, ma a nè tya' buketi"/"says yes, but her heart is not in it." Gradually our conversation meandered into the unwritten rules of relationships between women. One fragment about the unwritten rules of engagement between mati:

MILLY (confident, right arm on her hip, moving shoulders and throwing her head back just slightly): "Luku no, sonlesi di mè go na wan fesa, mè wan' ab' mi vrij"/Look, sometimes when I am going to a party, I want to be free. I do not want be bothered by my lover. So we have an under-standing, we have made this agreement that we will both be free that evening. "Dus m' e breni, mi n' e yere noti. Ef' m' e si wan tra sma, a yeye wan' en, dan m' o suk' en."/So I'm blind, I don't hear anything. If I see somebody else, if "my soul" wants her, then I will pursue her.

LYDIA *(moving forward in her chair, pointing her index finger): "Ma kon mek' mi du en … yu b' io kir' mi!!"/But I should have tried… . You would have killed me!! (Both burst out laughing.) "Ala den feti nanga den krutu san un ben krutu f'a san disi!!"/All the fights and quarrels we had because of this stuff!! You wouldn't even let me dance with somebody else. The thing I hated most was when you would start yelling at me at the party, with all those peo-ple around. It was free amusement for all. I feel: let's go home and talk it over. It's nobody's business but our own.*

DELANI *"Mhmmm?!?? Ma fa dat kan? Unu na mati, unu na krin visiti, a sma na yu skin, ma dan a mus' tap' en ai di a' e si dat' yu e wan' wan tra sma? Yarusu no sa kon bij dan? Hoe dan, Milly?"/But how is that possible? You are lovers, you are best friends, the woman is yours, literally, "the woman is your body," but then she has to close her eyes when she sees that you are into some-body else? Won't jealousy play a part? How does that work, Milly?*

LYDIA *(laughing, gesticulating): "Mi s'sa!! Now y'e taki!!!"/Sister!! Now you're talking!!!*

MILLY *(slightly on the defensive now): Nononono, you have to look at it this way: I am older and more experienced than she. I know the sharks that are out there. I know that when some of these women dance with her, d' o vrij-postig/they are going to take liberties with her and later boast to their friends: "M'e sak' a san' gi a sma yere!"/I sure let her have it! I won't stand for it. I know the ropes: she doesn't have to worry about me in that respect.*

DIANA *(laughs expansively): "Ee-hee!! Gado sab' saide a n'e gi asi t'tu … !!"/ God knows why he didn't give the horse horns … !*

In the fragment above Milly first made a general claim about the rights and privileges of both partners in the relationship. When it was contested by Lydia and Delani asked for clarification, it turned out that the privilege to pursue another woman was, in Milly's view, only reserved to herself. Diana rounded off the conversation and eased potential tension with a quip, where-upon everybody burst out laughing. The discussion subsequently moved on to different roles in relationships between women, their economic coordi-nates, and their attendant privileges and obligations.

The liveliness and richness of the language used by the women is well illustrated in this fragment, as is Delani's technique to ask for clarification and elaboration. She essentially summed up what was known already and asked the participants to clarify their standpoints. Diana's contribution to the discussion, the last phrase, was interesting and illustrative of linguistic complexity. Her comment was characteristically ambiguous and indirect, a common phenomenon for black language use in the Diaspora. One of the verbal art forms of Creole working-class women, as we already saw, is the use of odo, often in clipped form, to comment on a situation. Diana's utterance might have meant several things. While she literally said "God knows why he didn't give the horse horns," she might have alluded to the fact of life that there are different entitlements in any relationship: Lydia's entitlements were clearly not the same as Milly's. But Diana was also implying that she applauded God for his sagacity: if the horse, Milly, was so impetuous when she did not have horns, one could only imagine (and fear for) what she would be like if she did have them. The same ambiguity was inherent in Lydia's description of Diana. The cultural richness of "A' e bar' hip hip hoere, ma a n' e tya' buketi"/She shouts hip hip hurray, but does not carry a bouquet is not adequately expressed by the translation I offered above: "She says yes, but her heart is not in it." The expression refers to the institution of the birthday in mati circles, which will be elaborated upon later in this chapter. The odo, again, might be interpreted in several ways. Lydia might have been implying that Diana will pretend to be interested in the mati work, but will not come through when push comes to shove. Alternatively, she may have been saying that Diana pretends that she is experienced in the mati work, yet that is all it is: pretense.

The landscape, punctuated by rich nuances, unexpected turns, and serious contestations, in this conversation would not have been captured equally well by separate interviews with Milly, Lydia, and Diana. Folk seminars were so rich in content and productive, I suggest, because they mimicked a situation that mati created for themselves anyway. It is part of mati culture to talk about the most intimate details of sex openly and jokingly. During these sessions, particularly, I felt at the height of anthropological bliss because, once underway, the women's words, symbols, and meanings soared like eagles and directive questioning was seldom needed. Egged on by each other's stories, one bolder than the other, the women would compete in telling "tall tales" of their exploits. In general, I found that talking with mati about sex was much easier and more open than it was with women who were sexually involved only with men.

Delani's phrase in the fragment where she summed up the modalities in which Milly and Lydia related to each other was a beautiful poetic litany, demonstrative of the plethora of terms mati command to talk about their relationships. The lexicon for "girlfriend" is extensive and sometimes untranslatable:

TABLE 5.1 Women's Expression for "Girlfriend"

mi vriendin	my "girlfriend" (ambiguous)
mi mati	my "friend" or "girlfriend" (ambiguous)
mi skin	(lit.) my body (has sexual connotations)
mi visiti	(lit.) my "visitor"
mi krin visiti	my true friend
mi sma	(lit.) my person
mi speri	my peer
mi eygi gebruik	(lit.) my own use (has sexual connotations)
mi spul[13]	my "girl," "sweetheart"
mi meid	my "gal" (a little "rough")
mi yappi	(untranslatable)
mi libi	my life
mi lobi libi	my love life
mi kabel	my "comrade"
mi kabber	my "comrade" (probably a variation of kabel)
mi kompe	my friend, comrade, buddy (ambiguous)

It is no coincidence that so many of these expressions are ambiguous, i.e., depending on the context they may or may not have sexual meaning. The word *mati* itself is, as we saw, used with those two meanings: friend (m/f) in a neutral sense and friend (m/f) in a sexual sense. It fits within the indirect and the metaphorical character of Sranan Tongo, which is so rich in odo, riddles, and narratives, not to name matters directly. In the verbal arts, which are so abundantly present in black languages in the Diaspora,[15] fundamental West African patterns were joined with the necessity, already manifesting itself during the Middle Passage, to be ambiguous in one's utterances, so that only insiders could fully understand what was being said. Depending on the context in which they found themselves, mati, too, have had ample reasons to keep their conversations ambiguous.

Mati were quite graphic in their language use when their sexual activities were challenged or ridiculed in a public setting: A couple in their late thirties told me that when a man insists on dancing with one of them, and he does not want to take no for an answer, they tell him: "Luku no, yongu, no wer' mi ede, want m'e griti"/Look, man, don't tire my head, because I rub. When a man on the street, called out *mat' mat' meid*[16]/heavy mati girls to them, Carla yelled back: *Tya' i s' sa kon, no?*/Bring your sister, no? Outsiders may use the same expressions mati use, but they are then often used in a denigrating way: (Surinamese Dutch) *schuurmeiden* or (Sranan) *griti meid*/"rubbing gals"; (Sranan) *plata preti* or (Surinamese Dutch) *platte borden*/"flat plates." Beside the linguistic aspect, there is a behavioral repertoire within mati culture, both at the personal and interpersonal level and including paralinguistic features and motor habits, that is quite characteristic.

Initiation Into the Mati Work

A pattern in the mati universe, which we encountered in Juliette's narrative and persists to this day, is the initiation of young girls into the "work" by older women. Generally, it was the older woman who took the initiative in expressing interest in a young girl. In general, the initiator simultaneously stakes a claim to the dominant position in the relationship.

During my research several women across generations pointed out this pattern to me. Olivia Bijlhout, now sixty, had her first relationship when she was fifteen. Her mati was thirty-nine at the time. Josephine Emanuel, forty-three, was initiated at age thirteen by a woman of forty-six. Two other women, now in their early thirties, fondly recalled their first lovers, again appreciably older. Stella Einaar, a thirty-six-year-old handywoman, also known as Stanka, recalls her first "affair":

> I met my first lover, when I was at school in the city. I was fifteen years old.
> I always used to pass her house and one day she invited me in, to sit down
> and chat with her a little while. A year passed in which nothing happened
> between us, then one day she asked me to play with her breasts. Pretty soon,
> I would tell my mother that I was spending the weekend with a friend from
> school, but I would be with my mati.

After the first involvement with an older female partner, there is no clear-cut ongoing pattern. Some women may choose to stay with an older partner, others go on with a peer. In general, there are no feelings of "impropriety" connected to large age differences between partners either in same-sex or cross-sex relationships. Indeed, there are several odo that hint at situations where a significant age difference is present between partners. One of them is "Yongu kaw e nyan owru grasi"/Young cow is eating old grass, another is "Owru kaka e bor' krakti supu"/An old rooster makes strong soup. The expression Juliette used for the age differential between us was "Pikin aksi e fala bigi bon"/The little ax fells the big tree. These expressions are used for same-sex as well as opposite-sex relationships. Van Lier (1986) also noted this age-differentiated pattern in the mati couples he interviewed in 1949. I interpret his phenomenon, which is in opposition to the ideal of equality in age bracket, valued in many Western relational patterns, as an African "grammatical principle" guiding behavior in sexual relationships. The literature offers several examples of such female age-differentiated same-sex relationships. In marriages between women in Nigeria and Kenya an older woman expressly chose a younger woman with the intent that she would help with household work and bear children (Amadiume 1987;[17] Tietmeier 1991). In the case of "mummies" and "babies" in Lesotho, an age difference was customary, as was the notion of a teaching relationship (Gay 1985; Kendall 1999). Judith Gay first documented the custom among Lesotho boarding school girls of forming same-sex couples composed of a slightly more "dominant" partner, called a "mummy," and a slightly more "passive" partner, a "baby." The girls engaged in kissing, body rubbing, possessiveness and monogamy, the exchange of gifts and promises, and, sometimes, genital contact. In the wider Afro-Caribbean region Elwin (1997) recorded the lives of contemporary lesbian girls and women from different Caribbean islands and came across the same age-differentiated pattern: e.g., Rhonda Sue from Dominica at fourteen liked the mother of a girlfriend who was forty-two and had six children; Pulcheria Theresa Willie of St. Lucia had her first relationship, at eighteen, with a woman who was twenty-two years her senior.

This pattern has been around for quite some time within a Surinamese context. Everaert (1999) studied the late period of slavery in Suriname and discerned a pattern whereby older prosperous male and female slaves had younger opposite-sex partners. Currently, both in Suriname and in the Netherlands, large age differences exist within female and male mati couples. Obviously, the cultural forms vary in different regions but the persistence of the underlying "grammatical principle" in the organization of sexuality in various parts of the black Diaspora points to a broad-based repertoire, in which (large) age difference does not signal inappropriateness, but, as I understand it, an eroticization of that difference. Let's look at what contemporary mati have to say about their relationships with young girls.

In talking about the interaction between mature women and young girls, several women admitted to me in private that they were simultaneously involved in an affair with an adolescent girl apart from their steady relationship. In Josephine's circles it is considered good mati practice to initiate a young girl, to impart sexual and general mati knowledge to her.

> *Everything that has to do with love is good, no matter in what form it comes. If you feel love for women, then you have to live accordingly. Adults have to help you, so that the feeling that is in you can express itself. I have recently had a relationship with a seventeen-year-old girl, a teaching relationship. The girl kept on phoning me, she wanted to meet with me, so I finally gave in. The thing was too strong in her. I taught her how the life is. From one generation to the next people teach each other the work, and it is getting better all the time.*

From the perspective of the older woman, it has definite advantages to mold and train the young girl, according to how she wants to see her behave. The young girl is variously called *yong' doifi*/young dove, *yong' fowru*/young chicken, or *yong' krakun*/young turkey. Several women stressed the importance of the "young dove" treating her older lover with respect in public, addressing her with two words, including her age-related title of address, as in *Mis' Elfride*/Miss Elfride. At parties, for instance, the young woman has to be solicitous of her needs, providing her with food and drinks; she should not give the older woman *bigi taki*/a big mouth and in general abstain from being *grofu*/rough. The young girl gets her first introduction to the obligations that mati have toward one another, such as taking care of the other when she is ill, sharing resources in time of need, and the sexual obligations. When the older woman is in a good economical position, either because she has adult children who support her or because she herself has good sources of income, she will spoil the girl with presents, jewelry, and clothes. In exchange, she will demand absolute fidelity from the girl, while she herself will not necessarily keep to such standards.

Talking about her preference for "young chickens," Lena Sluisdom, thirty-nine years old, said:

> *"Mi abi gril fu yongu pikin. M' e wan set' en, pot' en fa m'e wani"*/I feel capricious toward young girls. I want to make her, mold her like I want. It has more power when you lie down with her, after you have taught her what you want. With an older woman you cannot do that. I want to play the man, that is, be on top, while she has to be the woman. *Di mi de nanga speri*/when I am with a peer, I mostly want to be the man too, but then maybe she wants it, too, and then you have to compromise and switch around every so often, and then still it never works out in the end. That is my experience. With young girls it is less complicated; they are more curious, they want that thing all the time, no matter how, they just love it.

Most women see twelve as the minimal age for girls to become sexually active, though a few others indicated that in special cases, when the girl is unusually *lepi*, literally, "ripe, mature," they would do it with a younger girl. From the patterns of transmission of the mati work that were evident in Juliette's narrative, and judging by current practices, it is evident that there is continuity in the ways in which girls get socialized into the institution. Young girls often get initiated into the work by older women in their thirties and forties, who in their turn have been initiated by older women. Sexual and other mati knowledge is thus transmitted from one generation to the next. Sexual relations with women often precede those with men. The mati option evidently is in abundant supply in working-class neighborhoods and is in general not surrounded by negative value judgments.

I have not found any indications that women experience psychological difficulties, like those found in Euro-American societies, such as "having to come to terms with it" around self-acceptance or "how do I tell my mother?" Mother, typically, is not told; she has eyes to see. When Misi Juliette's oldest daughter Matsi was fifteen years old, she had her first relationship with a neighbor, a woman who was Juliette's peer. Although Matsi and Juliette never discussed what was going on, Juliette, in her own words, was not stupid. Later, when Matsi found a lover her own age, the neighbor came over and wanted to talk to Juliette about the unhappy fate of her relationship with Matsi. Juliette's rhetorical question: "Well, what was I supposed to do about it?" Among experienced mati it is taken for granted that as an older woman one does not become too attached to a younger partner, since there is always the chance that she will begin a relationship with a peer. Among younger mati, too, none ever "came out" to their children, since one's sexual behavior simply is not conceived of or talked about in that way. In chapter 6 we will see that Lydia de Vrede, who had then been in the Netherlands for a couple of years, adopted a different policy, a "coming out" policy, with her children, who had stayed behind in Suriname. But, in general, children see and hear and "are not stupid."

Making the Right Moves

Talking with mati, for instance at the folk seminars I described earlier, it became clear that a lot of the same joie de vivre that characterized the lives of the women of Juliette's generation is still present in the mati world. Sex with women was felt to be inherently good, healthy, joyous, and fun: *sport*. Lydia (thirty-seven) and Milly (fifty-six), whom we encountered before in a folk seminar, were former mati who had kept in close contact and were best friends, each other's confidantes. They opened windows unto the fine art of making the right moves when you are interested in a woman. Their stories were as lively as those of the generations before them. Milly definitely had a preference for playing the "male" role in her relationships and she had a nickname that paid homage to her particular style of courting women: Robe Milly. As she explained it:

> When I went to parties, I would wear this big robe. As soon as I saw a woman I liked, I would make my move, because my policy was this time is as good as any other. Maybe I will never get another opportunity.
>
> "I mu' ab' dre ai, ef' i wan' feni"/you have to have dry eyes, courage, when you want to score. So if the lady is sitting in company, I walk up to her, bend over, and say: "Lady, can I have a word with you?" Then I walk over to the bar and wait for her to walk up. When she comes, it does not really matter what you say, e.g., "your face is really familiar to me" or "didn't you live in Abrabroki?" It does not really matter, because you already have her halfway, let's say. Pretty soon I will suggest to her to go outside for a while, because it is too hot inside. Another good one is to ask the woman to go pee with you, out in the back. The part where my robe comes in, is when I spread it out on the ground, out back, and we lie down on it. Baya!! I did not go anywhere without that robe!!!

This style which Milly described is the prerogative of the "male" role. It is not likely that Milly's partner would get away with this behavior. Consequently, what may very well be the case is that Milly's lover would stay at home, having had this experience before. It is not seldom that a party ends in a skirmish. Milly was probably not exaggerating when she said Ef' mi mu' ter' den oso, pe m'e waka, pe m'e go mek' mi muiterij.… ."/If I had to count the houses where I walked, where I went to make my mutiny … Juliette would also repeatedly muse about the number of (older) women she had been with and she expressed it in almost the same terms: "If I had to count the women … " Even though the women who uttered this expression experienced it as a highly individual and personal part of their autobiography, I look upon this theme as a collective narrative element of how a strong, successful, and pleasurable mati life is presented. These women were, in emic terms, making a statement about the strength of their Apuku, the male spirit that is foregrounded in their personhood and who is pivotal in their wanting to lie down with other women.

Asked to give some examples of their experiences, one of the stories that tumbled out vividly illustrated the naughtiness and joy Milly had in her sexual exploits and again the rich language mati deploy:

*I had this lady that I was really infatuated with, Ingrid. She and Lucia were
mati and I was living with a man at the time, who often had to work the
nightshift at Paranam.*[18] *One Saturday afternoon, I went to the market to do
my shopping. I bought two bags of groceries for myself and one bag for her,
including two ice cold bottles of beer. I took the bus to her place and she let me
in. However, she was expecting her Mati that afternoon, too. So she told me to
lock the door from the outside and climb through a window. Pretty soon we
were upstairs in bed. "Un ben f'furu, so na wan snelle werk a ben mus' de. A
slag kon aan de boord, i sab' san m'e taki, toch? A hoogtepunt fu a wroko"/We
were "stealing," so it had to be fast work. We were almost hitting, you understand what I am saying, don't you? the climax of the work. Pam-pam-pam,
who comes knocking? But the key was not in its regular place; it was inside. I
was not afraid, but Ingrid was shaking. I asked her: Saide y'e befi so"?/Why are
you trembling so? I wanted to go on, mi ben wan' doro na Heiligeweg,*[19] *literally, "I wanted to arrive at Heiligeweg," I wanted to climax. But Ingrid was so
nervous, she jumped from the bedroom window unto her neighbor's roof. "Pe
y'e sie mi in' a oso, mi no ben dyompo. Mi ben go suk' mi libi, mi no ben wan'
pur' Inke f' en mati anu"/Where you saw me in the house, I did not jump. I
had gone to seek my life, I did not want to take Ingrid from her mati's hands.
It turned out that Lucia had a spare key to the house, so she came upstairs. I
was only wearing a black slip, sitting on the bed. She said: "Good afternoon." I
said: "Good afternoon to you too." Ingrid stayed outside, did not dare come in.
"Lucia ben suku mi so meni langa keba, so un fen' makandra gelijk"/Lucia
had been after me for a long time, so we found each other right away.*

This narrative, which depicted a scenario that was known as *plei kisi*,
literally, "play get," ends here, but I would venture that Lucia, once she was
through with Milly, went in search of Ingrid and gave her some good thrash-
ing. *Plei kisi* is illustrative of the sometimes insidious power games that mati
play; older women are most adept at it. *Plei kisi* ultimately resulted in one's
getting together with one's lover's lover; the older mati A, who had a relationship with B, effectively destroyed what was going on between B and C by
having sex with C. Younger women tend to accept this scenario less. But new
games have come into vogue that are at least as insidious.

The narrative above again shows the language that is used by mati in the
sexual domain, a language at once rich in images, precise, and inventive. The
language is deliberately difficult for outsiders to understand. "We were stealing"; "A slag kon aan de boord," half in Dutch and half in Sranan Tongo, calls
up images of a ship, where a direct hit is about to take place, thus appropriately
referencing (almost) climaxing. Like the expression Milly used before: "Ef' mi
mu' ter' den oso, pe m'e waka, pe m'e go mek' mi muiterij … "/If I had to count

the houses where I walked, where I went to make my mutiny ... " these images, interestingly, bespeak a maritime universe. From the start of the colony, Paramaribo was the main seaport. Seamen and naval officers, newly arriving in the harbor, were, according to several historical sources, very popular with white, enslaved, and freed women alike (Stedman 1974). From the earliest days on, laundrywomen found employment washing clothes for maritime personnel, and they probably also traded sex for money. Beckles (1989) described a similar scenario for enslaved women in another seaport, Bridgeport, Barbados, where enslaved women were forced by their owners to bring in a fixed amount of money per week. In Bakhtinian fashion, a word not forgetting where it has been, I assume that these sexual expressions, originating in a maritime milieu, have kept on circulating also in the same-sex sexual domain.

"I wanted to arrive at Heiligeweg" is another splendid image, especially if one imagines the Heiligeweg itself: lots of stores and a busy intersection, where the buses from the outlying districts and neighborhoods arrive in the city center. That is the place where one wants to be in a sexual encounter: I wanted to come.

In another conversation with Milly, she spoke to me, drawing on her rich experience, inviting caution: "A no ala pe y' e go, y' e feni gesluiten ondrosey'"/It's not everywhere you go that you find closed "down there." This referred to disappointing experiences: women who "down there" are just like the sea or Ansu: too salty and too wet.[20] She and other mati also informed me in depth about the many qualifications and types of *noso,* literally, "nose, clitoris," that may cross one's path.

The detailed language that mati have developed to describe their experiences with sex, its explicitness, nuance, and the ease with which they use it, has made an extraordinary impression on me. It certainly formed a contrast to the language-poor sexual environments, in Euro-American contexts, that I knew best.

Beside the information about roles within a relationship to which I will turn in the next section, the above narratives illuminate the mati landscape from an insider perspective. You can "search for your life," that is to say, have a passing sexual connection, but also have the intention to "take someone out of the hands of her mati." In the last chapter we saw that *mi ben go suk' mi libi*/I was searching for my life indicated transactional sex with men in order to keep one's head above water. Other emic divisions that mati use to order their world include the distinction between sexual acts, where women just sleep with other women, *den didon gewoon*/they are just lying down, and acts where mutual obligations are involved, *den mati*/they are in a committed relationship. Other graphic terms for the just-lying-down modality are *nyan p' sa*, literally, "eat," here in the sexual sense, and be gone, and *boro p' sa*/sneaking in and disappearing. Just sleeping with a woman carries no mutual obligations. But doing the mati work, expressed by the verbs *de in' a wroko, de in' a bewegey, de in' a zaak, de in' a libi*/to be in the work, to be in the movement, to be in the business, to be in the life, means that you have obligations toward your partner. In fact, the "work" in the term *mati wroko* in itself implies that there are obligations. These obligations consist, as we have seen in Juliette's narrative, of mutual help, of nurturance and emotional support and sexual obligations. Part of the mati sensibility also involved, as you will recall in Juliette's narrative, that children given to one's mati to be raised by her should not be demanded back. In addition, mati believe that when one of the partners feels sexual need, the other has to oblige her. Not fulfilling one's *kamra prikti*/chamber obligations, here in a same-sex framework—but the principle is operative in the opposite-sexed domain as well—leaves the other partner free to go and seek redemption with another woman. But it is understood that when she is suspected of infidelity she will be confronted with the jealousy of her partner. The code of ethics and entitlements in such situations demands that the "wanderer" keeps denying her infidelity, unless she is caught with her pants down, so to speak.

Before we consider the division of roles in a relationship, it is necessary to visit a current debate about sexuality as identity versus sexuality as behavior and to explore how the mati work fits into these different understandings.

The Mati Work as Behavior

The cross-cultural study of homosexualities is still plagued by some basic conceptual shortcomings that carry the fingerprints of North American conceptualizations of sex. An indication of such shortcomings is the fact that the concept of "homosexual identity" still plays a privileged and tenacious part in discussions about sexuality[21] (cf. D'Emilio 1984; Vance 1989; De Cecco and Elia 1993). The concept is inserted as a particularly powerful mediator of gay and lesbian behaviors. Sometimes these discussions are limited to the Western world, but the concept is also, apparently without much hesitation, used in cross-cultural contexts. Even though, in constructionist approaches, the relationship between sexual acts and sexual identities is thought to be variable, scholars often do not question the notion of homosexual (or homoerotic) identity in itself or its ubiquitousness. Whether homosexual identity is conceived of as an essentialist category, with biological and physiological influences preceding and setting limits to cultural ones, or as a constructionist concept, privileging social and cultural experiences, it is striking that a concept used with such frequency in the literature is not subjected to more reflection. However the concept is perceived, it apparently speaks to deeply ingrained, ethnopsychological notions in Western subjects that the core of our being, our essence, the privileged site in which the truth about ourselves and our social relationships is to be found corresponds to something that we call (homo-)sexual identity. What has generally been lacking is an exploration of the implication in and the embeddedness of "sexual identity" in hegemonic, Western thought, even if in feminist and "queer" versions.

The static nature of sexual identity is in line with the ways personhood in general has been envisioned within a Western universe. The troubled Western relationship with homosex, naturalized, compartmentalized, medicalized, consecutively made into sin and into the "deepest, truest" expression of the self, of one's identity, is historically and culturally embedded. Whether a homosexual identity is understood as the pure sediment of biological or physiological processes, or whether some kind of interaction between the biological and the cultural is envisioned, or whether primacy is entirely given to sociocultural experiences, the notion of a sexual identity in itself carries deep strands of permanency, stability, fixity, and near impermeability to change. Furthermore, the mere existence of a sexual identity is usually taken for granted.

The particular Euro-American understanding of a person as a bounded, fixed, rational, and self-determining agent is produced and reproduced in and by modern political, legal, social, and aesthetic discourses. Subjectivity has, until recently, implicitly been envisaged along masculine lines, thus leaving femininity no conceptual space but the nonmasculine; femininity is not just different, but in a hierarchically subordinate position to the masculine. While male sexuality is seen as aggressive and potent, female sexuality has by and large been conceptualized as passive and weak, needing to be awakened by a stronger force. One, furthermore, is either heterosexual or homosexual, with bisexuality muddying these clear waters. Dichotomous, either/or, hierarchical thinking characterizes this system.

The Creole working-class universe is characterized by additive, inclusive, both/and thinking (cf. Hill Collins 1990). As we saw, a person is conceived of as multiple, malleable, dynamic, and possessing male and female elements. Furthermore, all persons are inherently conceived of as sexual beings. A linguistic reflection and construction of this multiple, dynamic conceptualization of personhood is that in Sranan Tongo there are infinite possibilities to refer to "I." A human being, in this universe, is understood to be made up out of human and "godly" elements. From conception until death, a person is "carried" and protected by Winti. Women who engage in the mati work are thought to be carried by a strong male God, an Apuku, who is jealous of his "child," the woman, engaging in permanent sexual relationships with flesh-and-blood males. The

Apuku is believed to be so strong and demanding, that his child will have difficulty relating to men and will be more attracted to other women. An emic explanation of the mati work does not claim a core homosexual identity but is conceived of as engagement in a pleasant activity, desired and instigated by one particular instance of the "I." It is the Apuku who is sexually attracted to women and there is no emic reason to privilege this instance of the "I" above others by making him the decisive, "truest" element of the self.

In keeping with the multiplicity of the "I," a multiplicitous sexual repertoire was realized in the Creole working-class. There is no significant stigma attached to parts of this repertoire. Girls growing up in Creole working-class neighborhoods are confronted with different sexual choices and engaging in one variety, e.g., the same-sexed one, does not generally expose the girl to disapproval, nor does it predispose her to stay in that part of the sexual system forever. Thus we see women who are alternately or simultaneously active in either part of the system. Women express their same-sex sexual activities by means of a verb: *m'e mati*/I am doing the mati work, not by means of an "I am" construction.

Conceiving of same-gender sexual behavior, embodied in the mati work, in terms of "identity" inscribes and reproduces Western thought categories with their legacy of dichotomy, hierarchy, and permanency, thus distorting a phenomenon that is emically experienced in quite different terms. "Homosexualities" cross-culturally have in common same-sex sexual acts, but these acts are also critically different and contextually conceived in multiple ways. What is viewed as sexual varies widely cross-culturally and even when there is convergence between Western and non-Western contexts as to which acts count as sexual, it cannot be assumed that the landscapes in which these acts are embedded and acquire meaning are interchangeable. It is clear that mati conceive of their same-sex activities as sex, but they conceive of these acts in terms of behavior, not identity. Emically it makes more sense to conceive of sex as a relational activity, where the sex of one's object of passion is less salient than sexual fulfilment per se. This is a radically other configuration than dominant Western conceptualizations of homosexuality as identity. In the mati work no real, authentic, fixed self is claimed, but one particularly strong, masculine instance of the multiplicitous "I," who loves to lie down with women, is foregrounded.

Roles in the Relationship

In most mati relationships both women participated in paid labor and had children to care for. Many mati agreed, however, that in every relationship there has to be a gendered role division, where one of the partners will have the "male" role and the other one will play the "female." Although many mati subscribed to this notion, it was by no means the only model to pattern a relationship. The words that are used in Sranan for these roles are, literally, *man*/man and *uma*/woman. Sometimes this role division was readily apparent by different appearances, behavioral styles, and dress codes of a couple; other times it is not outwardly clear. Among older couples *par' weri* was still customary: women wore dresses made from the same fabric. The woman who made the first move indicating her interest in the other had staked a simultaneous claim to the "male" role. The roles say something about the sexual division of labor in the relationship; the "male" lies on top or can tell the "female" to be on top. Among couples who have an outspoken division of roles, there are also often differential entitlements, in the sense that the "man" can demand more privileges and freedoms.

Unless the male role has been clearly determined from the beginning, and is of paramount importance to one partner, this role division can become a topic of discussion and negotiation. In some couples the role division is fluid, since there are couples who switch roles every so often. In van Lier's seven case studies of mati, collected in 1949, the majority of women did not switch roles in the relationship; only one couple reported switching every two weeks. There are also women who have had a "masculine" role in one relationship and take a "feminine" role in the next. The polarization in roles is deemed necessary and "natural," and almost all women agreed that two "women" or two "men" cannot be together. The odo "Tu kapasi no man tan in wan olo"/Two armadillos cannot live in one hole applies to this understanding. It is apparent that, unless someone has an absolute preference for one role or the other, there is variation and flexibility in the gender system.

This flexibility is elaborated by Lydia de Vrede, the mother of five children, who has played both "male" and "female" roles in relationships. Addressing the gendered division of labor in mati relationships, Lydia states:

> *Den mannengre-meid/those manly types have a whole series of demands. You are not supposed to have a man, others do not want you to have children. Sometimes she does not want you to go out at all. When you go to a party you are not supposed to talk, much less dance with anybody else. Some women think they have to beat you up, to make you obey. They are really laying down the law for you. As a woman, I am not into those women. Because a mati libi/the mati life still is not accepted 100 percent everywhere; I do not like to go out with a woman who is too masculine. Right away when they see her, people know what the score is. It is not only the fact that she is wearing men's trousers and shirts, it is her whole attitude. I like more feminine women.*

While most women readily agree that the "male" role has more privileges than the female role, there are women who will not take the male role under any circumstances. Maureen Fernandes has always had a feminine role in her relationships with women, whether her partner was "masculine" or "feminine":

For me, the character of the person is the most important. If I love you, I love you and I will defend you against everybody. I will give you everything I own. I don't care what you look like, whether you look like a "man" or a "woman." You have to treat me sweetly, that is all. I for myself want to look the way I do: well taken care off, very feminine, very attractive to both men and women.

Stella Einaar, on the other hand, known to friend and foe as Stanka, always plays the "male" role in her relationships. She wears very smart men's clothes and a man's hat or baseball cap, according to the image she is projecting. Stanka mostly hangs out with the guys in a local café, playing billiards and card games. In mati language she is referred to as *wan effektieve mati meid*/a true mati gal, since her demeanor and behavior leave little question as to her sexual style. Effektieve mati meid are seldom sexually involved with men and may simultaneously have more than one female lover. Stanka says:

I never have just one mati at one time. I have my tru visiti/"steady," and then two or three other lovers. If my steady is a Creole woman, I take care that the others are not: I will take Jampanesi/a Javanese or Koelie/a Hindustani (woman) or someone who is here on vacation from Holland. Creole women are difficult, san!!!what!! She is going to call the others and curse them, if they are Creoles too. I really handpick my lovers, I do not take any Jan, Piet, en Klaas.[22] Mi skin mu tek' den /My "I" has to take them. I can't afford to begin looking, after I and my tru visiti have broken up. It takes too long, so I keep them in reserve.

Inherent tensions are built into relationships by this division of labor, contributing to the recurrent jealousy in the mati world. The parallels between relationships in cross-sex and same-sex spheres are striking in this respect. In Juliette's younger days, when life was appreciably cheaper and the Surinamese guilder had not embarked on its inflationary course, some women could afford to support another woman by paying her rent and providing for her. The balance of power in those relationships favored the economically powerful partner and many women indicated to me that they would not want to be in such an arrangement, because it would make them too dependent. Nowadays, most women agreed that "keeping a woman" was no longer possible, at least not on a Surinamese income. There were, of course, mati who were in the favorable position to have a (male or female) lover in the Netherlands who supported them. Interestingly, many "male" mati were not economically dominant in their relationships. Some worked only irregularly, while others did not work outside the home. Stanka, for instance, financed herself by being in multiple relationships with partners who did work outside the home and, importantly, by a lover in the Netherlands.

While the discourse around polarized roles is strong, it does not mean that all women in fact conform to this strict division of labor. My impression is that many couples, in reality, wavered around the middle ground of an imaginary continuum. Like Lydia, other women indicated that they did not want to be with a woman who was too "masculine"; they did not want to be "under" someone, and in the sexual domain they expected both partners to be on top sometimes and do some work. These conceptualizations of different roles in a relationship have been around for quite some time since Juliette narrated that when she was a young woman there were women who projected very "masculine" styles. They dressed strictly in men's suits with men's hats. Juliette did not like to be in a relationship with one of them, because just as she did not want to be "under a man," her yeye did not allow her to be "under" a woman, either. Even then there were women who resisted extreme role conceptions.

While there is thus continuity in the division of roles among younger women, it bears repeating that such patterning is not inevitable. There is a lot of variation in sexual roles chosen, concomitant with a flexible gender system. The polarized roles are reminiscent of the butch/femme phenomenon described for Euro-American working-class lesbian couples in the 1940s, 1950s, and 1960s (Nestle 1992; Hollibaugh 2000). It is intriguing that of the limited number of studies we possess of female same-sex cultures cross-culturally[23] this pattern seems so prominent (see Lorde 1982; Kennedy and Davis 1993; Nestle 1992; Faderman 1981, 1991, 2003; Blackwood 1995, 1999; Wieringa 1999; Murray 1999). Interestingly, my Dutch colleague Saskia Wieringa (1999) questions the ability of social constructivist theory to account for the ubiquity, uniformity, and persistence of this pattern, globally, in female same-sex desire. According to her, social constructivists tend to ignore aspects of embodiment in their analyses of sexuality and her plea is to look harder at the interplay of the environment and embodied desires. How is it, Wieringa poignantly asks, "that individual women exhibit such levels of rebellion that they prefer to face physical maltreatment, prison or social ostracism rather than not live their desires"? (1999:207). Based on her fieldwork with lesbians in Jakarta and Lima, among whom she found the same polarized pattern, she proposes that we take more seriously the "materiality of the body" (255), bodies that are endowed with sexualities of varying intensities (ibid.).

I do not **agree** with Wieringa's line of argument. There are three points I want to make, which collectively signal the prematurity of an assessment that bases the prevalence of b/f cultures in bodies or even in the interaction between bodies and environment. In the first place, I am not sure that it is possible to state with any degree of validity that the majority of same-sex relationships in all these varied places are ordered according to polarized roles. It does seem certain that those relationships that are structured according to this principle are more visible than others. Two women who structure their relationship along—what locally counts for—"feminine" lines will not be as conspicuous and will possibly not even be registered as being in a same-sex relationship. I am suggesting that the supposed universal ubiquity of relationships exhibiting polarized roles may be a trick the eye is playing on us. Second, and more generally, the code of the complicated relationship between biology/"nature" and culture is far from being cracked. How is the connection between genes and complicated sexual behavior to be made? How can (stronger sexuality?) genes ever express themselves outside a cultural environment? Even if it were the case that the sexualities of particular individuals were stronger than that of others, why would that find expression in taking the butch role? Third, I believe that of the different ways to create erotic tension within a relationship, polarized roles are but one possible avenue. Apparently, within the mati universe age difference functions as another eroticizer, so conceivably so may other modalities in other cultures. We do not have enough knowledge yet of what counts as erotic in different cultures and we lack these data precisely for female same-sex relationships.

In chapter 6, where I will describe the unfolding of Lydia's life as she moved to the Netherlands in the beginning of the nineties, we will explore an extremely polarized relationship, with its attendant rights and privileges and economic coordinates, in more detail. I found that women who strongly believe in occupying the "male" role in their same-sex relationships and who are more or less inflexible in this role playing foreground their being "carried" by Apuku more than other women who have more flexibility. The former presented behavior that displayed similarity with masculine behavior in the opposite-sex sexual arena.

Jealousy and Obligations

Mati have, as we saw in Juliette's case, different attachments and feelings toward men and women. In most women's accounts the companionship and camaraderie of another woman is valued. Even if there is a man more or less regularly present, the homosocial fabric in society makes it fairly unlikely that a woman will receive the same support from him as from her mati in the sharing of everyday concerns such as money, care of the children, going to the doctor, and the like.

Sex also figures prominently in relationships between mati and men, but for altogether different reasons than it does among mati. Children are an important way to realize one's personhood, and in relationships with men the exchange relationship between money and sex is much more prominent. While some women stress that sexual contact with a man is necessary for a woman's *insey*/insides, this is not accepted by everyone. Lydia, who was married and only in the position to just "lie down" with women, explains the difference in her feelings toward men and women:

> *I see it like this: love between two women is stronger than between a man and a woman. Maybe emancipated women will tell a man what they like or do this or that. But to satisfy that man most women will pretend that they have come. But, with a woman, you know what you like sexually and so does she, "dus a san' kan law yu ede zodanig, a kan tja' yu go na Kolera"/thus that thing can make you so crazy, that you will have to go to Kolera (a psychiatric institution).*

Just as in cross-sex connections, a pattern of violence between mati is very much a part of life and it is one of the reasons many outsiders advance in their refusal to associate with mati. There are many scriptlike stories being told in "straight" circles, both working and middle class, about physical violence among mati brought about by jealousy. Mati are looked down upon and are not considered "decent" because of this behavior pattern. Several younger women spoke on the issue of violence. While some did not like it at all, the more general feeling in the group of women with whom I worked, especially among women who play the "male" role in their relationships, was that it was necessary to beat one's lover regularly if her behavior demanded it. Without violence she would presumably not be socialized into knowing who was the dominant partner and her own role as the submissive one. Take Stella, for instance. It has always been her style to exert force in her relationships:

> *When I know that someone really loves me, "m'e tron vrijpostig. M'e lob' tak 'fok' op'"/I start behaving out of line, I love to talk "fok' op." I will say, for example, I need sg. 100; give it to me or I am going to beat you. Life is like that. You have to beat your woman every day, till she wants to hear. Some of them really are hard of hearing. Same thing when she will cook something that is mi trefu/ritually forbidden dish, I will beat her up. One day, I really*

beat my lover badly with a chair, because I did not like the way she was look-
ing at another woman. I am telling you, I am bad news.

There is a certain pride in Stella's last words; she knows how to control
her women and to inspire awe. There are, of course, individual differences
between women and the flair with which they play their roles. Women
who play the "male" role but do not like to beat their mati are sometimes
considered to be at a disadvantage: not "tough" enough. In some relationships, where both partners have agreed to their gender division of labor,
the "female" partner, while she may not necessarily like the beatings, pretty
much takes them in stride. There were also women who had left their partners because of the intensity of the beatings. According to the "males,"
"females" like to be beaten. The beatings come with the territory, and both
parties essentially look upon them as a sign of continuing love and devotion.
There is matter-of-factness and openness in mati circles about the beatings.

In the domain of violence the feelings are different as well. For Juliette a
beating by a man spelled the end of the affair. With her mati it was different:

I think women should go to the police when men hit them. Even if it is your
own son who hits you. "Ma di mi nanga mi mati ab' trobi—mek ' un taki en
ben uru, no so mi ben uru—mi kan nak' en, en kan nak' mi. Dat na neks."/
But when my mati and I are having problems—let's say she has run around
or else I have done it—I can hit her, she can hit me. That is nothing. If you are
not jealous when your girlfriend is walking out on you, and if you do not hit
her, it is no true love. Even if a visiti/your mati, beats you up badly, you do
not go the police. How can you do that? "Na mi mati, na fu mi fu tek' a fon-
fon, m'e tan"/It is my mati. It is for me to take the beating, I will stay. With
a man it is different.

There is a paradox built into this element of the mati work that, on the
one hand, mirrors the dominant cross-sex relationships and connections,
while, on the other hand, the dangers and tensions in the polarized roles
of mati are attractive and seductive. Relations between men and women
are marked with asymmetry and often with physical violence. This model
also influences relations between members of the same sex, because women
especially move back and forth in this fluid dual sexual system. Additionally,
the continual contestation of boundaries and roles, "male"ness/"female"ness,
dominance/submission, sexual faith/promiscuity may very well add an element of seduction and eroticization to the sexual experience. And, there is,
moreover, an underlying explanation for the violence within the parameters
of the Winti religion, which may make it acceptable for many women.

Attitudes of Men Toward the Mati Work

Just as women do not all think similarly about the mati work, men do not either. It struck me at mati parties that men would be standing alongside the dance floor drinking beer, talking with one another, seemingly completely undisturbed by the fact that their wives were dancing in an intimate embrace with their mati. The women I interviewed about men's attitudes identified a whole range of attitudes and arrangements that can best be imagined as a continuum. There are men who radically reject the mati work, find it neither proper nor respectable and would absolutely not tolerate it if "their" wife would join in. There are also men who take part in the same culture and who understand the desire that their wife has for other women. Juliette's older partner Dorus was, as we saw, very indulgent toward her sexual activities with women, whereas Coba's male partner did not give her much space in that regard. When a woman has a strong masculine Apuku, a husband can agree to an arrangement where the three live together. Josephine Emanuel told me that as a young woman in her late teens she lived with her mati, Ilse, and Ilse's man, Harold, who were both in their late thirties. Ilse was a dominant woman who owned a diner and she also was dominant in her relationships. Harold would not dare approach Josephine sexually, *dan kon hij het vegen*/then he could forget it, i.e., forget about his relationship with Ilse too. Only when Ilse was in a good mood with Harold was he permitted, periodically, to have sex with Josephine.

Between the two extremes are men who know that their woman is in the mati work but do not talk about it or make a point of it, so long as it does not become too much of a problem or too visible. There are also men who pressure their wives and insist on being allowed to have sex with her mati. This happened to Lydia, and it was one of the reasons that she did not want to do the mati work anymore within the context of her marriage.

Relationships Between the Mati Work and Winti

Cultural-religious activities were an important part of the lives of Misi Juliette and her friends. Nowadays Winti Prey are predominantly held in the city and in adjacent districts, but in Juliette's "awakening" days, with little transport available, the reality was that people often had to walk for miles and miles to get to the *boiti* or *prenassi*/outside or plantation, where the Prey was held. They carried their clothes, food, and drinks in big baskets and bundles, often on their heads. Consequently, they would often stay for a number of days or even a week. During the nights there was the dancing. Early in the morning, at six, everyone went to sleep in the wooden huts surrounding the *kampu*/camp and during the afternoon women sat around, cooked, exchanged stories, *ben tyallans makandra*/flirted, sought each other out, and made appointments to see each other in town. Sex during the time they were at *boiti*, though ritually dangerous and frowned upon, did sometimes occur out back. Juliette explained to me the dangers entailed and women's reasons for their transgressions:

> *"F' a de, a no tak' alasma san de in' a wroko, ab' winti, ma furu sma abi. Verschillende winti n' e lob' a mati wroko kwet' kweti. Ingi lob' en, den lob' prisiri, ma den bigi winti, den Nengrekondre Koromanti n' e lob' en. Son Obia ooktu n' e lob' en. Aisa sref' no de nanga den tor' dati. A gewone matirij n' e tref' a winti so. Ma ef' i de tap' i futu, a no bun. Den winti fir' y' e tref' den, y' e morsu den. D' o siki yu, kan de d' o kir' yu... . Ma te i de yongu, yu n' a te maken nanga den san' dati."*/How it is; not everybody who is in the mati work has Winti, but a lot of us do. Some Winti cannot stand the work. Indians love it, they love making pleasure, but the big Winti, the African Koromanti do not love it. Some Obia also do not love it. Aisa herself is not into it. The regular mati work does not pollute the Winti so much. It is not good to do it when you are menstruating. The Winti feel you are polluting them, you are making them dirty. They may make you sick, other people have been killed. Also they are not going to come to your dreams anymore, to show you things, to warn you. But when you are young you do not have any business with what the Winti want. You are young, you feel lust all the time, you do it, whether you are menstruating or not.

This quote shows some of the deep reverberations Winti culture has within the mati world. There is a connection between the jealousy and the cultural-religious domain in Juliette's view. When you have certain Winti, e.g., *Motyo-Ingi*/Whore-Indian, *Motyo-Obia*/Whore-Obia, or Apuku, a jealous male god, you will always know when your lover has slept with another woman. The Motyo-Ingi will show his *asi*, literally, "horse," in her sleep where and with whom her loved one has slept. Even though the Motyo-Ingi loves to sleep around a lot, too, he cannot stand it when the lover of his asi does the same thing. That is why sometimes deaths or serious wounds are inflicted, because the Ingi gets so angry, but he cannot help it, that is the way he is. Not surprisingly, many mati report that they have Motyo-Ingi or Apuku.

The "cultural" explanation for the jealousy and violence in mati relationships illustrates again the concept of multiplicitous selves: Motyo Ingi, one of the incarnations of "I," loves to sleep around but cannot stand it when the mati of his asi ("I") does likewise. It is not "I" who hits, but Motyo Ingi. Not all women agree with this "cultural" reading of the mati work or the jealousy. Some say, "Gi den Winti por' nen!"/This gives the Winti a bad name.

My friend Lydia explained that for her there is a quite different connection between the mati work and Winti. Since she is married and can't reconcile this with the mati work, when she wants to be with women she goes to a Winti Prey. The advantage is that there are hardly any men around. Those that are there, according to her, are, with the possible exception of the drummers, all *boelers*/men who are into men, anyway. Going to a Prey gives her something of the atmosphere that she so misses—the joking, talking, laughter, nearness of and bodily contact with women. Especially when there are many women at a prey, to be in close physical contact is unavoidable and as such it is a favorite pickup opportunity.

Lobi Singi

A favorite passtime of women in the olden days was *lobi singi,* literally, "love songs." We owe the most elaborate description of lobi singi, festive gatherings where women sang for each other, to the music connoisseur Comvalius, whom we encountered before. Lobi singi, according to Comvalius, are a transitional form between African and European songs. Originating after the abolition of slavery (1863), lobi singi are modeled after the *Du,* a uniquely Surinamese dramatic play in which feuding factions of the plantocracy during slavery fought out their disputes through drama performed by their slaves (Comvalius 1935, 1939; Voorhoeve and Lichtveld 1975). Upperclass people, particularly women, who were interested in staging these lavish affairs could afford to begin and keep Du-associations going. Voorhoeve and Lichtveld compare the Du, which were staged from the middle of the eighteenth century until 1873, with the chambers of rhetoric in the Netherlands. After slavery the plantocracy lost interest in these costly performances, which often were so acerbic that they forced some planters to leave the colony. Some of the dramatic characteristics of the Du have been retained in lobi singi, but one important difference is that, with the exception of the musicians, all the participants in lobi singi are women. Lobi singi can be considered to be odes to love and are dedicated to Kibido/Cupid, the god of love (Comvalius 1935). Lobi singi sings the praises of the friendships between women, the virtues and faults.

Right after slavery, higher-class women, both of European and mixed descent, would hire working-class women to sing the praises and decry the vices of their peers. The patrons would not be present themselves at the performance but would hear a report from their servants. Later on working-class women would sing love songs for each other. Around 1900 lobi singi came to be used in a heterosexual context as well.

In Comvalius's time, the thirties, lobi singi consisted of three parts:

1. *Langa singi,* literally, "long song," an epical-lyrical song, consisting of verse with three lines.
2. The scene with *Aflaw,* a piece of drama, in which Aflaw, literally, "she faints," is the central character. Aflaw is the metaphorical image for the morally elevated woman who cannot bear gossip, hate, and deceit. Shaken by what she has heard during the langa singi, she faints and has to be treated by *Datra/* Doctor, who wears glasses and a high hat, sometimes complemented by such figures as the doctor's assistant and a nurse. The scene of Aflaw and Datra is in its entirety taken from the Du.[24]
3. *Kot' singi,* literally, "cut song," i.e., short song, refrain, that keeps the same melody while the words change. When Aflaw has fainted, the doctor is called with a kot' singi by the singer of the langa singi who has caused Aflaw's affliction:

> Kar' wan datra kon gi mi,
> kar' wan datra kon gi mi.
> Aflaw e dede na mi anu.
>
> [Call a doctor,
> call a doctor.
> Aflaw is dying in my hands.]

> (COMVALIUS 1939:11, 12)

This lobi singi is still sung today. Imagine, on the basis of Comvalius's description (1935, 1939), a large terrain in Saramacca Street on a Sunday afternoon from 4 to 7 P.M. Formerly the yard had been owned by a Jew, Abraham de Vries, also known as *Abraham kot nikkie,* Abraham with the crooked neck. De Vries made a living by buying dilapidated merchant marine ships, so the terrain was strewn with masts, chains, anchors, pumps, etc. The yard also harbored the only hand-operated merry-go-round in Paramaribo. Days in advance the news had circulated that Misi A would sing about her mati or another woman, and crowds of women showed up, waiting to hear the story of what happened between the two female friends. The public stood in a wide circle around the musicians and the singers. The woman who would sing the new self-composed songs walked slowly and in stately fashion in the circle, followed by the other participants. One by one, she sang her songs, first without and then accompanied by the musicians and the song was repeated by the bystanders. According to Comvalius, this choral song is an African characteristic. The beat of the music was indicated by the singers who waved their colorful angisa.

The content and meaning of the song were quickly understood, and in appreciation of the singer's talents the public offered her money, which she kept in a little lace bag tied around her waist. Comvalius (1939:357) mentions the following langa singi:

> Ef' wan lobbi ben lobbi mi
> A no lobbi mi moro (2x)
> Mi no kan kiri mi srefi
> Vo dati ede.
>
> [When a loved one has loved me
> But now she does not love me anymore (2x)
> I cannot kill myself
> For that reason.]

The long song was the main ingredient of the performance, because it always contained some new information that caught the women's attention. The long song was followed by a kot' singi, which was repeated over again, with the women dancing in pairs and in European style. The melody was upbeat and differed from the long song, which was stately. One such "cut song" was

> Wan dei wan dei, Kibido (3x),
> M'ee go lassie mie lieb'a ja-noe.
>
> [One day, one day, Cupid (3x),
> I am going to lose my life in your hands.]

Continuing the earlier tradition, it occurred that upper-class women wrote songs for their peers and had working-class women perform them. The songs could either be full of praise or expose another woman for her moral or physical faults.

Comvalius makes a strange, inverted connection when he observes:

> Through or because of the Lobbie Siengi unusual relationships among women in Suriname were generated, which were not dependent on social rank, intellectual development, race or country of origin. Love (?) brought women and young girls of very different walks of life together as intimate friends. Maybe this form of friendship should rather be considered as a form of servitude, and let's not talk about another, dark side to it, the discussion of which is no concern of ours. Probably it was blown over here from the French West Indies.[25]

(COMVALIUS 1935:11, 1939:356)

In their description of lobi singi the Herskovitses stress the West African origin. They consider it to be an established form of social criticism that ridicules the blameworthy behavior of women. They published the texts of thirteen lobi singi (Herskovits and Herskovits 1936:23–31). Voorhoeve and Lichtveld later published the texts of eighteen lobi singi (1975:38–49) that were recorded between 1957 and 1961 and partially overlap the collections of Comvalius and the Herskovitses.[26]

Lobi singi still are performed today, but in much leaner form (only the kot' singi) and less frequently than apparently used to be the case, but I was lucky enough to witness two of them in 1990–1991. Among the songs performed during the lobi singi that I attended I noted the following:

> Wan wan bun lobi de ete
> Wan wan bun lobi de ete
> Ma ala de na sma anu.
>
> [There are still some good loves
> There are still some good loves
> But they are all with somebody.]

The song comments on the predicament of a woman who is looking for a mati but finds that everyone is already taken. A subtext of this song is its tongue-in-cheek statement that nobody ever knows whether her mati is really hers alone.

> Ini wan lobi, na lobi.
> Ini wan lobi, na lobi.
> Ma echte lobi, a no wan lobi.
>
> [Every love is love.
> Every love is love.
> But true love is not just any love.]

And:

> Wer' moi krosi na noti.
> Wer' moi bruku na noti.
> Wer' moi koto na noti.
> Ma na sroto fu yu ondro na basi.
>
> [Wearing pretty clothes is nothing.
> Wearing pretty pants is nothing.
> Wearing a pretty skirt is nothing.
> But the key to your bottom is most important.]

FIGURE 5.2. Three women at a celebration, 1991. *Photo by Gloria Wekker*

Another song is quite old and typical in its metaphorical, flowery language:

> Roos e flauw a de fadon.
> Roos e flauw a de fadon.
> Ma stanvaste dat e tan sidon.

> [The rose is weak, it has fallen down.
> The rose is weak, it has fallen down.
> But "steadfast" stays upright.]

The qualities of women are symbolized here with flowers: the rose sags quickly, but the flower stanfaste (Gomphrena globosa, Amaranthceaea) is, as the name suggests, long-standing, steadfast. Stanfaste does not fall quickly for seductions, in contrast to the rose, which is beautiful, but on which one can build nothing. Mati often call a beautiful woman a rose. As Lena Sluisdom put it: "Moro betre mi ab' wan takru fes' sma, dan een roos"/Better someone with an ugly face than a pretty young rose. Since you never know if the rose will stay with you.

Another favorite pastime of women, one with a long history that is still carried on today, is the institution called *tya' boskopu*, literally, "to carry the message." In chapter 4 we saw a different manifestation of tya' boskopu, but here it takes the form of a match in exchanging and challenging each other with valued cultural knowledge, i.e., odo.

> *Diary May 28, 2001.*
> *Went to a party, this afternoon, of two well-known twins, in my old neighborhood, who celebrated their sixtieth birthday. The two birthday girls and their female relatives were all dressed in purple, the color that is appropriate for this crown year. Ninety-five percent of those present were women. Two different bands played back to back. When the party was well underway, a cross-dressed man initiated tya' boskopu, starting with the odo: "Mi na kapelka, mi sidon tap' ala den bromtyi, ma mi n' e soigi ala"/I am a butterfly, I sit down on all flowers, but I do not suck all of them. Great hilarity, applause!! An exchange followed between him and various women who answered him back with other, ambiguous odo, all with embedded sexual meanings: "Te yu wan' stanfaste lobi, sorgu yu kamra doro no abi tu sroto"/If you want true love, make sure that the door of your bedroom does not have two keys. This went on for about half an hour, after which the band resumed.*

Changes

Those who have seen the evolution of the mati work over several decades lament that the golden days of the institution are over. Juliette and her peers characterized the changes with a heavy dose of nostalgia: "Den dey dati noit' d' o kon moro"/those days will never come again. But younger women, who have memories of earlier times, are disillusioned and disappointed, too. It would be foolish to maintain that the institution of the mati work, like everything else in Surinamese society, has not suffered under the political-economic downhill course of the past thirty years, since political independence (1975). Also influential has been the fact that a sizable proportion of the population, including mati, has relocated to the Netherlands. Although there is considerable traffic between the two countries and bonds are maintained, the institution, like the rest of the society, has suffered from a certain anemia. The clearest mark of this is in the fact that the ceremonies, such as the birthday party and lobisingi, are organized with great difficulty. Oftentimes, no young women in their twenties and thirties are involved. In addition, the Civil War between the military and the Maroons and Indigenous people (1989–1992) meant that the outlying districts were inaccessible for years, so that the traditional outings and boat tours also became a thing of the past. Lack of money led to malnourishment among women, during the nineties, and it stands to reason that many activities that embellished their lives have been given up.

From the middle of the eighties a new phenomenon connected to the deteriorating economy presented itself. Lydia has a lot of insights in how things have changed. Her grandmother was also in the mati work, and since Lydia grew up in her household, her own mother having died when Lydia was an infant, she is able to make comparisons between the fifties and sixties and how things stood in the early nineties:

> *My grandmother and her mati were poor people, each had a man and chil-*
> *dren, but they helped each other where they could. If one needed money, the*
> *other would help out. "Let' anu ben was' krukt' anu"/the right hand washed*
> *the left. They discussed all their problems together and were wearing parweri*
> *a lot/the same dresses. I would like to take my example from them when I go*
> *into the work again. Nowadays there is a lot of competition between women.*
> *When two mati go to a party and one lends the other something to wear, she*
> *will go tell other people "She did not even have shoes to wear, I had to lend*
> *her mine." People have become more materialistic, they love gold, soso strey*
> *libi/life is motivated solely by greed. The een-op-tien matimeid/one-in-ten*
> *mati girls from Holland are making things worse.*

By one-in-ten mati girls Lydia was referring to Dutch Surinamese women, who with their Dutch guilders could get a handsome exchange rate of, in 1990–1991, one in ten. A theme that regularly cropped up in conversations was the way Surinamese people from Holland are mak-ing life more miserable for those who have stayed behind by throwing their money around. This is a double-edged sword because while, on the one hand, the Surinamese economy is kept afloat by remittances from Surinamese in the Netherlands to family members in Suriname, existing trends in the sexual domain, on the other hand, whether in a male-female or a mati context, were exacerbated by the free-floating cash. The rise in prostitution reported during the past two decades (Stichting Maxi Linder 2000) is linked to the increase in poverty and the influx of money from Dutch Surinamers. Many women emphasized that one of the new phe-nomena is that "Dutch" mati act outrageously and that the Surinamese mati lower themselves for money. Another side of this pattern is that the "Dutch" insult Surinamese women by elaborately describing the sexual acts to which the latter were prepared. Lydia stressed that nowadays one of the games people play is that they talk a lot about what a sexual partner did to them in bed:

> *What is happening now is den hebihebi p'tata meid, literally, "the heavy-*
> *heavy potato girls," Surinamese girls from Holland, they come here and get*

somebody to do oral sex with them for money. It is really shameful to the woman who is doing the oral sex, she has no self-respect, a' e saka en yeye/she is lowering her "soul." Then, later, somebody may be telling her girlfriends: "Te m' e taig' i, fa a sma ben pot' mi volledig, fa a sma ben bari, fa a sma ben nyan mi wreed"/When I am telling you, how she made me come, how she was screaming, how she ate me "cruelly," i.e., really baaad!!!

Whether the role that is attributed to Surinamese Dutch mati is factually true or not, what matters is that it is perceived as true by many Surinamese mati. Generally, the latter feel they are being treated as *pikin dagu*/little dogs, by the more economically viable Dutch women. It is easy to see that the balance in Surinamese mati relationships can be seriously distorted by this new situation.

Especially from the perspective of the "male" partner who may or may not be economically dominant, the new situation is a definite setback. By virtue of the fact that generally she who has the money calls the tune, the sexual opportunities for Surinamese *mannengre mati* /"male" mati are diminished. Just as many working-class and even lower middle-class Surinamese guys are complaining about the fact that they are outmatched by Dutch Surinamese men for the favors of Surinamese women, so the "male" mati is experiencing severe competition. As far as "female" mati are concerned, some maintain that they will not have anything to do with Dutch Surinamese girls, though others want involvement as a way out of their situation.

Still, during the fifteen years in which I have now followed the mati work, I have been led to believe that the institution is very much alive. It has adapted to different circumstances, yet it survives, as we will see in chapter 6.

Earlier Approaches to the Mati Work

In the remainder of this chapter I want to take some steps back and investigate what, historically, is known about the mati work. In addition, I will describe different historical, sociological, and anthropological explanations that have been proposed for the phenomenon. From the beginning of the twentieth century, 1912, but actually even earlier, the institution caught the attention of several observers, because it so flew in the face of implicit and explicit hegemonic assumptions about women's sexuality. I will offer my own approach to the mati work, which is novel, in that it offers a black diasporic understanding of the sexual subjectivity under study here. In doing so I will also address the vexed relationships between sex, gender, and sexuality, a current hotbed within lesbian and queer studies.

Mati relations are tantalizingly mentioned before 1900, which is regarded by most scholars of the phenomenon as the vital moment for its emergence. Due to the absence of men in the rain forest, where they were laboring in profitable industries like gold digging and balata bleeding, women turned to each other, according to this interpretation. Maria Lenders describes the conversion activities of Moravian brothers and sisters among Creoles in Suriname, 1735–1900, in her dissertation "Strijders voor het Lam" (1994). Around 1850 the missionary Sister Hartmann writes letters to her coreligionists in Europe that are full of complaints of converted men about the behavior of their women. A tantalizingly short passage from one such letter reads: "The wife of Gottlieb is a mati (female friend) of another woman. Gottlieb does not want it, but he cannot do anything about it, because he has been hit by her" (Lenders 1994:261). Sister Hartmann unfortunately does not digress on the nature of the relationship between the two women, but the context suggests that it is a sexual relationship.[27]

The mati work is first mentioned in official, colonial literature in 1912 in a memorandum to a report to the Dutch government. Concerned about the health problems of the indigent urban population, mainly the women, a report was made by a high-ranking Dutch official, A. J. Baron Schimmelpenninck van der Oye. In a memorandum to this report—"Eenige aantekeningen omtrent sommige minvermogenden"/Some notes concerning some indigents—anemia, general weakness, and concommitant complaints are mentioned as afflicting many women, often making it impossible for them to do labor on a regular basis. Beside their lack of money and the generally inferior quality of their food intake, consisting of bread, bananas, salt fish, and bacon, Schimmelpenninck van der Oye notes that there is another reason why many young women are so weak:

> Returning to the already discussed physically weak condition of so many young women, there is, in my opinion, still another reason, that is however of a delicate nature and about which I would be diffident to say anything, were it not that my advanced age and my tendency to investigate social ills of whatever nature would be excuses in this regard. I am referring to the sexual communion between women ("*het matiespelen*"/*the mati play*), which immorality has, as I gather, augmented much in the past decades and alas! has penetrated deeply into popular mores. It is not only that young girls and unattached women of various ranks make themselves guilty of this, the poorest often going and living together in pairs to reduce the cost of house rent and food for each of them, but also women living with men and even schoolgirls, following the example of others, do the same.[28]

(CITED IN AMBACHT 1912:98–99)

Schimmelpenninck van der Oye marks as the most important reasons for the augmentation of "the matie play," the introduction and expansion of the gold-and balata industries, which make men stay in the rain forest for many months. Moreover, the circumstance that—according to the official statistics—the population in the city has about twenty-five hundred more women than men, adds to these "immoralities."[29]

The trend set by Schimmelpenninck van der Oye is followed up by later scholars like Buschkens (1972). In what was a marked departure from the colonial voyeurism in the early part of the century, Melville and Frances Herskovits, studying Creole folklore in 1928 and 1929, described the ceremonial dimensions of the mati work. They are relatively open-minded in their descriptions of the birthday party and lobi singi. The birthday party they described is an aspect of social ceremonialism that was wholly in the hands of women. Usually given by the older partner for her younger lover, the institution is most often associated with female mati. The festivities opened during the late afternoon and, if there was dancing, continued through the night. It was customary for the special "friend" of the person who was celebrating her birthday to come late and to bring flowers for her mati. These she carried on her head and, as she approached the door of her friend's house, she stopped some paces away and called out:

"Mis'misi, mi kan kon na ini? Nowan doti no de na pasi? Nowan maka? Nowan sneki? Nowan storm no sa wai mi fadon?"

"No, no, misi, yu kan kon doro."

"Nanga baka?"

"Ya."

"Nanga fesi?"

"Ya."

"Nanga se? Fa mi e kanti de, mi no sa fadon?"

"No, yu no sa fadon."

["Little miss, can I come inside? Is there no dirt on the path? Are there no thorns? No snakes? Will the storm not blow me over?"

"No, no, Miss, you can come in."

"And backwards?"

"Yes."

"And forward?"

"Yes."

"And sideways? As I lean over, won't I fall down"?

"No, you will not fall down."]

As these formulaic words were being spoken the partners engaged in dancing steps, moving toward and away from each other. When the last phrase had been spoken, the woman whose birthday was being celebrated brought wine to the visitor, the music began to play, and the people who were gathered shouted "Hip, hip, hura! Sopi no de, ma kuku de"/Hip, hip, hooray! There is no rum, but there are cakes (Herskovits and Herskovits 1936:32, 33). The entire formula and the culturally charged symbols that the older woman uses—dirt, thorns, snakes—give expression to her fear of losing face and that the party that she is hosting will be spoiled by the presence of a competitor. A recurring theme I have found in older mati circles is that a younger partner will be attracted more to a peer. Sometimes trouble did arise, so the Herskovitses:

> It happens at times that when the ceremony we have just described is concluded, and the special "friend" bearing her flowers enters the house of her mati, she discovers that there are other flowers already in the room. The one just arrived thereupon seizes these flowers, crushes them, and throws them out, for they are the symbol of a rival claimant to the affection of her mati. If she knows the identity of this rival, she will, in addition, slap her, to show before the assembled guests that she will not have her rights disputed. If she does not know who had brought these flowers, she goes from one woman to the next to find out who it was. This byplay adds to the zest of the party, and while it goes on, such observations are made as will not fail to heighten the tension between the rivals, with the precaution, however, that the angered woman does not turn her attention to those who are making these remarks. It may happen, too, that the woman who had first sued for the affections of the mati in whose honor the party is being held is not at all intimidated, and makes a stand for her own prerogatives as "friend." In that case the matter is settled by blows, and the stronger of the two ejects the other; for while it is not uncommon for a woman to have more than one mati, neither will tolerate the presence of the other, nor yield her place if the challenge is thus made public. While the quarreling is going on, the woman who is celebrating watches passively, accepting the appeal to force and when the dispute is settled, the party proceeds with new impetus.

(HERSKOVITS AND HERSKOVITS 1936:33, 34)

As you will recall, fourteen-year-old Juliette in 1921 was involved in a similar scenario. She was not quite up yet to fully challenging the mati of Mis' Yaya, the older woman she was infatuated with at the time, but she knew the "grammar" of the situation. Since Juliette was not allowed to go to the birthday party, she found other ways to make her presence felt. It is also worth noting that while the Herskovitses write "it is not uncommon for a woman to have more than one mati," Juliette and other "informants" put the matter more precisely: idealtypically one only has one mati, while one may have multiple women with whom one "lies down."

The description above sounds absolutely familiar in a 1990s context. The formulaic opening and institutionalized form of jealousy at the birthday were not done at the beginning of the party anymore, but I observed that they were staged, if everyone was in good spirits, midway through the party. Older women and—often—male mati knew the words by heart, without failing. While the Herskovitses' scholarship, characteristic of the Boasian school of anthropology (Stocking 1968), called attention to the African character of Creole folklore and institutions in general, they did not develop a full-fledged analysis of the mati work along diasporic lines. The birthday party and lobi singi simply were institutions they came across, but they did not foreground the mati work.

The Surinamese historian van Lier, reports on data he collected among mati in 1949 in his beautifully titled *Tropische Tribaden*/Tropical Tribades (1986). While doing research for his standard work *Samenleving in een Grensgebied* (1977 [1949]), he stumbled across the mati work, but since he did not want to put *Samenleving* in jeopardy and people around him were beginning to question his activities, he abandoned the collection of data for *Tropische Tribaden* after having collected only seven cases. Very interesting is the fact that van Lier and his male, working-class, Creole assistant apparently had no problems at all eliciting data from their mati informants. This shows "the natural, unproblematical acceptation of the women themselves of their own homosexual behaviour" (1986:2). Some mati were prepared to describe in meticulous detail what their activities consisted of. Van Lier aimed to show that, among the diversity of homosexual forms, there are some that can be called "normal" homosexuality, i.e., those forms that ultimately did not result from physical determinants or psychodynamic disturbances but originated in women's conscious choice for a same-sex partner (1986:60). After reviewing several sociostructural factors, the sex-ratio, stratification, homosocial worlds, and certain tendencies within the family, that is, paternal deprivation, which can ostensibly psychologically predispose women to homosexuality, van Lier concludes that these factors ultimately do not force women into homosexuality. It is a matter of choice in an environment that is rich in alternative sexual styles. While I obviously agree with this conclusion, it is understandable, though unfortunate that van Lier located his research within a psychoanalytic framework that leans so heavily on the white, heteronormative psychic economy of a middle-class environment (Childers and hooks 1990; Christian 1997).

The main theme of contention between the various authors who have studied the mati work and my own work is that I do not believe there is reason to assume that the mati work only started around 1900, when men were absent in substantial numbers (e.g., van Wetering 1998). Underlying this different periodization is a black diasporic approach to the mati work that builds on West African "grammatical principles" (Mintz and Price 1992 [1976]) in the domain of (sexual) subjecthood.

A Black Diasporic Approach to the Mati Work

My own contribution to an understanding of the mati work builds upon research by the Herskovitses (1936, 1941, 1967 [1938]), Mintz and Price (1992 [1976]), and Wooding (1972, 1988). It employs a black diasporic approach that assumes that black people, within varying constraints and with varying results, have elaborated upon a common West African cultural heritage in the domain of (sexual) subjecthood in the Diaspora. One of the advantages of using such an approach is that it is attuned to continuities and variations found in constructions of selves, sexualities, and genders in different parts of the Diaspora. I imagine the West African grammatical principles governing personhood and sexuality in the black Diaspora like jazz: improvising upon certain basic themes—a notion of personhood in which the secular and the spiritual are intertwined; a conceptualization of female same-sex behavior as governed by the "carrying" of the women by a strong, "masculine" spirit; a flexible gender system that offers opportunities rather than constraints; the importance of fertility and parenthood for both men and women; the full sexual subjectivity of both women and men; sex as an extraordinarily pleas-ant part of life that does not have to end at an advanced age; a conception of sexuality that insists on and foregrounds sexual fulfillment rather than giving weight to the sex of one's object of passion; sexuality as activity, not exclusive identity—musicians in various parts of the black Diaspora have produced riffs, that are remarkably similar. Focusing on working-class women in the black Diaspora, we see a configuration where, in various places, women typically have children and sexual relations with men and women.

This formulation of diasporic sexual subjecthood dovetails with Sidney Mintz's and Richard Price's programmatic statement for African American studies, "The Birth of African-American Culture" (1992 [1976]). They argue that the aim of the discipline should not be to show concrete, comparable social and cultural forms in different parts of the Diaspora, but to iden-tify underlying principles, common basic assumptions (which will often be unconscious) about, for instance, social relations or the workings of the universe. Such principles can define the perceived similarities in African and African American cultural patterns. They show that the Herskovitses' pioneering project of the 1930s and 1940s, in which African "retentions" and "survivals" in the New World were traced by levels of intensity, was valuable, but also evinced a static conception of culture. In its attention to the formal elements of culture, it virtually ignored important processes of acculturation. Mintz and Price want to refine the Herskovitsian project and propose:

> An African cultural heritage, widely shared by the people imported into any new colony, will have to be defined in less concrete terms, by focusing more on values, and less on sociocultural forms, and even by attempting to identify unconscious "grammatical" principles, which may underlie and shape behavioral response.
>
> (1992 [1976]:9–10)

They propose to submit the "cognitive orientations" of blacks in the Diaspora to further research: what are the fundamental assumptions about social relations? Which values motivate people? How did one interact in social situations? What are the characteristics of interpersonal style? The "basic assumptions and expectations about the way the world functions phenomenologically (e.g., beliefs about causality)" form another important terrain for research (1992 [1976]:10). My project, which fundamentally references the shaping and the content of what it means to be human, pertains to conceptions about subjectivity, about gender, and about passion, something we now call sexuality that circulated among the slaves who set foot in Suriname.

At this moment there is no literature available that readily answers these questions. It is exceptionally difficult to excavate the "grammatical principles" underlying the cognitive orientations of sixteenth- , seventeenth- , and eighteenth-century Africans in the areas that we now call subjectivity, gender, and sexuality. What do we know about how these social processes and formations played out in the minds of those enslaved who, after an atrocious journey across the ocean, first set foot on Surinamese soil? The pieces of their conceptions of being human will have to be put together by all kinds of indirect and inventive methods since official historiography, from a hegemonic perspective, never allowed that there could be a category called subjectivity among the enslaved. Those who wrote the sources were only interested in the culture or the personal lives of the slaves to the extent that they could contribute to their labor productivity (Oostindie 1989). The elaborate lists describing various African tribes in Suriname—Mandingo, Ibo, Hausa, etc.—bring together a body of pseudo knowledge that is informed by the desire, on the part of whites, for the protection from and hyperproductivity of the enslaved. Since the planter class regarded the sexuality of black women as their property, a phenomenon like the mati work would have been disagreeable to them, since it did not contribute to reproduction and bespoke the sexual agency of enslaved women. Female slaves had no interest in informing the planter class about their sexual activities.

We can safely assume that many slaves who arrived in Suriname were aware of the existence of sexual bonds between women. Sources describing sexual behavior of women in various parts of Africa, partly prompted by contemporary political agendas, often contradict one another. While, from various, including feminist sides, considerable resistance is raised against the idea of sex between women in Africa (Amadiume 1987; Oyewumi 2001), the sources are too persistent to reject. For each author who claims the historical "sexual chastity" of women in Africa (Simson 1984; Omolade 1984), another can be called upon who speaks of the "broad sexual freedom" of Dahoman women in the early nineteenth century (Lombard 1967:74) or of "the high frequency of infidelity among Ashanti women" (Fortes 1950:275). Evans-Pritchard (1970) described that Azande women formed intimate bonds of friendship with other women, including cowives. With a ceremony called *bagburu* the women publicly stated that they were partners and would give each other preference in trading and other social needs. Women had strong networks of relationships with women, and erotic attachments were a part of those relationships.

In my project I again rely on the data of Melville Herskovits. He provides the most intriguing and relevant data for Suriname. In his study of Dahomey he stated that thirteen different categories of partnership are distinguished. Homosexuality is present among women as well as men and, according to some of his informants, more so among women (1967 [1938]:1:289). In this patrilinear and patrilocal society an emic distinction is made between unions where the father has control over the children born out of a partnership and relationships where the children are the property of the mother (1:301–302). There is a category under this last type of contact described as "giving the goat to the ram" that stands out because the contours of its underlying gender ideology most markedly reach across the Atlantic. Women in Dahomey can formally marry another woman, while the children born within such a union are the children of the first woman. In these marriages, which are frequent among upper-class women marrying girls of commoner or slave status, the woman of means

causes a house to be built near her own, and installs the young woman there. She is regarded by the inhabitant of this house as a husband, and is called "husband" by her "wife." From among her male acquaintances, or perhaps from the men of her husband's family, she chooses a man to whom she "gives" the young woman she has "married." He is told that the girl is his to live with, that he may come to her as often as he likes, but that he may not take her to his own compound. ... All children born of this mating, consequently, belong to the woman who is the nominal husband of the girl and after her death come under the control of her heirs. ... It now becomes clear why this type of marriage is given the name it bears. The native statement is: "When a goat becomes big, one does not ask which buck had caused her to conceive."

(1:320)

Herskovits warns that all of this does not imply a homosexual relationship, although "it is not to be doubted that occasionally homosexual women who have inherited wealth or have prospered economically establish compounds of their own and utilize their relationship to the women they 'marry' to satisfy themselves" (1:318–19).

There are also data about sexual relations between women in various other parts of Africa, e.g., the Nupe (Nadel 1951), Azande (Evans-Pritchard 1970), the Nyakusa (Wilson 1963), "mummies" and "babies" in Lesotho (Gay 1986; Kendall 1999), and in Zimbabwe (Epprecht 1998; Aarmo 1999). Ashanti women who have relations with one another are described as *obaa banyins*/ feminine men. These women were regarded as having a heavy *sumsum*/soul or second soul (Christensen, quoted in van Lier 1986:25). The comparable conceptualization of these obaa banyins with mati, who are thought to have a masculine Apuku, is striking. Interestingly, this same conceptualization is used in Zimbabwe. Epprecht (1998) notes:

> Women who had strong homo-erotic feelings, it should be noted, also had means to express them in ways that were not perceived as sexual. Principally this involved claiming possession by a male spirit such as *svikiro* or *tokoloshi*. A woman so possessed could take multiple female "wives," or refuse to be married, without challenging the dogma of heterosexual appearances.[30]

This similar conceptualization, thus far found in Zimbabwe, among the Ashanti, and among mati in Suriname, strongly points in the direction of an underlying "grammatical principle" that traveled in the black Diaspora, organizing the domain of female same-sex sexuality. Of course, this finding needs additional research in various parts of Africa and the black Diaspora.

Thus, marriages between women in Africa are more widespread than many realize. They are present, at least, among the Ba-Venda in Southeast Africa, Nilot peoples in Sudan, the Kikuyu in Kenia (Tietmeyer 1991), and the Igbo in Nigeria (Amadiume 1987). Whether these marriages were consummated or not is less important in my eyes than the radically different gender ideology upon which they are founded.

Ifi Amadiume, a Nigerian anthropologist, has described the gender ideology of the Nnobi in East-Nigeria, an Igbo people, in the nineteenth century. She writes that in traditional Igbo society, where ideas about gender proceeded from ecological factors and production methods, the social relations between men and women were mediated through a flexible gender ideology and a linguistic system with certain gender-free aspects. That ideology and the linguistic system made it possible for both genders to possess the same roles and status. Such flexibility in conceptions of gender encouraged institutions like the "female husband" and the "masculine daughter" within which women could occupy positions of wealth, power, and authority that, under strict gender definitions, would have been reserved for men. The correlation between sex and gender was not emphasized, but rather the relationship between gender and power was emphatically asserted. Men as well as women, "female husbands," could have multiple wives and, with this expansion of labor force, could aquire wealth and power (Amadiume 1987). Amadiume's findings are especially important by virtue of the parallels between her arguments and my own regarding the flexibility of gender ideologies, the linguistic system with gender-free aspects, and the detachment of sex and gender.

These diverse data from Africa provide a base from which to establish continuity between formations in the West African and the Surinamese contexts. What is most striking in both contexts is that women are autonomous subjects, both in the arena of property and property transfer, power, control over children (i.e., the possibility of establishing one's own lineage), and in the area of sexuality. Such autonomy is only possible when full subjectivity is conferred on both men and women. The relationship between sex and gender must then be loose and flexible; in other words, a male or female body should not prefigure the kinds of social roles, status, and power one can attain. So must the relationship between gender and sexuality; that is to say, "feminine" gender should not be assumed to predispose toward a passive, muted heterosexuality.

At the origin of the new, Surinamese society and culture, bonds between individuals of the same sex must have been important:

> Various shreds of evidence suggest that some of the earliest social bonds to develop in the coffles, in the factories and, especially, during the Middle Passage, were of a dyadic (two-person) nature. Partly perhaps, because of the general policy of keeping men and women separate, they were usually between members of the same sex. The bond between shipmates, those people who

shared passage on the same slaver, is the most striking example. In widely scattered parts of Afro-America, the "shipmate" relationship became a major principle of social organization and continued for decades or even centuries to
shape ongoing social relations.

(MINTZ AND PRICE 1992 [1976]:43)

We have a historic eyewitness account of the "presentations of self" of
the slaves upon their arrival in Paramaribo. They had marked each others'
heads with different designs, suns, half moons, without the help of a razor,
even without soap, only with a piece of glass. The women wore rings, cor-
als, and jewelry around their necks. The slaves staying on board spent the
time laughing, jumping, shouting, and clapping their hands.[31] The cultural
vitality expressed in these images, amidst the horror, fixing each other's hair,
wearing jewelry, and making the unbearable bearable by way of creatively
expressing themselves, is as impressive as it is shattering. Apparently, these
shipmates, with their diverse places of origin, languages, and backgrounds,
had already been able to find a common idiom with which to encourage
themselves and each other. It is worth noting that part of the performance of
their subjectivity was its beautification by means of jewelry.

I see the mati work as one idealtypical expression of black female sexuality in the Diaspora (Wekker 1993). The significance of Suriname is that
it may well be the place in the Diaspora that evidences the starkest, most
public configuration of mati work.[32] A combination of three elements forms
a possible explanation. First, there is the extreme preponderance of blacks
over whites during the period of slavery. The ratio of blacks to whites was,
taken over the entire colony, 25:1 during most of the seventeenth and eighteenth centuries. In the plantation districts, where the majority of slaves were
located, that ration amounted to 65:1 (van Lier 1977 [1949]; Price 1976).[33]
Second, the continual replenishment of African elements in the Surinamese
black population by the Dutch plantocracy's preference, certainly until the
abolition of the slave trade (1814), for new imports of slaves versus creating
circumstances that were favorable for reproduction (van Lier 1977 [1949];
Price 1976) needs to be taken into account. Third, the cultural colonial policies of the Dutch, which—with the exception of sexual encounters—essentially consisted of removing blacks geographically, culturally, and linguistically as far as possible from whites (Voorhoeve and Lichtveld 1975; van Lier
1977 [1949]). These three conditions resulted in a unique cultural constellation for Surinamese blacks. Not only was it forbidden for slaves to speak
Dutch, the plantocracy did not see it as advantageous to convert blacks to
Christianity or to baptize them until about 1830 (van Lier 1977 [1949]; Lenders 1994). Blacks were thus able to develop their languages, cultures, and

religion(s) relatively unhampered during slavery, as long as their activities and behavior did not interfere with labor on the plantations.

After the abolition of slavery (1863) it was especially the dark-skinned Creole working class that acted as the conservators of the African heritage. While the lighter-skinned Creole middle class aspired to Dutch standards and generally adopted Dutch as its linguistic vehicle and also refrained, as best they could, from *vernegerd*/"negrolike" behavior, the working class held onto and developed their own orientations on reality.

It is from this specific cultural configuration that I infer that Surinamese working-class women have been in a particularly favorable position, in a diasporic perspective, to elaborate upon constructions of sexualities, selves, and gender arrangements that build upon the African heritage. As such I consider it quite possible that the mati work has been present in Suriname since the beginning of the colony.

Data About Other Parts of the Black Diaspora

If my argument that the mati work in Suriname bespeaks West African "grammatical principles" in the domains of self, gender, and sexualities has any validity, we should be able to find comparable forms elsewhere in the black Diaspora. With few notable exceptions, however, black diasporic women have yet to start talking about their sexualities. Thus an important component of the "pleasures and dangers" in the lives of black working-class women in the Diaspora, what has made them survive emotionally and erotically and what continues to give them joy and pleasure, has been omitted from the canon of anthropology or any other discipline.

Some of the rather sketchy findings on the prevalence of the phenomenon of women loving women in other parts of the Caribbean suggest that it may not be as public and institutionalized as in Suriname but that it most certainly does occur. Audre Lorde's biomythography *Zami: A New Spelling of My Name* (1982) situates women who are sexually active with other women on Cariacou and Grenada.[34] M. G. Smith (1962) had done so before her, explaining the phenomenon, in familiar ways, by the absence of men overseas. In a number of studies on the Caribbean the subject is mentioned but not treated in depth. Apart from Suriname, the Herskovitses noted the phenomenon of women being sexually involved with other women on Haiti (1837) and on Trinidad (1947). The term used on Trinidad is also *zami*.[35] Curaçao knows *kambrada* relationships between women (Marks 1976; Clemencia 1995). Rubenstein states that on St Vincent *bulling* (male homosexuality) and *zammie* (lesbianism) are rejected (1987:257).

Vera Rubin (1976) has mentioned female same-sex sexuality on St. Martin, Saba, and Anguilla, while Kerr (1952) first brought Jamaica into our purview. Of a more recent date is the beautiful description that Makeda Silvera (1992) gives of her mother's and grandmother's recollections of Jamaican working-class "Man Royals" and "Sodomites" before the current violent climate of oppression of "queer sexualities" was put into place. It is evident that, like mati, "Man Royals" had relationships with men, often had children, but they were also sexually active with women. Elwin (1997) has collected interviews with women-loving women from various parts of the Caribbean, St. Kitts, Dominica, St. Lucia, and Jamaica.

African–North American historical data on the phenomenon of women loving women can be culled from women's blues and poetry and increasingly nowadays from fiction and academic work. In the classical women's blues of the twenties we find the voices of working class women who constructed themselves as sexual subjects (Carby 1986; Davis 1998). Ma Rainey expresses the anger of women at men's infidelity, but she also sings "Prove It on Me Blues," a provocative confirmation of the protagonist's relationships with women:

> They said I do it, ain't nobody caught me
> Sure got to prove it on me
> Went out last night with a crowd of my friends
> They must have been women, 'cause I don't like no men
> It's true I wear a collar and a tie
> Make the wind blow all the while
> 'Cause they say I do it, ain't nobody caught me
> They sure got to prove it on me
>
> …
>
> Wear my clothes just like a fan
> Talk to the gals just like any old man
> 'Cause they say I do it, ain't nobody caught me
> Sure got to prove it on me

In this chapter I have explored the institution of the mati work, looking at it from a historical perspective and in its contemporary forms. I have speculated that in its "underlying" behavorial principles the mati work is an elaboration of the West African heritage as it pertains to constructions of selves, sexualities, and gender.

First, mati and women who engage exclusively in relationships with men have a lot in common with each other. They are all embedded in a gender ideology that stresses independence, self-worth, and self-respect. Motherhood is for both the ultimate characteristic and fulfillment of womanhood. They all see relationships with men predominantly as a locus of exchange between sex and money.

Second, mati have more sexual knowledge and pleasure because in the all-female arena they freely exchange sexual knowledge and transmit the knowledge to younger generations. They do not see each other as competitors for scarce resources. They have a more independent understanding of their own sexualities.

Third, the mati work undermines a number of received feminist paradigms. The notion that men maintain universal hegemony over women's sexuality is contradicted by these data (Rich 1980). Bonds between women in their own behavioral environment are institutionalized, validated, and celebrated.

The mati work shows a sexual configuration where women unabashedly enjoy sex, are active sexual partners, and can disengage sex from love. From all accounts, I have concluded that mati sex is genitally oriented and not the "vanilla," cuddly brand that has so normatively been considered as the hallmark of feminine sexuality by mostly white women. It seems to me that part of the excitement in mati sex may stem precisely from the "dangers" inherent in the play with and the constant contesting of boundaries, the rights of both partners, and dominance/submissiveness. The mati work underscores the need to study sexuality and gender as two distinct arenas of social practice: one can be a woman and not have a muted, passive sexuality nor a fixed, cross-sex sexual orientation.

Finally, the mati work offers a radically alternative configuration to the historical genesis of homosexual "identity" under capitalism (cf. D'Emilio 1984; D'Emilio and Freedman 1988; Faderman 1991). The line of reasoning I have adopted is that the institution can be most profitably understood as an elaboration of an African set of principles guiding the construction of selves, genders, and sexualities. Sexuality is not conceived as expressive of a "core," "essential," "authentic," "true" self, but as behavior.

Chapter 6 will follow women in their transatlantic travels, during the nineties, to the postcolonial space of the Netherlands.

Sexuality is intimately and immediately felt, but publicly
and internationally described and mediated. Sexuality is
not only not essence, not timeless, it is also not fixed in
place; sexuality is on the move.

PATTON AND SÁNCHEZ-EPPLER 2000

This is why the study of specifically colonial cultures is an
essential prerequisite for the study of many contemporary
post-colonial and post-imperial ones.

KING 1991B

6

Sexuality on the Move

This chapter aims to explore the ways in which one of the sexual configurations that has been central in this book, the mati work, is on the move
transnationally. Taking women's lives as points of departure, it addresses
the question of how Afro-Surinamese women who engage in same-sex and
opposite-sex relationships have participated in sexual globalization in the
past decades. By sexual globalization I mean the various ways in which the
rapid flow of capital, people, goods, images, and ideologies across national
boundaries, which continuously draws more of the world into webs of interconnections, structures the domain of sexuality (Inda and Rosaldo 2002).
I will focus on the globalization of women's same-sex sexuality, a phenomenon that has received little attention in the literature.

Sexual globalization is an as yet underexplored phenomenon, especially
in its same-sex varieties. Most of these studies thus far have mainly paid
attention to gay males (Altman 1996; Drucker 2000; Patton and Sánchez-
Eppler 2000; Donham 2002; Cruz-Malavé and Manalansan IV 2002). In
addition, in-depth, grounded research is frequently sorely missing in transnational studies of sexuality, because these settle too readily for a focus on
the surfaces and commonalities of same-sex sexual globalization without
adequately understanding the particular historical and social contexts in
which these sexualities are embedded. Unfortunately, in the literature there

is still a significant trope that foregrounds cultural homogenization. The direction of cultural flows has generally been seen to emanate from "the West to the Rest," with the Rest supposedly swallowing Western sexual constructions wholesale and adopting Western labels like *gay, lesbian,* and *homosexual.* The cultural homogenization thesis has found expression in the sexual domain under the rubric of "global queering" (Altman 1996). Altman understands the global spread of homosexual identities under the influence of the expansion of consumer society, new communication technologies, and the AIDS crisis. He remarks that "American books, films, magazines and fashions continue to define contemporary gay and lesbian meanings for most of the world" (1996:2). It is clear to him that ... "economic and cultural globalization is creating *a newly universal sense of homosexuality as the basis for identity and lifestyle, not merely for behaviour*" (1996:6; my emphasis).

I want to mark my resistance to this "master" model of globalization, which is deeply embedded in the various binaries that modernity has spawned. The model holds that because of the large-scale transfer of meaning systems and symbolic forms the world is increasingly becoming one, not only in political and economic terms but in terms of its cultural construction as well. Notwithstanding the many critiques of this model (Appadurai 1990; Hannerz 1991; King 1991a; Cruz-Malavé and Manalansan IV 2002; Grewal and Kaplan 2001), it remains a very influential, almost Pavlovian mold.

In the past decades globalization has become all things to all theorists, "a black box of the nineties akin to structure in the seventies" (Burawoy et al. 2000:x). Dominant approaches to globalization are characterized by an emphasis on either economic or political process, often presenting the total-izing abstractness of grand theory. The "master" narratives of globalization foreground the hypermobility of capital, space-time compression, interna-tional communication, information technologies, and the receding role of the nation-state, bypassed above and below by other significant forces such as transnational corporations and global movements. These mostly gender-blind approaches make it hard to imagine what globalization actually looks like from the perspective of working-class people who are living it , both in the so-called periphery and in the center. I have been led by what Burawoy et al. (2000) call "grounded globalizations," i.e., starting from the experi-ences of Surinamese mati, I want to explore their global and local contexts and how they are imbricated in each other.

We are still a long way away from a model out of which "something like a decent global analysis might flow," as Appadurai wrote generally in 1990. Without the ambition to offer such a general model for sexual globalization, I want to search for what some of the significant ingredients of such a model might be by attending to "the relationship of gender to scattered hegemonies such as global economic structures, patriarchal nationalisms, 'authentic' forms of tradition, local structures of domination, and legal-juridical oppression on multiple levels" (Grewal and Kaplan 1994:17).

Globalization is a new turn in the genealogy of my interest in the mati work, which presented itself forcefully during the last period in which I did research in Suriname in May and June 2001. A mati funeral, accompanied by symbols that drew from Surinamese and Dutch cultural repertoires, was pivotal in my realization of the prominence of globalization. I will come back to this event in the course of this chapter.

In the past decades, along with the accelerated rate of globalization, culture has become increasingly deterritorialized and circulatory instead of being tied to the nation-state. In the preceding chapters I mentioned several features of the globalization of the mati work, without necessarily bringing them under the rubric of globalization. Women in Suriname forged connections with male and female sexual partners on the other side of the Atlantic, mainly through visits of Surinamese-Dutch partners to Suriname or, less frequently—in view of the unequal economic conditions—of Surinamese partners to the Netherlands. Long distance relations with female (and male) partners in the Netherlands became part of the fabric of this transatlantic community. It was evident that women had taken the mati work with them to the Netherlands, at least since the middle of the seventies, but I did not foreground this phenomenon in my earlier work since it focused almost exclusively on Suriname. The cultural space to which the mati work belongs is no longer singular within the national space of Suriname, but it should be situated in a historically and culturally inscribed space of postcolonialism. In this chapter I want to explore, on the one hand, what happens to the mati work when it moves into former metropolitan space, i.e., the Netherlands, and, on the other, in which ways the mati work in Suriname is influenced by the traveling discourses that mati who are on the move transatlantically implant in Suriname.

The multiple directions of cultural influence under globalization necessitates focusing on the Netherlands as a postcolonial space and the meeting ground of two models of female same-sex desire, lesbianism and the mati work. Lesbianism, with or without children, is constructed as an exclusive desire for women, is ideologically invested in "equality" along several dimensions, e.g., age, income, and educational level, and is associated with "modernity," while the mati work, with its flexibility in terms of sexual partners, its often large age differences and polarized roles between partners calls up associations with "tradition." Generally, the often implicit and sometimes explicit expectation is that in the meeting of these two models lesbianism will, sooner or later, prevail; the mati work will give way to the dominant

Euro-American form of female same-sex desire. This expectation is alive in commonsense discourses, but it is also fed by academic discourses that see an unproblematic unidirectionality in the field of sexual globalization, a triumphant progress and transfer of sexual forms and identities from the West to the Rest. Into this rather simplistic, linear evolutionary equation I want to insert a set of complicating factors. In hegemonic versions of sexual globalization ahistoricism and an overlooking of continuing imbalances of power have shaped the definition of Euro-American sexualities as normative and non-Western sexualities as deviant. The actual meeting of lesbianism and the mati work in the Netherlands, from the middle of the seventies, is prefigured in the system of Dutch Empire. In contradistinction to the preferred standpoint in the Netherlands that imperialism is something regrettable that happened elsewhere, was perpetrated by other nations,[1] and is thus external to Dutch continental history and identity, one of my central understandings is that imperialism, the invention of race, and the hierarchization of sexual configurations were fundamental aspects of Dutch modernity. In Dutch postcolonial space new representations of gendered and racialized bodies reinvigorate existing structures of inequality through the work that these representations do in dominant imagery effecting legislation, the market, the state, and economies of desire.

Studying sexual globalization within the Dutch-speaking cultural ecumene requires acknowledgment of the inescapable and overarching prisms of postcolonialism, postimperialism, and migration. It is to this postcolonial, transnational cultural space that I have shifted my gaze in this final chapter. The Dutch colonial empire was not only an economic and political system but also a social and cultural system welded together through language as well as through "a mass of … common institutions ranging from administrative and religious practices to architecture, from university curriculae to literature" (King 1991b:6). In the domain of sexuality a by now impressive body of literature traces the epistemic and real violence of the circulation of discourses constructing black women's sexuality in opposition to white women's sexuality. In Stoler's rereading of Foucault, "race" was at the root of sexual constructions in the metropoles, which were transferred to the colonies and then, after having been doused in "porno-tropics," back again to the metropoles, normativizing white women's sexuality (Stoler 1995; McClintock 1995). The cultural sedimentation of the colonial system in the metropolis is a deep-seated conglomerate of imagery constructing black women's sexuality as overactive, deviant, excessive, closer to nature, not in control, and animal-like.[2]

Stuart Hall, writing from the perspective of British Empire, introduces the distinction between "Global Imperialism" and the "Global Postmodern," noting different constellations that are operative in organizing "racial" difference:

Global Imperialism is the era of empire, of British (English) domination in which other human races are deemed inherently inferior and denied their own voices, while the Global Postmodern refers to a decentered world of American mass culture. Ironically, it is a world in which the previously silenced have found a voice with which to fight for new places. Global Imperialism describes a world centered around nations organized in a hierarchy of domination, while the Global Postmodern has lost any such hint of totalizing logic. It describes a world in which homogeneity calls forth diversity, in which difference is pluralized, deployed and valorized rather than enclaved in water-tight compartments of superiority and inferiority.

(HALL 1991)

It remains to be explored, however, through grounded ethnographies such as the one I am attempting here, how these two templates—global imperialism and the global postmodern—are operative in the sexual domain and how they are connected in the Dutch-speaking postcolonial cultural ecumene. I will foreground the operation of gender and "race" in processes of sexual globalization. The transition between the two templates is not a smooth and teleological one; it is uneven, contradictory, nonsynchronous, and palimpsestic.

A marked characteristic of Dutch transnational space is migration. In the past five decades the Netherlands has increasingly become marked by migrations of different kinds involving different groups of migrants, which has put into place another, more complicated configuration where representations of sexualities of different groups of women are relationally pitted against each other. For Surinamese people these migrations are (semi-) permanent, repetitive, and seasonal and they are also connected to old age and ill health. A complete account of the Netherlands in these past five decades includes not only the settlement of postcolonial migrants from its former colonies, Indonesia and Suriname, and the Dutch Antilles, which still are part of the Dutch kingdom, but it also takes account of this space having become a place of settlement for labor migrants from the circum-Mediterranean region, with Turks and Moroccans as the largest groups. Labor migrants from Eastern Europe, too, have increasingly become part of transnational Dutch space. In addition, the Netherlands has also become an anchor point for a miscellaneous "group" of refugees and asylum seekers from Iran, Iraq, and various African and Latin American nations. Overall, migrants make up an estimated 10 percent of the Dutch population of 16 million, but in the four large cities their numbers are more sizable, making up to 50 percent of the cohort in the younger age brackets. Given the subject of this chapter, the sexual globalization of the mati work, I cannot possibly do justice to the positionings of all these various groups in Dutch society, but the presence of the large female migrant groups—Surinamese, Antillean, Turkish, and Moroccan women—is a significant framework, because of the relational ways in which women's positions on the labor market and in the domain of sexuality are structured, always already taking white Dutch women as the models to be emulated, the teleological endpoints of a desired evolution. I will show which processes of normalization and hierarchization are operative in both domains.

Thus an important prism through which to view sexual globalization can be found in its interfaces with post–World War II migration, especially as it manifests in gendered patterns. Significant work has been done on this topic (Anthias and Lazaridis 2000; Castles and Miller 1998; Kofman et al. 2000; Momsen 1999) and there is consensus on the sheer numbers of women on the move, leading to an understanding in terms of the "feminization of migration." Due to the deepening chasm in prosperity between the North and the South, female migrants, legal and illegal, are on the move in unprecedented numbers and over ever longer distances, mostly but certainly not exclusively from South to North. To an important extent female migrants from the South have come to specialize in the North in "something that can look very much like love" (Ehrenreich and Hochschild 2002:4; Salazar Parrenas 2001). That is to say that the care sector—child care, care of the elderly, the sick and disabled, house cleaning, cooking—has been transferred from double-burdened middle- and high-income women in the First World to Third World migrant women, after it had become abundantly clear that these care tasks were not going to be shared in any substantive way by their male partners (Wekker 2004). Within the Netherlands, too, as we will see, Afro-Surinamese women have come to fill the vacancies of carer for the sick and the elderly and we will explore in which binaries this division of labor partakes.

I begin this chapter with an elaborate case study of a relationship between two Afro-Surinamese women, Lydia de Vrede and Wonnie Winter, who met at a mati party in Amsterdam shortly after Lydia had migrated to the Netherlands. I will continue to focus on the empirical details of female lives, in which love for other women is central, but I will also pay attention to the political and economical circumstances under which the relationship took shape. I will describe how the relationship was forged, some characteristic patterns in female mati connections, and the way in which the relationship suffered under various internal and external pressures. I will also explore some aspects of the encounter between mati work and lesbianism in the Netherlands and how that encounter turns received notions of "tradition" versus "modernity" inside out, calling the usefulness of that and other binaries into question. In the second half of the chapter the mati work in Suriname and how it is influenced by traveling Northern discourses will take center stage. Throughout the chapter I will engage with theoretical notions that have been influential in thinking about sexual globalization, addressing in what respects my work refuses some of those notions while offering others.

On the Move in Postcolonial Space

I thought life was going to be a brilliant comedy, and that you were to be one of many graceful figures in it. I found it to be a revolting and repellent tragedy.

WILDE 1979 [1897]

Lydia de Vrede, the thirty-seven-year-old nurse's aide and one of my key interlocutors, left Suriname in the beginning of 1993. Her relationship with her husband and the father of her three youngest children had gradually deteriorated. Lydia thought that Raymond had another woman and her main concern was that she was not receiving any financial support from him, barely making ends meet on her own income. She decided, with the help of her siblings who live in the Netherlands, to make a new start.

Two themes surfaced in Lydia's discussions with me during the 1990–1991 period: that a woman be financially independent and therefore not reliant on a man and her desire to have another chance at developing a relationship with a woman. When she was young she never fell in love with men, but, following the dominant heterosexual script, she did what was expected of her. She had many *matisma visiti*/mati girlfriends and her most ardent dreams were about a particular woman with whom she had been for a short period in her early twenties. This woman had migrated to Holland. With Lydia's own migration, these two recurrent desires got a new purchase on life. Given another chance at love, she would surely choose a woman.

Her oldest children, Fred, nineteen years old, a student at the Faculty of Technical Sciences at the university, and Marylyn, eighteen years, studying at a teacher's training college, would take care of the three youngest children during her absence. The plan was that Lydia would set herself up and then, as she found a job, a permit to stay, or, better yet, Dutch nationality, she would send for the children one by one. Lydia's four siblings in the Netherlands could not put her up but were willing to help her financially through the first period. Between them they had also paid for her ticket, which at nf 2,500 remained an exorbitant amount.[3] She first lived with an aunt in Amsterdam until she found her bearings.

As she had been instructed to do in Paramaribo, Lydia soon found her way to the Albert Cuijp market in Amsterdam, a large all-day open air market, which is a significant hub in the Afro-Surinamese network in Amsterdam. The Surinamese market stalls, stores, and the cafés adjacent to the market, are an important entry point or survival circuit, as Saskia Sassen (1998) terms it, for newcomers. These survival circuits have arisen in global cities in response to the deepening crises in the South, linking newcomers to vital information and connections in their new surroundings. At the market Lydia met with old friends and acquaintances and hooked into a network that enabled her to find work as a nurse's aide. Lydia had entered the Netherlands with a tourist visa, which was valid for two months. After that time her stay would become illegal. Initially, she worked under a friend's name for a nursing recruitment agency, specializing in care of the elderly and disabled in their homes.

In taking this job, Lydia was entering a profession in which there was an acute shortage of personnel, a shortage that began in the 1950s and has since accelerated. That acceleration is also racialized and gendered. Many white Dutch women have either left the profession or have found jobs in management, leaving the work floor in many hospitals and nursing homes predominantly to people of color, with Surinamese and Antillean women as nursing personnel, while Turkish and Moroccan men and women serve as cleaners, making beds and serving meals.[4] The top rung of the management ladder is almost exclusively white males. This gendered, racialized picture is a result of the increased recruitment of nursing personnel from Third World countries, particularly South Africa, Indonesia, and the Philippines but also in recent years from Eastern Europe.

Thus, Lydia had no trouble finding a job as a live-in nurse of an ailing octogenarian living by himself in a villa in Amstelveen, a wealthy suburb of Amsterdam. She lived in her own wing of the villa for two years, presiding over the household and the cleaning woman until the old man died. The naturalization of women's work, e.g., nursing, meant Lydia was not well paid, earning a meagre nf 125 for a twenty-four hour shift in someone's home.[5] As is the case with other feminized occupations, the unspoken rationale is that (black) women are doing what they are "naturally" good at. Surinamese nurses are much appreciated in the Netherlands and for middle- and upper-class people, who can afford the price of private care, they are a godsend. In the wealthy south of Amsterdam and the suburbs surrounding the city, many a Surinamese nurse has found a niche. They perform labor in the privacy of someone's home, being largely invisible to the outside world. Dutch clients see them as reliable, warmhearted, good cooks, and generally possessing traditionally feminized qualities that white Dutch women—so the commonsensical reading goes—have largely discarded in the process of emancipation. This "positive" evaluation of Surinamese nurses and caretakers may also be tied to the perception that linguistically and culturally the Dutch share more with them than with the other large racialized groups, Turkish and Moroccan women. A gendered and ethnicized discourse thus evokes Surinamese nurses as essentially having more "heart" for their charges, being "naturally" good at their work, and simply loving caretaking. As Lydia's choices at a later stage will show, reality is more complicated than the lazy chain of thought embedded within the global imperial would permit. For now it is important to consider some aspects of the powerful juxtaposition that has been put into place and how it reverberates for different groups of women[6] in the postcolonial cultural space of the Netherlands.

In the first place, there is of course no inherent reason why caring qualities should not be distributed evenly across First and Third World cultures—or across men and women. In reality whole cultural edifices have been built upon the qualities attributed to different categories of people. In the same gesture in which Surinamese women with their warmheartedness and respect for the elderly are constructed as essentially different from "modern" white Dutch women, a hierarchy is set up which, according to the standards of the discourse of emancipation, privileges the latter category. During three decades, from the beginning of the seventies, this discourse was powerful in the Netherlands because it embodied official Dutch governmental policy goals.[7] The main goals evolved and changed somewhat during those three decades, but they always included an equal division of labor and care tasks between men and women in the household, a revaluation of feminized qualities and care, and an accelerated entry of women to the labor market. Given the, within a post–WWII European context, exceptionally low labor market participation of Dutch women, their entering the labor market was an important touchstone of emancipation policy. Thus women who from the seventies on entered the labor market were evaluated higher than those women who stayed at home on an imaginary yardstick measuring emancipation. In practice the policy was predicated on the situation of white women (Wekker 1996), since the labor market participation of Afro-Surinamese women, frequently single heads of household, had traditionally been high. Coming from a long line of women who had always worked outside the home, they had been drawn to the Netherlands to forge a better future for themselves and their children. The high labor market participation of Afro-Surinamese (and some other migrant) women went unnoticed for a long time, however, due to a combination of willful "colorblindness," which was reflected in the historically loaded reluctance to collect statistics on the basis of "race" or ethnicity,[8] and to the sheer impossibility of a cultural imaginary that would allow women of color to have higher labor market participation, that now cherished yardstick of emancipation.

In the goals embraced by emancipation policy, i.e., entry of the labor market, an implicit message is sent about traditional, feminized values. They are all well and good and necessary, the message goes, but we do not value them that much that we will pay well for them. Thus "traditional" femininity is placed in the paradoxical situation that it is valued at the same time that it is disparaged. In a sequence of implicit steps, we see an instance of the tradition-modernity opposition in which tradition—warmth, respect, caring—is nostalgically constructed as something that "we," moderns, have lost and "they," colored folks, especially women, still have. It is something that "we" value, that "we" would like an injection of, but that "we" are not prepared to pay well for nor are "we" prepared to do it ourselves. Modernity, understood here as the full capacity to take care of oneself, in a diabolical turn, comes to resemble masculinity, while tradition, standing for femininity, has to a large extent been relegated to Third World women. Instead of the revaluation of qualities that were seen as typically feminine, at the outset of the second feminist wave, we see the desire on the part of middle- and upper-class Western women to abandon those qualities and to share in the "luxuries" of masculinity.

Another point that Arlie Russell Hochschild has developed, with regard to child care in the U.S., is that we should not presuppose that the caregiving capabilities of Third World women are "natural." The argument holds equally well for care for the elderly in a Dutch context:

> Theirs [i.e., Phillipina women] is not an import of happy peasant mothering but a love that partly develops on American shores, informed by an American ideology of mother-child bonding and fostered by intense loneliness and longing for their own children. If love is a precious resource, it is not simply extracted from the Third World and implanted in the First; rather, it owes its very existence to a peculiar cultural alchemy that occurs in the land to which it is imported.
>
> (2003:24)

This assessment can be easily transposed to Lydia's situation. Lydia's good caretaking skills were not "natural" or genetically placeable. Although there are strong values attached to care for the elderly in a Surinamese context, Lydia made a rational assessment to accept the job. In a situation in which she had few certainties the demand for her nurturing skills brought with it a roof above her head, (scarce) remuneration, a certain measure of autonomy, the opportunity to support her children overseas, and the expectation that with time her legal situation would improve. As she calculated the advantages and disadvantages of the job, she was willing to invest in it. What is tradition here is indeed a bricolage that is assembled on Northern terrain.

In a global, gendered, and racialized division of labor, at the end of the twentieth century, "hands" from the Third World help to alleviate labor shortages in the domain of "love" and care in the First. This division of labor repeats patterns of the colonial era and is firmly situated within Hall's "Global Imperialism" (1991). In the postcolonial Netherlands we see predominantly dark-skinned women taking care of white, middle-class male and female bodies.

Meeting Wonnie Winter

Shortly after her arrival, Lydia met Wonnie Winter at a mati party in Amsterdam. Since the middle of the seventies, the mati work migrated with Creole women, especially to the big cities in the Western part of the country—Amsterdam, Rotterdam, Utrecht, and the Hague—as well as to new satellite cities like Almere, Zoetermeer, and Nieuwegein. As in Paramaribo, women in the Netherlands keep in touch with each other for leisuretime activities, playing bingo, dancing, and flirting with each other, but their networks also support each other financially and socially. Some Afro-Surinamese women supplement their income by organizing mati parties, either at their own homes, on a boat in summer, or in dancing halls, where music, food, and drinks are provided against a fixed price of entry.

Wonnie had lived in Amsterdam since the seventies and had two grown daughters. She augmented her social security income by playing the drums in a band and driving people and small freight in her minivan. Wonnie was attractive, with short wavy hair and, noteworthy in an Afro-Surinamese understanding, light skinned. She made a tough impression and had a reputation in mati circles that she should not be joked around with. Adamant about playing the dominant role in her relationships, she courted Lydia, who at first had misgivings because of Wonnie's reputation. At the end of their first evening together, Wonnie asked Lydia whether she wanted to have a relationship with her. Lydia needed time to think about it and gave Wonnie her phone number. After a couple of weeks, she agreed to go out with Wonnie on her day off. Lydia was impressed with Wonnie, thought she was *een sterke meid*/a strong woman, liked the way she had built a life for herself and her children in the Netherlands, her good physical shape, and the fact that she neither smoked nor drank.

Lydia's friends were not happy about the way things were developing. The friend who had introduced them to each other cautioned Lydia about starting a relationship with Wonnie. But Lydia gave in after a while, overwhelmed by Wonnie's ardent professions of love. She moved house from her aunt's to Wonnie's.

Wonnie talked more when Lydia was not around and I spoke alone with her several times. She talked about being an adolescent in Paramaribo. Her three older sisters were always after her to get dressed up, to use makeup and to go out. They told her how pretty she was and to wear dresses, but Wonnie always preferred pants. She never liked boys:

> Women like Lydia are real women. But me, I always have felt like a man. "Het zit in de geest of je een man bent of een vrouw, je lichaam heeft er niets mee te maken"/It is in your spirit whether you are a man or a woman, your body does not have anything to do with it. It is your spiritual guides that determine it. At a party, when a boy would wink an eye at me, I would become very aggressive, furious, but I did not know why.

Growing up, she was withdrawn, shy, she did not have many friends, male or female. She never liked lipstick, nail polish, miniskirts. She preferred to wear long skirts or pants, so that her legs would not show.

She went to Holland at twenty-one. One of the older sisters found a Surinamese man for her. She had a relationship with him because she wanted children. She conceded that he had a lot of patience with her and gave her everything she desired, but her heart was not in the relationship. When her youngest daughter was six months old, he left. Wonnie was twenty-six years old at the time.

She began to socialize in mati circles in Amsterdam and for the first time had a sexual relationship with a woman. She noticed that she responded much more strongly to this woman than she had ever done to the two men in her life. This relationship did not last long, but from that time on Wonnie knew that she wanted to be with a woman:

> I was living with a nurse. She was working all the time and I had a lot of time on my hands. At a bingo drive I met another woman who was with a man. They were not living together; he was allowed to visit twice a week and then she did nothing special for him. I went by every day and she would cook special for me all the time. In my experience women give more attention and love to their mati than to their masra. I had nothing to complain about, it was adventurous and I was not jealous, but I would never choose a woman like that. I want to have somebody for myself; I do not want to share. Many women take a man for the eyes of the world and for economic reasons, but they really like women better.

Wonnie has only had relationships with Afro-Surinamese women in the Netherlands. She preferred to be with a woman of her own community largely for cultural reasons, e.g., her partner should be aware of her spiritual needs and obligations. She explained that for women like her, coveting the "masculine" role in their relationships, the situation in the Netherlands was much better, since they did not have to depend on a man for income. One could either work or depend on a social security income, but one did not have to put up with men. Recalling the attitudes of *effectieve mati*/true mati, mati who prefer to be with women, toward men in previous chapters, it is clear that the Netherlands offers more economic opportunities for mati and nonmati alike to be self-supporting than Suriname does.[9] Doing the mati work in the Netherlands, according to Wonnie, was much better than in Suriname anyway. In Holland she felt much freer. Her definition of being free entailed that when the police came to your door, because of a disturbance, you just told them "This is a lovers' quarrel" and they didn't bother you.

Wonnie had endured many difficulties and disappointments with men and women in her life, yet ultimately she had come out on top. She had accomplished what she wanted to accomplish, having children, financial security, and a relationship with a "feminine" woman. Yet she appeared beleaguered, battling other people's jealousy and their coveting of her belongings: a car, a comfortable house, enough money, and the like. One of her favorite odo was "I am a gold coin … " which she had internalized and used against the friends who opposed her relationship with Lydia. When I asked Wonnie to tell me what she valued in a partner, she answered:

> *I like a woman who loves to go out, who dresses in a feminine way, who likes it that she is a woman. A mu' ab' moi skin, literally, "she has to have a nice body," i.e., she has to be robust. Then I feel happy and secure. It does not matter to me whether she has an income or not. "Ef' m' e lob' i, dan m' e lob' i"/If I love you, then I love you. We should be able to talk together. I do not like it when one of the partners plays boss. We have to feel equal. I do not like it when she feels small, she has to be at ease in the relationship.*

Balancing various discourses, this is an interesting tour de force. Although Wonnie stressed that she liked egalitarianism in the relationship—"We have to feel equal"—her behavior did not support that statement, nor did Wonnie emerge as the champion of egalitarianism from Lydia's narratives about their relationship. She seemed to be proferring a dominant article of faith from a white Dutch discourse on lesbianism after the "sexual revolution" (Wekker 1998) in which inegalitarianism in relationships, especially in the institutionalized form of butch/femme, was strongly rejected. In my estimation Wonnie's statement pointed to the extent to which mati in the Netherlands, including those who are playing the dominant role, were exposed to and influenced by that strong discourse of egalitarianism. I was rather intrigued by her statement, because I had never heard *mannengre uma*, literally, "male women," in Suriname express such a desire.

Later on in the same conversation, Wonnie threw a more illuminating light on her meaning of egalitarianism. She talked about her reactions when somebody asked Lydia to dance at a party:

> *I feel defeat when other women ask Lydia to dance. Sometimes they do not even ask me if I allow it. They just go to her and ask her. The other day we were at the market and we were invited to a party, but I knew that some of them were out to challenge me, so we did not go. As we were leaving, one of those bold sharks embraced Lydia, laughing loudly, you know how they do that—eeh-eeh, hands on her hips—she said to me: "M'e or'en, bika a no mag kowru dya in a kondre disi"/I am holding her, because she should not be cold here, in this country. "A man dat' n'e koti, a man dat' na wan hebi trefu gi mi yeye," literally, "That thing does not cut, it does not go like that; it is a heavy taboo for my 'I.'"*[10]

Here Wonnie is referencing the world of Winti. The mockery that she felt women were making of her by approaching Lydia and showing Wonnie that she might not be as "strong," "manly," and in command as she liked to think she was, was heavily taboo for her yeye. In this case the masculine part of her "I" was insulted and felt defeated because of it. Dancing with a "male" woman's partner at a party, without first asking the dominant partner for permission is, both in Suriname and in the Netherlands, a serious insult, a blow to her sense of her self, her feeling of honor. Dominant women, on the other hand, can dance freely with whomever they want without consulting their partner. Spatially the different roles and entitlements are often expressed by the seating arrangements: the "female" partner is sitting slightly behind her lover, so that it takes an effort to reach her. This spatial arrangement mirrors the ways in which the positioning of male and female Winti is envisioned for the "male" partner.

Underneath the outward call for egalitarianism, which so resembles hegemonic Dutch patterns in same-sex relationships, there is thus an Afro-Surinamese universe that exerts its influence on Wonnie's behavior. Interestingly, Lydia and Wonnie, although both embedded in Winti, make use of different discourses to understand themselves, each other, and the world. Lydia was always at pains to stress that "yu ab' den Winti, a no de tak' den Winti mu ab' yu"/you have Winti, but it must not be the case that the Winti have you. "You must be in control. They [the Winti] should not shame you, they have to listen to you, to protect you. They should not come and shout at all kinds of parties. I have not foregrounded the Winti in my life; I am a believer, but I am not superstitious. I do not allow any Winti to be dominant over me."

Lydia, having worked in medical circles for years, called on a scientific, biological discourse to explain Wonnie's behavior: she thought that, unlike her, Wonnie had more male than female hormones. Lydia thus objected to Wonnie's prerogatives on "wordly" grounds, she simply did not accept that Wonnie should be free to dance with everyone while forbidding her from doing the same. Wonnie, on the other hand, understood her own behavior in terms of spiritual notions that put egalitarianism beyond her control. It was the male part of her self, her Apuku, that behaved in this way and that wanted to control Lydia. "With me, *Apuku e knap' na fesi*/Apuku, the male principle, stands in front. I cannot stand to be with another "male" woman. You can immediately see it when in a woman *a man tan na fesi*/the man stands in front; it is what she exudes."

This elaborate exegesis of what is involved in egalitarianism for either of the partners shows that their cultural differences, even though they are both embedded within the same Afro-Surinamese working-class women's culture, can be quite substantial. In addition to being a warning against homogenizing mati, there is another point to be made. Extrapolating on the cultural homogenization thesis that is still too prominent in studies of sexual globalization, one would assume that globalization unidirectionally leads to the spread of lesbian identity. Thus, it would be reasonable to expect that it is Wonnie, having been in the Netherlands for almost thirty years and thus more thoroughly exposed to lesbianism as the model of same-sex desire, who would take egalitarianism most seriously. In fact, it is precisely the other way around, which amounts to a serious interruption of the tradition-modernity binary in the field of same-sex sexuality.

Visiting Suriname

One collective interview took place at Wonnie's home, shortly after Lydia and Wonnie had returned from a visit to Lydia's children in Suriname in the winter of 1994. Lydia reflected on the differences between being with a female partner in the Netherlands and in Suriname. In Amsterdam nobody paid attention to your business. In Suriname being with a woman was accepted, as long as you did not talk about it, did not name yourself. They went to several mati and other working-class parties together and, without words, presented themselves as a couple. They did not meet with negative reactions.

If it had been up to Wonnie, she would have preferred not to talk about their relationship at all with Lydia's children. Lydia, on the other hand, felt that because the children had only known their mother in a relationship with a man, they should know about the nature of her connection with Wonnie. Lydia had not exactly been looking forward to the conversation and explained how she talked with them:

> I sat down with the eldest two and I explained: *ik heb een vriendin*[11] *gevonden*/I have found a friend and she means everything to me. Marylyn asked, "Does Aunt Wonnie have a husband?" I said no. Marylyn then said, "You know what you are doing. You went through a lot with Raymond and you deserve a little happiness. So I won't talk back to you. But make sure that you pay Aunt Wonnie back everything that she gave you." "Mi n' e kon leg den uit dat' Wonnie na mi bedvriendin, dat' m 'e seks en"/I did not explain to them that Wonnie is my "bedfriend," that I have sex with her. Then my boy Fred asked, "Do you live in one house?" I said, "Yes, and we sleep in one bed." Fred, "Don't you want to take Raymond back? Has she taken his place?" I said yes, Wonnie has taken his place. In the end they both agreed that Aunt Wonnie must love me a lot, to take me with all my children.

The children's words, veiled as they are, revealed that they understood that their mother's relationship with Wonnie was more than just an ordinary friendship. No one named the relationship, but everyone understood what it was. Even Lydia's grandmother, who had raised her and who had done the mati work all of her life, was offered an ambiguous definition of the situation. Lydia told her: "Ouma, mi fen' wan vriendin"/Grandma, I have found a friend. Grandma responded: "Meisje, komopo na mi tapu, yere. Mi na sokiman, soki smeri no kan kor' mi."/Girl, leave me alone. "I know one, when I see one."[12]

Lydia told her siblings in the Netherlands that Wonnie was her partner. With that "Dutch" directness, she might be locating herself within the preferred Dutch gay and lesbian model of psychosexual development: struggling with one's homosexual identity, finding a new equilibrium, and then coming out of the closet (de Bruin and Balkema 2001). With her siblings and grandmother in Suriname she preferred ambiguity. With her older children she occupied a middle position: even though the word *mati* did not enter the conversation with them, she made sure that they were aware, as the Surinamese Dutch saying goes, "dat het zo lang en zo breed is"/that it is this long and this wide, i.e., how things stood. The way Lydia handled informing her family members in Suriname and the Netherlands about her relationship showed the differential assessments she made of what was called for in each of the contexts. It is indicative of her astute and multifaceted behavioral repertoire, which depended on context. While the openness toward the Dutch siblings might be understood by the influence that her stay in the Netherlands was exerting, Lydia said that she felt closer to them, and, had they been in Suriname, she would have told them there too. Lydia thus again made assessments and exhibited behavior that contradicts an easy and pervasive Euro-American narrative that makes teleological assumptions about the direction of change in sexual configurations. Thus, the lazy tradition-modernity reading would have it that exposure to the "modern" model of same-sex relationships in the West results in mati taking over features of the lesbian identity construction or even the whole package. In this case it would entail Lydia's automatic coming out to her family, especially the ones in the Netherlands. And while she did tell them, she located the reasons in the quality of her relationships with them in deciding to tell them about her relationship with Wonnie. The disappearance of the mati work in the Netherlands, once Surinamese women are exposed to lesbianism, is part of the grand narrative of the tradition-modernity template too, while other possibilities, e.g., the mati work thriving in the Netherlands and white Dutch women adopting sexual and familial patterns that have long been part of the behavioral repertoire of Surinamese women, hardly seem worth considering. Although it would be an essentialist gesture to equate the childbearing patterns in the Afro-Surinamese and white Dutch same-sex communities, and research needs to be done about the confluence of these patterns, it is worth noting that in the past two decades single motherhood and children born in lesbian relationships among white women have increased. Yet in binarist teleologic "tradition," that is, the mati work is still equated with backwardness and "modernity," that is, lesbianism, in its exclusionary variety, with progress/civilization (cf. Shohat 1998). As we saw earlier with the governmental discourse of emancipation policy, which has white women as its implicit subject, it is oxymoronic, not part of the cultural imaginary, to suppose that Surinamese women could organize their procreational patterns in a way that white women would want to emulate. I situate this impossibility, again, firmly in the realm of the global imperial.

I do not automatically escape this powerful global imperial narrative. In this conversation I heard Lydia for the first time calling herself alternately "a bisexual woman" and "a lesbian." I noted it with a slight pang of my own version of anthropological nostalgia (Rosaldo 1993) for the mati work. I wondered aloud if being a mati is the same as being bisexual and if nothing was erased for her in the translation. Lydia cheerfully answered that in Suriname you say *M' e mati*/I "mati" (verb) and in Dutch *Ik ben lesbisch*/I am a lesbian. I already dealt with this central opposition in the ways Afro-Surinamese and

Dutch same-sex relational patterns are conceptualized, signaling activity and identity respectively. Lydia did not share my nostalgia; in fact she now felt that mati should make an exclusive choice for women and discontinue keeping various options open. I realized that my (imperial) nostalgia is an emotional and intellectual investment in the mati work, which entailed that she should hold on to the mati work and not claim lesbianism. My feeling denied her the possibility of naming herself situationally and contextually, which is so deeply ingrained in working-class culture, and, as I have claimed in chapter 3, resembles the fragmented self postulated under the global post-modern, while it is not to be equated with it. To the extent that Lydia spoke about herself in terms of a lesbian identity, it could as convincingly be interpreted as practicing situational multiplicitousness. On the other hand, in my desire for Lydia to think about herself as doing the mati work, I was also freezing and essentializing the concept of lesbianism, precluding the possibility that lesbianism will be infused with other meanings when new groups claim the term.

Cracks

Gradually tiny cracks began to accumulate in the relationship between Lydia and Wonnie. In the spring of 1995, in an individual interview, Lydia shared that there were certain aspects of Wonnie that she could not accept, i.e., her manlike behavior. Now that Lydia had finally made an exclusive choice for a woman, she could not accept it that Wonnie behaved like a man. Wonnie, as we have seen, modeled her behavior after the masculine pattern that is characteristic in the domain of male-female relationships. It bothered Lydia that Wonnie was always telling her what to do and was extremely controlling of where she went, whom she met, and at what time she came home.[13] Wonnie also resorted to physical violence when she was angry.

In one conversation Lydia coined a significant new phrase in a mixture of Standard Dutch and Surinamese Dutch. She said that she knew that there are relationships where "twee vrouwen beiden van het lesbisch werk houden"/ two women both love the lesbian work, but both behave in a feminine way. This is an interesting turn of phrase, where Lydia translated and transposed the Sranan Tongo expression *a mati wroko*/the mati work, into Dutch; she coined a new phrase by saying "to love the lesbian work," showing the mixing and matching between two different models of same-sex desire. She illustrated, in fact, the ways in which lesbianism could be infused with new meaning, holding on—in the new formulation—to the mutual obligations implied by "work."

The four of us—Lydia and Wonnie, Delani and I—sometimes went to parties together. At one such party, in the winter of 1995, Lydia danced with another woman and Wonnie had been livid. She stopped talking to us, making it clear that we were to leave immediately and the party was over. On the way back home, with Delani and I sitting in the back, Wonnie started yelling at Lydia and pulled the van over to the curb of the freeway. Her yelling went on for a while, while Lydia hardly responded. Abruptly they got out of the car and Wonnie threatened to hit Lydia, so Delani and I got out too. All of us were now standing along the freeway between the southeast of Amsterdam and the center at three in the morning. It was bitterly cold, cotton clouds were forming out of our mouths, and shards of mist were chasing each other in the dull orange-yellow light. Wonnie wanted to know what Lydia had been thinking to dance with Norine, when Norine had not asked Wonnie for permission. It was clear that Lydia had committed a serious transgression. In a mixture of Sranan Tongo and Dutch, Wonnie yelled at Lydia, pushing her around:

> *I do not tolerate it when other women dance with you. Then they don't ask me anything. You know how those vulgar folks, those trashy women will talk: vers-vers-vers/fresh-fresh-fresh. "M'e dans' en kiri, yongu, a 'er' nyan"/I danced the hell out of her, man, [I felt] her whole pussy!! It is to ridicule me. They don't show any respect to me.*

With *vers-vers-vers* Wonnie was making a reference to the salient observation in mati circles that someone has just arrived from Suriname. The maligned mati were saying: *Wonnie fanga vers*/Wonnie has caught (a) fresh (one), thereby expressing a certain respect for Wonnie, while they were at the same time testing and challenging her to see if she was really sure of her conquest. It is a sport among some mati to make physical contact with the newly arrived woman while dancing with her.

There are at least three levels of meaning attached to the expression *vers-vers-vers*. It is, first, often used as an advertisement on Surinamese stores and in newspaper ads to advertise fresh merchandise, especially meat. The not so subtle association between a newly arrived mati and meat bespeaks a hetero-masculine worldview, also being deployed by mati. Second, a prevalent discourse in these circles is that a newly arrived mati is highly desirable because she has traditional values, such as being hospitable, a good cook, and having *bun maniri*/good manners, and has not yet been spoiled by becoming materialistic. Thus newly arrived women are more appreciated than women who have lived in the Netherlands for a longer time. The tradition-undesirability versus modernity-desirability binary shows up here again, but in reverse: mati in the Netherlands often prefer women who have just arrived from Suriname, bespeaking a preference for "tradition." Third, simultaneously, there is a construction operative, in which the newly arrived mati and women in Suriname are rendered desirable objects and are thus feminized, while the implicit subject imagining what and who is desirable has agency and is masculinized. I am arguing that, exceptions notwithstanding, newly arrived mati often find themselves structurally in a situation of economic, emotional, and psychological dependency, needing knowledge of the local situation possessed by their partners. This situation is exacerbated by the demand of the Dutch state to remain with that partner for three years in order to get a permit to stay, which sets up a division of labor whereby "Dutch" mati are positioned in ways that are comparable to a masculine position, while newly arrived mati are symbolically positioned as feminine. Unfortunately, there is more than one parallel here with the situation of white European and U.S. males seeking mail-order brides from Thailand, the Philippines, or Eastern Europe. M. Jacqui Alexander (1998) has proposed to think about global sexual cartographies, in which those providing or envisioned to provide service are never positioned as agents, as equal partners in a sexual exchange. Her model of transnational sexual consumption is grounded in a "historically intransigent colonial relationship, in which a previously scripted colonial cartography of ownership and production, consumption and distribution all conform to a 'First World/Third World' division" (1998:294). Unequal sexual exchanges are not only located in a North-South context, they clearly also take place in settings, where both participants are from the South.

Returning to the desolate scene described above, several readings of Wonnie's outburst that do not mutually exclude each other are possible. First, there is the Surinamese cultural context in which her masculine spirits were put into jeopardy by Lydia's behavior. Second, Wonnie's outburst can also be read as an expression of the indignation she felt at the tresspass Lydia had made on the unwritten rules of the contract between them, in which, backed by the Dutch state, she occupied the privileged, masculine position. Lydia tried to calm Wonnie down, giggling, obviously embarrassed that Wonnie would give her anger such free expression in our presence. We tried without much success to intervene. After a while, her worst anger subsided and all of us climbed back into the van. We got home that evening, feeling, needless to say, very uncomfortable.

Things Fall Apart

The next time Lydia and Wonnie came over for dinner, the tension was so rife it was unpleasant to be with them. It became difficult to find topics of conversation that were not sensitive. Several times Lydia offhandedly made remarks about starting a relationship without knowledge of the other person: "We zijn doodvreemden voor elkaar"/We are complete strangers to each other. Wonnie, as usual did not comment, but she looked like a rumbling volcano. Somewhat later Lydia told me on the phone that Wonnie was threatening to go to the police and tell them that the relationship was over. That would mean that Lydia's grounds for staying in the Netherlands and for getting Dutch nationality would be nonexistent. She would either be forced to leave the Netherlands or become illegal again.

Shortly after, I accidently met Wonnie at the opening of a Surinamese art gallery, where her band was playing. During intermissions we chatted. Wonnie indicated that things were falling apart. In her view she had made all the right moves to keep Lydia happy; she had helped her get on her feet in the Netherlands, had given her everything she might desire. She felt righteous about her expectation that Lydia would stay at home when she was not working or that they would go out only together. Wonnie suspected that Lydia had started seeing someone else since she often came home late, unable and unwilling to account for it. Wonnie was bitter that Lydia *a' e waka en eygi pasi*/was doing her own thing, after she had helped her get her permit to stay. "She goes her way and I go mine."

At the next intermission I heard that Lydia had moved out and I was jolted. When I ran into Diana, Lydia's niece, in the shopping center, she told me that Lydia moved out because Wonnie had become violent toward her. Lydia had to move out surreptitiously, on an evening when Wonnie was playing with her band. She left a note for Wonnie saying that it was better to be apart. She announced in the note that she would send her brother to get the rest of her stuff in the coming week. When he went to get her possessions, Wonnie had, in a symbolically charged gesture that is not uncommon in male-female dyads, destroyed all her possessions, clothes, books, and photographs.

Epilogue

Gradually, Lydia picked up her life again. She was lucky to be so close to the mandatory three-year period that she obtained her own permit to stay in the Netherlands and, after a while, Dutch nationality. She retrained as a subway driver, became active in the union of municipal transport workers, and rented her own apartment. By first "choosing" a profession that would allow her to stay in the Netherlands and obtain Dutch nationality and then retraining for another job that she really wanted, Lydia showed characteristic agency and strategic planning. In becoming a subway driver, she poked her nose at the prevalent construction of Surinamese women as proverbial caretakers who simply and naturally love the work. She has brought her three youngest children over to the Netherlands. The eldest children chose to stay in Paramaribo. Lydia became very careful in relationships. Recently she started seeing an older Afro-Surinamese woman who is "very soft and very feminine." She has finally found the relationship she had been dreaming about, and they both preferred a visiting relationship.

The relationship between Lydia and Wonnie did not work out. It combined some of the worst features, jealousy and violence, that mati relationships can harbor. The deepest source of conflict, internal to the relationship, were the different ways in which the partners envisioned their roles.

But the relationship did not proceed in a vacuum. It suffered severely from the legal circumstances that position migrant partners as dependent, adding features to the relationship, which may be structural to transnational sexual exchanges generally, setting up "Third World" partners as feminized objects and "First World" partners as masculinized agents. There are several observations that need to be made here.

While this relationship had some extreme features, it should not be taken as the typical outcome of transatlantic mati relationships. The broadest framework in which I have placed it is that of sexual globalization, in which the mati work travels transatlantically. This was facilitated by cultural changes and legal battles in the Netherlands, during the eighties and nineties, that resulted in the recognition of homosexual and lesbian relationships as a valid basis to form partnerships[14] and thus enabled same-sex partners to form recognized unions. The "Dutch" partner has to meet certain housing, income, and age requirements, which have shown the tendency in recent years, under the Centrum-Right cabinets Balkenende I and II (from 2002 on), to become ever stricter. Lydia and Wonnie's relationship was made possible by this legislation. Although at first sight this progressive state gesture only knows winners, there are price tags attached to it. It is clear that the construction of lesbianism, which stresses a stable sexual identity as the legal ground enabling entry into the Netherlands, exerts influence on those who stand to benefit from it, hailing them to embrace that identity. Thus it need not surprise us that Lydia felt interpellated by the discourse of lesbianism. One consequence of the dominant discourse acting as a borderguard is that it homogenizes all those engaging in same-sex sexual activity, leaving no conceptual space for alternative conceptualizations of sexual subjectivity. In the apt words of Cruz-Malavé and Manalansan IV:

> While globalization is seen to liberate and promote local sexual difference, the emergence, visibility, and legibility of those differences are often predicated in

globalizing discourses on a developmental narrative in which a premodern, prepolitical, non-Euro-American queerness must consciously assume the burdens of representing itself to itself and others as "gay" in order to attain political consciousness, subjectivity and global modernity.

(2002:6)

This is a powerful critique of the "fixing" of gay and lesbian identity as the only possible, viable, and respectable mode of same-sex desire. Various authors have recently embarked upon this critical route, which breaks through received notions constructing sexual globalization (Gopinath 2002; Strongman 2002; Santiago 2002).

Wonnie's and Lydia's union showed the extreme dependency in which the newly arrived partner is structurally placed. Helma Lutz (1997) has rightly pointed to the double standards that white Dutch women, i.e., "autochthonous" women, and women arriving in the Netherlands from particular Third World countries, so-called allochthonous women, are held to.[15] "General" policy aims, in the framework of governmental emancipation policy during the past thirty years, have, as we saw, been geared toward financial independence and autonomy, supposedly for all women. In practice, "allochthonous" women are tightly bound, at least for three years, to their (homo- or heterosexual) partners who already are in the Netherlands. The emancipation goal of autonomy and independence for all women is thus set aside, for newly arrived women of color, in the service of the more pressing goal of keeping their numbers limited and their not becoming dependent for income on the state.

The dependency on a partner causes untold misery should the relationship fail. Lydia initially was extremely dependent on Wonnie for money, for housing, for her permit to stay, for her naturalization papers, for knowledge about Dutch society. This dependency should not be underestimated. That power differential, clothed in love in the beginning, must have surely convinced Wonnie even more that she was the "man in the house." As Lydia's dependence diminished over time, Wonnie's demanding behavior, backed by the law, as it were, grew more excessive.

Second, although Wonnie had been in the Netherlands for decades, she modeled her behavior after traditional male Surinamese patterns. She felt entitled to control Lydia's comings and goings. It also meant that she believed she had claims over Lydia's sexuality. Not staking a claim would amount to an insult to her "I" and a blemish to her reputation. Lydia, on the other hand, "fresh from Suriname" had other ideas about how they should interact. She had left her husband because she wanted a more egalitarian relationship, but with Wonnie she found herself in a situation that resembled the one with

her husband. Lydia and Wonnie break through lazy, Eurocentric juxtaposi-
tions that would have Wonnie, having been in the Netherlands for decades,
be more "progressive," liberated, and egalitarian and Lydia more "traditional,"
old-fashioned, and into polarized role-playing. They demonstrated exactly
opposite behaviors from those expectations. Lydia and Wonnie called on various discourses to make sense of themselves and the world. Lydia called predominantly on a biological discourse, which utilizes hormones as a key to
understanding behavior, and Wonnie made use of a Winti discourse, which
foregrounds the Gods and spirits who have particular—masculine and feminine—characteristics. Again, the correlation of being embedded in one or the
other discourse with the length of one's stay in the Netherlands is not clear-cut
at all. Reality is much messier. Moreover, the same person may make use of
different discourses, either in the same utterance or at different moments.

Third, when addressing the ways in which female mati insert themselves
in sexual globalization, it is striking that they, generally, meet in person,
through mati networks in the big cities in the Netherlands or in Paramaribo.[16] Mati networks in the Netherlands engage in leisure time activities,
playing bingo, dancing, and flirting with each other, but their networks
also support each other financially and socially. Typically, relationships are
forged between Afro-Surinamese women, although relationships with Javanese and Hindustani women also occur. Relationships with women from
other ethnicized groups, including white Dutch women, are rare. The personal way of meeting and the preference for a woman from one's own community compose a specific configuration. It may be a matter of generation
and class. The women I have worked with, who are "on the move" transatlantically, are at least in their thirties and working class. There is another factor
that may contribute to the widespread preference for a relationship with
another Afro-Surinamese woman. It is my impression that, for large numbers of older working-class Surinamese men and women in the big cities in
the Netherlands, social life unfolds and takes place largely within the Afro-
Surinamese community.[17] My observations at parties and ritual gatherings
in the southeast of Amsterdam, where a significant section of Surinamese
Amsterdammers lives, show that there are only rarely people of other ethnic
groups present. This holds both for general and for mati gatherings. People
may go to work in white or multiethnic settings, but their leisure time is
spent in Afro-Surinamese circles. Mati I have interviewed in Amsterdam
confirmed that they preferred, for a variety of reasons, to be in a relationship
with another Afro-Surinamese woman, and this pattern was also obvious in
Suriname. Some of the reasons, as we have already seen in Wonnie's case, are
located in the cultural domain: it is more comfortable not having to explain

one's cultural do's and don'ts, e.g., observing one's *trefu*/food that is ritually taboo, or the nature of the spirits one is carried by and thus the obligations one has to honor, or how one should be treated. Another set of reasons that surfaced had to do with differences in perceived standards of cleanliness, pertaining mostly to care for the body, when one has a white Dutch partner. Several mati observed that their first preference was to be with a Creole woman, next would be a Hindustani or Javanese partner, and they could not quite imagine being with a white Dutch partner. The third set of reasons reported is a positive preference to be with a black woman, because they are thought to be aesthetically and sexually most pleasing. The firm orientation of many mati, like Wonnie, who have been in the Netherlands for quite some time on the Afro-Surinamese community may result in ossified attitudes, beliefs, and practices in the same-sex relational domain than those more recent arrivals, like Lydia, exhibit. As I noted, this overturns the tradition-modernity binary.

Globalization offers opportunities, but it also exacerbates existing inequalities between the North and the South. There is a misplaced light-heartedness connected to the triumphant march of "global queering" that is at odds with the realities experienced by women like Lydia. Lydia was "looking for her life," needing to survive and build a new home for herself and her children. Given the conditions of Fortress Europe, these opportunities come at a price, e.g., personal dependencies and reinscriptions of colonial scripts, no matter what the actual ethnicized positionings of the protagonists involved are. We should not underestimate the real, enormous difficulties that partners have to deal with in a Western setting, which is desperately set to limit the entry of immigrants from Third World countries, even if they can show they are card-carrying members of the "lesbian community" (Espin 1999).

Contemporary Hegemonic Scripts About Black Women's Sexuality

While Lydia and Wonnie were in the process of getting acquainted, the presence of black sexualities in Dutch society did not go unnoticed. *De Volkskrant*, one of the large national daily newspapers, published a column on March 15, 1993, entitled "White in the Bijlmer,"[18] written by white female journalist Bernadette de Wit. In this column another white woman, Pamela, living in the Bijlmermeer, was given the opportunity to vent her opinions about Surinamese people in general and Surinamese women's sexuality in particular. The Bijlmer is the southeastern part of Amsterdam where a large section of the population is black, with people from Suriname, the Antilles, and various African nations. I will critically analyze this column, because *de Volkskrant* is an influential daily reaching a large, highly educated white readership, many of whom most likely have never set foot in the Bijlmer. The column informed them about black women's sexuality. Pamela had lived with a Surinamese man for fifteen years and he had just left her for a Surinamese woman. She had a child with him, thus her biography lent her the status of reliable witness:

> *I am not a racist. I do not feel at home with my own people either, with my colored children. The dirty remarks I have had because of that: I am a negro whore. I have asked for a house in another part of Amsterdam, because I want to leave the Bijlmer. For my child. You want me to tell you something funny? I am sure that I will get homesick.*

Pamela's trustworthiness and her right to speak as an "experiential expert" are established in this passage. The opening phrase "I am not a racist" functions as a transparant opening bid, with her colored child as the proof of her trustworthiness and thus a license for all statements that are to follow in the interview. Her ambivalence both toward "her own people," who call her a negro whore, and toward the Surinamese group, from whom she wants to distance herself but whom she will miss in the future, heighten her authenticity: here we are dealing with an in-your-face, real Amsterdam woman who tells it like it is. With respect to both groups she presents herself as half insider/half outsider. This strategy allows the reader to get the impression that her multiple "marginality" gives her privileged insight. Pamela is allowed to say everything about Surinamers that she wants—"they will never integrate," "divide and rule is the only thing they know," "that hatred against us, they imbibe it with their mother's milk"—after all, she has already established that she is not a racist.

Her statements about black women's sexuality are especially significant. They are statements in a long historical tradition of white women constructing black women's sexuality. The strategies Pamela uses to other black women, while in the same movement establishing white women as the universal, normative, essential subject, are my focus here. Pamela informs us about the nature of Surinamese people:

> *Everything that Surinamese people do is calculated. You only hit the sack with him when he pays for your food. You take a child and then, on top of your social security and the child allowance, you get another nf 500, from*

him. That is the way all Surinamese women do it here. They take it for
granted that he has two, three other women. They are walking where their
cunts lead them, anyway, because they are all bisexual.

Pamela produces an utterly pejorative reading of Afro-Surinamese work-ing-class sexual configurations here. While some of the ingredients that I have outlined earlier in this book are present, the umbrella under which everything is put is one of rejection and negativity toward the sexualized Other, while it is entirely clear that the sexual systems of the white Self are superior. What is striking, first, about this statement is Pamela's certainty about the general validity of the model she offers for understanding Suri-namese people: "Everything that Surinamese people do is calculated; this is the way all Surinamese women do it; they are all bi." According to Mohanty (1991), colonization almost invariably entails the often violent suppression of the heterogeneity of the subject in question. Pamela is exercising discursive power by her litany and is constructing a homogeneous, inferior black Other by implicitly taking herself and other white women as another homogeneous frame of reference. White Dutch women, in Pamela's subtext, are obviously totally different from Surinamese women: they have sex with men out of love or, in circles where that is allowed since the Sexual Revolution, out of desire. Calculation and greed are not a part of this discourse.

Second, reading in between the lines it is clear that several assumptions about normative, white female sexuality are operative. I will comment on three characteristics of that sexuality as they become clear in Pamela's words. In the first place, where Surinamese women "take it for granted that he has two, three other women on the side," we have to assume that white women would not stand for that. Here an implicit self-image of white women is constructed: she is free to take decisions, in control of her own sexuality and her own body. Moreover, white women are capable of regu-lating the sexuality of their men. Here it is still ambiguous whether black women do not want to do the same (too emancipated) or are not capable of doing so (too unemancipated). Whatever it will turn out to be, it is clear that it is no good. In the chiaroscuro of white and black sexuality, we see the contours of monogamy between white heterosexual couples as the normal and normative state of affairs. In the second place, black female sexuality is depicted as excessive, as far too much. That Surinamese men have multiple partners is one thing, but Surinamese women too walk "where their cunts lead them." Thus it becomes clear that the women do not want to control the sexuality of their men. Subtext: this is not the way white Dutch women are. Despite the widespread notion that white female sexuality is the apex of self-determination and autonomy, apparently there are implicit, self-regulating norms that keep it in check. Black women, so Pamela is implying, are not the least bit interested in abiding by those norms. Sexual freedom is good, according to her, but when you take too much of it—"walking where their cunts lead them"—a woman places herself outside the norms of respectability.[19] In the third place, picking up on Pamela's statement that "they are all bi," it transpires that bisexuality cannot count on her approval. It transgresses the boundaries of acceptable white female sexuality. Subtext: normative white female sexuality is heterosexual, predictable, fixed on a partner of the opposite sex. The "naturalized" sexuality that Pamela is implicitly referring to all the time and that enables her to reject the sexuality of Surinamese women is thus monogamous, heterosexual, not excessive, and not calculated.

Finally, the statement lacks any kind of consciousness of the historical and cultural context. Representations of black women's sexuality did not spring up over night: they are part of a deeply rooted texture of excessiveness, exoticism, deviance, and pathology (Nederveen Pieterse 1990). Representational regimes of the sexuality of different groups of women do not come into being independently from each other; they are relational. In contemporary Dutch multiethnic society, Islamic women are represented as sexually backward and oppressed, while Afro-Surinamese women are "too liberated," with a rampant sexuality, doing it indiscriminately with men and with women, doing it for money, "walking after their cunts." White female sexuality is the only decent, normative variety. Thus we see not only a relational structuring of these representations but also an operative hierarchy. Moreover, dominant representational regimes of Islamic women in the West have undergone radical changes from hypersexuality, in the late nineteenth and early twentieth centuries, to current asexuality (Lutz 1991). But the sexual imagery constructing black women shows more continuity, paradoxically containing elements of desirability and abject otherness. Within racist discourse blacks are not exclusively depicted as inferior; there is also, and often simultaneously, jealousy, an unspeakable yearning, involved (hooks 1992).

Thus in everyday discourse in Dutch society, which insists on being nonracist, images of black female sexuality are recirculated that ensure the continuing operation of the global imperial.

In Pamela's bitterly racist words, she transforms the threat and the hurt that she must feel at being abandoned in the familiar tradition (Surinamese sexual culture) versus modernity (white Dutch sexual culture) binary. Evidently her sense of self has been so challenged that she must resort to racist imagery to shore up her self esteem. One cannot help but wonder what it will do to her children to hear their mother rant in such a way about half their family. White female sexual subjecthood, too, is interrogated under the influence of sexual globalization. It has to resort to violent measures to hold on to its superior positioning.

The Mati Work in Suriname and Sexual Globalization

Thus far I have paid attention to how the mati work reinvents itself in a Dutch postcolonial space that is severely marred by a reluctance to address its colonial past and racist present. I now want to address some of the ways in which globalization makes itself felt in discourses on sexuality and on the mati work in Suriname.

I will briefly sum up the contexts in which sexual globalization in a female same-sex formation took place at the end of the twentieth and the beginning of the twenty-first centuries. The globalization of the mati work occurred in the context of and was produced by the displacement of old economic forms—that is, ever deepening spirals of economic crises, running inflation (Kromhout 2000), a state that had evacuated important tasks in the domains of care and education, and the supersession of national industries—glass, soap, building material, preserves, and juice—by transnational corporations extracting wood and gold. The rain forest, once a promise for an ecologically sound habitat, looked, at the end of the nineties, like a fragile and poisonous set of dentures from which so many teeth have been extracted. These conditions made it virtually impossible for the majority of the population, notably women who are single heads of households, to survive without access to foreign currencies. Many younger women migrated to the Netherlands and, in one case, to the U.S. Connections with resources outside of Suriname were vital social, economic, and erotic capital.

Politically, we saw the dislodgment of old political forms—that is, the nominal replacement of a dictatorship by a civilian government in the nineties—while in practice an almost inextricable nexus of political, military and commercial interests, the so-called Tarantulas, which had aligned themselves with transnational corporations, ruled the state. Politics orchestrated the resources of various sectors of the population in gendered ways, with women in structurally less favorable positions than men. From above we saw the influence of multinational corporations and transnational bodies (the UN, the World Bank, and the IMF, but also the international women's and indigenous rights movements) impinging on the state, whereas, from below, the state is challenged by a diverse array of forces: NGOs in the fields of women's and indigenous rights, trade unions incessantly demanding higher wages, unknown numbers of immigrants from mainland China

and an estimated forty thousand Brazilian garimpeiros, gold diggers, pointing to the unwillingness or inability of the state to police its borders.

At the most general level global cultural forces, i.e., the international
women's movement and donor organizations like Dutch Cordaid, Novib,
Mama Cash, Unifem and Unicef, the Canadian Fund for Gender Equity,
and the Global Fund for Women have increasingly impacted on the gender
and sexual landscape in Suriname. In the nineties and the early years of the
twenty-first century the Surinamese women's and NGO movements have,
with the help of these foreign donors, flourished and became more visible.
This is an aspect of globalization that has recently started to receive attention in the literature (Cruz-Malavé and Manalansan IV 2002; King 2002).
The women's movement has, among other targets, focused on domestic violence (Ketwaru-Nurmohamed 2000:68). Violent acts of men against women
received widespread coverage in the media in 2001. In Foucauldian fashion a discourse was forged between international donors and Surinamese
women's organizations in which sexual violence, which had been around
for a long time—recall Mis' Juliette's narrative about the sexual harrassment
she faced in the homes where she worked in the 1920s—could now for the
first time be discussed in the public sphere. The newspapers in May and
June 2001 brought an avalanche of cases of violence against women (Wekker 2001, 2004b). The framework is still that of a dominant, unequal gender
ideology, so justice is not necessarily served in these court cases, but at least
the message is transmitted that male sexual behavior is not "naturally given"
and that men can be held accountable.

There are other issues the women's movement has put on the public
agenda in the past decade that have impacted on the lives of all women,
including mati, and men: commercial sex work, HIV/AIDs, sustainable
livelihoods for women in the interior, broader representation of women
in politics, training of female entrepreneurs and women in nontraditional
occupations, provision of schooling and care for teenage mothers and their
infants. In 2000 a report was published by the Maxi Linder Foundation[20]
in collaboration with the Canadian Gender Equity Fund, that charted the
nature and extent of the sex industry in Suriname.[21] Strikingly, for a small
population of 440,000 people, 35 registered sex clubs were counted as well
as 152 informal locations where sex was transacted. While sex work is illegal
in Suriname, it is tolerated, and the foundation had registered 248 street
workers and another 500 workers, mostly from Columbia, Guyana, Brazil,
and the Dominican Republic, who worked in the club circuit.[22] As noted in
chapter 2, it transpired that male sex workers are very popular and were able
to charge higher rates for the same acts that women perform. For example,
for a whole day or evening a female sex worker could ask between sf. 40,000

and 60,000 while a male prostitute could charge between sf. 60,000 and 100,000.[23] Several sources confirm that male same-sex sexual behavior is hidden but rampant.[24] M. Jacqui Alexander's (1991, 1994) argument that the neocolonial Caribbean state, i.e., Trinidad and Tobago and the Bahamas, has a lot of interest in constructing some bodies as citizens while others—gays, lesbians, and prostitutes—are constructed as not being part of the nation, as a threat to the continuity of the nation by supposedly being nonprocreative, holds only partly in Suriname. While the Surinamese state naturalizes and tries to enforce compulsory heterosexuality for men, mainly by ridiculing and animalizing male homosexuals in public debates and speeches,[25] it has mainly ignored female mati, who are not in the habit of naming themselves. It remains to be seen how the state responds when young, educated women start to call themselves lesbian in public.

On a more personal level, the uneven economic circumstances, which were exacerbated by globalization, were intimately felt in the relationships between mati who are differently positioned on either side of the Atlantic. In chapter 5, on the mati work, I described how some mati, like Maureen Gonzalvez, were able to establish a satisfactory long-distance relationship with a woman in the Netherlands. On the other hand, in the beginning of the nineties the stronger financial situation of "Dutch" mati, who were visiting Suriname, sharply brought their privileges and the more precarious situation of Surinamese mati into focus. Many Surinamese mati felt that the "Dutch girls" sought to humiliate vulnerable Surinamese mati, who were tempted by their money to engage in compromising sexual encounters.

In the summer of 2001 globalization presented itself forcefully when I attended the funeral of a well-known mati who was in her late sixties. Prominent at the funeral were her male concubine and her mati, both resident in Paramaribo, and several female friends, her *speri*/peers, who had traveled from the Netherlands, some of whom were her ex-mati. The funeral was spectacular, because all the women wore the same color dresses and hats: a light beige. With this old *parweri*/wearing-the-same-outfit statement, they stressed their belonging together. In another symbolically charged gesture, droves of white doves and balloons were sent into the air. This event was special, because of the sheer numbers of people attending the funeral and the mixture of symbols that was invoked. The transnational character of the Surinamese community spoke loudly from the event: the deceased had, like many other retired Surinamese people, lived alternately in Suriname and with her children in the Netherlands in the last decades of her life. The balloons and doves were gestures from a Dutch cultural universe, symbolizing the space of freedom that the deceased was now entering, and the fabric of the dresses had come from the Netherlands as well. The presence of her two partners and the practice of parweri bespoke a Surinamese universe.The contours of a global mati funeral were transparent in the mixture.

I also spent time with two different sets of young women: a group of university students, in their middle twenties, and several mati couples who were in their twenties and thirties. I was struck, first, by the adoption of northern sexual labels by the educated young women and, second, by the continuity of the pattern of gendered roles among both sets of women. As far as the division of roles was concerned, the only young couple in the middle-class crowd, a school teacher and a sales representative in the electronics department of a large shopping mall, self-identified as lesbian and clearly were into a division of roles. Ethnically, one of them was *moksi* or, as young people also say nowadays, a "cocktail"—mixed—while the other one was a Hindustani girl, pointing to the purchase that the mati model has on girls and women of other ethnic groups. They dressed in a polarized "feminine" and "masculine" style and called each other *mammi*/mommy and *pappi*/daddy. Thus calling oneself lesbian does not make a universal statement about one's identity.

The female students, all childless, self-identified, with the exception of one, who called herself mati,[26] as lesbian or gay or tomboy. The students expressed that they did not have much appreciation for mati and talked about them with a certain disdain: "Ah, those women who do it with men, too. That has got to stop." Arguing from a lesbian identity perspective as fixed, true, and authentic, they saw mati sexual behavior as untrustworthy, self-serving, and too pragmatic, too interested in money. If they, at some point in the future, want to have children, they would prefer to have an artificial donor instead of going to bed with a man. The dismissal of mati on the grounds that they do it with men speaks of the internalization of a dominant Euro-American narrative in which one should be either hetero- or homosexual, not both. While I had not specifically asked them about it, they volunteered that it was difficult for them "to come out" at the university, again reproducing a dominant Euro-American narrative about what one is to do when one discovers one's sexual "nature." As I noted before, the coming out scenario is not part of the mati configuration. The self-identifications and the statements of the students would seem to invoke unproblematically a new, "global lesbian identity."

In my reading it is not surprising nor overly significant that the university students adopted global labels. These young women had access to the Internet and had no overt local middle-class models or concepts for female same-sex desire. This does not mean at all, however, that they had thrown all the elements of mati sensibility and understanding overboard. As one of the girls, Beverly Koorndijk, a twenty-five-year-old law student, recounted, her family did not officially know that she was gay but had its suspicions. They regularly asked when she was going to bring "Johnny" home, and her mother had suggested a ritual bath to turn around her Apuku—that is, her daughter should consult a ritual healer to *sreka en Apuku*/settle her Apuku,to make him recede more into the background. The contours of mati sensibility have not gone too far underground among these young women, who seemed, on first acquaintance, to inhabit a space of Western sexual identity formation.

Among working-class women, in 2001, the mati work was very much alive, and so was the gendered division of roles. All these women referred to themselves as mati. In this period a group of mati was planning to hold a Mr. Gay Suriname contest, which in the end failed to materialize.[27]

In the sexual domain, there was, especially in the case of young, highly educated men and women, an emergence of self-referentiality in terms of gay and lesbian identity, which in my reading does not signal that a homogenized global gay or lesbian identity is in formation. The labels are adopted, through access to the Internet, gay and lesbian movies, and visits to the Netherlands, but that does not mean mati sensibilities among young women have vanished. The mati work remains a significant source of meaning. It is not frozen in time, but they accommodate and change it as needed. Older working-class women, in their thirties and forties and up, are engaged in the mati work and thus do not claim an exclusionary sexual identity.

Few theoreticians of sexual globalization have focused on the empirical details of lives, organized around sex with same-sex persons, as they are lived in specific settings in the so-called Third World. I have tried in this chapter to provide depth and thick description to a transnational sexual phenomenon pertaining to women, which is rare enough in itself. My problems with the cultural homogenization thesis are numerous. The powerful narrative that underlies it reinstates the binary logic of "tradition" being associated with the mati work and "modernity" with lesbianism, the former inevitably giving way to the latter. This constitutes part of the global imperialist script. Yet something else is at stake; teleological scripts of Western gay and lesbian identities inexorably spreading across the globe and being swallowed wholesale everywhere overlook the agency of Afro-Surinamese women and their cultural situatedness. The often painful and mundane processes involved are not well captured by such concepts, which not only do not pay attention to power differentials involved in such relationships but also offer a totalizing misreading of the triumphant, global march of homosexual and gay identity out of disparate, messy, hybrid, on-the-ground phenomena. Finally, this discourse reinstates global imperial relations in the domain of same-sex sexuality. Sooner rather than later we will have to let go of the entire tradition-modernity binary because it is not helpful—indeed, it obscures more than it illuminates.

This chapter suggests that both women who travel transatlantically and women who are living in Suriname partake in and shape the phenomenon of sexual globalization. Both categories engage in bricolage to make sense of their sexual activities, but the content of their psychic-spiritual-sexual economy is still in place. Globalization does not only affect them, however: the sexualities of other groups of women, including white Dutch women, are also implicated in this process, as was demonstrated in the case of Pamela. In many recent queer studies that call for a "transnational turn" the ethnically unmarked position in (former) metropoles has escaped attention.

Coda

This study, *The Politics of Passion,* has captured (part of) life as it has been lived by Afro-Surinamese working-class women in Paramaribo and in the Netherlands over the last decade of the twentieth century and the dawn of the twenty-first, as refracted through the lenses of a female anthropologist of Surinamese descent. Black women have taken a central role in few studies on sexual subjecthood. Here the politics of passion as enacted by working-class women—street sweepers, market women, cleaning women, and newspaper sellers—received attention. Studies of black working-class life in the hemisphere have overwhelmingly targeted the family system, notably the "oddness" and undesirability of matrifocality, and have thus focused on the trials and tribulations in the relationships between men and women. By contrast, this book addresses the meaningful, nurturing, sexual, and emotional relationships that Afro-Surinamese women carve out for themselves.

The framework of my understanding of female selves, gender, and sexualities is that of the black Diaspora. I believe that Afro-Suriname has much to contribute to our understanding of how a particular people elaborated on a set of West African principles they had taken with them, embarking on the Middle Passage and in establishing communities in the "New World" from "scratch." One of the intriguing questions my work raises is since Afro-Surinamese women have found nurturance and sexual and emotional bonding with female partners, has this "model" found more widespread proliferation elsewhere? The few existing leads point to similar constructions of sexual subjecthood in West Africa, the Caribbean, and black America as a most fruitful field for further exploration.

Another question concerns the future of this black diasporic sexual knowledge system and set of practices. If globalization continues to accelerate, will these practices continue to frame the ways in which Afro-Surinamese women both in Suriname and in the Netherlands think about themselves and shape their subjectivities, or will they eventually become black "lesbians"? Will they come to think of sexual activity as sexual identity? Clearly, I can only speculate about this question, but the longevity and tenacity of the sexual culture Afro-Surinamese women embody point to a deeply anchored set of beliefs and understandings that will not be shed easily, as one removes a coat. There is a deep history that precedes this historical moment. As Mis' Juliette said: "Mi s' sa, un kon mit' a wroko dya, a no un mek'en"/My sister, we found the mati work when we got here, it was not us who invented it. In addition, the preference of many Dutch Surinamese women to spend their life in Afro-Surinamese circles means that the conditions are favorable that collectively the cultural heritage may be kept alive. Even if the macrostructures women live in continue to change, it is the everyday practices that will go on to shape their understandings of themselves as sexual beings.

Notes

Acknowledgments

1. I use the terms *Afro-Surinamese* and *Creole*, the local designation, intermittently for the descendants of slaves, an urban population that comprises about 32 percent of Suriname's 440,000 inhabitants.
2. My translation. Published first in the Surinamese newspaper *De ware Tijd Literair* (1990), the poem was reprinted in G. Oostindie and R. Hoefte, eds., *Echo van Eldorado* (Leiden: KITLV Uitgeverij,1996) and in M. van Kempen, ed., *Spiegel van de Surinaamse Poëzie* (Amsterdam: Meulenhoff, 1997).
3. The preceding lines—*motyo tie*, let them talk, sailor's tie—are names of *angisa*, the traditional headdresses Creole women wear. The names refer to different ways of tying the headwraps.
4. See Scholtens et al. (1992).

1. *No Tide, No Tamara* / Not Today, Not Tomorrow

1. The way I speak Sranan is inflected by having become fluent under Juliette's guidance. It is an archaic form of Sranan; I use many old fashioned expressions that make younger people laugh. It is very polite on the one hand—always addressing older people in the third person—"Does Juliette want something to drink"?—and at the same time it is very direct and graphic, e.g., in its

sexual lexicon. Parts of this chapter have appeared in Wekker 1992a, 1994, and 1998.

2. There are striking parallels in the relationship between Surinamese Dutch and Standard Dutch and that between Black English Vernacular (BEV) and Standard American English (SAE) (see Wekker and Wekker 1991).

3. *Nyan prisiri* literally means "to eat pleasure," to have fun. Nyan is a culturally salient metaphor.

4. Desi Bouterse was the military commander and leader of the sixteen soldiers who overthrew the democratic government in February 1980 and killed fifteen opponents in December 1982. He later became founder of the multiethnic political party NDP, Nationale Democratische Partij (National Democratic Party).

5. NPS is the Nationale Partij Suriname (National Surinamese Party), a largely Creole political party.

6. I was interested in the fate of PVVU, Politieke Volks Vrouwen Unie, an initiative by working-class Creole women to found a political party for women in the spring of 1991 (see Wekker 1997).

7. Giving Juliette a big box of Dutch cigars, *pastoorssigaren,* clergymen cigars, was always a big hit. Either she would smoke them herself or if she temporarily did not feel like smoking, being the trader she was, she would sell them on the market. Juliette also sometimes smoked a pipe. In eighteenth- and nineteenth-century representations of Surinamese slave women there are numerous images of older women with pipes.

8. In mati relationships both women may serve the other, but in relationships with sharply polarized roles the one performing the "male" role will usually not serve the other.

9. According to Comvalius (1935:11), Boss Kupu, a well-known clarinet player, was a favorite musician at lobi singi, together with his group.

10. *Tyuri*, chups, is the sucking of teeth, a dismissive black diasporic way of expressing oneself, mostly done by women.

11. My emphasis.

12. The poem is printed in the preface and acknowledgments and I have dedicated it to Juliette.

13. EBG is Evangelical Brethren Gemeinschaft, also called Hernnhutters, a Protestant group that came to Suriname in 1735, from Herrnhut in Germany, to evangelize the slaves.

14. Kasnika is the Sranan Tongo name of a river and a plantation in the district Commewijne. It is located between the rivers Commewijne and Cottica in a region where Amerindians and slaves mixed during slavery times. Conversation with Nel Sedoc, August 24, 2004.

15. *Sargi* is Dutch *zaliger,* the Christian term for the deceased.

16. With colleagues of the Ministry of Culture I had gone to the interior, to Asindoopo, Gaama konde, the seat of government of the Saramaka Maroons in November 1990, to witness and record limba uwii, the end of the period of mourning for Paramount Chief Aboikoni, who had died in January 1989 (see Scholtens et al. 1992).

While the Civil War (1986–1992) between the army and the Maroons was going on, there was no spraying against malaria in the interior. Even though I had taken medication, I came back to the city with malaria, which plagued me for weeks.

17. Juliette had another empty house in her backyard, smaller and more rickety than mine. During the year and a half that I lived with her, several people came by, looking for housing. She always refused. She also did not want to consider her age-mate Pa Otto, the father-in-law of her youngest daughter, as a renter. She explained to me: "I have been washing men's clothes and cooking for them all my life, I don't need the money. Let him go pester someone else."

18. Okra soup, a particularly elaborate and favorite broth, is considered very nourishing and it contains various ingredients: saltmeat, fish, okra, onions, tomatoes, and black pepper.

19. The odo is mentioned in a collection published in 1835 (Teenstra II 1835:212, no. 17).

20. This tradition has continued. In 1990 I was present at the yearly celebration of a working-class women's organization; all the women were beautifully clad in purple.

21. Blaka Watra is the name of a resort, close to Zanderij Airport or Johan Adolf Pengel Airport, where people go to picnic and swim.

22. *Masra,* during slavery, was the word for the master and the word for "husband," the steady male partner. It is still used in the latter sense as well as being a respectful term of address for a male. See chapter 4 for terms women use to refer to their male partners. The comparable term for a woman is *Misi.*

23. A biography of Pengel's life has been written by Hans Breeveld (2000).

24. This, again, is a feature with historical continuity, as it was one of the valid reasons to end a relationship during slavery (Everaert 1999).

25. *Nengredoro,* literally, "negro entrance." The concept stems from slavery, when there was a separate entrance to a house for the enslaved; it became a generic term for entrance.

26. Citrus aurantifolia (Rutaceae) (Sordam and Eersel 1989).

27. The IIAV is the International Information Center and Archives for the Women's Movement, in Amsterdam, which took the initiative for the chair in gender and ethnicity that I have held at the University of Utrecht since 2001.

2. Suriname, Sweet Suriname

1. According to van Stipriaan (1993) this representation might have been a successful export product of the British in their struggle for colonial hegemony with the Dutch. Parts of this chapter have appeared in Wekker 1992a, 1994, and 2004b.

2. According to Toni Morrison, black cultures under slavery can be considered as the first modern cultures, because of the problems of "dissolution, fragmentation and loss" with which the slaves were confronted and had to come to terms (Gilroy 1993b).

3. But see the work of Richard and Sally Price on Saramaka Maroons, Dew (1978), Gary Brana-Shute (1978, 1979), and Rosemary Brana-Shute (1976, 1992).

4. ABS (Algemeen Bureau voor de Statistiek): demographic figures over the years 1972–1999.
5. Literature on the Maroons is abundant, see, among others: Herskovits and Herskovits (1934); R. Price (1976, 1979, 1983, 1990); S. Price (1984); Price and Price (1980, 1991, 1999); Köbben (1968); de Groot (1969); van Velzen (1966); van Wetering (1973); de Beet and Sterman (1981); van Velzen and van Wetering (1989).
6. On the Hindustani population, see Speckmann (1965).
7. On the Javanese population, see de Waal Malefijt (1963); Suparlan (1976); van Wengen (1975); Derveld (1982).
8. On the Lebanese, see de Bruijne (1974).
9. Earlier, during the sixties, Javanese and Hindustani women had, to a significant degree, replaced Creole women in the marketplace (Tjoa 1992).
10. In 1990 there were 7,124 registered foreign laborers or approximately 7 percent of the labor force (Coopers, Lybrand, and Deloitte 1990:11).
11. Hyperinflation has characterized the Surinamese currency in the nineties. In the years between 1990 and 1993 annual inflation rose from 22 percent to 144 percent. In 1994 the percentage rose to the highest point ever: 394 percent. Stabilization was reached in 1996, under President Venetiaan, with an annual inflation of 1 percent, but in 1997 it rose again. In 1999 inflation was 30 percent again (Kromhout 2000:43).
12. However, in 2001, after many years, a report on poverty was published by the ABS, again, however, without data on gender.
13. At the beginning of my research period in 1990, 1 Dutch guilder (nf) was worth 10 Surinamese guilders (sf) and 1 U.S. dollar ($1) was 20 sf. In the middle of 1994 the value of 1 nf had risen to 110 sf, while $1 was appriximately 200 sf. In the middle of 2003, the last moment at which I recorded the exchange rates, the Euro had been introduced and 1 E = 2.20 nf = 3,300 sf and $1 was 2,900 sf.
14. Only President Venetiaan (NPS) tried to break with this tradition (1992–1996), but it was quickly undone by his successor, Wijdenbosch (NDP), who was in office between 1996–2000.
15. ABS, *Suriname in Cijfers* no. 191–2001/02:7. The percentage of poor persons lies between 49 and 74 percent (ibid., 10).
16. From a conversation with Juanita Altenberg, director of Stichting Maxi Linder, June 17, 2001.
17. Even the Dutch Embassy, in 2001, wanted payment for visa and other services in dollars or Dutch guilders.
18. They simply need to make sure that they are in the Netherlands when they need to see their benefits officer.
19. One of the consequences of this development is a further impoverishment of the governmental machinery, when the most skilled workers leave it behind. Such reports include the very useful United Nations Development Fund for Women's *Situational Analysis of Women in Suriname* (Ketwaru-Nurmohamed 2000). The Convention on the Eradication of all Forms of Discrimination Against Women (CEDAW) report (see note 20) was also drafted with the help of foreign donors.
20. See Sassen (1998), who proposes two key sites for research into gendering processes within the current moment of economic globalization: the debundling of

exclusive territoriality and sovereignty of the modern state. I believe that post- or neocolonial societies may be further drawn into globalization on the governmental level by the expansion of international agencies and the ratification of international treaties, such as CEDAW. Suriname produced a CEDAW report in 1999.

21. Suriname serves as an important point of transit for cocaine from Colombia to the U.S. and Europe. Buddingh, (2000), citing H. Tjin Liep Shie, the director of the Surinamese narcotics brigade, states with regard to the cocaine trade that a yearly 26,000 kilos of cocaine are transported. He estimates that the results from the cocaine trade are comparable to the export value of the bauxite sector.

22. It would be most instructive to explore the emergence of contrasting racialized stereotypes of different women: the submissive Indian housewife, the lazy and alcohol prone Amerindian woman, the independent, sexually hyperactive black matriarch, the seductive, unreliable, and materialistic Javanese woman, the downtrodden and submissive Maroon woman who makes children like rabbits. It is striking how much sexuality is shot through these various images. Images of female sexual propriety and heteronormativity frame the positioning of all women, including female heads of households, mati, and prostitutes, as threats to the reproduction of the postcolonial Caribbean nation-state (Alexander 1994; Trotz 2003). We need to seek insights into the relationality of these images and to explore how they have been invoked as unchangeable cultural essences and how and in whose interests they have been allowed to lead unquestioned lives of their own, both in academic and in commonsense knowledge. We need to ask what the implications of these notions are for the women involved. These lines of questioning, however, have hardly been undertaken yet in a Surinamese context.

23. *Making zami*: "that means you're going with a woman instead of a man," as one of Elwin's interviewees is quoted (1997:22). I want to call attention to the agency inherent in the expression, comparable to *doing* the mati work.

24. Personal communication with Audre Lorde.

25. There are approximately 440,000 Surinamese in Suriname and 300,000 in the Netherlands.

26. Large department stores and some butchers in Paramaribo employ women, on a commission basis, to sell credit notes to customers, notably women, in their neighborhoods. The customers go to the store with their credit note and buy for the amount that is written out. They do not start paying until the fifteenth of the next month. As a credit system it is extremely lucrative for the "brokers," who get an average of 15 percent on the credit they sell. They are liable to the store, however, when the customer fails to pay.

3. Winti, an Afro-Surinamese Religion, and the Multiplicitous Self

1. Female part of the "soul." Parts of this chapter have appeared in Wekker 1992a and 1994.
2. Male part of the "soul."

3. Usually Winti Prey take place at night, from 11 p.m. till *broko dey*/the break of day.

4. Princess Juliana, the mother of the current Queen Beatrix, was on the Dutch throne from 1948 to 1980. The Dutch royal family has been and continues to be quite popular in Suriname, especially among Creoles and Maroons. In the course of time Surinamers have written numerous letters to successive queens asking for their personal intervention in getting a permit to stay in the Netherlands or undoing the political independence of Suriname, folding the country back into the Dutch kingdom again. In 1991 I went to Asindoopo, the seat of government of the Saramaka Maroons, to attend the termination of the period of mourning for Paramount Chief Aboikoni, at two days travel from Paramaribo (see Scholtens et al. 1992). I was surprised to find, in the middle of the rain forest, a huge state portrait of a young Queen Juliana and her husband, Prince Bernhard, adorning the walls of the house where Aboikoni had presided.

5. Orgeade is a concentrated mixture of coconut and almonds that is diluted with milk or water.

6. Pemba doti is white clay, necessary to placate Winti. It, supposedly, has a calming function, symbolizing tranquillity and quiet. It can also be drunk, by mixing it with water or other beverages, and sometimes it is eaten (cf. Stephen n.d.:80).

7. People need to consult a bonu to have their Winti "set, arranged," so that they do not come at inappropriate moments. This procedure is called *broko maka*/breaking the thorns.

8. At the time, sf 20,000 was worth about $1,000.

9. During the colonial era Winti Prey were repeatedly forbidden by the colonial government.

10. I agree with McCarthy Brown that the term *God*, because of its overdetermination in a Christian context, is not really a good gloss for *Winti*, or *loa* in Voodoo.

11. Other researchers, for instance Erica Bourguignon (1978) in her study of Voodoo on Haiti, call this state "dissociation." I find this description unduly medical, but, more important, reflective of the unitary Western conceptualization of the self. I prefer to think of this state as temporarily foregrounding certain unconscious aspects of the multiplicitous self.

12. Information from an interview with bonuman Nel Sedoc, August 2004.

13. This is one of the instances when different interpretations, based on research in different regions, may be the case.

14. Here again there are striking parallels with other black religions in the Diaspora, like Voodoo on Haiti and in New York City. Karen McCarthy Brown (1991) describes how Haitian immigrants in New York experience their religion. Gods will make themselves known by taking possession of a person and identifying themselves.

15. This foundational mode of additivity, inclusion, fusion, mixing and matching, may also be a West African principle.

16. I agree with Fry (1986:140), who takes the position that "spirit mediumship is a social role whose credibility is defined by the actors themselves: a medium is possessed by a spirit for those who believe he is, and is a fraud for those who don't."

17. A moving documentary by Surinamese filmmaker Frank Zichem, *Geketend door het Verleden*/Chained by the Past (2003), shows—in mirror image—the confrontation of a Surinamese and a Ghanese man with slavery. When the Ghanaian Korsah visits a Maroon village in the Surinamese interior, he and the villagers are able to speak with each other in Koromanti.

18. To tap into the consciousness of Surinamese slaves and their descendants, it would be very interesting to do a systematic analysis of the lyrics and themes in Winti singi/Winti songs. Lawrence Levine did a comparable exercise in his brilliant study *Black Culture and Black Consciousness* (1977) with African American spirituals, gospel music, blues, and work songs.

19. Tusren is two sren. A sren is an old coin, not in use anymore, worth sixteen cents. In the olden days bonu were not allowed to ask people for more than four sren in return for their services. A recurrent complaint these days is that many bonu are asking people too much: they are said to be earning "blood money."

20. Wooding (1988 [1972]:15) mentions Kobi here. These day names are also known among Akan speaking peoples, like the Ashanti (ibid.).

21. Yeye consists, as we have seen, in a male and a female part, and thus I use a plural verb in English when both are intended. In Sranan Tongo to discern whether one or both parts of the yeye are implied depends on the context, since the verb has the same form in the singular and the plural.

22. *Pangi* are pieces of cotton cloth, worn by Creole and Maroon women, tied around their waists. They are also used for decoration.

23. Strongman (2002) notes the same phenomenon in Candomblé.

24. I am of course aware of the dangers of reading such paintings and sketches as if they would transparantly disclose "the truth" about enslaved lives, their likes and dislikes, to us. However, it would also be taking away from the limited agency they could exercise if we could not attach any significance to the way they dressed, e.g., the striking color combinations.

25. Brana-Shute probably worked with working-class women, closer to the (lower) middle class.

26. See the forthcoming dissertation of Rudy Uda on the transmission of odo.

27. An angisa can be named for the design in the fabric from which it is folded, e.g., "Mi na gowt' moni … " and for the way of tying it, e.g., *lowede*, an angisa worn for mourning, *oto baka*, the back of a car, or *Mis' de Neef*, named after Miss de Neef (van Putten and Zantinge 1988).

28. Thanks to Rudy Uda and Hein Eersel who helped me to approximately date the odo.

29. "Mi na af' sensi, no wan sma kan broko mi"/I am half a cent, no one can break me expresses an indomitable spirit in the face of much adversity. This odo transmits pride in a poverty-stricken background. "Mi na af' sensi" is used by both genders. "Mi na gowt' moni … " deals centrally with the subjects that I am interested in: women, relationships, sex, and self.

30. This is not an exclusively Afro-Surinamese phenomenon but a connection found in divergent urban working-class female settings, such as nineteenth-

and early twentieth-century white New York (Peiss 1986), contemporary white American (Rubin 1976), African American (Liebow 1967; Stack 1974), Nairobian (Nelson 1979), and Jamaican working-class cultures (Harrison 1988; Tafari-Ama 2002). Moreover, the "transactional" attitude of women in relationship to men may be more widespread than just working-class settings. North American socio-psychological research in mainly the white middle class fairly consistently points to men making "romantic" choices for mates, believing that "true love lasts forever, comes but once, is strange and incomprehensible, and conquers barriers of custom and social class," while women tend to be more "pragmatic," "knowing that we can each love many people, that economic security is more important than passion, and that when a women chooses a companion, she at the same time chooses a standard of living" (Peplau and Gordon 1985:264).

31. When a baby is sickly, its mother or parents may decide to "sell" it to a relative, e.g., for a dime. This symbolical gesture is meant to ward off the dangerous spell that the child might be under.

32. This is a soup meant to strenghten the kra.

33. During a pilot study I did on the UCLA campus (fall 1989), under the direction of Dr. Jim Turner, to discover ways to profitably talk about self, we discovered that a very good way was to ask people to talk about their best friend and what they valued in this person. This was not always possible in Suriname, since quite a few women said that they did not have a best friend and did not trust other women. In those cases it sometimes proved fruitful to ask them about their relation with a sister or about their disappointments in friends.

34. Wisi is the evil side of Winti.

35. Cf. Janssens and van Wetering (1985) and van Wetering (1989).

36. See Bijnaar's (2002) in-depth study of kasmoni in Suriname and the Netherlands.

37. Sranan Tongo *griti* means "to rub" and is translated into Surinamese Dutch *schuren*. It is the most colloquial and familial expression used for tribadism by mati themselves. Used by outsiders, *rubbing* has a negative connotation. Van Donselaar (1989:330) mentions the following meanings for *schuren*: 1. to press against each other, to pet with clothes on; 2. to make lesbian love; 3. to press against, etc., to neck.

38. NAKS, Na Arbeid komt Sport/After Work Comes Relaxation is a working-class theater and music ensemble. In 2001 they had one of the most popular kaseko bands, Naks Kaseko Loko.

39. A Miss Gay Suriname election for gay men was organized in the summer of 2001. At the same time, there were plans for a Mr. Gay Suriname contest for women, but this election never materialized.

4. *Kon Sidon na Mi Tapu* / Then He Comes and Sits Down on Top of Me

1. By this expression Andrea is indicating that he does not give her space, is cramping her style, referencing the desire for (sexual) control that men want to exert on women. Parts of this chapter have appeared in Wekker 1992a, 1994, and 2001.

2. The connection between sex and money has been observed in settings as disparate as nineteenth-century white working-class New York women's culture (Peiss 1984, 1986), the contemporary white North American working class (Rubin 1976) and middle class (Peplau and Gordon 1985), and in Nairobian (Nelson 1979) and Jamaican (Harrison 1988; Tafari-Ama 2002) slum conditions. The transactional character of sex is likely to be found in situations where there is a divergence in the access which males and females of the same class have to resources.

3. It is no coincidence that the study of heterosexuality elsewhere has not been overwhelming either (but see Katz 1996). In other fields of study, as well, we see the phenomenon that it has taken much longer, sometimes decades, for the so-called unmarked category, e.g., whiteness, masculinities, middle- and upper-class lives, to be taken up as worthy subjects of investigation (Wekker 2002).

4. Sex also is a favorite topic of conversation between men (Brana-Shute 1978, 1979).

5. NPS is the largely Creole Nationale Partij Suriname/National Party Suriname. In 1990 NPS formed part of the Front for Democracy and Development, a large coalition of three ethnically based political parties in the National Assembly.

6. This example was pointed out to me by Ilse-Marie Dorff.

7. Comparable attempts have been made, e.g., on Trinidad and Tobago, to make calypso less hostile to women (Reyes 1986).

8. The preoccupation with *konkru*/gossip, has been around for a long time. It is one of the minor themes in the collection of forty oral stories *Sye! Arki Tori!* that the anthropologist Trudy Guda brought together in the 1970s on the basis of the slavery narratives of master storyteller Aleks de Drie (1902–1982).

9. Surinamese people finely distinguish between a man's inside woman or *getrouwde vrouw*/married woman versus someone's *buitenvrouw*/outside woman. The Surinamese Dutch *buitenvrouw* is one of the words that has made it into the Standard Dutch lexicon.

10. Terborg (2002) finds that younger men increasingly condemn this behavior, finding it irresponsible.

11. Baking a cake does not take an entire canister of gas, so here is a little window for profit. On the other hand, gas bottles are seldom entirely full when they are delivered or they leak.

12. As we saw in chapter 2, a minimum social security income of about E 650 (or nf 1,450) represented a royal sum of more than sf 1,200,000.

13. The pun present in ST "den man tidey, den de moro lek' kaiman" is lost in translation; Andrea is saying men today are more like crocodiles.

14. The exchange rate for a Dutch guilder was sf 860 in May, June 2001.

15. Sieuw is a spicy, dark brown sauce used to marinate meat. A gas canister can be used for about a month and costs sf 19,000. On a daily basis, we counted sf 650.

16. The *verbontu*, which is meant here, was introduced among the slaves by the Moravian Brethren (EBG) as a substitute for marriage. It acquired another content among Creoles, certainly not meant by the brethren, as the oath that lovers take to be sexually faithful to each other all their lives. It is believed that it is the yeye of the two people who take the oath, so that breaking the oath may cause serious problems.

17. *Mannengre,* literally "man-negro," means men, generically. To my delight, Juliette also called my white male colleagues and friends mannengre.

18. I thank Gerda Havertong, Maggy Carrot, Desi Wekker, and Nel Sedoc for sorting out these different modalities with me.

19. Schalkwijk and de Bruijne note that endogamy within the different ethnic groups is preferential. In their sample survey of 1992 among 4,000 households in Greater Paramaribo, they found that 89 percent of Creoles, 92 percent of Hindustani, and 93 percent of Javanese preferred to be with a partner from the same ethnic group (1999:87).

20. But see Terborg (2002), who does not agree with this view. Our views can be reconciled by the distinction between ideology and practice.

21. Because I often walked in Paramaribo, I met a lot of men on the street. It happened frequently that men, who clearly did not have much money to spend, would try to impress me by offering to take me out to the most expensive hotel in town, where we would have dinner and presumably spend the night.

22. The etymology of *uitlopen,* literally, "walking out," is interesting. The term dates from slavery when slaves would often have relationships on other plantations, to which they had to walk after completing their day's labor and be back in time the next morning. I believe that it was mainly males who did the walking.

23. Bita wiri is a bitter green vegetable, Cestrum latifolium.

24. Very light-skinned Creoles are called a variety of terms, e.g., red, *kopro kanu*/copper cannon, brand 21. For a variety of terms describing nuances of skin colors and hair textures, see Wekker and Wekker 1991.

25. Thanks to Eddy van der Hilst for his help with these expressions.

26. The concept of "chamber obligations" is also applicable to men. A man who is not capable of observing his chamber obligations, e.g., because he is impotent, might typically go see a bonu, a traditional healer. Impotence is among the top four reasons why men consult traditional healers.

27. Terborg (2002:111) notes that many working-class men and women abhor (French) kissing—it makes them nauseous. Terborg sees it as part of the West African cultural heritage, without explaining why, however.

28. It would be interesting to make an inventory of black diasporic words in the sexual domain. I have reasons to believe and it makes perfect sense that the words designating the genitals would have common origins in West Africa and thus be related. In ST frequently used terms for female genitals, many starting with a p, are *poentje, poenta, poenie, panpan, pola, poenani, poenette, pima, pantje, pinkie.* Significantly, in circles of prostitutes the following terms are used: *a nyan*/the food, the money, *a ma*/mother, uterus, *a doos*/the box, *a boyo*/a particular cake, *a oni godo*/the honey pot. A young girl sitting with her legs apart might be told in Sur. Dutch: "Maak je portemonnee dicht" or "Maak je kinderbijslag dicht"/Close your purse or close your child support (from a conversation with Juanita Altenberg, director of Maxi Linder Foundation, June 2001).

29. By 2001 the attitude described for the police will likely have changed, because one of the strategic targets of the women's movement in the nineties has been

the battle against domestic abuse. According to the Stichting Stop Geweld tegen Vrouwen/Foundation Stop Violence Against Women, the average woman who seeks their help is a Hindustani or Creole woman, between twenty-five and fifty years of age. Her relationship with the aggressor has lasted between eight and twenty-five years and she has two or three children (Sumter and Zwanenbeek 2001:1). In addition, a Women's Rights Center was established and a national network against domestic abuse. The WRC trained 30 trainers from different ethnic groups and 460 police officers on how to do intakes with abused women. This training has also been given in 17 other Caribbean nations (from a conversation with Carla Bakboord, regional project manager, May 10, 2001).

30. By 1992 Lygia had indeed made it to Amsterdam She is one of the seven women who have migrated to the Netherlands since my research started.

31. The counterpart of *nyan blik* is *koren eten*/to eat corn (van Donselaar 1989:212) or *soigi pi*/to suck pi, male genitals.

32. With this combination I have moved from the position I took earlier (e.g., Wekker 1994, 1997), in which my focus was more or less exclusively on the West African cultural heritage. In Wekker 2001 I first expanded my analysis to include the colonial order.

33. Among scholars who have been engaged in excavating the West African cultural heritage in black family formation, we find the tendency, as noted before, to focus on everything but sexuality. Sudarkasa (1996:72), for instance, has formulated the 7 R's: respect, responsibility, restraint, reciprocity, reverence, reason, and reconciliation as African family values that "supported kinship structures ... that lasted for hundreds, perhaps even thousands, of years". Although I do recognize some of these principles operating in the Afro-Surinamese context, the seven R's are too general and do not address sexuality directly.

34. An intersectional analysis such as Ann Laura Stoler has made for the Dutch East Indies in her important text *Carnal Knowledge and Imperial Power: Gender, Race and Morality in Colonial Asia*, taking sexuality as its angle, has not yet been made for Suriname.

35. One of the best-known cross-racial relationships is described by the Scottish soldier John Gabriel Stedman, who came to Suriname to fight against the Maroons (1773–1778) and while there fell in love with the beautiful enslaved Johanna. Their relationship exemplifies on a microlevel the meeting of "two opposed cultural systems."

36. As teachers, nurses, photographers, as civil servants, as educated women, who had sometimes studied in Europe and who had returned to Paramaribo, they were the ideological inheritors of and the successors to the white female position in the asymmetrical gender, racial, and sexual ideology. My father's Jewish family forms an interesting case study of (un-)desirable scripts for upper-class women: my great-aunts Annie and Ria Gomperts, older sisters of my father's mother, studied French in Lausanne around 1910. They remained single all their lives, teaching private students, doing philanthropical works, raising gifted children of different ethnic groups in their home. Finding a suitable partner, a light-skinned, educated

man, was like looking for the proverbial needle in the haystack, in view of the out-migration of men of their class and their larger marital and sexual choices. Their younger sister, my grandmother, Eveline Gomperts, followed the undesirable, unspeakable script. She married a dark-skinned Creole man, Julius Wekker, an older widower. Eveline was disowned by her family and when Julius died, within a decade after their marriage, she was destitute, with four small boys to raise.

37. Conversion to Christianity did not mean that Winti was abandoned (Lenders 1994; Klinkers 1997).

38. My translation.

39. In Dutch *baasnegers* is used, which I have translated to *basya,* the black overseers on the plantation, who were generally better off than the ordinary slaves.

40. Trudy Guda gave me the following information: Apïaba was a historical figure, a well-known bonuman, who was still known in the oral tradition in 1949 when van Lier asked an informant to write down what he knew about Apïaba. The governor who gave her her house and yard most likely was van Sypensteyn, governor from 1873–1882. Apïaba acted as a diviner and a therapist; great value was attached to her prophecies and healing powers. She allegedly had many clients from prominent families.

41. The anomaly of a rich, free black woman seeking marriage with a white man is represented in the case of Elizabeth Samson. She brought her case before the Court of Justice in Suriname in 1764 and subsequently before the States General, the Netherlands. Pending her court case, the first marriage candidate died, but she came up with a second white suitor who was twenty-two years younger than she. Ultimately, the case was decided in her favor and she married him in 1767. The motivation of the States General was that her riches would evolve to white hands upon her death (McLeod 1996).

42. The advantages, in terms of mobility or obtaining freedom, to enslaved women who had a relationship with a white man should not be overestimated (cf. Beckles 1989; Barrow 1996).

5. The Mati Work

1. This chapter draws on Wekker 1992a, 1992b, 1994, 1998, and 1999.

2. See van Donselaar's *Woordenboek van het Surinaams-Nederlands.*

3. Translation: Lammens's "Contribution to the knowledge about the Colony of Suriname, in the era 1816 to 1822."

4. My translation and my emphasis. *Baas,* i.e., "boss," is still an old-fashioned and deep term of address for men.

5. Kappler named Albina, ST: Kapleri, on the river Marowijne, after his fiancée Alwine Lietzenmayer. It was founded around 1846.

6. Translation: Six Years in Suriname, 1836–1842.

7. My translation and my emphasis.

8. Brackette Williams mentions the term *mati* in her study of cultural struggle in Guyana: *Stains on My Name, War in My Veins* (1991). In that context it means the

ethos of egalitarianism among working-class villagers. Tracing the genealogies of the term in these two neighboring countries would be an interesting enterprise.

9. "That story" carries the connotation of the quarrel, the difficulties, the misunderstandings that you and I had.

10. Banya songs are, of course, very hard to date. This particular song was sung to me by ritual specialist Nel Sedoc on August 16, 2004. Masra Sedoc continued to explain that many of the shipmates had died on board and had been thrown overboard; others were sold to distant plantations, never to lay eyes on each other again.

11. I am not implying that the mati or sibi relationship among Saramaka meant a sexual relationship. I am not convinced, however, that mati work does not occur among Saramaka women, although it stands to reason that in a highly patriarchal society, such as Saramaka, it would not be as visible as among Creole women (Price, S. 1984).

12. No study of male mati has been undertaken as yet, which is remarkable given the scholarly attention that the female mati work has received. In this text, too, I will only pay attention to male mati in passing, when it is relevant, but I submit that study of the male mati work is exceedingly important. It, like the female mati work, offers a template for constructions of black diasporic male sexuality. In important respects the male mati work is a mirror of the female mati work, although there are some differences, most notably in its public visibility and the extent of its social condemnation.

It is common knowledge in Surinamese male mati circles that same-sex sexual behavior among men, even those who are married or in a steady, publicly displayed relationship with a woman, is quite common. Some well-known politicians and other public figures, who flaunt their heterosexuality in public, regularly show up at male mati parties. According to one of my gay male informants, Suriname has the highest density of "married homosexuals." A second tell-tale sign is that male prostitutes, overwhelmingly targeting men, do excellent business, better than female prostitutes. Their rates for the same sexual activities are higher than those of women and they are the first ones to be picked up from the street. From a conversation with Juanita Altenberg, director of the Maxi Linder Foundation, which supports prostitutes, June 2001. See also chapter 6.

From other parts of the black Diaspora, too, tantalizing bits and pieces of evidence point to the frequency of men engaging in sexual activity with both women and men. In view of the often hidden, secretive character of the male mati work and the dangers that this behavior possibly carries with it, in the age of the AIDS/HIV pandemic, an opener attitude that might be facilitated by research would be beneficial.

13. A bit rough (van Donselaar 1989:350).

14. Can also be said of a good male friend. The Surinamese soccer players in the Dutch national team call each other "kabel."

15. See Kochman 1972.

16. The doubling of mati in *mat' mat' meid* acts as an intensification.

17. Amadiume vehemently opposes the interpretation that there is sex involved in these relationships and has taken Audre Lorde to task about this, as I have been by some African feminists.

18. The Surinam Aluminium Company, the elite industry, is located in Paranam.

19. Besides *doro na Heiligeweg*/to arrive at Heiligeweg, *doro na Maagdenstraat*/to arrive at Maagdenstraat is also used. These are two busy streets in the center of Paramaribo.

20. Ansu, also called Meerzorg, is a little place opposite Paramaribo, on the river Commewijne.

21. This section is based on Wekker 1999.

22. Stanka is using a (Surinamese) Dutch expression, calling on men's names—John, Pete, and Charley—to indicate her pickiness; she will not take just anybody as a lover.

23. Although, admittedly, the majority of these studies, as I noted in a previous chapter, have North America as their setting.

24. Surinamese playwrite Thea Doelwijt has recently, to great acclaim, staged two Du—*Na gowtu Du*/The golden Du (1998) and *Na Dyamanti Du*/The Diamond Du (2003)—that were performed in Paramaribo and in Amsterdam.

25. My translation.

26. The translations of these lobi singi by Verny February are often very poetic and creative, but they suffer from the fact that he has frequently put them in a heterosexual context.

27. Lenders herself thinks it is "not improbable" that it was a sexual relationship (1994:261, note 285).

28. My translation.

29. When I told Juliette in 1991 about this report in which mati play is first mentioned and what this government official had to say about her activities, she reacted by sucking her teeth loudly, proclaiming: "Ai, Gloria, lib' mi 'anga law"/don't bother me with nonsense. "Individual women who, in the face of hegemonic rejection in their consciousness choose to be self-defined and self-evaluating are, in fact, activists. They are retaining a grip over their definition as subjects, as full humans, and rejecting definitions of themselves as the objectified 'other'" (Hill Collins 1986:24).

30. Wadzanai, recalling the experiences of an elderly female relative, interviewed by Marc Epprecht, Harare, March 25, 1997, in Epprecht 1998.

31. John Gabriel Stedman, the Scottish soldier who from 1773 until 1778 took part in an expedition against the Maroons and who kept an elaborate diary of his stay in Surinam, provides these data (1799) (1974: 276).

32. But Brazil is also very interesting in this respect (see Fry 1986 and Parker 1991).

33. By way of comparison, in the U.S. the ratio in the last decades of the eighteenth century was 1:15 (Price 1976).

34. Audre Lorde's interpretation of *zami* is that it might be derived from the French *les amies*. Another term used is *ma divines* (Smith 1962a).

35. Personal communication from Dr. Christine Ho.

6. Sexuality on the Move

1. I have called this syndrome, which entails the erasure of the Dutch colonial and imperial past, "Innocence Unlimited" and it is pervasive. It is evident in debates about Dutch identity, in history curricula at all levels of education, in monuments and public memory, in the organization of knowledge in the academy, and on the labor market (Wekker 2002).

2. In one of the rare research projects specifically focusing on the relationship between the history of slavery and representations of black women's sexuality in the Netherlands, Barnard student Lulu Meza quotes Oscar, one of her white, male informants as stating: "[Black women] have something wild, something animalistic … something less human, something tribal" (2004:27). The topic deserves fuller treatment and it confirms interview data I have gathered with young black women in the Netherlands, of both middle and working-class background.

3. Nf. 2,500 was approximately $1,200 and is, given comparable flight distances, an exorbitant amount of money. The Amsterdam-Paramaribo trajectory is a veritable gold mine, because the flights are almost always fully booked. The Surinamese national carrier SLM, which at its apex owned three 747 Boeings, has not been able to keep itself afloat. During the nineties SLM was taken over by the Dutch national carrier KLM, which now has a monopoly on that destination. Several attempts to break the monopoly, e.g., by Air France, flying from Paris to French Guyana and other private initiatives, taking Brussels-Paramaribo as their connecting points, have floundered.

4. In one of the few labor market studies that have collected statistical data by gender and ethnic group, it is shown that Surinamese and Antillean women work more hours outside the home than white women in the Netherlands, irrespective of their family situation. Turkish and Moroccan women occupy the lowest positions in terms of labor market participation (Hooghiemstra and Merens 1999).

5. At the time the currency was still Dutch guilders. This amount translates to about 56 Euros, which is roughly the same in U.S. dollars. Thus Lydia earned about 2.35 Euros per hour. By way of comparison, a cleaning woman in a private home in Amsterdam earned about E 4 per hour, in the same period.

6. I am only considering the positionings of white Dutch and Surinamese Dutch women here, while Turkish and Moroccan Dutch women are not taken into account. It bears noting that the chairperson of the Parliamentary Investigation Committee on the successes and failures of thirty years of integration policy in the Netherlands asked me to elaborate on the reasons for the failure or the refusal of these latter women to go into the care sector as nurses or nurses' aides (September 8, 2003). Apparently, this failure was read as an anomalous gesture, pointing to the cognitive dissonance that results from "ethnic" women not wanting to occupy the subordinate positions that are deemed appropriate for them.

7. In November 2003 the minister of social affairs and labor in the Centrum-Right cabinet, Balkenende-II, de Geus, declared the end of emancipation policy for white women. The goals had, according to de Geus, been reached. For so-called

allochtonous women, however, literally women who originate elsewhere, the widespread but disingenuous and racialized Dutch term to indicate women of color, there was stilll a long way to go.

8. In the Netherlands the term *race,* pertaining to people, has been evacuated since WWII, when the largest number of Jews in Europe was abducted to German concentration camps, and in its stead *ethnicity* is used, now doing much the same work that *race* used to do (Wekker and Lutz 2001).

9. Obviously, I have no statistical data to undergird my impression that mati who definitely prefer to be with women have more opportunities to avoid sexual contacts with men. But this emphatically does not go to say that the mati work is vanishing in the Netherlands and giving way to lesbianism.

10. *Trefu,* from Hebrew *treif,* is a food taboo with religious origin. See chapter 5.

11. Standard Dutch and Surinamese Dutch: *een vriendin,* a female friend, is ambiguous.

12. Grandma is using an old Sranan Tongo expression. *Soki* literally is to suck, meaning to have sex. Literally, the expression says, "I am someone who sucks, the smell of sucking does not seduce me." It glosses to "I am an old hand at this, you don't have to tell me anything."

13. This is, as we have seen, typical masculine behavior in male-female relationships, too.

14. In 2001 legal marriage was made possible for people of the same sex. Homosexual and heterosexual couples are not equal in all respects, however. The former are not able to adopt children together.

15. The largest allochthonous groups in the Netherlands are from Suriname and the Dutch Antilles, Turkey, and Morocco.

16. Through interviews with young gay males it became apparent that they, in their late teens and twenties and more educated than the women I have worked with, used the Internet in the latter part of the nineties intensively to make connections with males in the Netherlands and Belgium. Connections are forged with different sets of partners. Whereas working-class female mati preferred other mati, young gay males seemed to seek white middle-class partners. Against the background of the inequalities that processes of globalization express and exacerbate, the survival techniques of young gay Surinamese men make sense. In a world that offers limited possibilities for advancement, being young, gay, and black, is an avenue out of Suriname, even though it reinscribes Global Imperial patterns. The old representations of black male bodies in the economies of desire of white men, which regrettably are all too often internalized by the black men themselves, precede, accompany, and construct this global sexual cartography. A powerful, "natural," and often overendowed sexuality is ascribed to black men, a being at ease with their bodies, also finding expression in fantasies and projections of insatiability and wildness. Since the colonial part of Dutch history has by and large been excised from Dutch consciousness, the possibility of racism in personal relationships is seldom entertained.

17. Although the number of interethnic relationships in the Surinamese community in the Netherlands is considerable—the second highest percentage after Antilleans—I submit that these "mixed" couples are not overwhelmingly working class.

18. In Dutch: "Blank in de Bijlmer." The translations are mine.

19. Where in earlier historical periods black women were objectified and their buttocks and genitalia were treated as *pars pro toto* (Gilman 1985; Nederveen Pieterse 1990), now it is again "their cunt" that is taking a walk with them.

20. The Maxi Linder Foundation, founded in 1994, is named after Maxi Linder, a well-known Creole prostitute, who was the first labor organizer for female commercial sex workers in Suriname. Her life has been fictionalized in the immensely popular novel *De Koningin van Paramaribo* (Amsterdam: Accord, 1999), which has also been made into a theater play, staged both in Amsterdam and in Paramaribo. The aims of the foundation are to optimize the social, economic, mental, and physical health and well-being of female commercial sex workers.

21. The report was discussed during a two-day workshop on June 16 and 17, 2000.

22. See also Kempadoo (2004) for a reading of prostitution in Suriname.

23. From section 2, "Identification of Non-registered Brothels," 2.3. Explanatory notes on different sexual acts performed by sex workers and the prices as of April 2001, p. 18.

24. From a conversation with Juanita Altenberg, director of the Maxi Linder Foundation, June 2001.

25. In June 2001 a public debate took place in the National Assembly after gay men had proclaimed at the Miss Gay Suriname contest that they wanted to have a place for anonymous sex. Representative O. Rodgers of Nieuw Front spoke in the National Assembly of "sex bestiality" and "total moral decline" (Handelingen Nationale Assemblé, Paramaribo, June 5).

26. It may be the case that this young woman called herself mati to please me because she had read my Dutch book.

27. The Mr. Gay Suriname contest was envisioned after a Miss Gay Suriname contest for gay men took place in June 2001. It was intended for female mati projecting "masculine" personae. While there is ample space for female mati to gather and to celebrate each other in their own circles, the public space that needs to be claimed to stage a Mr. Gay Suriname contest is apparently out of their reach.

Works Cited

Aarmo, M. 1999. How Homosexuality Became "Un-African": The Case of Zimbabwe. In E. Blackwood and S. E. Wieringa, eds., *Female Desires: Same Sex Relations and Transgender Practices Across Cultures.* New York: Columbia University Press.

Accord, C. 1999. De Koningin van Paramaribo. Amsterdam: Vassalucci.

Alexander, M. J. 1991. Redrafting Morality: The Postcolonial State and the Sexual Offenses Bill of Trinidad and Tobago. In C. Mohanty, A. Russo, and L. Torres, eds., *Third World Women and the Politics of Feminism.* Bloomington: Indiana University Press.

——— 1994. Not just (any) body can be a citizen: The Politics of Law, Sexuality, and Postcoloniality in Trinidad and Tobago and the Bahamas. *Feminist Review,* no. 48.

——— 1998. Imperial Desire/Sexual Utopias: White Gay Capital and Transnational Tourism. In E. Shohat, ed., *Talking Visions: Multicultural Feminism in a Transnational Age.* New York: Museum of Contemporary Art.

——— 2005. *Pedagogies of Crossing.* Durham: Duke University Press.

Alexander, M. J., and C. T. Mohanty, eds. 1997. *Feminist Genealogies, Colonial Legacies, Democratic Futures.* New York: Routledge.

Algemeen Bureau voor de Statistiek. 1980. *Algemene Volkstelling: Suriname in Cijfers.* Paramaribo: ABS.

——— 1989. *Manpower Survey.* Paramaribo: ABS.

——— 2001. *Suriname in Cijfers.* No. 191. Paramaribo: ABS.

Altman, D. 1996. On Global Queering. www.lib.latrobe.edu.au/AHR/archive. July.

Amadiume, I. 1987. *Male Daughters, Female Husbands: Gender and Sex in an African Society*. London: Zed.

Ambacht. 1912. *Het Ambacht in Suriname*. Rapport van de Commissie Benoemd bij Gouvernementsresolutie van 13 januarie 1910, no. 13. Paramaribo.

Amin, K. 1980. The Class Structure of the Contemporary Imperialist System. *Monthly Review* 31, no. 8.

Anthias, F., and G. Lazaridis, eds. 2000. *Gender and Migration in Southern Europe: Women on the Move*. Oxford and New York: Berg.

Anthias, F., and N. Yuval Davis. 1995. *Racialized Boundaries: Race, Nation, Gender, Colour, and Class and the Anti-Racist Struggle*. London: Routledge.

Appadurai, A. 1999. *Modernity at Large: Cultural Dimensions of Globalization*. Minneapolis: University of Minnesota Press.

Bakboord, C. 1998. Verslag van het congres *"Bestrijding huiselijk geweld."* Paramaribo: Caribbean Association for Feminist Research and Action.

Barrow, Ch. 1996. *Family in the Caribbean: Themes and Perspectives*. Kingston: Ian Randle.

Beckles, H. 1989. *Natural Rebels: A Social History of Enslaved Black Women in Barbados*. London: Zed.

———1999. *Centering Woman: Gender Discourses in Caribbean Slave Society*. Kingston: Ian Randle.

Beeldsnijder, R. 1994. *"Om werk van jullie te hebben'*: Plantageslaven in Suriname, 1730–1750."* Utrecht: Universiteit Utrecht.

De Beet, C., and M. Sterman. 1981. Aantekeningen over de Geschiedenis van de Kwinti en het Dagboek van Kraag (1894–1896). Bronnen voor de Studie van Bosnegersamenlevingen, no. 6. Utrecht: Centrum voor Caraibische Studies.

Besson, J. 1993. Reputation and Respectability Reconsidered: A New Perspective on Afro-Caribbean Peasant Women. In J. Momsen, ed., *Women and Change in the Caribbean*. Kingston: Ian Randle; Bloomington: Indiana University Press; London: James Currey.

Bhabha, H. 1984. "Of Mimicry and Man: The Ambivalence of Colonial Discourse. *October* 28.

Bijnaar, A. 2002. *Kasmoni: Een spaartraditie in Suriname en Nederland*. Amsterdam: Bakker.

Blaaspijp, L. 1983. *Sranang Krijoro Koeltoeroe Foe Deng Kongvo Singi: Singi Foe Deng Nootoe Di E Kwinsi Wi Na Ini Na Ala Dei Libi*. Paramaribo: JJB.

Blackwood, E. 1986a. Breaking the Mirror: The Construction of Lesbianism and the Anthropological Discourse on Homosexuality. In E. Blackwood, ed., *The Many Faces of Homosexuality: Anthropological Approaches to Homosexual Behavior*. New York and London: Harrington Park.

———ed. 1986b. *The Many Faces of Homosexuality: Anthropological Approaches to Homosexual Behavior*. New York and London: Harrington Park.

———1995. Falling in Love with An-Other Lesbian: Reflections on Identity in Fieldwork. In D. Kulick and M. Willson, eds., *Taboo. Sex, Identity and Erotic Subjectivity in Anthropological Fieldwork*. London and New York: Routledge.

————— 1999. Tombois in West Sumatra: Constructing masculinity and erotic desire. In E. Blackwood and S. E. Wieringa, eds., *Female Desires: Same-Sex Relations and Transgender Practices Across Cultures.* New York: Columbia University Press.

————— 2002. Reading Sexualities Across Cultures: Anthropology and Theories of Sexuality. In E. Lewin and W. L. Leap, eds., *Out in Theory: The Emergence of Lesbian and Gay Anthropology.* Chicago: University of Illinois Press.

————— 2005. Wedding Bell Blues: Marriage, Missing Men, and Matrifocal Follies. *American Ethnologist: The Journal of the American Ethnological Society* 32, no. 1.

Blackwood, E., and S. E. Wieringa, eds. 1999. *Female Desires: Same-Sex Relations and Transgender Practices Across Cultures.* New York: Columbia University Press.

Bolton, R. 1996. Coming Home: The Journey of a Gay Ethnographer in the Years of the Plague. In E. Lewin and W. L. Leap, eds., *Out in the Field: Reflections of Lesbian and Gay Anthropologists.* Urbana and Chicago: University of Illinois Press.

Bookman, A., and S. Morgen, ed. 1988. *Women and the Politics of Empowerment.* Philadelphia: Temple University Press.

Boston Lesbian Psychologies Collective, eds. 1987. *Lesbian Psychologies: Explorations and Challenges.* Urbana and Chicago: University of Illinois Press.

Bott, E. 1957. *Family and Social Network: Roles, Norms, and External Relationships in Ordinary Urban Families.* New York: Free.

Bourguignon, E. 1978. Spirit Possession and Altered States of Consciousness: The Evolution of An Inquiry. In G. Spindler, ed., *The Making of Psychological Anthropology.* Berkeley and Los Angeles: University of California Press.

Brana-Shute, G. 1978. Some Aspects of Youthful Identity Management in a Paramaribo Creole Neighbourhood. *De Nieuwe West Indische Gids* 53, no. 1.

————— 1979. *On the Corner: Male Social Life in a Paramaribo Creole Neighborhood.* Assen: Van Gorcum.

Brana-Shute, R. 1976. Women, Clubs, and Politics: The Case of a Lower-Class Neighborhood in Paramaribo, Suriname. *Urban Anthropology* 5, no. 2.

————— 1993. Neighbourhood Networks and National Politics Among Working-Class Afro-Surinamese Women. In J. Momsen, ed., *Women and Change in the Carribean.* Kingston: Ian Randle.

Brand, D. 1994. *Bread Out of Stone: Recollections, Sex, Recognitions, Race, Dreaming, Politics.* Toronto: Coach House.

————— 1996. *In Another Place, Not Here.* New York: Grove.

Breeveld, H. 2000. *Jopie Pengel, 1916–1970: Leven en werk van een Surinaamse politicus, Biografie.* Schoorl: Conserve.

de Bruijne, G. 1974. De Libanezen van Suriname. In *Sociaal-Geografisch Spektrum, een Bundel Studies aangeboden aan Prof. Dr. A. C. de Vooys.* Utrecht.

de Bruijne, G., A. Runs, and H. Verrest. 2001. De NGO-wereld als bron van nieuwe Transatlantische contacten. *Oso. Tijdschrift voor Surinaamse Taalkunde, Letterkunde en Geschiedenis* 20, no. 1.

de Bruin, K. A. P., and M. Balkema, eds. 2001. *Liever vrouwen: Theorie en praktijk van de lesbisch-specifieke hulpverlening.* Amsterdam: Schorer.

Brydon, L., and S. Chant. 1989. *Women in the Third World: Gender Issues in Rural and Urban Areas.* Aldershot: Elgar.

Buddingh, H. 2000. *Geschiedenis van Suriname.* Utrecht: Het Spectrum.

Burawoy, M., J. Blunt, S. George, Z. Gille, T. Gowan, L. Haney, M. Klawiter, S. Lopez, S. Ó Riain, and M. Thayer. 2000. *Global Ethnography: Forces, Connections, and Imaginations in a Postmodern World.* Berkeley and Los Angeles: University of California Press.

Buschkens, W. 1974. *The Family System of the Paramaribo Creoles: Verhandelingen van het Koninklijk Instituut voor Taal- , Land- en Volkenkunde, no. 71.* 's Gravenhage: Martinus Nijhoff.

Bush, B. 1990. *Slave Women in Caribbean Society: 1650–1838.* Kingston: Heinemann; Bloomington: Indiana University Press; London: James Currey.

Butler, J. 1990. *Gender Trouble: Feminism and the Subversion of Identity.* New York: Routledge.

Carbado, D., D. McBride, D. Weise, eds. *Black Like Us: A Century of Lesbian, Gay, and Bisexual African-American Fiction.* San Francisco: Cleis.

Carby, H. 1986. "It Jus Be's Dat Way Sometime": The Sexual Politics of Women's Blues. *Radical America* 20, no. 4.

Castles, S., and M. Miller. 1998. *The Age of Migration: International Population Movements in the Modern World.* New York and London: Guilford.

Centraal Bureau voor de Statistiek. 1991. *De Demografische Ontwikkeling van de Surinaamse en Antilliaanse Bevolking, 1971–1991.* Den Haag.

CESWO. 1993. *Beknopt overzicht van de levensomstandigheden van huishoudens uit de lagere inkomensgroepen van Groot-Paramaribo.* Paramaribo.

Childers, M. and b. hooks. 1990. A Conversation About Race and Class. M. Hirsch and E. Fox Keller, eds., *Conflicts in Feminism.* New York and London: Routledge.

Chin, H., and H. Buddingh'. 1987. *Surinam: Politics, Economics, and Society.* London and New York: Frances Pinter.

Christensen, J. 1950–1951. Double Descent Among the Fanti. *Human Relations Area Files,* FE 12–15.

Christian, B. 1997. Fixing Methodologies. Beloved. Ed. E. Abel, B. Christian, and H. Moglen, eds. *Female Subjects in Black and White: Race, Psychoanalysis, Feminism.* Berkeley and Los Angeles: University of California Press.

Clark Hine, D. 1989. Rape and the Inner Lives of Black Women in the Middle West: Some Preliminary Thoughts on the Culture of Dissemblance. *Signs: Journal of Women in Culture and Society* 14, no. 4.

Clemencia, J. 1995. Women Who Love Women. A Whole Perspective from Kapuchera to Open Throats. Paper delivered at the Caribbean Studies Association conference. Curaçao. May 23–26.

Cliff, M. 1987. *No Telephone to Heaven.* New York: Dutton.

——— 1995 [1984]. *Abeng.* New York: Plume.

Coleridge, P. 1958. Vrouwenleven in Paramaribo. In *Suriname in Stroomlijnen.* Amsterdam: Wereld Bibliotheek.

Comvalius, Th. 1935. Het Surinaamsch Negerlied: de Banja en de Doe. *West-Indische Gids,* no.17.

───── 1939. Een der Vormen van het Surinaamsche Lied na 1863. *West-Indische Gids*, no. 21.

Condé, M. 1986. *Moi, Tituba, sorcière … : Noire de Salem*. Paris. Mercure de France.

Constantine-Simms, D., ed. 2000. *The Greatest Taboo: Homosexuality in Black Communities*. Los Angeles: Alyson.

Coopers, and Lybrand Deloitte. 1990. *Het Programma voor Sociale Bijstand en Werkgelegenheid*. Deelrapport 7.

Cruz-Malavé, A., and M. Manalansan IV, eds. 2002. *Queer Globalizations: Citizenship and the Afterlife of Colonialism*. New York: New York University Press.

Danticat, E. 1994. *Breath, Eyes, Memory*. New York: Soho.

───── 1996. *Krik? Krak!* New York: Vintage.

───── 1998. *The Farming of Bones*: A Novel. New York: Soho.

Davis, A. 1989. *Women, Culture and Politics*. New York: Random House.

───── 1998. *Blues Legacies and Black Feminism: Gertrude "Ma" Rainey, Bessie Smith, and Billy Holiday*. New York: Pantheon.

De Cecco, J., and J. Elia. 1993. *If You Seduce a Straight Person, Can You Make Them Gay? Issues in Biological Essentialism Versus Social Constructionism in Gay and Lesbian Identities*. San Francisco: Haworth.

De Costa-Willis, M., R. Martin, and R. Bell, eds. 1992. *Erotique Noire–Black Erotica*. New York: Doubleday.

D'Emilio, J. 1984. Capitalism and Gay Identity. In A. Snitow, C. Stansell, and S. Thompson, eds., *Desire: The Politics of Sexuality*. London: Virago.

D'Emilio, J., and E. Freedman. 1988. *Intimate Matters: A History of Sexuality in America*. New York: Harper and Row.

Derveld, F. 1982. *Politieke Mobilisatie en Integratie van de Javanen in Suriname: Tamanredjo en de Surinaamse Nationale Politiek*. Groningen: Bouma's Boekhuis.

Dew, E. 1978. *The Difficult Flowering of Surinam: Ethnicity and Politics in a Plural Society*. The Hague: Martinus Nijhoff.

Donham, D. 2002. Freeing South Africa: The "Modernization" of Male-Male Sexuality in Soweto. In J. X. Inda and R. Rosaldo, eds., *The Anthropology of Globalization: A Reader*. Malden and Oxford: Blackwell.

van Donselaar, J. 1989. *Woordenboek van het Surinaams-Nederlands*. Muiderberg: Dick Coutinho.

de Drie, A., and T. Guda, eds. 1984. *Wan Tori Fu Mi Eygi Srefi*. Paramaribo: Ministerie van Onderwijs, Wetenschappen en Cultuur.

───── 1985. *Sye! Arki Tori*! Paramaribo: Ministerie van Onderwijs, Wetenschappen en Cultuur.

Drucker, P. ed. 2000. *Different Rainbows: Same-Sex Sexualities and Popular Movements in the Third World*. London: Gay Men's.

DuBois, W. E. B. 1982 [1903]. *The Souls of Black Folk*. New York: New American Library.

Duggan, L. 1992. Making it perfectly queer. *Socialist Review* 22, no. 1.

Echols, A. 1984. The New Feminism of Yin and Yang. In A. Snitow, C. Stansell, and S. Thompson, eds., *Desire: The Politics of Sexuality*. London: Virago.

Ehrenreich, B., and A. R. Hochschild, eds. 2002. *Global Woman: Nannies, Maids, and Sex Workers in the New Economy*. New York: Holt.

Ellis, P., ed. 1986. *Women of the Caribbean*. London and New Jersey: Zed.

Elliston, D. 1995. Erotic Anthropology: "Ritualized Homosexuality" in Melanesia and Beyond. In *American Ethnologist* 22, no. 4.

Elwin, R., ed. 1997. *Tongues on Fire: Caribbean Lesbian Lives and Stories*. Toronto: Women's.

Epprecht, M. 1998. The "Unsaying" of Homosexuality Among Indigenous Black Zimbabweans: Mapping a Blindspot in an African Masculinity. *Journal of Southern African Studies* 24, no. 4.

Espin. O. M. 1999. *Women Crossing Boundaries: A Psychology of Immigration and Transformations of Sexuality*. New York: Routledge.

Evans-Pritchard, E. 1970. Sexual Inversion Among the Azande. *American Anthropologist* 72.

Everaert, H. A. M. 1999. *Een zoektocht naar de aard van man-vrouw relaties onder Surinaamse slaven: De suikerplantages Fairfield, Breukelerwaard, Cannewapibo en La Jalousie in de periode voorafgaand aan de emancipatie*. Universiteit van Amsterdam.

Faderman, L. 1981. *Surpassing the Love of Men: Romantic Friendship and Love Between Women from the Renaissance to the Present*. New York: William Morrow.

—— 1991. *Odd Girls and Twilight Lovers: A History of Lesbian Life in Twentieth-Century America*. New York: Columbia University Press.

—— 2003. *Naked in the Promised Land*. Houghton Mifflin.

Ford-Smith, H. 1986. *Lionheart Gal: Life Stories of Jamaican Women*. London: Women's.

Fortes, M. 1950. Kinship and Marriage Among the Ashanti. In A. Radcliffe-Brown and D. Forde, eds., *African Systems of Kinship and Marriage*. London: Oxford University Press.

Foucault, M. 1978. *The History of Sexuality*. New York: Pantheon.

—— 1980. *Power/Knowledge: Selected Interviews and Other Writings, 1972–1977*. Ed. C. Gordon. New York: Pantheon.

Frazier, E. F. 1939. *The Negro Family in the United States*. Chicago: University Press.

Fry, P. 1986. Male Homosexuality and Spirit Possession in Brazil. In E. Blackwood, ed., *The Many Faces of Homosexuality: Anthropological Approaches to Homosexual Behavior*. New York and London: Harrington Park.

Gay, J. 1986. "Mummies and Babies" and Friends and Lovers in Lesotho. In E. Blackwood, ed., *The Many Faces of Homosexuality: Anthropological Approaches to Homosexual Behavior*. New York and London: Harrington Park.

Geertz, C. 1973. *The Interpretation of Cultures: Selected Essays*. New York: Basic.

—— 1984. "From the Native's Point of View": On the Nature of Anthropological Understanding. In R. Shweder and R. LeVine, eds., *Culture Theory: Essays on Mind, Self, and Emotion*. Cambridge: Cambridge University Press.

Gevisser, M. 2000. Mandela's Stepchildren: Homosexual Identity in Post-Apartheid South Africa. In P. Drucker, ed., *Different Rainbows: Same-Sex Sexualities and Popular Movements in the Third World*. Gay Men's.

Gilman, S. 1985. Black Bodies, White Bodies: Towards an Iconography of Female Sexuality in Late Nineteenth-Century Art, Medicine, and Literature. *Critical Inquiry* 12, no. 1.

Gilroy, P. 1993a. *The Black Atlantic: Modernity and Double Consciousness.* Cambridge: Harvard University Press.

—— 1993b. *Small Acts: Thoughts on the Politics of Black Cultures.* Serpent's Tail.

Goffman, E. 1959. *The Presentation of Self in Everyday Life.* New York: Doubleday.

—— 1963. *Stigma: Notes on the Management of Spoiled Identity.* Englewood Cliffs: Prentice-Hall.

Gopinath, G. 2002. Local Sites/Global Contexts: The Transnational Trajectories of Deepa Mehta's *Fire.* In A. Cruz-Malavé and M. Manalansan IV, eds., *Queer Globalizations: Citizenship and the Afterlife of Colonialism.* New York: New York University Press.

Gowricharn, R., and J. Schuster. 2001. Diaspora and Transnationalism. The Case of the Surinamese in the Netherlands. In R. Hoefte and P. Meel, eds., *Twentieth-Century Suriname: Continuities and Discontinuities in a New World Society.* Leiden: KITVL.

Gray White, D. 1985. *Ain't I a Woman? Female Slaves in the Plantation South.* New York: Norton.

Grewal, I., and C. Kaplan, eds. 1994. *Scattered Hegemonies: Postmodernity and Transnational Feminist Practices.* Minneapolis: University of Minnesota Press.

—— 2001. Global Identities. Theorizing Transnational Studies of Sexuality. *GLQ* 7, no. 4.

de Groot, S. 1969. *Djuka Society and Social Change: History of an Attempt to Develop a Bush Negro Community in Surinam, 1917–1926.* Assen: van Gorcum.

Gwaltney, J. L. 1980. *Drylongso: A Self-Portrait of Black America.* New York: Vintage.

Halberstam, J. 1998. *Female Masculinity.* Durham: Duke University Press.

Hall, S. 1991. The Local and the Global: Globalization and Ethnicity. In A. King, ed., *Culture, Globalization, and the World System: Contemporary Conditions for the Representation of Identity.* Minneapolis: University of Minnesota Press.

Hallowell, A. 1955. *Culture and Experience.* Philadelphia: University of Pennsylvania Press.

—— 1960. Personality, Culture, and Society in Behavioral Evolution. In S. Tax, ed., *The Evolution of Man,* vol. 2: *Evolution After Darwin.* Chicago: University of Chicago Press.

Hammonds, E. 1997. Black (W)holes and the Geometry of Black Female Sexuality. In M. J. Alexander and C. T. Mohanty, eds., *Feminist Genealogies, Colonial Legacies, Democratic Futures.* New York: Routledge.

Hannerz, U. 1970. What Ghetto Males Are Like: Another Look. In N. Whitten and J. Szwed, eds., *Afro-American Anthropology.* New York: Free.

—— 1996. *Transnational Connections.* London: Routledge.

Haraway, D. 1988. Situated Knowledges: The Science Question in Feminism and the Privilege of Partial Perspective. *Feminist Studies* 14, no. 3.

—— 1991. *Simians, Cyborgs, and Women: The Reinvention of Nature.* London: Free Association Books.

Harding, S. 1991. *Whose Science? Whose Knowledge? Thinking from Women's Lives.* Ithaca, NY: Cornell University Press.

———— 1998. *Is Science Multicultural? Postcolonialisms, Feminisms, and Epistemologies.* Bloomington: Indiana University Press.

Harrison, F. 1988. Women in Jamaica's Informal Economy: Insights from a Kingston Slum. *Nieuwe West-Indische Gids* 62, nos. 3 and 4.

Herdt. G. 1987. *The Sambia: Ritual and Gender in New Guinea.* New York: Holt, Rinehart and Winston.

Herdt, G., and R. J. Stoller. 1990. *Intimate Communications: Erotics and the Study of Culture.* New York: Columbian University Press.

Herskovits, M. 1928. Personal Diary, Kept in Suriname. New York: Schomburg Center for Research into Black Culture.

———— 1937. *Life in a Haitian Village.* New York: Knopf.

———— 1941. *The Myth of the Negro Past.* Boston: Beacon.

———— 1967 [1938]. *Dahomey: An Ancient West African Kingdom.* Vols. 1 and 2. Evanston: Northwestern University Press.

Herskovits, M., and F. Herskovits. 1934. *Rebel Destiny: Among the Bush Negroes of Dutch Guiana.* New York: McGraw-Hill.

———— 1936. *Suriname Folk-lore.* New York: Columbia University Press.

———— 1947. *Trinidad Village.* New York: Knopf.

Hill Collins, P. 1986. Learning from the Outsider Within: The Sociological Significance of Black Feminist Thought. *Social Problems* 33, no.6.

———— 1989. The Social Construction of Black Feminist Thought: An Essay in the Sociology of Knowledge. *Signs: Journal of Women in Culture and Society* 14, no.4.

———— 1990. *Black Feminist Thought: Knowledge, Consciousness and the Politics of Empowerment.* London: Harper Collins.

Hochschild, A. R. 2002. Love and Gold. In B. Ehrenreich and A. R. Hochschild, eds., *Global Woman: Nannies, Maids, and Sex Workers in the New Economy.* New York: Holt.

Hoetink, H. 1958. *Het patroon van de oude Curaçaose samenleving: Een sociologische studie.* Assen: Van Gorcum.

Hollibaugh, A. L. 2000. *My Dangerous Desires: A Queer Girl Dreaming Her Way Home.* Duke University Press.

Hooghiemstra, E., and J.Merens. 1999. Variatie in Participatie: Achtergronden van arbeidsdeelname van allochtone en autochtone vrouwen. Den Haag: SCP.

hooks, b. 1992. *Black Looks: Race and Representation.* Boston: South End.

———— 1996. *Bone Black: Memories of Girlhood.* New York: Holt.

Inda, J. X., and R. Rosaldo, eds. 2002. *The Anthropology of Globalization: A Reader.* Malden: Blackwell.

Jagdeo, T. 1992. *Suriname Contraceptive Prevalence Survey 1992.* Stichting Lobi. Paramaribo: Drukkerij Boschman.

Janssen, A. M. 1986. *Suriname: Ontwikkelingsland in het Caraibisch Gebied.* Amsterdam: Uitgeverij SUA.

Janssens, M., and W. van Wetering. 1985. Mati en Lesbiennes, Homoseksualiteit en Eth nische Identiteit bij Creools-Surinaamse Vrouwen in Nederland. *Sociologische Gids* no. 5 and 6. Meppel: Boom.

Kambel, E. R. 2002. *Resource Conflicts, Gender, and Indigenous Rights in Suriname: Local, National and Global Perspectives.* Ph.D. diss., University of Leiden.

Kambel, E. R., and F. MacKay. 1999. *The Rights of Indigenous Peoples and Maroons in Suriname.* Copenhagen: International Work Group for Indigenous Affairs (IWGIA).

Kappler, A. 1983 [1854]. *Zes Jaren in Suriname, 1836–1842.* Zutphen: de Walburg.

Katz, J. 1996. *The Invention of Heterosexuality.* New York: Plume.

Keil, C. 1966. *Urban Blues.* Chicago: University of Chicago Press.

Kempadoo, K. 2004. *Sexing the Caribbean: Gender, Race, and Sexual Labor.* New York: Routledge.

Kendall. 1999. Women in Lesotho and the (Western) Construction of Homophobia. In E. Blackwood and S. E. Wieringa, eds., *Female Desires: Same-Sex Relations and Transgender Practices Across Cultures.* New York: Columbia University Press.

Kennedy, E. L., and M. D. Davis, eds. 1993. *Boots of Leather, Slippers of Gold: The History of a Lesbian Community.* New York: Routledge.

Kerr, M. 1952. *Personality and Conflict in Jamaica.* Liverpool: University Press.

Ketwaru-Nurmohamed, S. 2000. *Situational Analysis of Women in Suriname.* United Nations Development Fund for Women.

Kincaid, J. 1983. *Annie John.* New York: New American Library.

—— 1992 [1978]. *At the Bottom of the River.* New York: Plume.

—— 1996. *The Autobiography of My Mother.* New York: Farrar Straus and Giroux.

King, A., ed. 1991a. *Culture, Globalization, and the World System: Contemporary Conditions for the Representation of Identity.* Minneapolis: University of Minnesota Press.

King, A. 1991b. Introduction. Spaces of Culture, Spaces of Knowledge. In A. King, ed., *Culture, Globalization, and the World System: Contemporary Conditions for the Representation of Identity.* Minneapolis: University of Minnesota Press.

King, K. 2002. There Are No Lesbians Here: Feminisms, Lesbianisms, and Global Gay Formations. In A. Cruz-Malavé and M. Manalansan IV, eds., *Queer Globalizations: Citizenship and the Afterlife of Colonialism.* New York: New York University Press.

Kirtsoglou, E. 2004. *For the Love of Women: Gender, Identity, and Same-Sex Relations in a Greek Provincial Town.* London and New York: Routledge.

Klinkers, E. 1997. *Op hoop van vrijheid: van slavensamenleving naar Creoolse gemeenschap in Suriname, 1830 – 1880.* Utrecht: Vakgroep Culturele Antropologie. Universiteit Utrecht.

Köbben, A. 1968. Continuity in Change: Cottica Djuka Society as a Changing System. *Bydragen tot de Taal-, Land-, en Volkenkunde* 124.

Kochman, T. 1972. *"Rappin' and Stylin' Out": Communication in Urban Black America.* Urbana and Chicago: University of Illinois Press.

Kofman, E., A. Phizacklea, P. Raghuram, and R. Sales. 2000. *Gender and International Migration in Europe: Employment, Welfare, and Politics.* New York and London: Routledge.

de Kom, A. 1971 [1934]. *Wij Slaven Van Suriname.* Amsterdam: Contact.

Kondo, D. 1990. *Crafting Selves: Power, Gender, and Discourses of Identity in a Japanese Workplace*. Chicago: University of Chicago Press.

Kromhout, M. Y. 2000. Gedeelde smart is halve smart: Hoe vrouwen in Paramaribo hun bestaan organiseren. Ph. D. diss., Universiteit van Amsterdam.

Kruijer, G. 1973. *Suriname: Neokolonie in Rijksverband*. Meppel: Boom.

Kulick, D., and M. Wilson, eds. 1995. *Taboo: Sex, Identity, and Erotic Subjectivity in Anthropological Fieldwork*. London: Routledge.

Ladner, J. 1971. *Tomorrow's Tommorow: The Black Woman*. New York: Anchor.

Lammens, A. 1982. *Bijdragen tot de Kennis van de Kolonie Suriname: Tijdvak, 1816–1822*. Meppel: Krips Repro.

Lamur, H. 1985. *De kerstening van de slaven van de Surinaamse plantage Vossenburg, 1847–1887*. Amsterdam: Universiteit van Amsterdam, Antropologisch–Sociologisch Centrum.

Lancaster, R. N. 1992. *Life Is Hard: Machismo, Danger, and the Intimacy of Power in Nicaragua*. University of California Press.

Lancaster, R. N., and M. di Leonardo, eds. 1997a. *The Gender/Sexuality Reader: Culture, History, Political Economy*. New York: Routledge.

Lancaster, R. N., and M. di Leonardo. 1997b. Introduction: Embodied Meanings, Carnal Practices. In R. N. Lancaster and M. di Leonardo, eds., *The Gender/Sexuality Reader: Culture, History, Political Economy*. New York: Routledge.

de Lauretis, T. 1991. Queer Theory: Lesbian and Gay Sexualities, an Introduction. *Differences* 3, no. 2.

Leavitt, R., B. Sykes, and E. Weatherford. 1975. Aboriginal Woman: Male and Female Anthropological Perspectives. In R. Reiter, ed., *Toward an Anthropology of Women*. New York: Monthly Review Press.

Lenders, M. 1994. Strijders voor het Lam: Leven en werk van Herrnhutter-broeders en-zusters in Suriname, 1735–1900. Ph.D. diss., Universiteit van Amsterdam.

Lenders, M., and M. van de Roer. 1983. *Mijn God, hoe ga ik doen? Creoolse alleenstaande moeders in Amsterdam*. Amsterdam: Uitgeverij SUA.

Levine, L. 1977. *Black Culture and Black Consciousness: Afro-American Folk Thought from Slavery to Freedom*. Oxford: Oxford University Press.

Lewin, E. 2002. Another Unhappy Marriage? Feminist Anthropology and Lesbian/Gay Studies. In E. Lewin and W. L. Leap. eds. *Out in Theory: The Emergence of Lesbian and Gay Anthropology*. Urbana and Chicago: University of Illinois Press.

Lewin, E., and W. L. Leap, eds. 1996. *Out in the Field: Reflections of Lesbian and Gay Anthropologists*. University if Illinois Press.

—— 2002. *Out in Theory: The Emergence of Lesbian and Gay Anthropology*. Urbana and Chicago: University of Illinois Press.

Lewis, D. 1975. The Black Family: Socialization and Sex Roles. *Phylon*.

Liebow, E. 1967. *Tally's Corner: A Study of Negro Streetcorner Men*. Boston: Little, Brown.

van Lier, R. 1977 [1949]. *Samenleving in een Grensgebied*. Een Sociaal-Historische Studie van Suriname. Amsterdam: Emmering.

—— 1986. *Tropische Tribaden: Een Verhandeling over Homoseksualiteit en Homoseksuele Vrouwen in Suriname*. Dordrecht and Providence: Foris.

Lombard, J. 1967. The Kingdom of Dahomey. In D. Forde and P. Kaberry, eds., *West African Kingdoms in the Nineteenth Century*. London: Oxford University Press.

Lorde, A. 1978. *The Black Unicorn*. New York: Norton.

—— 1982. *Zami: A New Spelling of My Name*. Trumansburg, NY: Crossing.

—— 1984. *Sister Outsider: Essays and Speeches*. Trumansburg, NY: Crossing.

Lutz. H. Migrant Women of "Islamic Background": Images and Self-Images. MERA occasional paper no. 11.

—— 1997. The Limits of Europeanness: Immigrant Women in Fortress Europe. *Feminist Review*, no. 57.

Mburu, J. 2000. Awakenings: Dreams and Delusions of an Incipient Lesbian and Gay Movement in Kenya. In P. Drucker, ed., *Different Rainbows*. London: Gay Men's.

McCarthy Brown, K. 1991. *Mama Lola: A Vodou Priestess in Brooklyn*. Berkeley and Los Angeles: University of California Press.

McClintock, A. 1995. *Imperial Leather: Race, Gender, and Sexuality in the Colonial Contest*. New York and London: Routledge.

McLeod, C. 1996. *Elisabeth Samson, Een vrije zwarte vrouw in het achttiende-eeuwse Suriname*. Schoorl: Conserve.

Malmberg-Guicherit, H. 1993. De Positie van het Vrouwelijk Hoger Kader, Den Sabiuma fu Sranan. In Congresbundel, *Vrouwen, Ontwikkeling en Leiderschap*. Paramaribo.

—— 1999. Strijdbaar zwak geslacht. *Kompas* 4, no. 48.

—— 2000. Meer vrouwelijk Leiderschap. Unpublished paper. March 8.

Manderson, L., and M. Jolly, eds. 1997. *Sites of Desire, Economies of Pleasure: Sexualities in Asia and the Pacific*. Chicago: University of Chicago Press.

Marks, A. 1976. *Male and Female in the Afro-Curaçaoan Household*, no. 77. 's Gravenhage: KITLV.

Martin, E. 1987. *The Woman in the Body: A Cultural Analysis of Reproduction*. Boston: Beacon.

Mbiti, J. 1969. *African Religions and Philosophy*. London: Heinemann.

Meza, L. 2004. "(De-)Colonizing Black Women's Bodies and Sexualities: Afro-Surinamese Women and Sexual Violence in the Netherlands." B.A. thesis, Barnard College.

Ministerie van Arbeid. 1993. *Arbeidsmarkt Informatie*. Paramaribo.

Mintz, S., and R. Price. 1992 [1976]. *The Birth of Afro-American Culture: An Anthropological Perspective*. Boston: Beacon.

Mohammed, P., and C. Shepherd, eds. 1988. *Gender in Caribbean Development*. Mona: University of the West Indies.

Mohanty, C. T. 1991. Under Western Eyes: Feminist Scholarship and Colonial Discourses. In C. T. Mohanty, A. Russo, and L. Torres, eds., *Third World Women and the Politics of Feminism*. Bloomington: Indiana University Press.

Momsen, J. 1999. *Gender, Migration,and Domestic Service*. London: Routledge.

Moynihan, D. 1965. *The Negro Family: The Case for National Action*. Washington, DC: United States Department of Labor.

Murray, A. 1999. Let Them Take Ecstasy: Class and Jakarta Lesbians. In E. Blackwood and S. E. Wieringa, eds., *Female Desires: Same-Sex Relations and Transgender Practices Across Cultures*. New York: Columbia University Press.

Nadel, S. A. 1951. *Black Byzantium: The Kingdom of Nupe of Nigeria*. London: Oxford University Press.

Nash, J. 1983. The Impact of the Changing International Division of Labor on Different Sectors of the Labor Force. In J. Nash and M. Fernandez-Kelly, eds., *Women, Men and the International Division of Labor*. Albany: State University of New York Press.

Nash, J., and H. Safa. 1980. *Sex and Class in Latin America: Women's Perspectives on Politics, Economics, and the Family in the Third World*. South Hadley: Bergin and Garvey.

Nederveen Pieterse, J. 1990. *Empire and Emancipation: Power and Liberation on a World Scale*. London: Pluto.

Nelson, N. 1979. How Women and Men Get By: The Sexual Division of Labour in the Informal Sector of a Nairobi Squatter Settlement. In R. Bromley and C. Gerry, eds., *Casual Work and Poverty in Third World Cities*. Chichester: Wiley.

Nestle, J. ed. 1992. *The Persistent Desire: A Femme-Butch Reader*. Boston: Alyson.

Newton, E. 2000. *Margaret Mead Made Me Gay: Personal Essays, Public Ideas*. Durham: Duke University Press.

Nichols, M. 1987. Lesbian Sexuality: Issues and Developing Theory. In Boston Lesbian Psychologies Collective, ed., *Lesbian Psychologies: Explorations and Challenges*. Urbana and Chicago: University of Illinois Press.

Obeyesekere, G. 1981. *Medusa's Hair: An Essay on Personal Symbols and Religious Experience*. Chicago and London: University of Chicago Press.

Omolade, B. 1984. Hearts of Darkness. In A. Snitow, C. Stansell, and S. Thompson, eds., *Desire: The Politics of Sexuality*. London: Virago.

Oostindie, G. 1989. *Roosenburg en Mon Bijou: Twee Surinaamse Plantages, 1720–1870*. Dordrecht and Providence: Foris.

Ortner, S. 1981. Introduction: Accounting for Sexual Meanings. In S. Ortner and H. Whitehead, eds., *Sexual Meanings: The Cultural Construction of Gender and Sexuality*. Cambridge: Cambridge University Press.

Oyewumi, O. 2001. Ties That (Un)bind: Feminism, Sisterhood and Other Foreign Relations. *Jenda: A Journal of Culture and African Women Studies* 1, no. 1.

Padgug, R. 1989. Sexual Matters: On Conceptualizing Sexuality in History. In K. Peiss, C. Simmons, with R. Padgug, eds., *Passion and Power: Sexuality in History*. Philadelphia: Temple University Press.

Park, R. G., and J. H. Gagnon, eds. 1995. *Conceiving Sexuality: Approaches to Sex Research in a Postmodern World*. New York: Routledge.

Parker, R. G. 1991. *Bodies, Pleasures and Passions: Sexual Culture in Contemporary Brazil*. Boston: Beacon.

———— 1999. *Beneath the Equator: Cultures of Desire, Male Homosexuality, and Emerging Gay Communities in Brazil*. New York: Routledge.

Patterson, O. 1967. *The Sociology of Slavery: An Analysis of the Origins, Development, and Structure of Negro Slave Society in Jamaica*. London: MacGibbon and Kee.

Patton, C., and B. Sánchez-Eppler, eds. 2000. *Queer Diasporas*. Durham: Duke University Press.

Peiss, K. 1968. *Cheap Amusements: Working Women and Leisure in Turn-of-the-Century New York.* Philadelphia: Temple University Press.

———1984. "Charity Girls" and City Pleasures: Historical Notes on Working-Class Sexuality, 1880–1920. In A. Snitow, C. Stansell, S. Thompson, eds., *Desire: The Politics of Sexuality.* London: Virago.

Peiss, K., C. Simmons, with R. Padgug, eds. 1989. *Passion and Power: Sexuality in History.* Philadelphia: Temple University Press.

Peplau, L., and S. Gordon. 1985. Women and Men in Love: Gender Differences in Close Heterosexual Relationships. In V. O'Leary, R. Kesler Unger, and B. Strudler Wallston, eds., *Women, Gender, and Social Psychology.* Hillsdale, NJ: Erlbaum.

Pieper, I. 2000. *Suriname's elite in het buitenland: Aard en betekenis van externe relaties.* Surinaamse Verkenningen. Paramaribo: Leo Victor.

Pierce, B. 1971. "Kinship and Residence Among the Urban Nengre of Suriname: A Reevaluation of Concepts and Theories of the Afro-American Family." Ph.D. diss., Tulane University.

Portelli, A. 2001. *The Death of Luigi Trastelli and Other Stories: Form and Meaning in Oral Stories.* New York: State University of New York Press.

Povinelli, E., and G. Chauncey. 1999. "Thinking Sexuality Transnationally." *GLQ* 5, no. 4.

Price, R. 1976. *The Guiana Maroons: A Historical and Bibliographical Introduction.* Baltimore: John Hopkins University Press.

——— ed. 1979. *Maroon Societies.* Rebel Slave Communities in the Americas. Baltimore: Johns Hopkins University Press.

——— 1983. *First Time.* The Historical Vision of an Afro-American People. Baltimore: Johns Hopkins University Press.

——— 1990. *Alabi's World.* Baltimore: Johns Hopkins University Press.

Price, R., and S. Price. 1991. *Two Evenings in Saramaka.* Chicago: University of Chicago Press.

Price, S. 1984. *Cowives and Calabashes.* Ann Arbor: University of Michigan Press.

Price, S., and R. Price. 1980. *Afro-American Arts of the Suriname Rain-Forest.* Los Angeles: Museum of Cultural History, University of California; Berkeley and Los Angeles: University of California Press.

——— 1999. *Maroon Arts.* Boston: Beacon.

van Putten, L., and J. Zantinge. 1988. Let Them Talk. *Mededelingen van het Surinaams Museum,* no. 43. Paramaribo: Stichting Surinaams Museum.

Radcliffe-Brown, A., and D. Forde, eds. 1950. *African Systems of Kinship and Marriage.* London: Oxford University.

Reiter, R., ed. 1975. *Toward an Anthropology of Women.* New York and London: Monthly Review.

Reyes, E. 1986. Women in Calypso. In P. Ellis, ed., *Women of the Caribbean.* London: Zed.

Rich, A. 1979. *On Lies, Secrets and Silence: Selected Prose, 1966–1978.* London: Virago.

——— 1980. Compulsory Heterosexuality and Lesbian Existence. *Signs: Journal of Women in Culture and Society* 5, no. 4.

Robertson, J. 1998. *Takarazuka: Sexual Politics and Popular Culture in Modern Japan.* Berkeley and Los Angeles: University of California Press.

Rodman, H. 1963. The Lower-Class Value Stretch. *Social Forces* 42.

Rosaldo, R. 1993. *Culture and Truth: The Remaking of Social Analysis.* Boston: Beacon.

Rose, T. 2003. *Longing to Tell: Black Women Talk About Sexuality and Intimacy.* New York: Farrar, Straus and Giroux.

Ross, D. 1998. *Wrapped in Pride: Ghanaian Kente and African American Identity.* Los Angeles: UCLA Fowler Museum of Cultural History.

Ross, E., and R. Rapp. 1997. Sex and Society: A research note from social history and anthropology. In R. N. Lancaster and M. di Leonardo, eds. *The Gender/Sexuality Reader: Culture, History, Political Economy.* New York: Routledge.

Rubenstein, H. 1987. *Coping with Poverty: Adaptive Strategies in a Caribbean Village.* Boulder and London: Westview.

Rubin, G. 1975. The Traffic in Women: Notes on the "Political Economy" of Sex. In R. Reiter, ed., *Toward an Anthropology of Women.* New York and London: Monthly Review Press.

——— 1984. Thinking Sex: Notes for a Radical Theory of the Politics of Sexuality. In C. Vance, ed., *Pleasure and Danger: Exploring Female Sexuality.* Boston and London: Routledge and Kegan Paul.

Rubin, L. 1976. *Worlds of Pain: Life in the Working-Class Family.* New York: Basic.

Sacks, K. 1982. *Sisters and Wives: The Past and Future of Sexual Equality.* Urbana: University of Illinois Press.

Said, S. 1993. *Culture and Imperialism.* London: Chatto and Windus.

Salazar Parrenas, R. 2001. *Servants of Globalization: Women, Migration, and Domestic Work.* Stanford: Stanford University Press.

Sang, T. 2003. *The Emerging Lesbian: Female Same-Sex Desire in Modern China.* Chicago and London: University of Chicago Press.

Sansone, L. 1992. *Schitteren in de Schaduw: Overlevings-strategieen, subcultuur en etniciteit van Creoolse Jongeren uit de lagere klasse in Amsterdam, 1981-1990.* Amsterdam: Het Spinhuis.

Santiago, S. 2002. The Wily Homosexual (First—and Necessarily Hasty—Notes). In A. Cruz-Malavé and M. Manalansan IV, eds., *Queer Globalizations: Citizenship and the Afterlife of Colonialism.* New York: New York University Press.

Sassen, S. 1998. *Globalization and Its Discontents.* New York: New.

Schalkwijk,A., and G. A. de Bruijne. 1999. *Van Mon Plaisir tot Ephraimszegen: Welstand, etniciteit en woonpatronen in Paramaribo.* Surinaamse Verkenningen. Amsterdam: AGIDS/UvA; Paramaribo: Leo Victor.

Scheper-Hughes, N. 1992. *Death Without Weeping: The Violence of Everyday Life in Brazil.* Berkeley and Los Angeles: University of California Press.

Schiltkamp, J., and J. de Smidt, eds. 1973. *Westindisch Plakkaatboek: Plakkaten, Ordonnantieen en andere Wetten Uitgevaardigd in Suriname.* Amsterdam: Emmering.

Scholtens, B. 1985. *Suriname tijdens de Tweede Wereldoorlog.* Paramaribo: Anton de Kom Universiteit van Suriname.

Scholtens, B., G. Wekker, L. van Putten, and S. Dieko. 1992. *Gaama Duumi, Buta Gaa-*

ma: Overlijden en Opvolging van Aboikoni, Grootopperhoofd van de Saramaka Bos-negers. Paramaribo: VACO.

Shepherd, V., B. Brereton, and B. Bailey, eds. 1995. *Engendering History: Caribbean Women in Historical Perspective.* New York: St. Martin's.

Shohat, Ella. ed. 1998. *Talking Visions: Multicultural Feminism in a Transnational Age.* New York: New Museum of Contemporary Art.

Shweder, R., and R. LeVine, eds. 1984. *Culture Theory: Essays on Mind, Self, and Emotion.* Cambridge: Cambridge University Press.

Silvera, M. 1992. Man Royals and Sodomites: Some Thoughts on the Invisibility of Afro-Caribbean Lesbians. *Feminist Studies* 18, no. 3.

Simson, R. 1984. The Afro-American Female: The Historical Context of the Construction of Sexual Identity. In A. Snitow, C. Stansell, and S. Thompson, eds., *Desire: The Politics of Sexuality.* London: Virago.

Smith, M. G. 1962a. *Kinship and Community in Carriacou.* New Haven: Yale University Press.

—— 1962b. *West Indian Family Structure.* Seattle: University of Washington.

—— 1965. *The Plural Society in the British West Indies.* Berkeley and Los Angeles: University of California Press.

Smith, R. T. 1956. *The Negro Family in British Guiana.* London: Routledge and Kegan Paul.

—— 1996. *The Matrifocal Family: Power, Pluralism, and Politics.* New York: Routledge.

Snitow, A., C. Stansell, and S. Thompson, eds. 1984. *Desire. The Politics of Sexuality.* London: Virago.

Sordam, M. I., and Ch. H. Eersel. 1989. *Surinaams woordenboek, Sranantongo: Een korte inleiding tot het Sranantongo met uitgebreide woordenlijst.* Baarn: Bosch and Keuning.

Spalburg. J. G. 1913. *Bruine Mina de koto-missi.* Paramaribo: Wekker.

Speckmann, H. 1965. *Marriage and Kinship Among the Indians in Surinam.* Assen: van Gorcum.

Spillers, H. 1984. Interstices: A Small Drama of Words. In C. Vance, ed., *Pleasure and Danger: Exploring Female Sexuality.* Boston and London: Routledge and Kegan Paul.

Spiro, M. 1987. Culture and Human Nature. In E. Spiro, B. Kilborne, and L. L. Langness, eds., *Theoretical Papers of Melford E. Spiro.* Chicago: University of Chicago Press.

Staal, P. 1992. Women, Food, Sex, and Survival in Candomble: An Interpretive Analysis of an African-Brazilian Religion in Bahia, Brazil. Ph.D. diss., University of California, Los Angeles.

Stack, C. 1974. *All Our Kin.* New York: Harper and Row.

—— 1986. The Culture of Gender: Women and Men of Color. *Signs: Journal of Women in Culture and Society* 11, no.2.

Stam, R., and E. Shohat. 1994. Contested Histories: Eurocentrism, Multiculturalism, and the Media. In D. T. Goldberg, ed., *Multiculturalism. A Critical Reader.* Oxford: Blackwell.

Stedman, J. 1974 [1799]. *Reize naar Surinamen en door de binnenste Gedeelten van Guiana.* Parts 1–4. Amsterdam: Emmering.

Stephen, H. N.d. *Lexicon van de Winti-Kultuur*. Paramaribo: De West.

———1985. *Winti: Afro-Surinaamse Religie en Magische Rituelen in Suriname en Nederland*. Amsterdam: Karnak.

Stichting Maxi Linder Association. 2000. Report regarding commercial sex in Suriname. Paramaribo: Stichting Maxi Linder.

van Stipriaan, A. 1990. What's in a Name? Slavernij en naamgeving in Suriname tijdens de 18e en 19e eeuw. *Oso: Tijdschrift voor Surinaamse Taalkunde, Letterkunde en Geschiedenis* 9, no.1.

——— 1993. *Surinaams contrast: roofbouw en overleven in een Caraïbische plantagekolonie, 1750–1863*. Leiden: KITLV Uitgeverij.

Stocking, G. 1968. *Race, Culture, and Evolution: Essays in the History of Anthropology*. Glencoe, Ill.: Free.

Stoler, A. 1995. *Race and the Education of Desire: Foucault's History of Sexuality and the Colonial Order of Things*. Durham, NC: Duke University Press.

——— 2002. *Carnal Knowledge and Imperial Power: Gender, Race, and Morality in Colonial Asia*. Berkeley and Los Angeles: University of California Press.

Strongman, R. 2002. Syncretic Religion and Dissident Sexualities. In A. Cruz-Malavé and M. Manalansan IV, eds., *Queer Globalizations: Citizenship and the Afterlife of Colonialism*. New York and London: New York University Press.

Sudarkasa, N. 1996. *The Strength of Our Mothers: African and African American Women and Families, Essays and Speeches*. Trenton, NJ: Africa World.

Sumter, T., and M. Zwanenbeek. 2001. *Onderzoek intake formulieren*. Paramaribo: SSGtV.

Suparlan, P. 1976. *The Javanese in Surinam: Ethnicity in an Ethnically Plural Society*. Ph.D. diss., University of Illinois at Champaign.

Tafari-Ama, I. 2002. Blood, Bullets, and Bodies: Sexual Politics Below the Poverty Line, the Political Economy of Violence, Power, Gender and Embodiment in Jamaica's Inner City. Ph.D. diss., The Hague: Institute of Social Studies.

Teenstra, M. D. 1835. *De Landbouw in de kolonie, voorafgegaan door eene Geschied- en Natuurkundige Beschouwing dier Kolonie*. Parts 1 and 2. Groningen: Eekhoff.

——— 1842. *De Negerslaven in de Kolonie Suriname en de Uitbreiding van het Christendom onder de Heidensche Bevolking*. Dordrecht: Lagerweij.

Terborg, J. R. H. 2002. *Liefde en conflict: seksualiteit en gender in de Afro-Surinaamse familie*. Ph.D. diss., Universiteit van Amsterdam.

Thoden van Velzen, H. 1966. Politieke Beheersing in de Djuka Maatschappij: Een Studie van een Onvolledig Machtsoverwicht. Ph.D., diss., University of Amsterdam.

Thoden van Velzen, H., and W. van Wetering. 1989. *The Great Father and the Danger: Religious Cults, Material Forces, and Collective Fantasies in the World of the Surinamese Maroons*. Dordrecht and Providence: Foris.

Thompson, R. 1983. *Flash of the Spirit: African and Afro-American Art and Philosophy*. New York: Vintage.

Tietmeyer, E. 1991. *Gynaegamie Im Wandel: Die Agikuyu zwischen Tradition und Anpassung*. Kulturantropologische Studien. Muenster: Literatur.

Tjoa, T. 1990a. Vrouw Zijn in Suriname. Inleiding in het Kader van de Vierde Lustrumviering van de Vereniging van Medici in Suriname, February 5.

———1990b. Presentatie in het kader van de Internationale Vrouwendag, March 8.

———1992. Women in the Caribbean. Five Hundred Years of History. Political Participation of Women, Legal Status of Women. Caracas: Instituto Venezolano de Estu-
dios Sociales y Politicos.

Trefossa. 1990 [1957]. Mi Go—M'e Kon. *Mutyama: Surinaams Tijdschrift voor Cultuur
en Geschiedenis* 1, no. 1.

Trotz, A. 2003. Behind the Banner of Culture? Gender, "Race," and the Family in Guyana. *New West Indian Guide* 77, no. 182.

Trouillot, M. R. 1992. The Caribbean Region: An Open Frontier in Anthropological
Theory. *Annual Review of Anthropology* 21.

Turnbull, C. 1986. Sex and Gender: The Role of Subjectivity in Field Research. In T.
Whitehead and M. Conaway, eds., *Self, Sex, and Gender in Cross-Cultural Field Research*. Urbana and Chicago: University of Illinois Press.

Vance, C. 1989. Social Construction Theory: Problems in the History of Sexuality. In
D. Altman, C. Vance, M. Vicinus, and J. Weeks, eds., *Homosexuality, Which Homosexuality?* London: GMP.

Venema, T. 1992. *Famiri Nanga Kulturu: Creoolse Sociale Verhoudingen en Winti in Amsterdam*. Amsterdam: Het Spinhuis.

Voltaire. 1993 [1759]. *Candide or Optimism*. Trans. Shane Weller. London: Penguin.

Voorhoeve, J. 1982. Het Sranan als Cultuurtaal. *Oso: Tijdschrift voor Surinaamse Taalkunde, Letterkunde en Geschiedenis* 1, no. 1.

Voorhoeve, J., and U. Lichtveld, eds. 1975. *Creole Drum: An Anthology of Creole Literature in Suriname*. New Haven: Yale University Press.

Walker, A. 1982. *The Color Purple*. Orlando: Harcourt, Brace, Jovanovitch.

Weeks, J. 1981. *Sex, Politics, and Society: The Regulation of Sexuality Since 1800*. New
York: Longman.

———1986. *Sexuality*. Chichester: Ellis Horwood.

Wekker, G. 1981. Die in het Donker Ziet Men Niet: Een Ethnografische beschrij-
ving van de Socio-culturele Context en de Historisch-filosofische beperkingen
van het Matrifokaliteitsbegrip van M. J. Herskovits. M.A. thesis, Universiteit van
Amsterdam.

———1990. Creole Women. *De ware Tijd Literair*.

———1992a. "I Am Gold Money" (I pass through all hands, but I do not lose my value):
The Construction of Selves, Gender, and Sexualities in a Female, Working-Class,
Afro-Surinamese Setting. Ph.D. diss., University of California, Los Angeles.

———1992b. "Meisje, is bobi krijg je, nô?" Creolse Vrouwen in Suriname en hun ero-
tische relaties met kinderen en pubers. In M. Sax and S. Deckwitz, eds., *Op een oude
Fiets moet je het leren*. Amsterdam: Schorer.

———1993. Mati-ism and Black Lesbianism. Two Idealtypical Constructions of Female
Homosexuality in Black Communities of the Diaspora. *Journal of Homosexuality*
24, nos. 3/4.

———1994. *Ik ben een gouden Munt: Subjectiviteit en Seksualiteit van Creoolse Volksklasse Vrouwen in Paramaribo*. Amsterdam: Feministische Uitgeverij Vita.

———1996. Praten in het Donker: De Praktijk van het Weten in Nederlandse Vrouwen studies. In G. Wekker and R. Braidotti, eds., *Praten in het Donker: Multiculturalisme en Anti-Racisme in feministisch Perspectief.* Kampen: Kok Agora.

—— 1997. One Finger Does Not Drink Okra Soup. Afro- Surinamese Women and Critical Agency. In M. J. Alexander and C. T. Mohanty, eds., *Feminist Genealogies, Colonial Legacies, Democratic Futures.* New York and London: Routledge.

—— 1998. Of Sex and Silences: Methodological Considerations on Sex Research in Paramaribo, Suriname. *Thamyris: Mythmaking from Past to Present* 5, no.1.

—— 1999. What's Identity Got to Do with It? Rethinking Identity in Light of the Mati Work in Paramaribo, Suriname. In E. Blackwood. and S. E. Wieringa, eds., *Female Desires: Same-Sex Relations and Transgender Practices Across Cultures.* New York: Columbia University Press.

—— 2001. Of Mimic Men and Unruly Women: Social Relations in Twentieth Century Suriname. In Rosemarijn Hoefte and Peter Meel, eds., *Suriname in the Twentieth Century.* Leiden: KITLV; Kingston: Ian Randle.

—— 2002. Building Nests in a Windy Place: Thinking about Gender and Ethnicity in the Netherlands. Oration, Faculty of Arts, University Utrecht.

—— 2004a. Still Crazy After All These Years. Feminism for the New Millenium. *European Journal of Women's Studies* 11, no.4.

—— 2004b. Sranan, swit' Sranan: Populaire beeldvorming over etnische en gend-ergelijkheid in Suriname. In M. van Kempen, P. Verkruijsse, and A. Zuiderweg, eds., *Wandelaar onder de Palmen.* Leiden: KITLV.

Wekker, G., and R. Braidotti. *Praten in het donker: Multiculturalisme en Anti-Racisme in feministisch perspectief.* Kampen: Kok Agora. 1996.

Wekker, G., and H. Lutz. 2001. Een hoogvlakte met koude winden. De geschiedenis van gender- en etniciteitsdenken in Nederland. In Botman, M., N. Jouwe, and G. Wekker, eds., *Caleidoscopische visies.* De zwarte, migranten- en vluchtelingen vrouwenbeweging in Nederland. Amsterdam: Koninklijk Instituut voor de Tropen.

Wekker, G., and H. Wekker. 1991. Coming in from the Cold: Linguistic and Socio-Cultural Aspects of the Translation of Black English Vernacular Literary Texts into Surinamese Dutch. *Babel: Revue Internationale de la Traduction* 37, no. 4.

van Wengen, G. 1975. *The Cultural Inheritance of the Javanese in Surinam.* Leiden.

Weston, K. 1992. *Families We Choose: Lesbians, Gays, Kinship.* New York: Columbia University Press.

—— 1998. *Long Slow Burn: Sexuality and Social Science.* New York and London: Routledge.

van Wetering, W. 1973. Hekserij bij de Djuka: Een Sociologische Benadering. Ph.D. diss., Universiteit van Amsterdam.

—— 1989. Liefdesrelaties onder Mati: Creools-Surinaamse Vrouwen in Nederland en in Het Land van Herkomst. In G. Hekma, D. Kraakman, M. van Lieshout, and J. Radersma, eds., *Goed Verkeerd: Een Geschiedenis van Homoseksuele Mannen en Lesbische Vrouwen in Nederland.* Amsterdam: Meulenhoff.

—— 1998. Mati: The Lures and Dangers of Utopianism in Lesbian Studies. *Thamyris: Mythmaking from Past to Present* 5, no. 1.

Whitehead, T., and M. Conaway, eds. 1986. *Self, Sex, and Gender in Cross-cultural Field-work*. Urbana and Chicago: University of Illnois Press.

Whitehead, T., and L. Price. 1986. Summary: Sex and the Fieldwork Experience. In T. Whitehead and M. Conaway, eds., *Self, Sex, and Gender in Cross-Cultural Fieldwork*. Urbana and Chicago: University of Chicago Press.

Whitten, N., and J. Szwed, eds. 1970. *Afro-American Anthropology*. New York: Free.

Wieringa, S. E. 1999. Desiring Bodies or Defiant Cultures: Butch-Femme Lesbians in Jakarta and Lima. In E. Blackwood and S. E. Wieringa, eds., *Female Desires: Same-Sex Relations and Transgender Practices Across Cultures*. New York: Columbia University Press.

Wilde, O. 1979. De Profundis. In R. Hart-Davis, ed., *Selected Letters of Oscar Wilde*. Oxford and New York: Oxford University Press.

Williams, B. 1991. *Stains on My Name, War in My Veins: Guyana and the Politics of Cultural Struggle*. Durham: Duke University Press.

Wilson, M. 1963. *Good Company: A Study of Nyakusa Age-Villages*. Boston: Beacon.

Wilson, P. 1973. *Crab Antics: The Social Anthropology of English-Speaking Negro Societies of the Caribbean*. New Haven: Yale University Press.

de Wit, B. 1993. Blank in de Bijlmer. *De Volkskrant*. March 15.

Wolbers. J. 1861. *Geschiedenis van Suriname*. Amsterdam: Emmering.

Wooding, C. 1988 [1972]. *Winti, een Afro-Amerikaanse Godsdienst: Een cultureel-historische analyse van de Cosmologie en het Etnomedische Systeem van de Para*. Rijswijk: Wooding.

Yelvington, K. A., ed. 1995. *Producing Power: Ethnicity, Gender, and Class in a Caribbean Workplace*. Philadelphia: Temple University Press.

Young, L. 1996. *Fear of the Dark: "Race," Gender, and Sexuality in the Cinema*. London and New York: Routledge.

Young, M., and P. Wilmott. 1957. *Family and Kinship in East London*. London: Routledge and Kegan Paul.

Index

Healing, traditional/spirituality-based, 8, 89, 90, 98–99, 264n7, 265n19

Health insurance and formal sector employment, 124

Hemelrijk, Roy (Zorgzaam's lover), 131–33, 146–49, 150, 155

Herskovits, Frances, 205, 211, 212, 214, 215, 220

Herskovits, Melville, 120, 159, 205, 211, 212, 214, 215, 216–17, 220

Heterosexuality: commodification of working-class, 31; competitive relations between women, 153; as dominant public discourse for men, 253; Euro-American naturalization of, 75–76, 160–61, 250; invalidity of compulsory, 173; see also Opposite-sex relationships

Hilda (Cummings's neighbor), 42, 114–15

Hindustani ethnic group, 135–36

Historical perspective: Creole ethnic group, 161–62, 164–65, 218; and etymology of *mati,* 174–78; mati work, 31, 209–14; opposite-sex relationships, 158–70; plantation regime gender system, 106–8, 119–21, 159, 161–65, 167; subjective nature of, 6; see also Slavery

Hochschild, Arlie Russell, 232

Homogenization, cultural, 224, 226, 237, 244–45, 255

Homosexuality: African context, 22; as essentialist category of identity, 191–92; gay vs. lesbian perspectives in anthropology, 16, 173–74, 223; male Surinamese, 253, 271n12, 274n16; see also Same-sex relationships

Humans in Winti cosmology, 95–99

Humphrey (Burgzorg's lover), 125

Hymen, 26

Identity: and Afro-Surinamese personhood, 85; Afro-Surinamese women's challenge to binaries of, 72–73; Euro-American vs. alternate

cultural approaches, 68–69; and exclusivity of European lesbianism, 19; vs. mati sexuality as behavior, 2, 13, 174, 191–93; sexuality as identity, 118, 122; static vs. flexible, 244–45; Surinamese adoption of language of, 239–40; see also Selfhood; Sexual fulfillment; Subjecthood

Igbo society, same-sex sexuality in, 218

Immigration issues in the Netherlands, 229–33, 241–42, 245–51

Immortality of soul, Winti religion, 90

Imperialism, global, 226–27, 233, 239–40, 255

Incidental sex vs. long-term committed relationships, 48, 190–91, 213

Independence, social and economic: and avoidance of marriage, 30, 34, 140; as basic life theme, 3, 25; colonial-era manifestation of women's, 165; importance for women, 114, 134–35; and inequalities in Dutch emancipation policy, 245; and land ownership, 43; Netherlands as opportunity for, 235; younger women's struggle for, 154

Inequalities: Afro-Surinamese women's sexuality as alternative to, 68; and global perspective, 226, 228, 247; increases in socioeconomic, 208–9; and labor division in the Netherlands, 230–33, 245; in mati work, 46, 48, 68, 181–82, 184, 186, 188, 193–97, 233–37, 240–42; in opposite-sex relationships, 24–25, 231; political/economic, 42–44, 118, 126, 251; in same-sex relationships in Dahomey, 216–17; and transnational feminism, 79; see also Class, socioeconomic; Marriage

Informal vs. formal sector employment, 80–81, 124

In-law relationships, 143–45

Inside woman/concubine, 138–39; see also Concubinage; *Getrouwde vrouw/* married woman

BETWEEN MEN ~ BETWEEN WOMEN
Lesbian, Gay, and Bisexual Studies

Terry Castle and Larry Gross, Editors

Richard D. Mohr, *Gays/Justice: A Study of Ethics, Society, and Law*

Gary David Comstock, *Violence Against Lesbians and Gay Men*

Kath Weston, *Families We Choose: Lesbians, Gays, Kinship*

Lillian Faderman, *Odd Girls and Twilight Lovers: A History of Lesbian Life in Twentieth-Century America*

Judith Roof, *A Lure of Knowledge: Lesbian Sexuality and Theory*

John Clum, *Acting Gay: Male Homosexuality in Modern Drama*

Allen Ellenzweig, *The Homoerotic Photograph: Male Images from Durieu/Delacroix to Mapplethorpe*

Sally Munt, editor, *New Lesbian Criticism: Literary and Cultural Readings*

Timothy F. Murphy and Suzanne Poirier, editors, *Writing AIDS: Gay Literature, Language, and Analysis*

Linda D. Garnets and Douglas C. Kimmel, editors, *Psychological Perspectives on Lesbian and Gay Male Experiences* (2nd edition)

Laura Doan, editor, *The Lesbian Postmodern*

Noreen O'Connor and Joanna Ryan, *Wild Desires and Mistaken Identities: Lesbianism and Psychoanalysis*

Alan Sinfield, *The Wilde Century: Effeminacy, Oscar Wilde, and the Queer Moment*

Claudia Card, *Lesbian Choices*

Carter Wilson, *Hidden in the Blood: A Personal Investigation of AIDS in the Yucatán*

Alan Bray, *Homosexuality in Renaissance England*

Joseph Carrier, *De Los Otros: Intimacy and Homosexuality Among Mexican Men*

Joseph Bristow, *Effeminate England: Homoerotic Writing After 1885*

Corinne E. Blackmer and Patricia Juliana Smith, editors, *En Travesti: Women, Gender Subversion, Opera*

Don Paulson with Roger Simpson, *An Evening at The Garden of Allah: A Gay Cabaret in Seattle*

Claudia Schoppmann, *Days of Masquerade: Life Stories of Lesbians During the Third Reich*

Chris Straayer, *Deviant Eyes, Deviant Bodies: Sexual Re-Orientation in Film and Video*

Edward Alwood, *Straight News: Gays, Lesbians, and the News Media*

Thomas Waugh, *Hard to Imagine: Gay Male Eroticism in Photography and Film from Their Beginnings to Stonewall*

Judith Roof, *Come As You Are: Sexuality and Narrative*

Terry Castle, *Noel Coward and Radclyffe Hall: Kindred Spirits*

Kath Weston, *Render Me, Gender Me: Lesbians Talk Sex, Class, Color, Nation, Studmuffins . . .*

Ruth Vanita, *Sappho and the Virgin Mary: Same-Sex Love and the English Literary Imagination*

renée c. hoogland, *Lesbian Configurations*

Beverly Burch, *Other Women: Lesbian Experience and Psychoanalytic Theory of Women*

Jane McIntosh Snyder, *Lesbian Desire in the Lyrics of Sappho*

Rebecca Alpert, *Like Bread on the Seder Plate: Jewish Lesbians and the Transformation of Tradition*

Emma Donoghue, editor, *Poems Between Women: Four Centuries of Love, Romantic Friendship, and Desire*

James T. Sears and Walter L. Williams, editors, *Overcoming Heterosexism and Homophobia: Strategies That Work*

Patricia Juliana Smith, *Lesbian Panic: Homoeroticism in Modern British Women's Fiction*

Dwayne C. Turner, *Risky Sex: Gay Men and HIV Prevention*

Timothy F. Murphy, *Gay Science: The Ethics of Sexual Orientation Research*

Cameron McFarlane, *The Sodomite in Fiction and Satire, 1660—-1750*

Lynda Hart, *Between the Body and the Flesh: Performing Sadomasochism*

Byrne R. S. Fone, editor, *The Columbia Anthology of Gay Literature: Readings from Western Antiquity to the Present Day*

Ellen Lewin, *Recognizing Ourselves: Ceremonies of Lesbian and Gay Commitment*

Ruthann Robson, *Sappho Goes to Law School: Fragments in Lesbian Legal Theory*

Jacquelyn Zita, *Body Talk: Philosophical Reflections on Sex and Gender*

Evelyn Blackwood and Saskia Wieringa, *Female Desires: Same-Sex Relations and Transgender Practices Across Cultures*

William L. Leap, ed., *Public Sex/Gay Space*

Larry Gross and James D. Woods, eds., *The Columbia Reader on Lesbians and Gay Men in Media, Society, and Politics*

Marilee Lindemann, *Willa Cather: Queering America*

George E. Haggerty, *Men in Love: Masculinity and Sexuality in the Eighteenth Century*

Andrew Elfenbein, *Romantic Genius: The Prehistory of a Homosexual Role*

Gilbert Herdt and Bruce Koff, *Something to Tell You: The Road Families Travel When a Child Is Gay*

Richard Canning, *Gay Fiction Speaks: Conversations with Gay Novelists*

Laura Doan, *Fashioning Sapphism: The Origins of a Modern English Lesbian Culture*

Mary Bernstein and Renate Reimann, eds., *Queer Families, Queer Politics: Challenging Culture and the State*

Richard R. Bozorth, *Auden's Games of Knowledge: Poetry and the Meanings of Homosexuality*

Larry Gross, *Up from Invisibility: Lesbians, Gay Men, and the Media in America*

Linda Garber, *Identity Poetics: Race, Class, and the Lesbian-Feminist Roots of Queer Theory*

Richard Canning, *Hear Us Out: Conversations with Gay Novelists*

David Bergman, *The Violet Hour: The Violet Quill and the Making of Gay Culture*